Teaching the Old Testament in English Classes

JAMES S. ACKERMAN, Associate Professor of Religious Studies at Indiana University, is author of *On Teaching the Bible as Literature*.

ALAN WILKIN JENKS is Dean of Freshmen and Lecturer in Religion at Duke University.

EDWARD B. JENKINSON is Associate Professor of Education, Coordinator for School English Language Arts, and Director of the English Curriculum Study Center at Indiana University.

JAN BLOUGH is currently working at MarkeTrends, Indianapolis, a market research and analysis firm.

Published for the
Indiana University English Curriculum Study Center
EDWARD B. JENKINSON, Director

PREVIOUSLY PUBLISHED

On Teaching Literature:
Essays for Secondary School Teachers

Teaching Literature in Grades Seven Through Nine

Two Approaches to Teaching Syntax

On Teaching the Bible as Literature: A Guide to
Selected Biblical Narratives for Secondary Schools

What Is Language? And Other Teaching Units
for Grades Seven Through Twelve

Teaching Literature in Grades Ten Through Twelve

Books for Teachers of English:
An Annotated Bibliography

Writing as a Process of Discovery:
Some Structured Theme Assignments for Grades
Five Through Twelve

Essays on Teaching Speech in the High School

On Teaching Speech in Elementary and
Junior High Schools

Teaching the Old Testament in English Classes

BY

JAMES S. ACKERMAN,
Senior Author,

and

ALAN WILKIN JENKS

and

EDWARD B. JENKINSON,

with

JAN BLOUGH

148113

BLOOMINGTON   *Indiana University Press*   LONDON

Published in Canada by Fitzhenry & Whiteside Limited,
Don Mills, Ontario
Library of Congress catalog card number: 72–93907
ISBN: 0–253–35785–3 cl.
0–253–28850–9 pa.

MANUFACTURED IN THE UNITED STATES OF AMERICA

CONTENTS

ACKNOWLEDGMENTS

The portion of the project of the Indiana University English Curriculum Study Center reported herein was supported through the Cooperative Research Program of the Office of Education, United States Department of Health, Education, and Welfare.

The Center received additional financial support from the Cummins Engine Foundation, which awarded a grant providing funds for meetings and equipment that could not be financed by the grant from the United States Office of Education.

The authors are deeply indebted to the forty-one teachers who attended the first Indiana University summer institute on teaching the Bible in secondary English. Those teachers wrote hundreds of study questions on various biblical passages that provided the base for at least fifty per cent of the suggested questions in this text. Their questions were edited to fit space and to conform with the style followed herein; therefore, the contributing editors are responsible for any errors in the questions.

Grateful acknowledgment is given to the following teachers:

John E. Bates, Middletown, New Jersey; Miss Stella Bentley, Hammond, Indiana; Mrs. Jean Gorrell Blessing, Markle, Indiana; Miss Annie G. Bohannon, Waynesboro, Mississippi; Miss Marilyn V. Breeden, Indianapolis, Indiana; Sister Maureen Brinker, SSND, Burlington, Iowa; Mrs. Emma Jane Cagle, Brazil, Indiana; Mrs. Mary Ruth Carter, Amarillo, Texas; Mrs. Sarah Mills Chapman, Bloomington, Indiana; Mrs. Isabel G. Daressa, Port Jefferson, New York; Miss Phyllis Ebert, Garden City, New York; Mrs. Mary Lavon Elster, Fort Wayne, Indiana; James J. Garvey, Mineola, Long Island, New York; Mrs. Florence Gholz, Bakersfield, California; Mrs. Alice Gordon, Richmond, Indiana; Mrs. Ruth Hallman, Xenia, Ohio; Miss Donna Halper, Roslindale, Massachusetts; Mrs. Toni Aberson Hammer, Indianapolis, Indiana; Mrs. Darlene Harbuck, Bloomington, Indiana; Levi C. Hartzler, Elkhart, Indiana.

Also, Mrs. Martha B. Jones, Wabash, Indiana; Miss Susan A. Judge, Rochester, New York; Brother George Klawitter, CSC, Indianapolis, Indiana; Mrs. Harriet Koshar, Bedford, New York; Sister Grace Mannion, RS, Hartford, Connecticut; Mrs. Dorothy Maylott, Concord, California; Mrs. Patricia Medlock, Bloomington, Indiana; Melvin Merzon, Oak Park, Michigan; Miss Rosemary Monjure, New Orleans, Louisiana; Mrs. Marion Murphy, Ferguson, Missouri; Miss Kristen Norden, Worthington, Minnesota; Miss Martha Patton, Rome, Georgia; Mrs. Marion von Tiesenhausen, Huntsville, Alabama; Arnold J. Schilling, Armstrong, Iowa; Irwin M. Schmuckler, Philadelphia, Pennsylvania; Mrs. Marilyn Sedam, Richmond, Indiana; Sister Regina Shaughnessy, CSC, Vincennes, Indiana; Miss Yvonne Vish, La Grange, Illinois; Miss Judith Ann Wubben, Chicago, Illinois; Mrs. Sharon Wyman, Bloomington, Indiana; Frank Yuse, Spokane, Washington.

Grateful acknowledgment is given to Jane Stouder Hawley, who served as contributing editor to the forerunner to this volume. The authors also wish to thank Thayer S. Warshaw and Donald A. Seybold, teachers in that first summer institute. Grateful acknowledgment is also given to Philip B. Daghlian, whose sound advice on each of the books in the English Curriculum Study Series has been most welcome.

Various parts of this book were typed and tested over a five-year period. During that time, seven different secretaries accepted the chore of retyping the many revisions of this volume, assisted with the proofreading of mimeographed copies in various stages, and finally proofread the text itself. Grateful acknowledgment is given to Mrs. Julia Hamilton, Mrs. Victoria Hedrick, Mrs. Lynn Sears, and Mrs. Dorothy Spencer. Special thanks go to Mrs. Judy Benadum and Mrs. Glenna Bryant for the more than seven hundred hours that each spent on the final revision, typing and retyping, checking and rechecking every line, painstakingly proofreading again and again while knowing that, inevitably, readers will still spot minor errors, and for preparing the index. The authors gratefully acknowledge the work of Mrs. Jan Blough, who, in addition to compiling and writing a number of the suggested questions, typed one entire rough draft of this manuscript and assisted Edward Jenkinson with the editing at that stage. And special thanks also go to the able editors of the Indiana University Press for their invaluable work on this and all other books in the English Curriculum Study Series.

Introduction

No other collection of books has influenced Western culture more than the Old Testament.* No other collection has been printed in as many languages and in as many editions. No other collection is more worthy of study in the schools.

The variety and quality of the literature in the Old Testament justify its close reading in English classes in junior and senior high schools. The biblical narratives are also appropriate matter for study in any course in social studies or in the humanities, since they serve as a record of a small—but significant—group of people. If we understand the way of life described in the Old Testament, we should be able to understand a little more fully some of the forces at work in our own. A study of biblical narratives also helps a student understand the illusions and symbols in thousands of classical and contemporary works of literature. Such study further helps him to appreciate much of music and art—and all of life; for he can detect the influences of the Old Testament daily in many of the names he hears, in many of the places he visits or reads about, and in many of the expressions that he and others use.

When the forerunner to this volume was published five years ago, its authors found it necessary to point out in the introduction

---

* The writers have chosen the familiar term "Old Testament" for the literature to be covered. This is a Christian designation for what is called simply "the Bible" (or *Tanach*) within the Jewish community. Whereas many Christians see the events recorded here (Abraham, Moses, Prophets) as culminating in the New Testament, Jews do not accept the implication that their sacred literature is "old" in the sense that it is superseded by a new revelation. Similarly, the commonly used B.C. (Before Christ) and A.D. (In the year of our Lord) are Christian terms; Jews, and many Christian scholars, prefer B.C.E. (Before the Common Era) and C.E. (Common Era). The teacher should be aware that all these terms are controversial; he would do well to explain his choices among them to his classes.

that the Supreme Court decision banning prayer in the public schools did not prohibit the study of biblical literature. James S. Ackerman and Jane Stouder Hawley wrote:

> The public controversy surrounding Bible study in the schools has been calmed by a 1963 decision of the Supreme Court. The same decision, which ruled compulsory worship in the public schools a violation of individual rights, defined a place within the school program for comparative and historical study of the religions and their literature. Included in the decision of the Supreme Court of the United States in the case of *Abington v. Schempp* were these words:
>
> > . . . It might well be said that one's education is not complete without a study of comparative religion or the history of religion and its relationship to the advancement of civilization. It certainly may be said that the Bible is worthy of study for its literary and historic qualities. Nothing we have said here indicates that such study of the Bible or of religion, when presented objectively as part of a secular program of education, may not be effected consistent with the First Amendment.
>
> Since 1963, then, when this decision was rendered, teachers and curriculum writers in various parts of the country have been preparing materials for the objective and secular study of the Bible in English, history, and humanities programs. *

The predecessor to this volume in the English Curriculum Study Series contained background information for the teacher and suggested questions for discussion on selected biblical narratives from the two stories of creation through David. This volume follows much the same format as the first, but it contains background material and study questions on at least four times as many narratives. In addition, this book contains far more questions that focus on the literary qualities of the narratives, and it also contains suggested activities that might serve to help teachers think of better and more exciting activities for their specific classes.

---

* James S. Ackerman with Jane Stouder Hawley, *On Teaching the Old Testament as Literature: A Guide to Selected Biblical Narratives for Secondary Schools.* Bloomington: Indiana University Press, 1967, p. xi.

As in the first book, the approach to biblical scholarship herein attempts to represent the general consensus of those Protestant, Catholic, and Jewish scholars who, though they may differ in the interpretation of details, attempt to understand the development of biblical religion and history within the context of its ancient Near Eastern background. James S. Ackerman and Alan Wilkin Jenks, the writers of the notes for teachers, have tried to trace the crucial events that gave rise to early Israelite religion and to describe the major aspects of its development. Though the purpose of this volume is not to affirm religious faith, such faith certainly is not denied. The intent of this volume is to make the literary products of that faith more understandable and real by placing them in their proper setting. Although attempts are made throughout in the notes to incorporate various interpretations of the biblical narratives, it must be noted that the writers have adopted one particular approach to the scriptures, and even though that approach is a widely accepted one, the reader must be aware of the writers' bias.

The notes on each narrative were written primarily for the teacher, to help him illuminate the text when he thinks such elucidation would be beneficial to students. The writers believe that the historical and cultural background for many of the passages can provide the teacher with information that will add immeasurably to the students' study and understanding of the Old Testament. We fully realize, however, that such information, if read to the students or if given to them in lengthy lectures, can be dreadfully dull. Rather than lecture to the students, we hope that the teacher will guide them in lively discussions of the various passages, sharing with them his own knowledge only when it serves to enhance the students' understanding and appreciation of the passages.

Teachers attending the first summer institute on teaching the Bible in secondary English at Indiana University demonstrated that the study of the Old Testament definitely need not be dull and that there are as many approaches to that study as there are teachers. A summary of just four of the units prepared in the first institute indicates the range of possibilities for including study of the Old Testament in the English curriculum in junior and senior high schools.

Toni Hammer of Indianapolis, Indiana, designed twenty-nine activities to help ninth-grade students understand why and how man creates and to help them "realize the universality of man's role as a seeker for insight about the Creator and the Creation." Her six-week unit combines the study of selected biblical narratives with the study of films, paintings, poetry, short stories, and Egyptian, Babylonian, and American Indian legends. The students not only study various ways that man creates, but they do their own creating by writing stories, or by painting, or by making tape recordings, or by producing films. In brief, they make discoveries about themselves, their creation, and their ability to create.

In a unit entitled "Becoming a Hero," Marion Murphy of Ferguson, Missouri, acquaints ninth graders with heroic archetypes from the Old Testament. By focusing on biblical stories of Jacob, Moses, and David, she helps students explore the concept of the hero, first in the Old Testament and then in South Sea legends, poetry, songs, novels, biographies, and short stories. Each student can decide what activity he wishes to complete during the unit by selecting from a wide range of activities, including dramatizing their own stories, constructing crossword puzzles, preparing a wall hanging, finding appropriate music and art to dramatize one of the selections in the unit, setting to music one of the psalms of David, or presenting a tableau of one of the scenes from one of the biblical stories.

In a unit designed for high school juniors and seniors, John Bates of Middletown, New Jersey, explores some of the literature of dissent in the Old Testament. This two-week unit is part of a larger one entitled "Man Against the Establishment," in which students examine some of the literature of protest and dissent. While reading the writings of Amos, Hosea, Micah, and Isaiah, students study Hebrew prophetic literature, consider various meanings of prophecy, examine the role of prophecy assumed in the development of social justice, recognize the relevancy of prophetic writing, and evaluate possible meanings, purposes, and needs for creative dissent and protest.

Melvin Merzon of Oak Park, Michigan, developed five units on literature and the Bible for a one-semester elective course for high school students. The first unit focuses on what the Bible is, how it came to be, and how it influences Western literature. As they study unit one, students also examine some biblical narratives and consider the language of the Bible. Unit two focuses on the Bible *in* other literature, and unit three on the Bible *as* literature. The fourth unit introduces students to a study of comparative religion, and the fifth explores human experiences, concentrating on freedom of man, human suffering, morality, evil, and protest and dissent.

The forty-one teachers participating in the first summer institute at Indiana University (see Acknowledgments) proved that the study of the Old Testament at any level need never be boring for students. Their units provided students with every opportunity to increase their understanding of man and his literature, to improve their ability to use language and to understand its many different uses in history, and to sharpen their own ability to write and to make discoveries about themselves and their worlds through their own writing.

The unit approach to the Old Testament is, of course, not the only—or preferred—way to study the Old Testament in secondary English. The study of biblical narratives can be tied to the study of different pieces of literature at any grade level, or a study of the literature of the Old Testament can be conducted successfully as a separate subject in one or more courses in a phase-elective or traditional program. There is no end to the possibilities of including a study of biblical literature in the curriculum.

For virtually any approach to the teaching of the literature of the Old Testament, the teacher's framing of questions that prompt lively discussion is critical. The questions provided herein are merely suggestions for stimulating discussion. Approximately half of the questions are based on those written by teachers attending the first summer institute, and we are grateful for their help. (See

Acknowledgments.) For any distortion of the purpose of those questions written in the institute, we apologize.

Some of the questions merely elicit information about a specific biblical passage to make certain that the students understand it; other questions ask students to call upon their experiences and their knowledge to help them understand a particular passage; still other questions call for interpretation. It is in the area of interpretation that the teacher needs to be most careful. Whenever possible, the teacher needs to make certain that a full range of interpretations of a specific narrative or passage is given by various students. By doing so, the teacher can underscore the fact that almost every man approaches the Old Testament with a particular point of view that is neither right nor wrong but is based on the sum of his experiences. As students hear various points of view expressed and as they attempt to understand the basis for those views, we hope that students will become more tolerant of one another and will attempt to understand how a man's point of view influences everything he says, does, and thinks.

The suggested questions included in this volume are not geared to a particular translation of the Old Testament. We do not recommend any single translation for study; rather, we suggest that teachers permit students to bring their own Bibles to class. In writing the background material for the teacher, however, James S. Ackerman and Alan Wilkin Jenks found it necessary to refer to only one translation, so that they could be consistent and so that readers could easily follow the references—all of which are to *The Oxford Annotated Bible – Revised Standard Version.*

When he undertook the revision and expansion of the first English Curriculum Study Series volume on teaching the Bible as literature, James S. Ackerman called upon Alan Wilkin Jenks to write some of the notes. The division of labor follows:

JAMES S. ACKERMAN—The Origins of Man, Patriarchal Legends, The Story of Joseph, Moses and the Exodus, The Fall of Jericho, The Judges, The Early Monarchy (*Eli and Samuel, Samuel and Saul*), The Prophetic Movement (*Introduction, Amos, Hosea, Isaiah, Micah*), The Fall of Judah: Exile and Restoration (*The*

Fall of Jerusalem, Ezekiel, The Last Judgment), and The Literature of the Post-Exilic Period (*Wisdom Literature: Proverbs, Ecclesiastes, Job; Love Songs*).

ALAN WILKIN JENKS—The Early Monarchy (*Saul and David, David the King, Solomon*), The Divided Monarchy and the Rise of Prophecy, The Prophetic Movement (*Josiah's Reform, Jeremiah*), The Fall of Judah: Exile and Restoration (*Second Isaiah, Ezra and Nehemiah*), and The Literature of the Post-Exilic Period (*Short Stories: Ruth, Jonah, Esther, Daniel; The Psalms*).

The teacher who uses this book in its entirety will note some repetition in the questions, in the suggested activities, and in the text itself. Such repetition is intentional because the writers think that certain kinds of questions should be asked for every passage and certain kinds of activities might apply to almost every passage. But the important point that needs to be made here is that both the questions and the activities are only suggestions of the writers. We are convinced that teachers will pose far better questions in their classes, since they know the students, and we are also certain that they will design far more exciting activities. The activities herein cover a variety of ways that students can demonstrate an understanding of the biblical passages, as well as a variety of levels of sophistication. No attempt was made to label activities for students according to grade level or academic ability. We leave that task to the teacher because he, and only he, can make that decision. The suggestions here are only that—suggestions. The repetition is intentional because we know that many teachers will not read the book in its entirety; rather, they will examine only those passages they intend to teach.

EDWARD B. JENKINSON

PART I

Background
on the Old Testament

CHAPTER 1

Early Israelite History

Although the Old Testament* comprises a rich variety of literary types, its basic framework is historical narrative that tells the story of a people whose original existence as a nation came to an end almost two thousand years ago. Beginning with an Amorite herdsman wandering into Palestine, the Old Testament ends with the Jewish community experiencing intense persecution and producing an apocalyptic literature that eagerly anticipates the coming of God's kingdom. Through a variety of songs, stories, legends, prophecies, and visions, the Old Testament records a wide range of human experience within the context of specific events in the history of a particular people.

Biblical history is written from a particular point of view. The people of Israel understood their origin, existence, and destiny as arising out of the gracious will of a god who had called them to fulfill his purposes in the world. Every event was viewed from the perspective of their god's achieving his purposes: the world was the arena of God's activity, and only through human events did God reveal his purposes and work out his will.

Our study of the Old Testament will necessarily involve us in major tenets of biblical faith, since, by its very nature, biblical

---

*Concerning the use of the term *Old Testament,* see the footnote on page xi. This chapter is a revision by James S. Ackerman of the first chapter of *On Teaching the Bible As Literature,* by James S. Ackerman with Jane Stouder Hawley as Contributing Editor (Bloomington: Indiana University Press, 1967).

literature is inextricably tied to religion. But our focus will consistently remain on the ancient cultural setting rather than on contemporary sectarian interpretations. Modern interpretations are of course important and valid in their place; but the purpose of this book is to open up the literature of early Israel. Thus we will restrict ourselves to the ancient religious matrix which gave shape to the literature we will be studying.

Many of the early Old Testament historical narratives had as their setting the second millennium B.C. Only at the end of this period, during the reign of King David (about 1000–961 B.C.), did Israel become a great nation. Before David's time the Israelites were insignificant as a political power. The large nations—Egypt, Babylonia, Assyria, and the Hittite and Mitanni empires—did not regard Israel as a force to be reckoned with. Apart from the Old Testament, we have only one piece of evidence from this early period which would indicate that other nations even knew that Israel existed.[1]

Nevertheless, the ancestors of Israel were full participants in shaping the history of the second millennium. Though insignificant in themselves, they took part, with other peoples, in great migratory movements that destroyed cities and toppled empires. As seminomadic herdsmen, the ancestors of Israel were greatly influenced by the nations through which they passed. By the end of the third millennium, a highly sophisticated and complex civilization had developed in the ancient Near East. Although the sources of this civilization were in Egypt and Mesopotamia, migrations extended its influence to peoples throughout the Fertile Crescent.

As a preface to the biblical narratives, we will trace the broad outlines of ancient Near Eastern history. Abraham, whom tradition calls the forefather of the Israelite nation, lived sometime between 2000 and 1600 B.C. But we must go back beyond his time to set the narratives in their proper perspective.

Early Mesopotamia

About 4000 B.C., a swarthy, dark-haired people, who called themselves Sumerians, began settling in Mesopotamia near the mouth of the Tigris and Euphrates rivers. We do not know where they came from, but we do know that these amazing people were the prime movers toward the development of ancient Near Eastern civilization. By 3300 B.C. they had developed a system of writing based on the symbolic representation of uttered sounds rather than on pictures of objects or ideas. For the first time man was able, in writing, to express thoughts, record stories, and keep commercial and governmental records.

These writings tell us a great deal about Sumerian life and thought. We have examples of foreign policy, legal reforms, marriage and divorce contracts, court procedures, warehouse records and receipts, proverbs, school training, and the scientific pursuits of astrology, medicine, and agriculture.[2] Of particular interest are the prayers and lamentations, many of them filled with despair, and the lists of omens and rituals for warding off evil. More central to our study is the rich store of Sumerian mythological literature and legendary literature, including a flood story similar to the one in Genesis.

The Sumerian culture existed as a collection of city-states, not as a unified nation. Each city-state was fiercely independent from, and often quite hostile to, its neighbors. The city-state was originally governed by a council of elders in a system very similar to a modern-day republic. During major crises the entire town was called to assembly, and anyone owning land had a vote. Much of the land in a city-state was not owned by individual citizens, however, because each city-state was considered the personal estate of one of the major gods in the Sumerian pantheon. Therefore, the temple, the god's manor house, dominated the city's economy, using sizeable tracts of land for its own (that is, the god's) needs and renting much of the rest to private enterprise. Each citizen spent part of his time working the temple lands or maintaining and improving the temple property.

Why were the people so zealous in serving their god?[3] The Sumerians believed that all events, from disastrous floods to military victories, were determined in the heavens by the assembled pantheon of gods. Each god represented the best interests of his city-state to the extent that he was satisfied with the way he was being served in his temple manor. The Sumerians believed that a strong, well-run city-state in which the needs of the temple were more than fulfilled would not only please the patron deity, it would also increase his power and prestige among the gods.

Another reason for this attentive service lies in the Sumerian view of man's purpose on earth. Several myths combine to explain the reason for man's existence: he was created to serve the gods, so that they might enjoy lives of ease and pleasure. Each major god in the pantheon was the personification of one of the forces of nature (sun, moon, storm), and through serving its god, each city-state was enabling a particular natural phenomenon to continue to function. This reasoning was the Sumerian way of bringing order and stability to a universe which was often capricious and perplexing.

Sumerian democracy gradually became ineffective. Population growth pressured the city-states to expand their land holdings; boundary disputes among the Sumerians were frequent. It became increasingly difficult for the democratic assemblies, which traditionally handled problems through discussion, to cope with the demands of constant warfare. Because there was a need for quick, decisive action, which Sumerian assembly government could not provide, increased power was placed in the hands of a strong man whose military prowess could deliver the community from the enemy. This position of power soon normalized into the permanent institution of kingship.

After 2600 B.C., groups of uncivilized Semitic people, the Akkadians, began entering Mesopotamia from the northwest. Upon settling in Mesopotamia, they became enthusiastic converts to Sumerian culture. They adopted the Sumerian writing system to express their own language and incorporated into their heritage many of the Sumerian literary traditions. The Akkadian migrations provided the *coup de grace* to Sumerian democracy. The Akkadians became the dominant political force throughout Mesopotamia by 2350 B.C., ruling the land in a completely different way.

The Sumerians had attempted to order their baffling universe through the mythological principle of the divine pantheon. By this means each city-state, while maintaining political individuality, participated through its patron deity in the universal community. The Akkadians, however, were much more inclined to action than to mythological speculation. Under their great king, Sargon, they established an empire—the first known empire in history—which stretched from the Persian Gulf to the Mediterranean Sea. This tendency toward unity through empire dominated Near Eastern political life for the next two thousand years.

Various factors—invasions of barbarians from the East, revived Sumeran nationalism, an overextended governmental network—caused the breakup of the Akkadian empire within two centuries of its founding. By 2000 B.C., other groups of Semitic peoples, taking advantage of the power vacuum, came streaming into the land from the northwest. These invaders, called Amorites (Westerners) by the Mesopotamians, assimilated Sumero-Akkadian culture and gained political control of the land within two hundred years. By 1800 B.C., the land was divided into three great powers: the Amorite kingdoms of Babylonia and Assyria and the eastern kingdom of Elam (later called Persia). Elam and Assyria had brief moments of glory, but both were soon checked by Hammurabi, the brilliant Babylonian king, who succeeded in ruling over roughly the same empire which Sargon of Akkad had once controlled.

Abraham and the Patriarchs

Biblical tradition states that Abraham originally came from Ur, the ancient Sumerian city of the moon god Nanna, in Mesopotamia.[4] This tradition is probably the reason for the strong Mesopotamian influence in the law codes and in the early stories of Genesis. In Abraham's time the Mesopotamian cities were generally ruled by princes who were either administrative officials for, or vassals of, the current king. Other than this connection with the king and the broadened horizons which accompanied the establishment of empires, the general life and culture must have been quite similar to that of the Sumerian city-states. The ancestors of Israel observed and absorbed much of this culture from the cities through which they passed in their wanderings.

Abraham was an Amorite.[5] While thousands of Amorites entered Mesopotamia from the upper Euphrates valley, many other Amorite clans moved southwest along the Mediterranean coast into Canaan. Abraham's clan was a part of the latter migratory movement. The original inhabitants of the land, the Canaanites, who had been there since at least the fourth millennium B.C., settled in large fortified city-states which dotted the fertile valleys. They were an agricultural people ruled mainly by a feudal aristocracy. Although some incoming Amorites managed to conquer and establish cities, assimilating themselves into the Canaanite feudal-agricultural system, many tribes chose to retain their seminomadic existence in the hill country. Their choice may to some extent have been necessitated by Canaanite strength in the valleys, as it would have taken a sizable coalition of clans to breach the walls of a Canaanite city.

Some of the incoming clans established rural settlements in the sparsely populated central hill country of south Canaan, where they continued the pastoral life of the herdsman while probably relying upon some forms of primitive farming to supplement the produce of their flocks. Other clans which roamed farther south in the Negeb were forced to maintain their seminomadic life because of the arid land, though at times climatic changes seem to have supported a larger population in this area. One of these times (2000–1800 B.C.) was roughly contemporary with Abraham —a period in which the Negeb became part of a highly developed overland trade caravan system stretching from Egypt to Mesopotamia. The chief means of transportation was the pack-ass, not the camel.[6] Many of these Amorites, often referred to as "Hebrews" by the native inhabitants, were given a resident alien status in the land and probably took on such jobs as mercenaries or caravaneers.[7] Although these new groups often lived under the domination of neighboring Canaanite city-states, their social structure remained based upon family, clan, and tribe rather than upon identification with a particular city.

In general, the forefathers of Israel lived quietly in the sparsely populated hills. Occasional squabbles over water rights seem to have been the major interruptions to their otherwise peaceful existence. We should not picture Abraham as a weak loner, however, buffeted about between migrating tribes and entrenched city-states. We learn in Genesis 14:14 that he was able to marshal 318 fighting men to save his nephew Lot. Though the stories in Genesis are usually focused upon the feelings and actions of particular individuals, we must remember that Abraham, Isaac, Jacob, and Jacob's twelve sons were all chieftains of large clans. Many contemporary biblical scholars believe that the stories in Genesis often describe as the actions of individuals the complex intermingling and movements of whole clans and tribes. For example, such scholars believe that the city of Shechem was not destroyed by two brothers (Genesis 34:25), but rather by a confederation of two related tribes.

Abraham's religion differed from the beliefs and practices of his Mesopotamian and Canaanite urban neighbors. Surely he was aware of the divine pantheon concept, known throughout the Near East, in which each deity (sun, storm, death) exercised a particular function within the universe. Yet we find no evidence in the Genesis stories of Abraham's worshiping a host of gods. He is constantly portrayed as being guided and protected by one god—a personal god who has entered into a covenant with him. Although several leading scholars have concluded that Abraham was a monotheist, it seems more likely that he acknowledged that other tribes could worship their gods, but he worshiped only one—the god who watched over his people.

Recent scholarship has shown that Abraham's religion was closely related to the religion of the seminomadic peoples of that time.[8] Each clan or tribe was bound by contractual agreement to the personal god of its chief or founding father. This is clearly shown by the oath between Jacob and Laban, which was to be enforced by their respective clan deities (Genesis 31:53). The clan members felt a strong kinship toward their god, who was regarded as the head of their family.

The covenant between the clan deity and his family expressed the core of their relationship. In Abraham's case, the covenant involved two central elements: the divine promise that Abraham's clan would be led to a land which they would possess and upon which they would prosper and become a great nation; and the human response of faith—placing full reliance on their god's power and intent to fulfill his promises. The nature of this covenant is believed to account for the main difference between the religion of Abraham and that of his Near Eastern urban neighbors. The people of Mesopotamia and Canaan were often apprehensive, trying to placate capricious deities through numerous rituals. The Abrahamic covenant, on the other hand, allowed its followers to face life's vicissitudes with confidence in the eventual outcome. The signs of the strong sense of destiny which stands at the heart of Israelite faith are evident: life was moving toward the end which God had promised; God himself was working through history to achieve this end.

No sooner had the Amorites settled in the land than the Hurrians began migrating southward from the region east of the Black Sea. Their advance was greatly facilitated by two military innovations: the horse-drawn chariot and the composite bow. They swept across Upper Mesopotamia, some groups pressing as far as southern Canaan. Though the population of Canaan remained basically Semitic (Canaanite and Amorite), many of the Canaanite city-states came to be ruled by a Hurrian aristocracy. This Hurrian domination of Canaan, which was significant as early as 1700 B.C., had a domino-like effect on the land's earlier inhabitants. Large groups of Canaanites and Amorites chose, or were forced, to move southward into Egypt. The Egyptians called these invaders Hyksos (foreign chiefs).

The Egyptians and the Hyksos

Egyptian civilization had been flourishing for more than a thousand years before the Hyksos arrived. Within several centuries of the Sumerians' development of written symbols, the Egyptians had also developed a system of writing. Most Egyptian writing was done on perishable papyrus; consequently, many aspects of Egyptian culture have been lost. But inside the pyramids and in the tombs of other Egyptian nobility, texts have been discovered which give us insight into Egyptian thought. In contrast to the literature and art of Mesopotamia, that of early Egypt evidences a strong sense of dignity and serenity. The people led peaceful lives, unthreatened by man and nature. Since the Pharaoh was regarded as the incarnation of the mighty sun-god, the government was markedly stable. The land was protected from outside invasion by mountains, deserts, and the sea, and the Nile rose and ebbed with periodic regularity.

The easiest entry into Egypt was from Canaan—across the upper Sinai Peninsula into the Nile Delta region. Thus a part of Egypt's foreign policy was to protect herself through political control of Canaan. (Signs of Egyptian influence can be found in Canaan from the early part of the third millennium B.C.) Nevertheless, as we see from Egyptian paintings and government reports, small groups of Semitic herdsmen and traders were able to enter Egypt periodically. Occasionally, the Egyptians became involved in border skirmishes with the herdsmen, and the Egyptians often sent their prisoners to work as slaves in the copper and turquoise mines in Sinai.

The Hyksos invasion of Egypt took place during the seventeenth century B.C. Over a period of about one hundred years, the foreigners gained complete control of the country, and a succession of Hyksos princes ruled as pharaohs over Egypt for nearly a century. Their chief means of conquest was the horse-drawn chariot—an invention they had adopted from the Hurrians.

Some ancestors of Israel may have entered Egypt during this period of Hyksos rule. The account of Joseph's swift rise to power as the Pharaoh's prime minister would be more understandable during a time of Semitic control of the land. The Hyksos background of the Joseph story might also help to explain the puzzling change between the ending of Genesis and the beginning of Exodus. In the last chapter of Genesis, Jacob's death is mourned by the Pharaoh himself, but in the opening of Exodus, we learn that the Hebrew people are slaves in Egypt. After about one hundred years of Hyksos rule in the intervening time, the Egyptians rebelled against the hated foreigners. Many Hyksos were captured and kept in Egypt as slaves. The others were driven back into Canaan and subdued in a succession of battles. By about 1500 B.C., Egyptian power once more dominated all of Canaan.

The sole rival to Egyptian claims in Canaan was the Hittite empire, which controlled most of modern-day Turkey. The Hittites had enjoyed periods of glory earlier—most notably under Mursilis, who in 1531 B.C. led a raid deep into Mesopotamia and completely obliterated the Babylonian empire begun by Hammurabi. In that raid Babylon was plundered and burned, and her famous temple was destroyed. But the Hittites never achieved permanent power, seemingly because of their bitter fratricidal wars over succession to the throne, as exemplified by Mursilis' assassination during his victorious procession home from Babylon.

Hittite power gained some degree of stability under the empire's greatest king, Shuppiluliuma (about 1375–1340 B.C.). He expanded to the east by destroying the Hurrian empire of Mitanni, then pressed southward into Canaan at the expense of Egyptian power. The manner in which Shuppiluliuma and his successors incorporated smaller surrounding territories into the Hittite empire becomes important later in understanding the development of Israelite religion. Instead of subjugating people through battle, the king would send an emissary to the local prince with an offer: "Join with me, be loyal to me, and I will protect you." The prince was asked to submit himself as a vassal, acknowledging the Hittite king as his lord. The basis of the vassal's obligation to remain loyal and obedient was always given in terms of the kindnesses which the Hittite kings had done for the vassal in the past. If the prince acceded to the request, a formal contract, or suzerainty covenant, was made. In this agreement the vassal prince received the protection of the Hittite empire in return for complete loyalty, obedience, and annual taxes. He was not to rebel by seeking the aid or joining forces with another suzerain (for example, the Egyptian Pharaoh), nor was he to aid any other rebel prince. Furthermore, he was not to quarrel with any prince who was also a vassal to the Hittite king. Any controversy between vassals was to be brought before the king for settlement. Although most of the recovered examples of the suzerainty covenant are from Hittite sources, it was undoubtedly a well-known and commonly used instrument of foreign policy throughout the ancient Near East during the latter half of the second millennium.

Egyptian power recovered rapidly under the pharaohs of the nineteenth dynasty, especially under Seti I and Ramses II. Egyptian armies marched north to challenge the Hittites for the possession of Canaan. After a series of battles in which neither side seems to have emerged victorious, a peace treaty of friendship, wherein Egypt retained control of almost all of Canaan, was signed between Ramses II and Hattusilis III about 1280 B.C.

Moses and the Covenant at Sinai

Tradition unanimously credits Moses as the founder of the Israelite nation. Although the Pharaoh of the Exodus has not been definitely identified, the weight of evidence has led many scholars to suggest the early nineteenth dynasty—the time of Seti I (1313–1292 B.C.) and Ramses II (1292–1225 B.C.)—as the most likely period for the escape from Egypt. During this time, the Hebrews were engaged in two royal projects: the building of the cities of Pithom and Raamses. Raamses, far up in the northernmost part of the land, was the former capital from which the Hyksos had ruled Egypt. With his renewed interest in controlling Canaan, Ramses II was reestablishing it as his capital city so that he would have easy access to the north.

According to tradition, Moses had escaped from Egypt and through marriage had eventually become attached to some tribes of Kenite (or Midianite) herdsmen who were wandering through the Sinai Peninsula. (We do not know how long he was gone from Egypt.) Impelled by a divine revelation, which assured him that the promises made to Abraham long ago were about to be fulfilled, Moses returned to Egypt. The god who appeared to Moses at the burning bush was called by a new name—Yahweh, which is translated as Lord or Jehovah in most English Bibles. Yahweh eventually came to be regarded not as a completely new god, but rather as a new form of the god worshiped by the descendants of Abraham, Isaac, and Jacob (see Exodus 6:2ff).

Eventually Moses was able to lead a small (500 to 5000?) band of runaway slaves out of Egypt.[9] The event was too insignificant (or too embarrassing from the Egyptian point of view) to have been noted in Egyptian records. But the Exodus from Egypt, especially the miraculous deliverance at the sea, stands as the central event in the entire Old Testament. It had the same importance to the Israelite as Jesus' resurrection from the dead has to the Christian.

Instead of taking the quick route to Canaan, which would have been well-guarded by Egyptian soldiers, Moses led his band of escapees to the mountain of God where, according to tradition, Yahweh had previously revealed himself through the burning bush. Moses and his followers believed that, by their deliverance from Egypt, Yahweh had established his claim upon the Israelites as his people. Now it was up to them to fulfill the obligations involved in being Yahweh's people.

The agreement between Yahweh and Israel was formally defined in the covenant mediated through Moses at Mount Sinai. This covenant is based upon the same conceptual pattern and literary form as the Hittite suzerainty treaty described previously. Yahweh was conceived as the great king who, by delivering the people of Israel from the hands of the Pharaoh, had invited them to be his vassals.

Why did Yahweh choose Israel? Old Testament tradition describes the Israelites as being stiff-necked and rebellious from the beginning. They murmured against both Moses and Yahweh, and lacking confidence in the covenant promises, they yearned to return to slavery in Egypt. Thus Yahweh's selection of Israel was not to be considered as a sign of favor, but as a strict call to obedience—that the purposes of the suzerain might be served.[10]

Yahweh's demands were stipulated through the Ten Commandments. Just as the Hittite vassal was not to seek the aid of or put his confidence in another suzerain, so the Israelites were enjoined from giving their loyalty to any god other than Yahweh. Yahweh was no longer thought of as a clan deity, as in the time of Abraham, but as the cosmic ruler of heaven and earth. His power over the Egyptian gods had been clearly demonstrated. If nations worshiped other gods, it was because Yahweh had allotted them to the various deities who served in his court (the Sumerian patron deity concept). These deities, however, had no power apart from Yahweh's commands. Other gods might exist in the minds of men, but to the Israelite they were but lifeless idols of wood and stone. Power was exclusively in Yahweh's hands; the religion of Moses and his followers had become monotheism.

There is no ancient Near Eastern deity with whom Yahweh can be compared. He was not a personification of the sun, moon, or stars; he did not represent, nor was his existence tied to, any of the forces of nature which periodically died and revived in accordance with the annual cycle of the seasons. He had no consort or offspring. He was Lord over nature and used it (for example, the plagues; Exodus 7–12) to accomplish his purposes. Whereas Abraham had viewed God as the benevolent head of his clan, Yahweh now became holy, unapproachable, uncontrollable. He was conceived as the Lord of history who governs the affairs of men and nations. No person could see him and live. Whereas idols could be built and nailed down in temples by other peoples in order to gain some measure of control over their gods, Yahweh could not be manipulated in this way. One of the commandments strictly forbids the making of any graven image of Yahweh. He was a god who could not be restrained or controlled by man.

The name Yahweh (meaning "he brings into existence" or "he causes to happen") is in itself an indication of his nature. He was not a Lord of the status quo, but the God who regulated history in accordance with his ethical demands and expectations. Pagan religion and society were trapped within the status quo. Every effort was directed toward maintaining the present order of the universe, the regular pattern of nature, and the given structure of society. Israel felt herself called beyond the status quo—out of slavery in Egypt toward a future whose quality depended upon her obedience to her Lord. With this strong sense of destiny, which had begun with the promises to Abraham, Israel saw herself moving toward the fulfillment of God's purposes. Her exodus from the land of slavery and her journey through the wilderness toward the land of promise symbolized this destiny.

Israel's relationship to her suzerain Lord was governed by three commandments of the Mosaic covenant. Again following the Hittite pattern, the other basic demands from the suzerain regulated the vassals' behavior in relation to each other. Justice was the basic principle upon which Israelite society was to be structured: each member was expected to give and receive his just due in the community. That one Israelite should permanently gain power or control over a covenant brother was considered anathema to Yahweh's demands for social righteousness among his vassals. Therefore, Israelite laws have a strong egalitarian orientation. Remembering well their days of slavery in Egypt, the Israelites had a strong sympathy for the downtrodden. Israel—alone among all nations of the past—saw the structuring of a just society as one of the keystones of her religious obligation.

Thus we see that some distinct changes took place in Israel's religion during the time of Moses. At the heart of the covenant with Abraham was the simple faith that God would one day fulfill his promises—that Israel would receive land and become a great nation. Though no ethical demands were laid upon Abraham, the heart of the Mosaic covenant was Israel's obligation to obey in return for her having been rescued out of Egypt. Israel knew that the Mosaic covenant was a conditional relationship which Yahweh could terminate if his people failed to serve his purposes.

Following the covenant at Sinai, the Israelites began their trek through the wilderness to the Promised Land. It was a journey full of hardships, a journey in which Moses' leadership was constantly questioned and threatened. The band was forced to make several detours to avoid conflict with peoples whose strength was superior to theirs. During the several decades of wandering—before the Israelites finally sighted the Promised Land from the eastern bank of the Jordan River—they probably encountered related tribes who joined their ranks as covenant brothers.

The Emergence of Israel as a Nation in Canaan

Living directly between the Egyptians and the Mesopotamians, the Canaanites were middle men both economically and culturally. Facing the Mediterranean, with the major trade routes of the

Fertile Crescent running through their land, the Canaanites developed a special genius for commerce. One of the by-products of this talent was the development of a simplified system of writing, suitable for keeping business records. This writing system, adopted by the Greeks through commercial contact in the ninth century B.C., is the basis of our own alphabet. The Canaanites reached their zenith around the middle of the second millennium B.C., freely borrowing from both Egypt and Mesopotamia in the areas of art, architecture, literature, and religion and transforming them into a vibrant, synthetic, yet unique culture.[11]

There are various conflicting theories as to how Israel came into being as a nation. The one point on which scholars can agree is that the thirteenth century B.C., was an opportune time for radical social and political changes in the land of Canaan. After driving the Hyksos out of Egypt (about 1550 B.C.), the Egyptians gradually pressed into Canaan. Their intent in regaining control was to establish Canaan as a buffer to prevent future invasions into Egypt and to profit from the trade outlets of the highly developed Canaanite commercial system. But the result of several centuries of heavy-handed Egyptian rule was the severe weakening of the fabric of Canaanite society. Oppressive Egyptian taxation eventually stifled Canaanite commerce, virtually destroying the vital middle class which had dominated the culture. The result was a gradual polarization of Canaanite society in which a small landed aristocracy, supported by Egyptian power, ruled over a population of serfs. Another factor which played into the hands of the Egyptian overlords was the rugged, hilly terrain in Canaan which isolated the city-states from each other, creating bitter rivalries and feuds among them.

The most serious disruption of Canaanite society was caused by a tremendous maritime invasion from the Aegean Sea, beginning about 1250 B.C. (The destruction of Troy celebrated in *The Iliad* was but a minor episode in this massive movement.) The results for all peoples living along the eastern Mediterranean coast were disastrous. The Hittite empire was completely annihilated, and the Egyptians, who had recalled their troops from Canaan to meet the onslaught at the Nile Delta, battled the sea peoples to a bloody standoff. The sea peoples went elsewhere to settle—along the coast of Canaan and as far off as Sardinia. But Egypt was so weakened by the battles that she never regained the dominant role in Near Eastern history that she had formerly enjoyed.

There are three major theories regarding Israel's emergence as a nation in south Canaan some time in the latter part of the thirteenth century B.C. Although they are not mutually exclusive, each has a distinctive emphasis. The first cites evidence that Hebrew clans were already migrating into south Canaan in the fourteenth century B.C., one hundred years before Moses and Joshua.[12] Non-biblical texts (the Amarna letters) show that Shechem was already a Hebrew center in this early period, a fact which is perhaps corroborated by Genesis 34. Furthermore, there is no archeological evidence that Shechem was destroyed during the time of Joshua, who gathers the Israelite tribes there to enter into a covenant relationship with Yahweh and with one another. Thus it may be that Shechem was an early Hebrew covenant center. The first theory, then, posits a gradual buildup of the Hebrew population in south Canaan with diverse clans and groups entering from different places over a long period of time. Encouraged by the disruption caused by the sea peoples' invasion and by the entry of a Hebrew group which had recently escaped from Egypt, the Hebrews felt strong enough to challenge the Canaanites for control of the land. As indicated by Judges 1, the struggle went back and forth until complete Israelite control was finally established by King David.

A second theory tries to fit together what appears to be contradictory evidence within the biblical tradition: Joshua 1–11, which describes a sudden invasion by a united Israel, resulting in an almost total devastation of the major south Canaanite centers, and Judges 1, which indicates that many Canaanite cities were in fact not incorporated into Israel right away.[13] Noting archeological evidence, which indicates widespread massive destruction in the latter part of the thirteenth century followed by intermittent layers of destruction for the next two hundred years, some scholars posit a major attack upon the cities of south Canaan carried out by a united group of tribes. However, Israel was not strong enough nor its population large enough to take complete possession of the land all at once. As the Israelite army moved on, the survivors of destroyed cities would often return and resettle in the cities. Several of the larger cities remained in Canaanite hands, as the struggle for land possession continued for the next two centuries. Other cities would change hands among Israelites, Canaanites, and Philistines four or five times in several hundred years until the time of David, when the land was brought fully under Israelite control.

A third theory begins by pointing out that a tribally structured nation does not necessarily indicate seminomadic origins.[14] The basic social split in ancient times was not between the farmer and the seminomad—but between city and village, and villages were commonly organized into tribal units for mutual protection. The rural peasants, who combined the role of small farmer and herdsman, were constantly in conflict with the nearby city-state whose feudal prince attempted to extend his tax power and economic control at their expense. The Amarna letters, it is argued, do not mention a Hebrew invasion from the wilderness, but rather they talk of segments of the population and certain cities "becoming Hebrew." What does this mean? It has long been known that "Hebrew" is not an ethnic designation, and here it is suggested that the term means a "rebel"—a person or group which has cast off the established authority in the land. The Canaanite princes, who ruled the land as puppets supported by Egyptian power, became increasingly vulnerable to overthrow once the sea peoples' invasion caused the withdrawal of Egyptian troops. Furthermore, there is no way to explain how a group numbering 5,000 at the most at the exodus from Egypt could become a nation of 250,000 within three generations without positing a massive influx of peasants who had suffered under the Canaanite feudal system into the new nation of Israel. The appearance of a small group of escapees from Egypt who proclaimed a new god, Yahweh—a god who sets oppressed peoples free—was the catalyst that triggered a widespread social revolution within Canaan. Thus, according to this theory, Israel was born in a setting of political and social turmoil whereby the urban Canaanite feudal stranglehold on the land was broken by a coalition of peasants and seminomads who attempted to set up a new society based more on the egalitarian ideals of seminomadic life.

We have gone into greater detail on this point in order to emphasize the complexity of Israel's origins. It is virtually certain that the group which escaped from Egypt was vastly augmented by other clans and tribes in the process of Israel's becoming a nation. The merger of tribal groups must have been accompanied by the gradual oral amalgamation of the traditions of the various groups, so that all Israel came to acknowledge Abraham as their forefather and the escape from Egypt as their act of deliverance, in the same way that nineteenth century immigrants to America accepted George Washington as their founding father and the Revolutionary War as their struggle for freedom. As the stories of the patriarchs and of the Exodus from Egypt came to be told after the formation of the twelve tribes, it was a natural expression of unity for the tribes to speak of themselves as all having descended from one man—all having sojourned in Egypt, having been enslaved, and having been miraculously set free. For the tribes of Israel, whether their ancestors had been delivered from the crushing oppression of Pharaoh or of the Canaanite prince up on the hill, the story of the Exodus expressed their collective experience of having been set free by the power of Yahweh.

The Judges and the Tribal League

According to Joshua 24, the official formation of the twelve tribes of Israel took place at Shechem. Joshua told those who had joined the Israelites during the invasion of Canaan about Yahweh —how he had revealed himself to Moses, delivered his people from Egypt, and was in fact a new manifestation of the clan deity which the descendants of Abraham had always worshiped. The people were told to put away their foreign gods and to "choose this day whom ye will serve." Those who chose Yahweh covenanted to be his servants by accepting the stipulations laid down by Moses at Sinai. Though the twelve tribes of Israel were of diverse origin, the contractual alliance to Yahweh constituted their unity. The land was then apportioned among the tribes. After the opening invasion, each tribe, to some extent, had to secure the land which had been allotted to it.

The first two hundred years during which the Israelites struggled to maintain and expand their foothold in Canaan are commonly called the period of the judges. Unlike other nations, Israel was not ruled by a king. As stipulated in the Mosaic covenant, Yahweh alone was king. He laid down the terms by which his people were to be governed, and he also provided protection in times of danger. The Israelites believed that whereas a king could win and protect land by leading troops into battle himself, Yahweh performed this kingly function by raising up a man to lead the army against the enemy. When an emergency arose, the people were able to recognize the leader designated by Yahweh through the charismatic power which had suddenly come upon him. This power, they believed, was the effect of Yahweh's spirit, and the man became the unquestioned leader. His authority was neither lifelong nor hereditary; it lasted only until the crisis of the moment had passed.

These charismatic leaders were called judges. In Hebrew the word judge refers to an individual who actively intervenes to secure justice. A judge was a righter of wrongs. As the strongest person in the community, he had the power to protect others against injustice. At the national level, the judge was looked upon as that person empowered by Yahweh to secure for the people of Israel what was rightfully theirs.

Israel had no standing army. The clans rallied to face a crisis. Each Israelite was a kind of minuteman who stood ready to answer the call to arms. Furthermore, when another tribe was threatened, all Israel was obligated to come to its aid. Any war in which Israel's freedom was at stake was regarded as Yahweh's war. Just as the Hittite vassals, even if they were not directly involved in the conflict, had to send their troops to march with the Hittite king, so Yahweh's vassals; even the tribes which were not immediately threatened, were supposed to send military help.

Warfare was a sacred event for ancient peoples. The battle

between nations was regarded as a struggle between their respective gods. Thus, not the relative strength of the opposing armies but a mightier god was thought to determine the outcome. The most important quality of a soldier was absolute faith that his god had given the enemy into his hands. Ritual purification and sacrifices and the recitations of oracles preceded the great battles. The people of Israel were confident that Yahweh was mightier than any other god and that he would give them the victory if they faithfully adhered to the covenant. Since any war was primarily Yahweh's war, they believed that they did not deserve to profit from the outcome. Thus all human and material spoil was destroyed—sacrificed to Yahweh.

The twelve tribes of Israel, called the Tribal League, were united, then, essentially through their mutual adherence to Yahweh as suzerain. Israel was a sacral confederation; there was no central government. Each tribe ran its own affairs as it saw fit, with clan elders and local leaders presiding. Only in religious matters was there a centralized administrative structure.

Throughout the period of the judges, a central place of worship was maintained for all the tribes. Although they worshiped in local shrines as well, the tribes gathered periodically at the central sanctuary to renew the covenant and to remember the mighty acts of Yahweh which had made them into a nation. Intertribal disputes were also settled at these assemblies.

The fragile institutions, designed to preserve maximum local autonomy while at the same time creating a sense of national unity, are understandable when one considers the oppression which the ancestors of Israel had experienced in Egypt and Canaan.[15] The concept of Yahweh as king, with the insistence upon temporarily empowered charismatic military leadership, was Israel's attempt to safeguard personal freedom by refusing to give permanent, dynastic power into the hands of any family. The refusal to support a full-time standing army, which could be used to buttress the claims to power of a popular or ambitious leader, reflects the same concern. The belief that battles are justified only when they are Yahweh's wars—when Israel's freedom was at stake—reflects the revulsion of peasants who remembered how their land and possessions had been ravaged time and time again by the booty raids conducted by one city-state prince against another.

And yet the central place of worship (where the Ark of the Covenant was kept) was Israel's way of producing a tribal solidarity which had not existed before Joshua. At Shechem, Joshua demanded that new peoples joining Israel put away the gods they had been serving and swear exclusive allegiance to Yahweh. Monotheism emerged at this time as a political necessity. The fragile union of tribes would disintegrate if lesser, local loyalties were maintained. A sense of corporate responsibility was created when all Israelites swore a common allegiance to Yahweh.

Although some tribes became weak (for example, Simeon) and were eventually absorbed into larger ones, others became so strong that they were forced to divide (for example, Joseph into Manasseh and Ephriam). Though we find differing lists of the twelve tribes in various parts of the Old Testament, the number twelve was strictly maintained.[16] In time, however, the Israelites discovered that a loose confederation of tribes was insufficient to deal with their enemies. They came to feel the need for a permanent leader who might command a well-trained and equipped standing army to deal with emergencies as they arose.

The emergence of the Philistines as a threat to Israel's national existence hastened the downfall of the Tribal League. The Philistines, descendants of the sea peoples who had invaded Egypt, had probably settled along the sea coast of south Canaan shortly before 1200 B.C.[17] Although they were quite small in number, living in only five cities, their army was unified and well-disciplined. By the middle of the eleventh century B.C., the Philistines had the Israelite army in complete disarray. The decisive moment came about 1050 B.C. with the fall of Shiloh, Israel's central place of worship. Samuel, who had been connected with the Shiloh sanctuary and had assumed national leadership following its destruction, was compelled by popular demand to find a permanent military leader who could deliver Israel from the Philistines. The anointing of Saul as the first king was the beginning of the end of one of the great periods in Israel's history.

Saul was in many ways a judge—part of the old order. He was an extremely charismatic individual with only a small band of personal retainers, and he was dependent upon the tribal levies for his army. At first Saul was quite successful against the Philistines. But eventually the continuous pressures of the Philistines and his conflict with Samuel caused Saul to fear that he had lost his charismatic power, his favor with Yahweh. With these self-doubts, he was driven into insane fits of jealousy by the rising popularity of David. Saul wasted the energy of the Israelite army pursuing David instead of the Philistines, and eventually Israel collapsed. The final battle was fought on the slopes of Mount Gilboa, where the Israelite army was smashed and scattered by the Philistines. Saul and several of his sons were killed.

David and the Emergence of Kingship

David had begun his career as a captain in Saul's army. His personal charm and charisma had won him wide popular acclaim, but Saul's jealousy soon forced David to flee the land. He hid out in caves as a fugitive outlaw while building a band of four hundred loyal soldiers. Finally he became the vassal of a Philistine king. But fortunately for David, the other Philistines feared treachery and would not allow him to fight against Israel at Mount Gilboa.

After Saul's death David returned to his home in Bethlehem, where he was made king over the tribe of Judah. The Philistines, who then controlled the land, allowed his kingship because they thought it would keep Israel divided. The northern tribes of Israel were ruled by Ishbaal, one of the few sons of Saul who had survived Mount Gilboa. But a series of intrigues, which culminated in Ishbaal's assassination, brought the elders of Israel to David's doorstep to make him king over all of Israel.

The Philistines discovered this new unity too late. When they marched out to divide Israel again, their army was cut to pieces by David's troops, whose striking power came mostly from that hard core of loyal followers who had joined him during his outlaw days. In quick succession David conquered the Edomites,

Moabites, Ammonites, and Arameans, and entered into a peace treaty with the Phoenicians. Within two decades of the disaster at Mount Gilboa, David had made Israel the strongest empire in the ancient Near East, controlling nearly all of Canaan.

David's internal policy ended the Tribal League. In a wise move to placate the rivalry between north and south, he selected Jerusalem as the new capital of Israel. He then brought the ancient Ark of the Covenant into Jerusalem, transforming the city of David into the new central place of worship—Mount Zion, Yahweh's holy dwelling place.

Perhaps the most far-reaching changes accomplished under David were those which affected religious behavior. The Mosaic covenant, with its strict ethical emphasis, was shoved into the background. Stress was placed instead upon David as Yahweh's servant through whom the promises made to Abraham had finally been fulfilled. Indeed Israel possessed the Promised Land; she was a great nation. A new covenant came into being: one between Yahweh and David. Unlike Saul, who was rejected for his disobedience, David and his descendants were to be maintained on the throne in Jerusalem eternally, regardless of their sins. The Israelites believed that since Jerusalem was Yahweh's holy city, his exalted dwelling place, it would always be protected against enemy attacks. In these changes we see the emergence of a religion which regarded Yahweh as a national guardian, regardless of the people's behavior, rather than as a suzerain who held his vassals accountable for their actions.

Under Solomon, David's son, Israel became a full-fledged monarchy. A lavish court was created, wives were imported from all over the Near East, and beautiful government buildings were built throughout the land. Israel was governed by a centralized administration which superseded the authority of local tribal units. To keep this power in the hands of the crown, a standing army was stationed throughout the empire.

Such rapid transition into a radically new way of life necessarily produced some reaction. But the story of this reaction, which culminated in the development of prophecy, as well as in the work of Deuteronomy, is beyond the scope of this introductory essay. We need only point out that Israelite protests against monarchy can be traced back prior to Saul. Many Israelites believed that Yahweh, and Yahweh alone, was king over Israel. The anointing of a human king was seen as the dethroning of Yahweh. This protest against monarchy explains, in part, Samuel's violent rejection of Saul and also the rebellions (one led by David's own son Absalom) against David's rule. The tenets of the Mosaic covenant were still adhered to by large groups of Israelites.

When Solomon died in 922 B.C., this anti-monarchial feeling led to the breakup of the empire. The northern tribes broke away from the house of David, forming the nation of North Israel, but Benjamin was eventually won over by the descendants of David, becoming a part of the southern nation called Judah.

CHAPTER 2

Israel's Literature

FROM ORAL TRADITION TO PRINTED BIBLES

Although several law codes may have been written during the time of Moses, no large-scale recording of early Israelite history was made until the reign of David. Therefore, the writers in David's court, as they looked back to the age of Abraham and beyond, were not eyewitnesses to the events they were recounting. They were relying instead upon traditions which had been passed down by word of mouth from generation to generation for hundreds of years. Thus many of these early traditions, especially those in the book of Genesis, can be called historical narrative only in the broadest sense of the term history.

Perhaps the stories in Genesis might be better referred to as legends. Although legend may be an earlier form of historical narrative, there are several clear-cut differences between legend and history.[1] Written history, though never free of interpretation, tends toward a camera-like representation of the events which it describes. The historian depends upon the accounts of eyewitnesses, insofar as possible, and he evaluates their testimony for credibility against other descriptions of the events. Furthermore, though the historian may explore minor details for the light they shed upon the personality of important leaders, he generally gives primary attention to the great events of the age.

This chapter is a revision by James S. Ackerman of the second chapter of *On Teaching the Bible As Literature,* by James S. Ackerman with Jane Stouder Hawley as Contributing Editor (Bloomington: Indiana University Press, 1967).

Whereas historical records are most often based on written observations made soon after the event, legends are usually preserved for long periods of time by word of mouth. Therefore it is not surprising that, though the legends were often based on actual events, the details of those events were modified as grandsons and great-grandsons saw new meanings and developed different emphases to accomodate the stories to their own times. As the stories were passed on around campfires or at local places of worship, it was natural that they would undergo changes. The material upon which legends are based is usually not related to the major events of the age. Only that information which is directly relevant and interesting to the listeners is selected. Since the legends in Genesis were told by the descendants of Abraham, for example, the great rulers of the nations are mentioned only insofar as they come into direct contact with the patriarchs.

We have mentioned before that the twelve tribes of Israel had lived separately, migrating by themselves or with one or two other tribes before they were united under Moses and Joshua. Each of these tribes undoubtedly had a store of tradition concerning its own formation long before it became a part of the larger nation. The stories in Genesis preserve only a small portion, centered around Abraham, Isaac, Jacob, and Joseph—men who probably were the forefathers of the more important tribal groups. Abraham was remembered as the founding father, and the tribes' newly established unity was expressed through Jacob's being called the father of twelve sons, each representing one of the tribes of Israel.

After 1200 B.C. (Joshua), these stories, which until then had probably existed as small, independent cycles of tradition, began to be grouped together into a larger pattern. The thematic framework around which these units were structured was already formulated by 1200 B.C., and it was based upon the divine promises to the patriarchs, which were fulfilled in the Exodus from Egypt and the conquest of the Promised Land. We find this theme succinctly stated in an ancient Israelite credo which was probably recited by the worshipers as the basis for annual renewal of the Mosaic covenant.

A wandering Aramean was my father; and he went down into Egypt and sojourned there, few in number; and there he became a nation, great, mighty, and populous. And the Egyptians treated us harshly, and laid upon us hard bondage. Then we cried to the Lord, the God of our fathers, and the Lord heard our voice, and saw our affliction, our toil, and our oppression; and the Lord brought us out of Egypt with a mighty hand and an outstretched arm, with great terror, signs and wonders; and he brought us into this place and gave us this land, a land flowing with milk and honey. (Deuteronomy 26:5–9)[2]

This short passage is Israel's sacred story. It is the framework around which all the earlier tribal traditions were structured.

The overall narrative, stretching from the time of Abraham down to the conquest of Canaan, continued to be developed, modified, and polished as it was transmitted orally throughout the period of the judges. Being preserved in oral form, the story might differ slightly from one Israelite village to another. But since it was regularly recited before all the people when the covenant was renewed at the central place of worship, we may assume that the variations were not extreme. If, as some believe, these cycles were transmitted as poetry, the rhythm of the language would provide a further check against drastic change.

In the tenth century B.C., some time during the reigns of David and Solomon, Israel's sacred story was probably first written down —in narrative prose. Scholars have called this unknown writer the *Yahwist* (and his document *J*)[3] because he consistently refers to God as *Yahweh*. The *Yahwistic* epic probably represents a southern version of Israel's sacred story. It is one of the great pieces of literature in the Old Testament. The style is free and flowing, moving rapidly to the climax of each scene; scenes and characters are sketched distinctly with a few words.

A joyful optimism permeates the whole work. The Yahwist writes with an exuberant confidence that the promises made to Abraham have been fulfilled through the conquests and kingdom of David. His confidence, however, is based on Yahweh, not on man. Perhaps the most significant contribution made by the Yahwist to the development of Israelite literature is the preface which he gave to his epic in Genesis 2–11. Here he modified ancient Near Eastern traditions in order to portray man as a creature who is uniquely capable of disobeying God at every opportunity. Man's sin, which had spread from the Garden of Eden to pollute the entire universe, caused Yahweh to intervene in human history through Israel so that his righteous order of creation might be restored.

After Solomon died, Israel split into two nations. The ten northern tribes broke away from the house of David in a partial attempt to return to the tenets of the Mosaic covenant. The Northern Kingdom, which regarded itself as the true successor of Israel, had its own epic tradition. Scholars call this version *E*, and its writer the *Elohist* because of this tradition's preferential use of *Elohim* (translated "God" in most Bibles) for the divine name. It can be assigned roughly to the latter half of the ninth century B.C. Although it tells the same story as the Yahwist epic, beginning with Abraham and extending at least through the conquest, there are certain regional differences. For example, there is a marked interest in the prophetic movement which had flourished in the North under Elijah and Elisha. Furthermore, whereas the Yahwist often depicts God in strongly anthropomorphic terms, the Elohist portrays him in a more distant fashion. God never "comes down" to walk and talk with man in *E*; rather he appears to man in dreams.

These two national epics, though dependent upon oral tradition as their source, originated independently and remained separate until 722 B.C., when North Israel was permanently destroyed by the Assyrian army. During this period of confusion, several documents, among them E, were probably brought into Judah by North Israelite refugees. When it was noted that E contained material different from that of the J version, an editor incorporated large portions from E, harmonizing them with the J narrative—thus forming a united epic tradition. This editing was probably done under King Hezekiah (about 700 B.C.), who had among his major policies the reunification of North and South into one nation.

Another document which must have entered Judah from North Israel at that time constitutes a major portion of the book of

Deuteronomy. This book contains Mosaic covenant traditions from the Tribal League period which were preserved and reworked in North Israel after they had been ignored and suppressed in the South by the descendants of David. The book is an ardent plea that Israel save herself from the Assyrian menace by obeying the ancient covenant teachings of Moses. Only then, it was believed, would Yahweh act to save his people.

After lying unnoticed in a storage room of the Jerusalem temple for a century, the document was discovered during a renovation project in 622 B.C. and brought before King Josiah, who set about making these ancient covenant demands the law of the land. Although the reform was short-lived on a national level—ending with the king's tragic death—it was continued by a small group of Deuteronomic theologians, whose contribution to the development of Israelite literature was extremely important. The Deuteronomists undertook to continue the history of Israel which had been begun by J and E. Gathering materials from various sources —ancient tales of the judges and early prophets, royal court records and annals, and other accounts—they tried to show that Israel's history had been determined by the extent to which she had obeyed Yahweh's demands. The Deuteronomic history was incorporated into the JE narrative, beginning with the speech of Moses before his death (Deuteronomy) and extending from the conquest to the Babylonian exile (Joshua-II Kings).

The final stage of this literary development took place while the Jews were exiled in Babylon.[4] A priestly writer (P) took JE plus the Deuteronomic history and added materials from sources which had not been available to the other writers. For the most part he included ancient palace and temple archive lists which had been rescued from burning Jerusalem. These included lists of tribes, ancient genealogies, boundary lists, rituals for sacrifice, law codes, and standards of measure for various temple objects. But the priestly writer also added several stories to the historical narrative, most notably the creation story (Genesis 1:1–2:4a) and alternate accounts of the covenants with Abraham (Genesis 17) and Moses (Exodus 6:2–8). (When we speak of a sixth century writer adding accounts to the biblical narrative, we are in no way implying that these traditions are less ancient or less genuine. These accounts probably represent the traditions as they were known and preserved by the priests of the Jerusalem temple.) The priestly writer added these stories to show the ancient origin of two institutions—observance of Sabbath and circumcision—which had become hallmarks of Judaism by the time of the Exile. The major part of the priestly material, however, follows Exodus 25 as a continuation of Moses' speech at Mount Sinai. A large portion of the Old Testament, from Genesis to II Kings, was now in finished form.[5]

Scattered among several nations by the Exile, the Jews were soon faced with the threat of being consumed and forgotten as a distinct people. How could the people of Yahweh function as a minority group, dispersed among the nations? All the previous factors of national identity—land, crown, temple—lay in ruins. The Jews desperately needed a common bond around which they could rally, no matter where they lived.

Under Nehemiah and Ezra, who led in bolstering the faltering Jewish community which had returned to Palestine after the Exile, this bond—holy Scripture—was established. The book of Deuteronomy, representing the covenant teachings of Moses, had already been proclaimed sacred during the reform of King Josiah. Ezra went even further. Taking the first five books of the Bible (Genesis—Deuteronomy), which include the patriarchal preparation for Moses, the Exodus deliverance under Moses, and the teachings of Moses at Mount Sinai, Ezra reunified the people in covenant renewal around this body of literature as their sacred teaching (called the Torah in Hebrew). The Torah remains the most revered part of the Old Testament in Judaism to this day.

Other writings, especially those of the prophets, were also popular and soon became authoritative among the Jews. By at least the third century B.C., this new group, called the Prophets, was accepted into the Old Testament canon as holy Scripture. These writings can be divided into two groups: (a) the Former Prophets (Joshua-II Kings), which provides the historical framework in which the prophets were active, and (b) the Latter

Prophets, composed of the three major prophets, Isaiah, Jeremiah, and Ezekiel, and the twelve minor prophets.

The centuries immediately preceding and following the Christian era were ones of strong religious ferment. More and more writings were produced, many claiming ancient origin, and it became increasingly difficult for religious authorities to determine which were to be accepted. Thus between A.D. 90 and 100, when the Jewish community in Palestine was once again threatened with disintegration after the severe treatment it had received from the Roman legions during the First Revolt (A.D. 66–70), a synod of leading religious authorities was convened at Jamnia to decide finally which books were to be included in the Old Testament canon. The place of the Torah and Prophets in the canon was reaffirmed, and a new group of books called the Writings was added.[6] These books, including such important texts as the Psalms and Job, completed the official collection of Old Testament literature.

Each Jewish community had its own edition of Scripture, which had been laboriously copied by hand on parchment scrolls. Long after the collection of thirty-nine Old Testament books was officially recognized, there remained significant regional variations in the word-for-word rendering of particular texts. After the Exile there were at least three major Jewish communities (Babylonian, Palestinian, and Egyptian), each of which maintained its own version of the Old Testament writings.

How do we explain these divergencies? There are many reasons for textual corruption. A scribe might have mistakenly omitted or repeated words, or incorrectly interpreted the poor penmanship of a predecessor. If the text was being read aloud to a group, he might have heard a word or phrase incorrectly. In rare cases a zealous scribe might have omitted or altered passages which offended his sensitivities. These changes, once they had entered the texts, were then often passed down faithfully from generation to generation.

Another factor which affected the development of the text was the fact that Hebrew, the language in which most of the Old

Testament was written, was gradually replaced as the spoken language by Aramaic, a related dialect. Between the time of Ezra and Jesus, Hebrew became increasingly difficult for many Jews to understand. The need for translations into other languages was apparent.

In the third century B.C., the Egyptian textual tradition was translated from Hebrew into Greek, the lingua franca of the day. The Greek version is called the Septuagint. Interestingly, it included a group of writings called the Apocrypha, which is not in the standardized Old Testament canon. The Septuagint became popular around the Mediterranean wherever Greek was spoken, and like the Hebrew text, it also was soon differentiated into regional recensions.

Although Nehemiah and Ezra had been partially successful in reestablishing a Jewish community in Palestine following the Exile, the center of Jewish learning remained in Babylon. It was there that what eventually became the standard Hebrew text for much of the Old Testament was preserved. It was probably brought to Palestine during the second century B.C., when Parthian invasions in the East forced a massive migration of Jews out of Babylon. The recently discovered Dead Sea Scrolls, our earliest evidence by almost 1000 years for any Hebrew text, clearly show the variety of textual traditions—Egypt, Palestinian, and Babylonian—which existed and interacted with one another in Palestine during the last two pre-Christian centuries. Eventually, especially under the influence of Rabbi Aqiba in the second century A.D., the Babylonian version won out over its rivals, becoming the standardized Hebrew text for much of the Old Testament.

After Rabbi Aqiba, the status of the Hebrew text continued to rise at the expense of the Septuagint version. This prompted both Jews and Christians (Aquila, Symmachus, and Theodotian) to rework the Septuagint to conform more closely to the Hebrew text. These efforts culminated in the edition of the Hexapla by Origen in the fourth century A.D. Translations were also made from the Hebrew into Aramaic, Syriac, and Latin and from the Greek into Coptic, Ethiopic, Latin, and Arabic during the early Christian centuries. These recensions and translations are valuable in establishing the original text of a particular passage because, though they too have suffered at the hands of the scribes, they indicate the state of regional versions in a time before the text was permanently fixed.

An important translation into Latin was made by the scholar Jerome at the end of the fourth century A.D. It was called the "Vulgate," because it brought the Bible into the vulgar (common) tongue of the day. The Vulgate was based primarily on the Hebrew text, but it also includes the books of the Old Testament Apocrypha. The Vulgate became the standard version for Western Christendom until the Protestant Reformation. It remains one of the versions used today in the Roman Catholic Church.

One final development in the Hebrew text should be noted. For many centuries it had been passed down in consonantal form, the form in which alphabetic writing had been first developed by the Canaanites. As Hebrew became an increasingly archaic language, however, ambiguities arose because of the missing vowels. Thus around the sixth century A.D. a group of Jewish scribes, called Masoretes, inserted vowels into the Hebrew text. The standard Hebrew version is today called the Masoretic text.

The first translation of the Bible into English was made by John Wycliffe in the fourteenth century A.D. It was based on Jerome's Vulgate, and its style greatly influenced the translations which followed. William Tyndale made the next significant translation in the beginning of the sixteenth century, just as the Protestant Reformation was beginning in Europe. The printing press had by then been developed so that copies of the Hebrew and Greek texts were available to him. His translation, which was roughly contemporary with Luther's German translation, was a milestone in the history of the English language, both for its beautiful phraseology and because it was the first English Bible to be reproduced in print.[7] A century later this flurry of translating was climaxed by the magnificent King James and Douay versions, which were to set the tone of English thought and language for many centuries to come.

There have been other translations, most notably the English Revised Version and the American Standard Version, completed near the turn of the twentieth century. But none has surpassed the King James and Douay versions in popularity. Only within the past decades, because of many recent textual discoveries and an increased sense of urgency to put the Bible into an understandable idiom, have several contemporary translations won widespread acceptance. Among these recent translations are the Revised Standard Version, the New English Bible, Catholic Confraternity Douay Version, the New American Bible, the Jerusalem Bible, the Torah (which is the first part of a new translation being done by the Jewish Publication Society of America), and also Phillips' paraphrase of the New Testament into modern English.

PART II

An Analysis
of the Literature
of the Old Testament

BY JAMES S. ACKERMAN
Senior Author
and
ALAN WILKINS JENKS

with Sample Questions for Discussion
compiled, edited, and/or written by
Edward B. Jenkinson
and
Jan Blough

Suggested Activities by
Edward B. Jenkinson

CHAPTER 3

The Origins of Man

The Two Stories of Creation

GENESIS 1:1–2:4A P[1]

Although the first story of creation included in Genesis was not recorded until the Exile, it is nevertheless based on ancient traditions. As it was repeated in priestly circles, the original poem was modified and adapted to liturgical use.[2] But the process of change did not alter the consistent structure of the story, which helps give it grandeur and force. Note the parallel structure and repetition in these two sentences:

(a) "And God said, 'Let there be a firmament in the midst of the waters, and let it separate the waters from the waters.'"
(b) "And God made the firmament and separated the waters which were under the firmament from the waters which were above the firmament."

Both sentences refer to the same act of creation. Their chief difference stems from the verbs *said* and *made*. Some scholars suggest that the Priestly writer added "And God said . . ." to the account to emphasize God's transcendence over all of creation and to show creation by divine fiat: all things are brought into existence by the power of his word.

The language in this narrative is simple and direct—yet ceremonious. Phrases are echoed throughout to enhance the theme of order and the concept of God as the great orderer of the cosmos. The dignity and ceremoniousness of the language add to the conception of an august, majestic god who creates by divine fiat.

The absence of particularly human motivation reinforces the idea of an utterly transcendent deity. Each *day* represents a higher level in the order of the creation, with man's creation as the final act symbolizing his place in the cosmos. Man is represented at the top of the scale of nature as God's most excellent creature—the only living thing made in the image of God.

In this version, the creation is presented as eight separate acts (two on the third and sixth days). Perhaps this tradition derives from a culture in which the creation was accomplished in eight days. If such is the case, the Priestly writer probably doubled up on two days (the third and the sixth) to accommodate the story to the six-day work week, plus the traditional Sabbath.

In this story, water is presumed to be the original substance; thus the separation of the waters was necessary to the creation of the world. This assumption coincides with a view of the universe which was commonly held in Mesopotamia. The earth was conceived as a flat square, floating on water, and the heavens, being blue, were also believed to contain water. The space of sky was thought to be maintained by the firmament (Genesis 1:6f), which separated the waters of heaven from those below the earth.

In most pagan accounts of the creation, order is established through a terrific battle in which the powers of chaos are subdued. In the Mesopotamian creation story, *chaos waters* is the monster killed by the storm god after a tremendous struggle. She is then sliced in two lengthwise—half to form the waters of heaven and half to form the waters below the earth. The Priestly writer uses the name of this monster (translated *the deep*) in verse two of his account, but there are no signs of a struggle. God is transcendent over all—even the powers of chaos and evil. Nevertheless, a definite relationship exists between Genesis and the Mesopotamian creation story, as suggested by the close similarities in the order of creation in the two accounts.

In verse 26, God says, "Let *us* make man in *our* image."* This

* Italics added.

statement is not puzzling to one who is aware of the divine pantheon concept as described in the historical essay.[3] God is addressing his host, designating that man be made in their likeness. The word *image* implies that man's physical, mental, and emotional faculties bear some similarity to those of the divine beings (compare with Psalm 8). Thus man is the crowning glory of God's creation. In 1:28, man is commanded to be fruitful and multiply, filling the earth and having dominion over all things. Whereas most ancient cultures deified the forces of nature and attempted to live harmoniously with them, biblical man believed that all of nature was God's creation and that it was man's role to subdue it to serve his purposes. By building dikes and canals and by irrigating and planting the land, man maintained and furthered the order of creation. He brought life and order from the harsh, conflicting and often barren forces of nature which he had experienced in the wilderness. (Today many ecologists are bemoaning this Judeo-Christian attitude toward nature which has until now dominated Western civilization.)

Some Questions for Discussion: According to the Priestly writer, what original substance existed prior to the creation? Why, according to the text, did God create the universe? How many stages were involved in the creation? What significance, if any, do you attach to the order of the creation?

What do you think is the meaning of man's having been made in the *image* of God? Note that in verse 26 God says: "Let us make man in our image, after our likeness. . . ." To who do you think the word *our* refers? Defend your answer.

Read Genesis 1:1–2:4a aloud, or listen to someone else read it. What effect does the language have on you? Why do you think the Priestly writer carefully selected words to achieve that effect? Do you think the language used in the account of the creation is appropriate? Explain your answer.

Do you think the Priestly writer structured his description carefully? If so, how did he structure it? What evidence of a *structure* can you find?

Note that at the completion of each of the acts of creation, there is a statement like this: "And there was evening and there was morning, a second (third, fourth, and so on) day." How does the account of the seventh day differ from the others? What significance do you attach to the seventh day?

This story of the creation has inspired other works of art, such as John Milton's "Paradise Lost," James Weldon Johnson's "The Creation," and Marc Connelly's *Green Pastures*. In what other works of art can you find references to Genesis 1:1–2:4a? What paintings, poems, plays, and so forth do you think were inspired by this story of creation? Why do you think so?

Suggested Activities: Some scholars have noted that the "real meaning" of the first creation story does not lie in what is said but in what is not said. They also note that the real meaning stems from the emotional overtones created by the language. Reread this passage carefully before you attempt to explain, orally or in writing, what you think the *real meaning* is. Before you write your answer or give it orally, you might consider questions like these:

> Was man created entirely for his own benefit, or for the benefit of someone else? What is the chief end of man? What is man to do on the Sabbath? What power is attributed to God? How do you know?

Without departing from the text, dramatize this story of creation. After you write a script, check it to make certain that the words uttered by God are faithful to the text. As you prepare the script, you need to answer questions like these:

> How would you describe the setting for this story of creation? Who will be present on your stage? What is the reason for this decision? How will you divide the dramatization into scenes—if you use scenes—to show time sequence? What effects can you achieve with lights? What

effect can you achieve by having no one on stage—only a voice or voices offstage?

GENESIS 2:4B–25 J

In the Yahwist's version of creation, verse 4 indicates that the entire creation took only one day. First, "a mist went up from the earth and watered the whole face of the ground." Thus a separation of the waters is not the key to creation; rather, it is the watering of parched soil. Secondly, God formed man from dust, giving him life by breathing into his nostrils. The remaining order of events differs from those in the first story of creation. The simultaneous creation of man and woman is the final act in the Priestly version, but J depicts man as being created first, followed by the creation of vegetation, beasts and birds, and finally woman. God is more human than transcendent in this second account.

The concept of man having been made from the earth can be found in several ancient Mesopotamian stories. The relationship between man ('adam) and ground ('adama) in Hebrew would reinforce this idea for the storytellers. We see a similar play on words in the man's poem of exaltation in verse 23, where he names the new creature *woman* ('ishsha) because she was taken from man ('ish). This passage expresses the closeness between husband and wife in Israelite culture. But why the rib, an actual part of Adam's body, rather than dust? A recent suggestion is that this story developed as a play on two Sumerian words, because in that language the word *rib* and a word closely related to *Eve* (living) are identical. The words are not identical in Hebrew, however, so we must assume that the Yahwist is basing his story on earlier Sumerian traditions in order to describe the mystery of marriage partners becoming "one flesh."

Man was permitted to name the beasts, the birds, and the woman. In ancient cultures, names were important indications of the character of a person or thing. Earlier man believed that the unknown could be known and controlled if it could be named. Thus knowing the name of a person or thing gave one a mysterious power over it, and the authority to designate the names substantially heightened this control. The Yahwist is saying essentially what the Priestly writer said in Genesis 1:1–29—that man has dominion over all God's creation. And since giving names was considered to be an act of creation in ancient cultures —bringing order and being out of the unknown—man is depicted by the J writer as a partner with God in the ongoing creative process.

Man was placed in the garden of Eden to guard and tend it. He could enjoy its fruits, except he must not eat from "the tree of the knowledge of good and evil." There is no scholarly consensus concerning the author's intent at this point. Some claim that eating from the tree brought sexual knowledge. But Genesis 2:22–25 implies that the man and the woman had already enjoyed sexual companionship. They had been enjoined to "be fruitful and multiply" in the earlier creation story (Genesis 1:28), so surely the Priestly writer did not regard this tree as transmitting sexual knowledge. Furthermore, eating from the tree was said to make man "like God" (Genesis 3:5, 22), whose sexuality is denied throughout the Old Testament.

Can the tree's fruit have given man a moral conscience— knowledge of what is right and wrong? Man must already have had that knowledge to understand God's admonition not to eat from the tree. There are several Old Testament passages in which "good and evil" refer to more than moral right and wrong, con- noting rather a knowledge of everything which affects man—from the highest good to the lowest evil (see II Samuel 19:35, King James Version). This is experiential knowledge from which one eventually learns to choose the good and refuse the evil (Isaiah 7:15–16). We would suggest, therefore, that the tree brought man total knowledge of the heights and depths of life. He had been created as a child of God, who provided for all of his needs. His knowledge (experience) had been limited to an existence which was in complete conformity with the divine will. Man in his innocence was still a child, completely dependent on God, his Father. Genesis 2:25 emphasizes this childlike innocence. As children the two were naked, but not ashamed.

The garden of Eden is pictured as an oasis watered by subterranean streams (Genesis 2:6). Whereas the waters in the first story were a potentially destructive force which had to be contained, which reflects the point of view of a delta culture, water in this second story is the substance which brings life to the parched soil, which reflects the point of view of a seminomadic culture. From the garden four rivers branched out toward the four corners of the earth. Scholars have tried to locate the spot by identifying the rivers. Their best hypothesis is that the garden was near the head of the Persian Gulf. The Hiddekel is the Tigris River. Cush is the biblical name for Ethiopia, south of Egypt. Thus many scholars have conjectured that the second river might be the Nile. It is more likely, however, that Cush refers to a land northeast of Babylon and that the garden was somewhere in Lower Mesopotamia.[4] The garden, incidentally, was quite close to, and shares many of the characteristics of, Dilmun—the mythical garden of the gods in Sumerian literature.

Some Questions for Discussion: Why do you, or don't you, think this creation story is a continuation of the first story of creation in Genesis? How does the language of the second account differ from the first? How does the style of the two accounts differ? Is the sequence of events the same? Is the tone of the first account different from the second? How would you classify the tone of each account?

What reason is given for the creation of woman? Why do you think Adam was given the task of naming the animals and the woman? Why is Adam's world pictured as a garden?

Study the two accounts of the creation and describe the kind of god presented in each account.

Suggested Activity: After you have studied both stories of the creation, construct an oral or written argument through which you can persuade a friend that there are two distinct accounts of the creation in Genesis. What evidence will you offer? How will an analysis of the language, structure, and tone of each account enhance your argument? What reference works can you use to support your argument?

The Expulsion from Eden (Genesis 3 J)

A primeval legend seeks to explain a particular aspect of universal reality by focusing on an event which occurred at the beginning of time. Thus the story of the expulsion is a poetic attempt to account for the misery and suffering that exists as part of the human condition. Although God created a perfect and harmonious universe, man has long recognized that such perfection does not exist in the world around him. The expulsion rationalizes man's misery in terms of his willfully disobeying his creator. Symbolically, the Yahwist has given us a portrait of all men by depicting the errant way of Adam, whose name means *man* in Hebrew.

The Yahwist, aware of the poetic milieu in which he is working, makes no attempt to account for a serpent who can speak. Talking animals are common in fables and legends, and serpents were once thought to be the most clever of animals, embodying characteristics we might today attribute to foxes.

The temptation scene is dramatic. The serpent begins by misquoting God. When the woman quickly rushes to God's defense, the serpent casts doubt upon God's motive for placing the tree out of bounds, and the willpower of the woman weakens. She eats and soon persuades her husband to follow her example.

The discovery scene is also a masterpiece. The Lord is portrayed as a wise parent who must ferret out the truth from his reluctant children. When Adam admits his nakedness, he also admits his guilt. And the Lord responds: "Who told you that you were naked? Have you eaten of the tree of which I commanded you not to eat?" In sorrowful wrath, God expels the two from paradise. Their lot is death (they are barred from the tree of life), enmity, and fruitless toil. He places members of his host (the cherubim) to guard the entrance to the garden with a flaming, rotating sword so that man can never re-enter.

There are many things which this primeval legend seeks to explain: why snakes crawl, why there is enmity between snakes and man, why woman suffers pain in childbirth, why man toils, why people wear clothes. At a deeper level, the story is trying to pinpoint the source of man's sinful misery. It lies in the breakdown of the childlike trust which man had in God. The serpent created doubt concerning God's motives for demanding obedience (Genesis 3:4–5). In eating the forbidden fruit, man attempted to gain knowledge of alternatives of behavior other than complete conformity to the divine will. Furthermore, since his faith in God had been shaken as evidenced by his feeling that he could no longer rely completely upon God's power and love, man sought to establish an independent source of power for himself. He found it in the forbidden fruit. Eating from the tree gave him wisdom-insight-understanding (Genesis 3:6–7), which, God remarks, made man "become like one of us"[5] (Genesis 3:22). This newly gained creative intelligence, coupled with his newly exercised capacity of choice, made man feel self-sufficient and independent —increasingly inclined to experience life as it exists apart from God's will.

The man and the woman are no longer innocent children. They have reached adolescence, declaring independence from their father's authority because they are no longer certain that he is commanding what is best for them. They seek autonomy, but a concurrent result is estrangement from God (they hide from him in Genesis 3:8). They are estranged from one another (they are ashamed of their nakedness in Genesis 3:7; Adam blames Eve for their disobedience in Genesis 3:12). Finally, they are estranged from the entire creation (Genesis 3:16–19). Set within the context of estrangement, man's freedom and creative intelligence become the source of his unhappiness, making him dissatisfied with his lot and always desiring something more. Thus the Yahwist seems to be saying that it is creative intelligence, coupled with the inclination toward its misuse, which constitutes both the grandeur and the misery of man.

Because the problem is complex, the Yahwist's analysis of the origin of evil is necessarily ambivalent. Although God created the serpent, he did not will evil in the world. The serpent acted against God's will; yet he is ultimately subject to God's control. Evil existed only as a potentiality until man willfully disobeyed. According to the Yahwist, then, man's disobedience brought evil into the world, resulting in divine wrath to this day.

Some Questions for Discussion: How is the serpent character-ized in Genesis 3:1? According to Eve, what does God say about the fruit in the garden? Why do you think the serpent could persuade Eve to eat the forbidden fruit? What knowl-edge do Adam and Eve gain from eating the forbidden fruit? How do they behave as a result of their new awareness? How is the serpent punished? Why are Adam and Eve banished from the garden?

Does man's eating the forbidden fruit give an adequate explanation of the origin of sin and evil? Why, or why not? What kind of relationship exists between God and man after the fall? What are the indications that man is still under God's care? What specific universal questions are explained by this story? Are they explained to your satisfaction? Why, or why not?

Man's expulsion from Eden has usually been termed "The Fall." Some scholars have maintained that the expulsion was an "upward fall" in human history. Can you see any possibility for a positive and/or creative good ensuing from the expulsion from Eden? What characteristics of man are revealed here that might be said to be responsible for both his grandeur and his misery?

Suggested Activities: When Adam and Eve ate the forbidden fruit, they were no longer innocent. Loss of innocence is a familiar theme in literature. Name as many literary works as you can in which the theme seems to be loss of innocence. Explain why you think each of the works fits this theme.

"The Fall" has inspired many works of art. Think about the stories, plays, paintings, and music with which you are most familiar. Which seem to be inspired by "The Fall"? Explain why you think so.

Prepare a collage in which you depict the creation and fall of man.

Dramatize the temptation and the expulsion from Eden. Who will be your principal characters? How will you describe them to your actors? How do you think each of the following should be portrayed: Eve, the serpent, Adam, God? Why do you think so? What evidence for your portrayals can you find in Genesis 3?

Cain and Abel (Genesis 4:1–16 J)

A favorite literary motif, well-known from other ancient Near Eastern legendary sources, is the rivalry between two occupational groups. A more recent example of this kind of conflict existed between cowboys and farmers and sheepherders half a century ago in the American West. The Cain-Abel story tells of the traditional rivalry between shepherds and farmers. Since Cain is the villain, this story must have become popular with Israelites during their seminomadic days—before they settled down in Canaan during the period of the judges to become primarily an agricultural nation. It reflects the traditional hostility and suspicion of the herdsmen for the farmers, who were the urbanized "city folk" of those days. (Note that Cain was the founder of the first cities.) As is still sometimes the case, the rural herdsmen felt that urban life was inherently sinister and treacherous. Such feelings are personified in the character of Cain. One should guard against comparing the personal characteristics of Cain and Abel, concluding that Cain had done some evil things not told in the story which caused his offering to be unacceptable. The story reflects the simple herdsman's prejudice that God would of course prefer the shepherd's sacrifice to that of any farmer.

The rejection of Cain's offering causes him to hate his brother, and the results of Adam's disobedience now become apparent. Jealously leads to murder, and the alienation between men who were born brothers is expressed by the haunting question, "Am I my brother's keeper?" Abel's blood cries out to God from the ground. Blood was the power of life in Israelite thought, possessing an independent, magical power of its own. If it were spilled through murder, a solemn obligation was laid upon the dead man's next of kin to take vengeance upon the murderer. The man's life was still evident in the spilled blood, which called out for vengeance. It was thought that until the obligation was fulfilled, the blood would continue to call out for divine requital against both the murderer and the kinfolk of the murdered man. Divine wrath would be manifested in the sterility which would come upon the land where the murder had taken place (see Genesis 4:11f, Deuteronomy 21:1–9).

In the Cain-Abel story, God places a curse upon the land and banishes Cain from the fellowship and protection of his family. This, as was noted before, is the most terrible curse of all, for Cain cannot long survive as an alien roaming in hostile lands. God yields partially to Cain's plea for mercy by placing a mark on his forehead—a mark of protection indicating that anyone who harms Cain will bring down sevenfold vengeance from God upon his family. Seven for one is an ancient concept of family vengeance, which was substantially modified by the "eye for eye, tooth for tooth" concept in the Covenant Law code (Exodus 21:24).

The origin of Cain's wife occasions no difficulty if we acknowledge that the Yahwist was not attempting to write a history of the human race in our sense of the term *history*. Rather, he was using several ancient traditions to provide some theological perspective for Israel's sacred history.

> *Some Questions for Discussion:* Why did the narrator have God favor Abel's sacrifice but not Cain's? According to the narrator, was God rejecting the offering itself, or the man who made it? What is Cain's reaction to the rejection? What is the meaning of the statement that Abel's blood cries out to God from the ground? What is Cain's punishment? Do you think it is just? How do you think the punishment would have been viewed by the Israelites?
>
> Why does Cain ask God, "Am I my brother's keeper?" What is he really asking God? Why does Cain fear that those who find him will slay him? How does God show mercy on Cain before sending him away? How do you explain the origin of Cain's wife? What is the purpose of the Cain-Abel story?
>
> Cain's question "Am I my brother's keeper?" has prodded man's conscience for centuries. What are some of the answers

that modern man has given to that question? What answers do you find in contemporary literature?

Suggested Activity: The "mark of Cain" has many interpretations. If possible, ask a minister, priest, rabbi, and layman what the "mark of Cain" means to him. Check commentaries and other references to see what can be discovered about the "mark." Report your findings to the class.

Noah and the Flood (Genesis 6:5–9:29 JP)

The flood story is given a brief mythological introduction (Genesis 6:1–4) to show that man's sin had corrupted not only the earth but the entire universe. Even members of the divine host were in rebellion against their Lord. (Genesis 6:1–4 is a fragment in the background of the Lucifer myth, which was expanded by Milton in *Paradise Lost.*) Adam's disobedience had resulted in fratricide, and the whole earth had been plunged into chaotic violence (Genesis 6:5). God was grieved by what he beheld and resolved to make a fresh beginning by blotting out mankind. The Hebrew word for *flood* in this account actually means that God intended to bring back the chaos waters which had been restrained by the firmament.[6] The waters above the heavens would come crashing down; the waters below the deep, with all restraints removed, would come churning up; and the entire cosmos would return to chaos. But God decided to save his creation, and mankind, through Noah.

As was stated in the historical essay, there are many flood stories in Sumero-Akkadian literature. The biblical version, sharing so many striking parallels with these stories, is undoubtedly based on the same flood tradition—brought by the Patriarchs when they migrated from Mesopotamia. Recent geological research upon Lower Mesopotamia indicates that the flood stories, although now immersed in myth and legend, may have been occasioned by a sudden rise in the sea level of the Persian Gulf which caused the inundation of large portions of the Lower Mesopotamian coastland.

There are some variations between the accounts, occasioned

mostly by the many centuries of oral tradition. The Babylonian Noah is named Utnapishtim. In addition to his family and the animals, he also saved the craftsmen. When the flood begins to abate, he sends out first a raven, then a swallow, and finally a dove. These changes are insignificant, of course; the most important difference is in the reasons given for the flood. In the Sumerian version, the flood results from a capricious decision of the gods, aimed for no particular reason at a certain Sumerian city-state. In the Old Testament, it is a just punishment wrought by a righteous God against the entire world for its sin. Thus the Yahwist has adapted the ancient account to his theological purposes.

Just as there are two stories of the creation (P and J), so are there two versions of the flood story. But, unlike the creation stories, the two accounts of the flood have been interwoven, forming one composite story. This causes duplications (Genesis 6:13–22 and 7:1–5, for example) and even contradictions within the story. According to P, Noah brought a male and female of every kind of animal on board, the flood lasted one hundred and fifty days, and the waters subsided in one hundred and fifty more. According to J, Noah brought eight pairs of animals on board, the flood lasted forty days, and the waters subsided in two weeks.

In Genesis 7:6, Noah is said to be six hundred years old. Some of his forefathers are said to have lived even longer (see Genesis 5). It was a common practice in antiquity to ascribe extreme longevity to forefathers. The Sumerian king list, which reaches back almost beyond the bounds of historical memory, tells us that some of the early kings lived from thirty to forty thousands years. Claims of such longevity may result from the natural tendencies to idealize the past and to consider a long life a good life.

At the end of Chapter 9, God acknowledges man's natural inclination to evil, but, apparently delighted with Noah's sacrifice, he determines never to destroy his total creation. This resolve is sealed with a covenant, the sign being the rainbow, which also symbolizes God's warrior bow, laid to rest from use against mankind.

Noah was thought to be the progenitor of all mankind: his sons were Shem (Semitic Near Eastern peoples), Ham (African peoples), and Japheth (European peoples). Because these peoples comprised the total known population at the time of the Yahwist, the covenant made with Noah is conceived as a universal covenant with all mankind.

Some Questions for Discussion: According to the narrator, why does God decide to destroy the earth? Which sentences explain why Noah and his sons were spared? Measured by feet instead of cubits, how big was the ark?

Some scholars believe that the Noah story is an interweaving of two stories by two different writers. What inconsistencies in this account can you find that might indicate that two accounts have been interwoven to make one?

When does the flood start? How does Noah determine that the flood has ended? According to the narrator, how does God react to Noah's sacrifice? What does God promise Noah?

For what two things is Noah given credit in Genesis 9:20? According to Professor John H. Marks in *The Interpreter's One-Volume Commentary on the Bible,* "tiller of the soil" is literally "man of the ground." Professor Marks asks: "Does this mean the first farmer, or the first man?" How would you answer that question? What are the reasons for your answer?

Suggested Activities: Attempt to state the entire message of God as it is recorded in Genesis 6:13–7:4 in fewer words. Why were you, or weren't you, successful? Compare your message with the biblical one. Which is the more forceful? Which is the more literary of the two? Why do you think so?

Reread the description of the flood (Genesis 7:11–8:13) and then write your own description of it, providing your reader with many details so that he will know exactly what you think happened. Then compare your account with one written by a classmate. Which account is more faithful to the biblical passage? Why do you think so?

What do you learn about the great flood by consulting an encyclopedia or some historical source? Is there geological evidence that the flood occurred? Is there any evidence that the ark existed? Report your findings to the class.

Compare the account of the flood in Genesis 7:11–8:13 with the story of the flood in the ancient Babylonian epic of Gilgamesh. How do you account for the similarities?

Read the entire Gilgamesh epic (see Nancy K. Sandars, *The Epic of Gilgamesh.* Baltimore: Penguin Books, 1960) and compare the context in which the Babylonian narrator places the account of the flood with the context in which the biblical narrator sets his flood story.

The Tower of Babel (Genesis 11:1–9 J)

The background of this story may be the Hittite destruction of the temple-tower of Babylon in 1531 B.C.[7] Babylon was one of the great cities of ancient times, and the destruction of its famous temple-tower must have been discussed with amazement throughout the Near East.

Mountains were the traditional dwelling places of the gods in ancient thought (Mount Sinai, Mount Olympus), but Lower Mesopotamia was extremely flat. Thus ancient Mesopotamian temples were built on top of huge, stepped mounds of earth—intended as artificial mountains—called ziggurats. Such a mountain, believed to reach almost to the gods' dwelling place in the heavens, provided a summit for the god to visit and reveal himself to his people. The people ascended the ziggurat in order to draw nearer to their god.

Babel is the Hebrew word for Babylon. In Babylonian, the word means "gate of god"; but in Hebrew, the word is closely connected with a verbal root meaning "to confuse, confound." Thus, as the story of Babylon's fall was rumored about, it is not surprising that a legendary development in the story should come to account for the confusion of tongues. Such a story would be particularly useful for the Yahwist, since his primeval history presupposes man's originating in one locale, using one common language. Thus the story explains why there are so many languages in the world today and why man is now scattered over the face of the earth.

God is portrayed as genuinely concerned about and amazed at the power of man's reason. Through cooperation with his fellow man, there is indeed little which man cannot accomplish, although he has irrevocably lost immortality (Genesis 3:22). After deliberating with his host, God decides to further limit man's power by the confusion of languages—precipitating untold misunderstanding and futile strife. The Yahwist is again seeking to explain presently observed phenomena (many languages, scattered peoples) as having been caused by man's continuous rebellion against God.

But the Yahwist saw something more in this story: it represented yet another instance of the arrogant disobedience of man —of his attempts to tear down the barriers between heaven and earth. The Yahwist believed that the true God in heaven and earth was holy, unapproachable—that there was an absolute cleft between God and man. Despite the tremendous power of reason which man had won through eating the forbidden fruit, he could never become God. He might seek immortality through enduring monuments, but ultimately he and his words would return to dust.

Some Questions for Discussion: What motivates the people to build the Tower? According to the narrator, what does God do after he sees the Tower? How is God characterized in this story? How is man portrayed? What is the relationship between God and man here?

According to the narrator, why did God need to confuse the languages and scatter the people? What purpose(s) would the ancient Israelites have seen in this story? Is there a common theme (or themes) which ties the Tower of Babel story to the stories of Adam and Eve, Cain and Abel, and Noah? In what sense do these stories constitute an introduction to the story of Israel beginning with Abraham? Why would the writer want to compose such an introduction?

CHAPTER 4

Patriarchal Legends

Whereas the primeval legends deal with universal themes and settings, the patriarchal legends are concerned with the lives of the founding fathers of Israel. Thus the scope of the stories is narrowed from the universal to the local. Nevertheless, these stories also attempt to answer questions about observed phenomena of a local nature which pertain directly to Israel. Why are there twelve tribes of Israel? The founding father, Jacob-Israel, had twelve sons. Why do the Benjaminites feel more closely related to the tribes of Joseph than they do to the people of Judah? Joseph and Benjamin were brothers—sons of the same mother.

In general, there are three major types of patriarchal legends:[1]

1. *Ethnological legends:* stories which seek to explain the present relationship between peoples as a result of the past actions of their ancestors. Why are the Canaanites our servants? Because Noah placed a curse on Canaan after the flood. Why are the Ammonites and Moabites, though related to us, such disreputable people? Because, although Lot was the nephew of Abraham, Ammon and Moab were born through Lot's sexual relations with his own daughters. Why do the Ammonites and Moabites live to the east of Jordan and we to the west? Because one day Lot selected that land, leaving Abraham the rugged hill country. Why is Reuben, the first-born of Jacob, no longer the most powerful tribe? Because he was cursed after sinning

against his father's concubine. Why does Beer-sheba belong to Israel? It was ceded to Abraham through a covenant after strife with another tribal chieftain.

2. *Etymological legends:* stories which try to explain how a certain place or person was named. Babel received its name through the confusion of tongues, Isaac from Sarah's laughter at the news that she would bear a son, Jacob from grabbing his twin brother's heel at birth, and Israel from the story of Jacob's wrestling with the angel.

3. *Cultic legends:* stories which attempt to explain the origin of various customs and places of worship. Why do we not sacrifice children? Because Abraham was restrained by the angel when he attempted to sacrifice Isaac. Why do we not eat the sinew around the hip? Because when Jacob wrestled with the angel, his hip was dislocated. Why do we journey to Bethel to worship God? Because God appeared there to Jacob in a dream when Jacob was fleeing from his brother Esau. These stories are often preserved in connection with a particular place. Just as Americans, in pointing to Plymouth Rock, might proceed to tell of the Pilgrims' first landing, the Israelites would point to the stone at Bethel, which served as Jacob's pillow on the night of his encounter with God.

The Migration of Abraham (Genesis 11:27–12:9 J)

This passage is a transitional section which the Yahwist has used to move from the primeval legends into the Abraham[2] stories. It tells of Abraham's forefathers moving from the Babylonian city of Ur[3] and settling in the region around Haran in Upper Mesopotamia. The details are partially confirmed by the fact that several towns in that region—Haran, Terah, Nahor—bear the name of Sarah's ancestors.

Chapter 12 begins abruptly. God addresses Abraham, demanding that he leave his family and his homeland to sojourn as an alien in an unspecified country. Abraham is asked to accept alien-ation similar to the banishment of Cain—leaving the protection of his family for the promise of protection and blessing by God. Accompanying this demand is the amazing promise that, although Abraham is seventy-five years old and Sarah is childless, God will make his name great[4] and multiply his seed into a great nation.

Abraham is told that other nations will be treated according to the way they deal with him. This promise is the perfect picture of a tribal god—one who is dedicated to Abraham's cause no matter what.

"And by you all the families of the earth will bless themselves" (or be blessed) is somewhat puzzling. The passage probably means that Abraham will serve as the model through whom all the nations will bring blessing upon themselves and upon one another. The blessing was thought to involve an increase in prosperity and fertility. Deuteronomy 28 enumerates the nature of blessings and curses at a national level.

The Yahwist has no interest in recounting the sociological, economic, or historical forces which may have also motivated Abraham's journey. For him the event is a test of religious faith. Abraham, the model of faith and obedience, makes no querulous response to God's demand. For the Israelite listeners, Abraham's obedience would have had great dramatic impact.

After Abraham arrives in Canaan, God appears to him and promises him the entire land. Thus the story explains why the sacred oak of Moreh at Shechem was an ancient shrine in Israel where Joshua later renewed the covenant with the twelve tribes. The end of verse 6, "At that time the Canaanites were in the land," is a clear indication of the processes of oral tradition—the story did not achieve its final form until the Canaanites had been driven out of the land.

Some Questions for Discussion: What is Abraham commanded to do? Do you think the command would be difficult for Abraham to accept? Why? In light of the above, what does his response tell you about Abraham? To what place does Abraham eventually migrate? Compare the terms of the promise made to

Abraham with the promise made to Noah. What similarities do you note? What differences?

How would you characterize Abraham in this story? On what information do you base your characterization? What seems to be the relationship between Abraham and God in this story? Considering what comes before and what comes after this story, what purpose do you think the biblical writer meant for it to serve?

God's Covenant with Abraham (Genesis 15:1–18 JE)

The description of God's covenant with Abraham is closely related to, or perhaps even an alternate version of, the preceding story in chapter 12. It is a composite piece which reads unevenly, evidencing editorial blending of several variant traditions. It is nighttime in verse 5; yet there is daylight in verse 12. Abraham is praised for his faith in verse 6, but two verses later he reveals doubts. Two sets of covenant promises are given (Genesis 15:13–16, 15:18–21). Most scholars propose that the main break in the text is between verses 6 and 7.

Chapter 15 focuses on Abraham's desire for an heir and the covenant God makes with him about his descendants. The chapter emphasizes the fact that posterity was extremely important in ancient thought. Because there was no concept of immortality, it was believed that one lived chiefly through one's descendants. A person could die happily only in knowing that he had descendants who would give him a proper burial and perform ritual ceremonies so that the departed could rest happily in Sheol. We have learned recently that it was customary for childless couples to contract with a relative or servant, establishing him as their heir if he would agree to serve them and give the couple a proper burial. Abraham had made such an agreement with Eliezer of Damascus. This agreement would be cancelled, however, should the couple eventually have children.

God states that Eliezer will not be Abraham's heir, that Abraham and Sarah will have a son, and from this son will come descendants more numerous than the stars in heaven. Abraham accepts the divine promises and challenges with equal equanimity, and God acknowledges him as a faithful servant.

The agreement between God and Abraham was sealed with a ceremonial covenant meal, for which Abraham slaughtered various sacrificial animals and birds. The animals were cut in two and "laid each half over against the other," a practice we also see in other covenant ceremonies (see Jeremiah 34:17–20). The agreement was sealed by both parties (or just the vassal) walking between the divided animals, magically bringing similar destruction upon the participants should they fail to live up to their covenant vows.

Abraham fell into a deep sleep, a common preparation for a divine act (see Genesis 2:21). What follows in the writings are two separate sets of covenant promises. In the first, Abraham is told about the Egyptian bondage, exodus, and conquest. These words, of course, entered the tradition *post facto*. But they were occasioned by the question which must have been constantly reiterated in Israel: Why did God wait so long before fulfilling his promises? The answer is given in verse 16: Israel is to possess the land as a divine retribution against the earlier inhabitants for their sins. The sins of the inhabitants continue to accumulate, for the moment of judgment is still several centuries away. Here these earlier inhabitants are called Amorites, the name used characteristically by the Elohist.

Preceding the second set of covenant promises, a smoking fire pot and flaming torch—ancient ritual implements—are passed between the divided animals. The fire and smoke are images of the divine presence. The Yahwist is aware that this represents God's presence, but he does not say it openly. The implication is that in this covenant agreement God is playing the role of the vassal. He is pledging to fulfill his covenant promises that the descendants of Abraham will one day become a great nation and possess the land of Canaan.

Some Questions for Discussion: Why is it so important to Abraham to have children? What does Abraham mean when he says Eliezer of Damascus is his heir?

What is the purpose of a covenant? What is the exact nature of the covenant God makes with Abraham? Why does Abraham seem to doubt the promises made to him? How is the covenant sealed? What do the flaming torch and burning lamp symbolize? How do you know?

To what does verse 13 refer? Why might the storyteller have included this explanation of the captivity in this story? Look at verses 6 and 8. Why does Abraham believe the Lord in verse 6 and not believe him in verse 8? What apparently has happened here? Do you see any other indications of two versions within this story? What is meant by "the iniquity of the Amorites is not yet complete" (verse 16)?

Sodom and Gomorrah (Genesis 18:16–19:38)

The destruction of Sodom and Gomorrah has already been anticipated in chapter 18, which should be read and referred to in discussing this story. Abraham has received three wayfaring strangers at the door of his tent, treating them with lavish hospitality. He eventually discovers that they are divine messengers who are on their way to Sodom and Gomorrah to see if the indictment against those cities actually warrants their destruction. Thus the grim purpose of the divine sojourners is known to us but not to Lot.

The angels left Abraham in the late afternoon, traveling the forty-mile distance before sundown. There are only two angels now; God had stayed behind to discuss the matter further with Abraham. There is something too repulsive in the sins of Sodom and Gomorrah for the narrator to allow God himself to become involved, except when the moment arrives for judgment to fall. Lot was sitting at the city gate (which was the "town hall" or community center of all Canaanite cities) in the cool of the evening. He greeted the strangers by bowing low to the ground— a common gesture of obeisance during that age. In an act of qualified hospitality, he offers the strangers one night's board and lodging. The angels' answer is an abrupt "no"; they are on a grim errand. Finally, however, they succumb to Lot's urging. They are

served a "feast" of unleavened bread—poor fare in comparison
with the sumptuous repast which Abraham had provided.

The inhospitable reception of the citizens of Sodom is used by
the narrator to provide a sharp contrast to the action of Lot. The
entire male citizenry, possessing homosexual inclinations, had
surrounded Lot's house in order to attack the strangers. This
situation created the supreme test of the rules of hospitality,
which obligates the host to protect his guests at all costs. Hospitality was, and still is, an extremely important custom in the Near
East. A sojourner traditionally was not entitled to the legal protection of the community. Thus it was Lot's responsibility to
protect his guests from violation.

Those listening to the story are supposed to be impressed by
the lengths to which Lot will go in order to fulfill the obligation
of hospitality. He appeals to the citizens as "brothers," implying
that he has lived long enough in the city to enjoy the legal rights
of a citizen. But his attempt at settlement is rejected by the
Sodomites, and they attack him.

The identity of the strangers is quickly revealed as they enter
the fray, striking the Sodomites with a blinding flash which leaves
them temporarily stunned. Lot, after regaining his composure, is
told of the impending disaster. At dawn the judgment will come.
The suspense builds, and Lot leaves the city just in time. Verses
23–24 are grammatically constructed to suggest three simultaneous
events: the sun rises; Lot reaches safety; the Lord rains fire and
brimstone on the doomed cities.

The statement that Lot's wife was turned into a pillar of salt
when she looked back on the burning cities illustrates legend's
common tendency to explain peculiar geological formations on
the earth's surface—as our Paul Bunyan stories "explain" the
formation of the Mississippi River and Rocky Mountains.

Sodom and Gomorrah have not been definitely located, but
they are thought to lie below the surface of the Dead Sea. It is
not known how the cities were destroyed, though earthquakes
are common in that area. Furthermore, there are large amounts
of natural asphalt which could have become ignited by the explo-
sion of one of the many natural gas pockets in that region.

Some Questions for Discussion: According to the narrator, why does the Lord decide to tell Abraham of the impending doom of Sodom and Gomorrah? How does Abraham react to the Lord's proposal? Why do you think the stoyrteller included the section on bartering between Abraham and the Lord? What does this show us about Abraham? What does this show us about God? about Sodom and Gomorrah?

Why, do you suppose, was Lot sitting at the city gate? What function did the city gate serve in ancient times? How does Lot's feast for the angels compare with Abraham's? What comment might the storyteller be making through this contrast? Why did the men of the city want Lot to turn the angels out into the street?

What does the phrase "know them" usually connote in the Bible? By making reference to this perversion, what is the storyteller implying about the nature of the life in the cities? Why is Lot willing to let his daughters be raped rather than the angels? Where else in literature do you find such strong feelings about hospitality and the rules that govern it?

Judging by verses 17–20, what trait has Lot in common with his Uncle Abraham? Is he as successful as his uncle was? Why is Lot's wife punished? Why does she become a pillar of *salt*? Why not a pillar of sugar or flour or something else? What connection has salt with the region where Sodom and Gomorrah were located?

Suggested Activity: In a brief oral report, explain why you think the destruction of other cities throughout history parallels the destruction of Sodom and Gomorrah. What cities suffered a similar fate? What were the social conditions in those cities before they were destroyed?

The Sacrifice of Isaac (Genesis 22:1–19 E)

This masterpiece of Israelite literature is one of the few Elohist stories which has not been spliced and harmonized into the Yahwistic account by later editors. Though we are told at the outset that God is only testing Abraham, a sublime suspense is main-

tained throughout as we watch the distressed father and unsuspecting son proceed to the sacrificial altar. No emotions are
revealed. The momentum is sustained and increased through a
staccato-like series of actions interspersed with sparse dialogue.

Abraham, the model of obedience, offers no resistance to this
horrible request. Instead of stressing the father's anguish, the text
simply states that Abraham got up the next morning, cut wood
for the sacrificial fire, saddled his ass, summoned his servants,
and departed with Isaac. The pathos of verses 6–8 is intense as
father and son leave the servants behind and go together to complete the sacrifice. The son, laden with the wood for his own
pyre, innocently asks his father where the sacrificial animal is.
Gently and evasively Abraham answers that the lamb will be
provided.

The drama moves rapidly to its climax in verses 9–13[5] through a
series of actions: they arrive; Abraham builds the altar, places
wood on it, ties up Isaac, places him on the altar, puts out his
hand, and takes the sacrificial cleaver. It has been suggested that
by describing the action in minute detail, the Elohist is trying to
indicate the benumbed, remote, automatic actions of the grief-
stricken father. He moves as one participating in a grotesque
dream.

This story was probably told to explain why Israel's ancestors,
unlike their ancient Near Eastern neighbors, did not practice
child (or human) sacrifice. The act was abhorrent to their god.
The story would also have served to reinforce the picture of
Abraham as God's obedient servant.

Within its larger sacred setting, the story means something
more.[6] Earlier stories established Isaac as the person through
whom God's promises would be fulfilled. Only if the child lives
can the seed of Abraham become a great nation. The real test,
then, was of Abraham's faith in God's ultimate purposes. Could
his trust be maintained even at the moment when it appeared that
God's purposes would fail?

Some Questions for Discussion: What do we, the readers, know
from the beginning of the story that Abraham does not know?

How does Abraham's reaction to God's command to sacrifice Isaac reinforce our understanding of Abraham's character?

Why do you think the storyteller did not include the thoughts and feelings of Abraham and Isaac? What emotions might the father and son be experiencing at this time? What effect does the lack of emotional quality have on the story?

What is the purpose of including in the story all the precise details of preparing for the sacrifice? What contradiction would result had God allowed Isaac to be sacrificed? What do you think are the purposes of this story?

Suggested Activities: Dramatize the sacrifice of Isaac. How will your actor portray Abraham? Isaac? What directions will you give the actors? What evidence from the biblical passage will you use to support your instructions to the actors?

Write a theme in which you explain why you believe Isaac is a young man with strong faith in God and his father. Explain why you think such faith is or is not believeable. To support your opinion, refer to characters in literature or history who have demonstrated such faith.

Compare the sacrifice of Isaac with that of Jephthah's daughter in Judges II and with the sacrifice of Iphigenia in the *Iliad.* What are the circumstances surrounding each sacrifice? How are they similar? How do they differ? Which sacrifices are carried out? Why? What are the results of the actual sacrifices? Of the attempted sacrifice?

The Betrothal of Rebekah (Genesis 24 J)

The solemn oath which Abraham exacts from his servants is similar to the last will and testament which an ancient man made on his deathbed (see Genesis 47:29). Aware of his approaching death, Abraham wanted to assure the continuation of his lineage by arranging the marriage of his son. The senior servant is entrusted with the task of securing the bride; Isaac is not even consulted. Abraham makes two stipulations: (a) Isaac's bride is not to be a Canaanite; the servant must return to Haran and find a young woman among Abraham's kin. (b) The servant is not to agree to any request that Isaac return to live in Mesopotamia. The tentative hold upon the Promised Land is to be maintained. The oath was guaranteed by the servant's laying his hand on Abraham's genitals—a procedure, demanded in only the most solemn agreements, which signified that the servant's failure to comply would bring sterility to his household.

The servant departs, his baggage full of expensive gifts for the prospective in-laws. Camels had not yet been domesticated; thus their mention in this narrative is anachronistic.[7] They are a symbol of great wealth, and the narrator probably used them to show how God had caused Abraham to prosper in Canaan.

The hardships of the thirty-day journey are not even mentioned: suddenly the servant is at the outskirts of the village. His prayer requests an omen from God that he might be guided to make the proper selection. Omens, incidentially, played an extremely important role in the life of ancient man. It is significant that the omen was also a test of the generosity and hospitality of the prospective bride.

A pastoral scene follows in which Rebekah comes, along with other maidens of the village, to draw water at the well. She complies with the tenets of the requested omen, and the delighted servant is brought home to the family. Her brother Laban is subtly characterized when he heartily welcomes the servant *after* beholding the expensive gifts. When the servant is received in the household, the entire story is retold to Rebekah's family. This repetition may be tedious for us, but such repetition is characteristic of ancient Near Eastern epic tradition.

The marriage is arranged between the servant and the head of Rebekah's family, who is apparently her brother Laban.[8] We have records of similar "sistership" marriage agreements from the middle of the second millennium B.C. They adhere to the same pattern as that used in the story: the groom is represented by an emissary of the family; gifts are presented to the prospective bride and her family; and, after the family's permission has been granted, the young woman must formally consent to the contract. The gifts to the family were quite substantial, representing the bridal price which the parties had agreed upon. This agreement partially explains the meager rights which the wife enjoyed in most ancient Semitic societies. She was considered the property of her husband.

The story concludes with a graceful description of the meeting of Isaac and Rebekah in the fields of Canaan.

Some Question for Discussion: Why does Abraham send his servant to find a wife for Isaac? What stipulations does Abraham make regarding the choice? What is the significance of each of these stipulations? How does the servant know that Rebekah is approved by God for Isaac? What does the sign itself tell you about the character of the "right" woman? On what basis do the members of Rebekah's family decide to allow her to marry Isaac?

What attitudes toward women are reflected in this story? Explain your answer. Are arranged marriages common in literature? Name several stories in which the bride was selected by someone other than the groom. What is your attitude toward arranged marriages?

The Jacob-Esau Conflict (Genesis 25:19–28:9 J)[9]

The major motif in the Jacob stories is the rivalry between two brothers. As in the Cain-Abel story, these brothers stand for opposing ways of life: the boisterous, aggressive, crude hunter contrasted with the quiet, clever, reflective herdsman. As these stories were repeated and developed over the centuries, Jacob, the herdsman, was appropriated as the representative of Israel. The older brother, Esau, became a symbol of Edom—Israel's neighbor to the southeast. And the intent of these stories is ultimately to account for Israel's dominance over Edom.

The twins supposedly receive their names through events which are connected with their birth. Esau is red (Edom) and hairy (a play on the word *Seir*, which is the central mountain range in

Edom). Jacob's name actually means "may (God) protect," but the Sematic root '*cb* had gone out of use, and popular etymology connected his name with the Hebrew word for heel. The incident in which Jacob grabs his brother's heel serves as a portent for the further development of the narrative.

In the first episode, Esau, famished from the hunt, trades his birthright to Jacob in exchange for a bowl of stew. The story illustrates the presumed superiority of the herdsman's way of life, where food is always available, to that of the hunter, who sometimes must go for a long period without finding game.

Recent archeological discoveries have helped us to gain a better understanding of the social customs basic to the birthright and blessing episodes. The birthright, a double portion of the family property, was traditionally the possession of the oldest son. It functioned somewhat as a piece of stock; it could be sold or traded for what it would bring. The father, however, might reallocate the birthright to another son, disregarding the priority of the first-born. Quite often this was done on the deathbed.

We have an instance of a father's wishing to reallocate the birthright in Genesis 27. Isaac, feeble and dying, was about to restore the birthright to Esau, his favorite son. Had it not been for the quick action of Rebekah on behalf of her favorite, Jacob would have lost out. In a sense Jacob is here acting to retain the birthright which had been forfeited to him. The suspense is high as Jacob succeeds in passing the tests proposed by his suspicious father. Permanent possession of the birthright, involving mastery over his brother, is determined by the old-man's blessing.

The listener's sympathies quickly change as Esau comes bursting in, triumphantly expectant after his quick kill. The change from joy to wrathful despair is poignant, as we watch the two broken men who have been duped by a cruel play. The blessing could not be recalled or revoked. In ancient thought the spoken word possessed a peculiar magical power. Once it was spoken, as a blessing or curse, it became an active force to bring about that which had been spoken.

Esau is not depicted here as the stupid bumpkin he was in the birthright story. One suspects that even the sympathies of the narrator were partially on Esau's side. Although J probably believed the cruel trick to be wrong, it was part of the tradition which he had received and which he felt obligated to perpetuate. How could he, the narrator, question the mysterious purposes of the god who had chosen Jacob over Esau?

The J narrative breaks off with Esau vowing murder, Isaac brokenly despondent, and Rebekah making plans to send Jacob to Haran until the controversy subsides. She knows that if murder is committed she will lose both sons—one to the murderer and the other to the demands of blood vengeance (Genesis 27:45).

At this point the editor has cleverly inserted Priestly material to provide another reason for Jacob's trip to Haran: to find a suitable young woman to marry. One can detect the break by the change to the stiff, formal style of the Priestly writer and by the different portrayal of Isaac. He is presented as being still in full possession of his faculties, no longer on his deathbed, and not the least bit angry with Jacob. (In Genesis 28:5, *Paddan-Aram* is P's designation for the region around Haran.)

Genesis 26 illustrates beautifully the processes of oral tradition. The first incident, in which Isaac attempts to pass off Rebekah as his sister to Abimelech, the King of Gerar, has been told twice before (Genesis 12:10–20; 20:1–18). These two earlier stories concerning Abraham and Sarah are the separate versions of J and E, both of which have been included by a later editor. In another region, the incident was attached to Isaac and Rebekah. It is obviously the same incident, since Abraham and Isaac both have the same protagonist, Abimelech—who probably would not have been fooled twice. Gerar belonged to the Canaanites during the time of Abraham and Isaac. Near the Mediterranean coast in the southwest part of Israel, Gerar became a Philistine possession (about 1200 B.C.), long after the time of Abraham and Isaac. But as the story was preserved in oral tradition, it was gradually forgotten that Philistines had not always lived there. It was assumed that Abimelech, who had a traditional Canaanite name, was a Philistine.

Genesis 26:17–33 describes a series of territorial disputes between Isaac and Abimelech over Beer-sheba. These incidents are variants of what has already been described in Genesis 21:22–34. We assume that it is the same Abimelech because Phicol, the army commander, is mentioned in both stories. E had received the tradition that the treaty at Beer-sheba had been made with Abraham, whereas J ascribed it to Isaac.

Some Questions for Discussion: According to the narrator, how did the Lord explain to Rebekah the unborn children struggling in her body? How did Jacob and Esau differ in appearance and inclination?

What did the birthright entail? Why and for what payment did Esau sell his birthright to Jacob? What sort of person do you think Esau was to have given up his birthright so lightly? What sort of person do you think Jacob was to have demanded such a payment for a small meal? Why did Rebekah encourage Jacob to steal the birthright? Is there any justification for her deceit? How does Jacob deceive his father?

What response does Esau's plight of arriving too late arouse in you? Contrast the weeping Esau with the one who sold his birthright to Jacob? Why can't Isaac take back his blessing? How does the information you receive at the birth of Jacob and Esau foreshadow the two blessings? Why will sending Jacob to Haran avert a double tragedy for Rebekah?

What two reasons does the account give for Jacob's leaving and going to Laban's house?

Suggested Activity: Write an account of this event using one of the four characters as the narrator. Why will your account differ from the original? What will the new narrator know and see that we are not aware of in the original account? What will he not know and see?

How does a change in narrator affect the telling of any story?

Jacob's Dream at Bethel (Genesis 28:10–22 JE)

Jacob's flight to Haran presented an excellent opportunity for the telling of his dream at Bethel in which God renewed the covenant promises and blessings which earlier had been made to Abraham and Isaac. In his dream, Jacob sees a stairway stretching to the heavens with the divine host ascending and descending upon it.[10] God stands at the peak; he speaks to reassure Jacob that his departure from the Promised Land is only temporary and that his descendants will one day possess it.

Jacob emerged from his dream, shaken and awestruck. He set up the stone which had been his pillow as a sacred pillar; then he poured oil over it to separate it from common use and dedicated it to God. Finally, he renamed the place *Bethel* (house of God). Bethel was a long-venerated shrine through most of Israel's history. Pilgrims journeyed to this holy place, doubtless to worship at the shrine which Jacob had established. The vow which Jacob made in verses 20–22 was probably repeated by the pilgrims as the story was retold and the experience was relived. Bethel eventually became a shrine for the kings of North Israel, whose cultic objects evoked prophetic rebuke (see I Kings 13). Finally, the site was razed during the reform of King Josiah.

Some Questions for Discussion: How do you think Jacob felt about going to Haran after Rebekah talks to him in Gen. 27:42– 45? What do you think he might have been thinking as he headed for Haran? Compare the hatred of Esau for Jacob with that of the eleven brothers of Joseph. What is the source of the hatred in each instance?

How does the force of the hatred affect the hated one?

What did Jacob see in his dream? What did God promise Jacob? What did Jacob vow? Why do you think the narrator inserted the account of Jacob's vision at this point in the Jacob cycle?

Suggested Activity: Where, outside of the Bible, have you read or heard the phrase "Jacob's ladder"? Bring to class any story, song, or poem that includes that phrase and share it with your classmates.

The Winning of Rachel (Genesis 29:1–30 J)

Jacob's arrival in Haran is described through another beautiful scene at the well. The young stranger, no doubt gregarious after his long, lonely journey, encountered some shepherds lounging at the well. Discovering where they were from, he asked about his relatives. The herdsmen were waiting for others to arrive so that the stone could be removed from the well and all the flocks watered together. Their answer to Jacob in verse 8 means that they were not permitted to remove the stone until all the flocks had arrived. The well was the property of several groups, and to avoid unfair use and hard feelings, the herdsmen had covenanted to ensure equal rights by removing the stone only when all the groups were present. The stone was also apparently quite large, and several herdsmen were needed to remove it. When Jacob saw Rachel arriving with her flock, he ran up and removed the stone single-handedly so that Rachel's flock could be watered. He was warmly greeted by Rachel and was welcomed into Laban's household.

Laban behaved properly toward his nephew for a month. But, probably sensing Jacob's feeling for Rachel, he realized that the situation presented an opportunity to strike an advantageous bargain. When Jacob asked for Rachel's hand, impulsively offering to work seven years for Laban in lieu of paying the bridal price, the marriage contract was formed. This extreme offer indicated to the ancient listeners the extent of Jacob's esteem and love for Rachel.

After seven years Jacob demanded his bride from Laban. At the wedding, however, the crafty father pulled a trick on the young bridegroom. The heavily veiled maiden was led into the bridal chamber, and Jacob woke the next morning to discover he had married the wrong sister. As the marriage had been consummated, the agreement was binding. When he went raging before Laban, Jacob was told that it would be a violation of social custom for the younger daughter to marry before the older. Jacob could do nothing but accept the harsh terms laid down by his new father-in-law: another seven years for Rachel. One senses that Jacob is receiving a just retribution for having tricked Esau. The injustice which had been done to one first-born (Esau) is now being somewhat avenged by Jacob's forced marriage to another first-born (Leah).

Jacob was permitted to marry Rachel directly after the week-long wedding festivities with Leah. Although the marriage of a man to two sisters may seem unusual and records of other such double marriages do not exist, one might assume that this was an acceptable social custom during the earlier part of the second millennium. This type of marriage was abhorrent to later Israel and expressly forbidden by biblical law (Leviticus 18:18), but the story was firmly entrenched and too important to the future development of Israelite history to be eliminated from her literary traditions.

Some Questions for Discussion: Describe the setting in which Jacob first meets Rachel. What reasons did Jacob have for weeping when he saw her? How does the removal of the stone from the well advance the plot of the story?

Explain your reactions to the story at the point of Laban's tricking Jacob. Was Laban justified in his trickery? Did Jacob deserve such a reversal? What irony is involved in Laban's deception? Compare the details of this deception with Jacob's earlier deception of Isaac. Has Laban changed since you encountered him in the Isaac-Rebekah story? What characteristics do you attribute to Laban?

Jacob's Reconciliation with Esau (Genesis 32:3–33:20 J)

The struggle between Jacob and Laban, in which each tried to outsmart the other, reached a peaceful resolution through the covenant at Mizpah. The narrator then creates new suspense by returning to a question which his impatient listeners had surely been asking: How did the conflict between Jacob and Esau end? Jacob still felt guilty about what had been done to Esau and was fearful that Esau's wrath would bring him ruin as he attempted to return to Canaan. He sent messengers to Esau, humbly seeking a favorable response. But when he heard that Esau was approaching, accompanied by four-hundred men, Jacob's worst fears were realized. To minimize the slaughter, he quickly divided his family and possessions into two camps. In a desperate effort to buy Esau's forgiveness, he sent lavish presents ahead, hoping that through them his brother's anger would be assuaged.

As the tension concerning the meeting with Esau continued to mount, the story of Jacob's wrestling with the angel breaks unexpectedly into the narrative. Jacob had expended all his concentration and energy preparing for his encounter with Esau. Suddenly he must use his last ounce of strength in an encounter which he had not anticipated. He had just finished praying to God for help (Genesis 32:9–12), reminding him of the promises which had been made long ago at Bethel. Is this struggle with the angel the answer to his prayer?

In many ancient stories men are attacked at night by evil spirits and win secret knowledge and blessing by overpowering them. The angel in this story begs to be released before dawn—a request which reflects the primitive belief that spirits are effective only at night. At first Jacob thought he was wrestling with a man. But the way by which his hip was dislocated indicated to him that the stranger was divine. Although painfully injured, he was strong enough to demand a blessing before the dawn. The angel could not bless him, however, until he knew something about him. One of the best clues to a man's character, it was thought by the ancients, was his name. So Jacob had to admit that he was a "heel-grabbing" rogue (Genesis 25:26; 27:36). The blessing follows immediately and Jacob's name is changed to *Israel*, indicating that his struggle had won God's acceptance and recognition. There are other stories in the Bible in which a person's name is changed through some dramatic personality-changing event (the change from Saul to Paul, for example). The Yahwist seems to be indicating in the later stories that such a change had taken place in Jacob-Israel. Surely this indication of divine acceptance is far more important to the Yahwist than the other phenomena for which the legend also accounts: (1) how Penuel received its name; (2) how Jacob's name was changed to Israel; (3) why Israelites do not eat meat from the sinew of the hip.

Jacob-Israel emerged from his experience awed and shaken: "For I have seen God face to face, and yet my life is preserved." Just as Abraham had been tested (Genesis 22), so Jacob-Israel also had been tested at the crucial moment of his life, and his perseverance had been accepted. This success was a good omen for the forthcoming encounter with Esau. Instead of bitterness and bloodshed, there was forgiveness and rejoicing. After the reunion, each group returned to its respective country.

Some Questions for Discussion: What reasons would Jacob have for sending a messenger ahead to Esau? Do you see any irony in the nature of the gifts Jacob sent to Esau? In what manner does Jacob present the gifts? What is the purpose of this manner of presentation?

Who is the "man" who wrestles with Jacob? What image of Jacob is the narrator building with the telling of his victorious wrestling match? What earlier event foreshadows this feat of strength?

In the Jacob stories cycle, the narrator describes two major confrontations between Jacob and God. What do you think these incidents add to the cycle? How does the narrator use these dramatic confrontations to help structure the cycle?

Using the information gained from previous incidents and episodes, contrast the personalities of Jacob and Esau. How does the author succeed in creating personalities for Jacob and Esau without actually telling the reader what they are like?

Were you surprised at Esau's reaction to Jacob's homecoming? Why or why not? Why is Jacob's name changed? What does the change in name symbolize?

CHAPTER 5

The Story of Joseph

The story of Joseph provides an appropriate conclusion to the patriarchal narratives. Yet it is different in several ways from the preceding stories. The most notable difference is its length, which allows the narrator far greater latitude in developing the character of Joseph. The story lacks many of the ethnological-etymological-cultic elements which characterize the earlier patriarchal narratives (see pp. 56–57). Further, there is no instance of God's personally appearing within the story.

Whereas the Abraham and Jacob stories are composed of independent traditions which have been clustered around two epic heroes of Israel's prehistory, the Joseph story is a single, continuous narrative.[1] There are individual scenes within the narrative—each a finished piece in itself—but there was never a time in which these scenes existed independently. Each is linked within the development of the story as a whole.

The Joseph story is a later development in the history of Israel's literature. Many of the episodes are probably derived from the Egyptian milieu of the mid-second millennium, during the time when Semitic peoples were settled in the Egyptian Delta. But the setting in which these episodes were shaped into their present literary form is quite different from the earlier epic cycles of Abraham and Jacob. Secular humanism is the prevailing tone in the Joseph story. Though there is a divine plan which overrides the schemes of envious brothers and Potiphar's wife, and which provides the continuation and preservation of the line of Abraham, Isaac, and Jacob in the context of impending famine (Genesis 45:4–8; 50:20), the stress throughout is upon man.

The many-sided character of Joseph is brought out in the sequence of episodes which portray his overcoming his brash, adolescent self-centeredness. Joseph emerges finally as a man of shrewd wisdom, integrity, modesty, and self-discipline, who is able to withstand the wiles of woman, who is able to control his emotions in public, and who is always ready with appropriate counsel when called upon in court. These are the very ideals of many of the Proverbs, which were used to train the young nobility to become the next generation of royal administrators. For these reasons it has been suggested that the final shaping of the Joseph story took place within royal court circles. It is great literature in itself; but it also would serve an excellent didactic purpose for the young nobility, portraying Joseph as the model court administrator whose ways were prospered by God because he developed the proper virtues.[2]

Although scholars have not yet found references to Joseph in Egyptian sources, it is quite possible that this narrative has some historical basis. It is well known that during this time people of Semitic origin were able to gain high offices in the Egyptian government.[3] Regardless of its historicity, the story is structurally important within the book of Genesis. In describing how the descendants of Abraham came to Egypt, it establishes the background for the period of enslavement which immediately follows in the book of Exodus.

The major sources for the Joseph story are J and E. Their versions are distinguished by the difference in the use of the divine name (see pp. 29–30) and the consistent reference to Jacob as *Israel* in the J version. As will be pointed out in our discussion of the story, J and E seem to have had slightly different versions, probably due to regional oral variations. These versions have been artfully edited to give further depth and quality to the narrative.[4]

Joseph and His Brothers (Genesis 37:2–36 JE)

Joseph is deftly portrayed as a pampered son who exalts himself at his family's expense whenever possible. He possesses a beautiful robe, a gift from his father, decorated with ornaments of precious metal.[5] It is a princely garment, which suggests the minimal amount of work required of Joseph in the family. He tattles on his brothers, we learn. His dreams, in which he sees himself as a royal figure before whom the rest of his family bow, betray a naive pride which further arouses the antagonism of his brothers and troubles his puzzled father. It should be noted that dreams were extremely significant in ancient thought. They were believed to have a prophetic character through which future workings of divine will were revealed. Therefore, although the brothers' ire at Joseph is made fully understandable, their attempt to get rid of him is presented as an effort to thwart the divine purpose.

Joseph is sent by his father to check on the welfare of his brothers, who are pasturing the flocks near Shechem. The reader has been prepared for the hostile reception he will meet, and the suspense is heightened when Joseph discovers that the brothers are not there and that he must proceed to Dothan to find them. The brothers see Joseph coming and plot to kill him. But remembering the possible dire results of incurring blood guilt (see pp. 49–50), they decide upon another means of getting rid of him.

Here the narrative becomes somewhat confusing and inconsistent. Reuben, hoping to save Joseph later, persuades the brothers to throw him into a pit (a bottle-shaped cistern dug into the ground for trapping rain water). Judah, who also wants to save Joseph, convinces the brothers to sell Joseph for twenty shekels to some passing Ishmaelite merchants who take him to Egypt. But Joseph is also stolen by some Midianites who take him to Egypt and sell him (Genesis 37:28, 36). Reuben then returns and is surprised to find Joseph gone.

One could suggest that verse 28 is saying that the Midianites stole Joseph from the pit and sold him to the Ishmaelites. But the brothers were dealing with the Ishmaelites (verse 27), and verse

36 states that the Midianites themselves took Joseph to Egypt. The problem is easily resolved when we recognize a conflation of the two traditions in verses 21–30.[6] In the E version, Reuben is Joseph's defender; Joseph is put in the pit and stolen out of it by Midianite traders, who take him to Egypt before Reuben returns to release him. In the J version, it is Judah who tries to save Joseph by suggesting that he be sold to Ishmaelite merchants.

When the brothers return home, they present Joseph's robe to Jacob. Upon recognizing the torn and bloody garment, Jacob rends his clothes and wears sackcloth for a long period of time. These are among the traditional acts of mourning in the Near East.[7] Mourning was more than an expression of sorrow; it was an acknowledgment that the mourner had been humiliated, weakened, and made unclean (see pp. 111–112) by the death which had struck his family. These acts of mourning set him apart from the normal life of the community until he had recovered his strength. Maintaining that he will continue to mourn even in death,[8] Jacob refuses the consolation of his children.

Some Questions for Discussion: Why did Joseph's brothers hate him? Are your sympathies with Joseph, or with the brothers? Explain your answer. Joseph has been described as a pampered son who tattled on his brothers. What evidence can you find to support this statement? Does Joseph encourage the hostility that exists between his brothers and himself? How?

Describe Joseph's dream as he told it to his brothers. How did his brothers interpret the dream? What did the dream prophesy for the future? What was Joseph's second dream? How did the interpretation of the second dream reinforce the prophecy of the first?

This chapter contains the skillful interweaving of the J and E strands. See if you can find the two strands. Pay careful attention of the two names for Jacob (Jacob, Israel), and to the references to Reuben and Judah. Can you determine exactly what the brothers do with Joseph? Have the brothers solved their problem wisely?

The "coat of many colors" is a frequently used allusion which originates in the story of Joseph. In this story, what part does the coat of many colors play? What does the coat of many colors symbolize today?

Suggested Activities: Make Joseph the narrator of Genesis 37. How would he tell the story? How might the account differ from what is told in Genesis 37? Why would it differ?

Rewrite Genesis 37 from Joseph's point of view. In your story, make certain that you do not add incidents to the account. However, by changing the narrative focus, you can tell your reader what Joseph thinks and how he feels.

Sibling rivalry is a common theme in literature. Name several stories, novels, and plays in which sibling rivalry is the basis of the plot. Do any of the stories seem to echo Genesis 37? Give reasons for your answer.

Reread Genesis 37:5–11. From those verses alone, write a character sketch of Joseph.

After you have written your character sketch, compare your version of Joseph as he appears in Genesis 37:5–11 with the character that is portrayed in the rest of the Joseph story. How does he change? What words would you use to describe him?

Joseph and Potiphar's Wife (Genesis 39:1–23 J)

In Egypt, Joseph is sold to Potiphar, a high official in the Pharaoh's court. Joseph's winning charm and a divine favor, which seems to cause the entire household to prosper quickly, bring Joseph to the responsible position of overseer to Potiphar's entire estate. (Verse 6 may be an illustration of the extent to which Potiphar had left things in Joseph's hands, or it may refer to Egyptian dietary taboos which forbad a foreigner to be involved in the preparation of meals.)[9]

But Joseph's charm places him in a dangerous situation. Potiphar's wife is attracted to him and tries to seduce him.[10] Joseph replies that such an act would not only be a violation of his master's trust, but—more important—a terrible sin against God. Adultery was a serious crime in all ancient Near Eastern countries, but it was especially serious in Israel. Whereas other ancient Near Eastern law codes often allowed the matter to be settled privately (for example, Hammurabi Law No. 129), adultery in Israel was always a community concern because one of God's most sacred laws had been violated. After repeatedly rebuffing the woman's advances, Joseph one day flees so quickly that his garment is torn loose. Using it as evidence, Potiphar's wife presses charges against the "Hebrew."[11] Such an accusation would customarily result in the death of the slave, but Potiphar has Joseph placed in the royal prison. Within the context of the story, the only explanation for such mild punishment is the never-ceasing divine favor, which causes Joseph to prosper even in prison.

Some Questions for Discussion: Why was Joseph made overseer of his master's house? To what extent was Joseph responsible for the household? What reason does Joseph give for ignoring Potiphar's wife? How does Potiphar's wife explain to the men of her house and her husband why she has Joseph's garment in her possession? Why do you suppose she presses charges against Joseph? What happens to Joseph as a result of this deception? How does the narrator depict the continuing presence of God despite Joseph's difficulties?

Interpreting the Prisoners' Dreams (Genesis 40:1–23 E)

There is a difficult transition from chapter 39, in which J had described Joseph's rapid rise to associate warden of the prison. In what follows, Joseph is portrayed as a lowly slave who has been charged with attending two noble prisoners—the chief butler and the chief baker (Genesis 40:5–23). Joseph complains of having been kidnapped (not sold) into Egypt (Genesis 40:15). Thus this chapter is a continuation from 37:36 of the E version, which does not record Joseph's difficulties with Potiphar's wife. In the E version, the Midianites had sold Joseph as a slave to Potiphar, who was the captain of the guard in the royal prison.

The context of the story indicates that the chief butler and the chief baker had offended Pharaoh and were in prison awaiting his decision regarding their fate. They knew that their dreams provided an omen for their futures, but, being in prison, they had no access to professional interpreters. We know that the interpretation of dreams and omens was a highly developed science throughout the ancient Near East. Joseph's sharp retort has a strong polemical tone: man's future cannot be determined by occult powers. It is in the hands of the god of history, the sole arbiter of human destiny, who alone can give insight into the meaning of dreams. The key to Joseph's interpretation is a play on the phrase "to lift the head," which has many idiomatic meanings in Hebrew and other Semitic languages. In this story, three usages are balanced against each other:[12]

(a) "To favor" connotes the gracious action of a king who accepts the obeisance of a prostrated subject by lifting his face. This is the most common meaning and is the key to the chief butler's dream.

(b) "To execute" is a rare, grossly literal rendering of the phrase which is particularly applicable in interpreting the chief baker's dream.

(c) "To review, give attention to" is the meaning in Genesis 40:20, which describes the day Pharaoh passed judgment on his two imprisoned servants—restoring the chief butler and executing the chief baker.

The reader is prepared for the story to reach its climax with the chief butler's deliverance of Joseph from prison (Genesis 41:14–15). But the narrator masterfully maintains the suspense: Joseph's plea is forgotten.

Some Questions for Discussion: What is the relationship at the beginning of the chapter between Joseph and Pharaoh's butler and baker? How does that relationship change as the story progresses? After saying that interpretations belong to God, why does Joseph then proceed to explain the meanings of the dreams? What meanings does Joseph give to the dreams of the butler and the baker? What does Joseph request for himself when the dream shall be fulfilled?

Why does the narrator include the fact that the butler forgot Joseph's request for a time after he was restored in Pharaoh's household? Why do you think this incident in prison was included in the Joseph story?

Interpreting Pharaoh's Dreams (Genesis 41:1–57 E)

Pharaoh's dreams abruptly open this scene, preparing the reader to anticipate the outcome. Knowing that his dreams are portents of the future, Pharaoh is troubled. He summons the professional interpreters, none of whom is able to render a satisfactory reading. The stage is now set for the young man who in the preceding scene has asserted the inefficacy of occult powers in determining the future. Impressed by the chief butler's account of his prison dream, Pharaoh summons Joseph into his court.

Joseph interprets the dream clearly, emphasizing that the divine plan is imminent and unalterable and urging that steps be taken to avert disaster. His advice goes beyond what would be required of an interpreter. Pharaoh is so impressed by the keen wisdom of such a young man that Joseph is appointed second in command (vizier) over all of Egypt. Furthermore, the tradition of seven-year famines is attested to in Egyptian literature.[13]

Although the precise time cannot be ascertained, Joseph's rise to power could best be explained if it occurred during the Hyksos period, when Semitic peoples ruled Egypt (about 1650–1550 B.C.). It has been noted that the Pharaoh in this story is extremely respectful toward God (Genesis 41:38f)—an attitude which might well characterize the Semitic mentality of the Hyksos period, but one which an Egyptian Pharaoh who considered himself a god would never adopt.[14]

By receiving a new name and marrying the daughter of the highest priest in Egypt, Joseph is made a full Egyptian. His success has surpassed even his youthful dreams. It is interesting to note that the following chapters, while providing many tests for

Joseph's unsuspecting brothers, also offer a test for Joseph himself: Has he forgotten his past—his family and his God? And when it is recalled to him, will he reject it in favor of the Egyption life and culture under which he has thrived?

Some Questions for Discussion: What is the turning point in Joseph's life? What has happened to make this the turning point?

What are Pharaoh's dreams? How does Joseph interpret them? Why, according to Joseph, was essentially the same dream presented to Pharaoh twice? How does Joseph advise Pharaoh to plan for the bad days ahead? How does this advice work to Joseph's advantage? How might it be interpreted to be a source of later trouble to the Hebrews (see Genesis 47:13–27 and Exodus 1–14, for example)?

Why do you think the reversal in Joseph's fortune was predictable? According to the narrator, what seems to be Joseph's relationship with God in the various incidents recorded in the Joseph story?

Dreams and the interpretation of dreams play important roles in the story of Joseph. What role have dreams or the interpretation of them played thus far? How does the story seem to revolve around dreams? What part do dreams play in the narrator's structure of the story? Explain your answer.

The Arrival of Joseph's Brothers (Genesis 42:1–38 E)

Joseph's rise to power in Egypt is only one of the story's major themes. Even more central within the overall narrative is Joseph's relationship with his brothers. Reconciliation is eventually effected through the famine, which has struck the land of Canaan as well as Egypt. The same event which has contributed to Joseph's power in Egypt is about to bring his brothers in Canaan under his control.

The brothers would have no way of knowing that the grand vizier who stands before them is Joseph. The childhood dreams have been fulfilled: Joseph's brothers are prostrated before him.

But Joseph, it seems, has not yet been avenged for their wrong to him. He accuses them of being an enemy reconnaissance force sent to spy out the land.[15] The brothers' entire defense hinges on their assertion that they are not mercenaries of a foreign power but brothers, representatives of one family (Genesis 42:13). Their defense plays perfectly into Joseph's hands, for he can demand that the missing brother (Benjamin) be produced in order to substantiate their story. They are put into prison and told that one brother should return to fetch Benjamin.

Joseph's initial outburst of wrath subsides. The brothers are released and told that only one must remain. Perhaps Joseph had decided that keeping all of them would have made Jacob fearful of sending Benjamin. The missing Benjamin is an important figure in this scene, but so is the brother who "is no more" (Genesis 42:13). The brothers' unspoken but keenly felt guilt finally explodes into the open, as their plight is attributed to a crime which they had been unable to forget or live down. The narrator notes that the vizier, who in fact needs no interpreter, is extremely moved by this sign of his brothers' remorse. Little do the brothers realize that the cruel vizier, the brother who "is no more," is even more shaken than they.

Joseph's emotions and actions, which show a strange mixture of love and severity, are difficult to understand. What is his final purpose? Why must Benjamin come? This uncertainty has yet to be resolved in the narrative.

Simeon, the second oldest, is bound and imprisoned before the brothers are sent home. Reuben, the first-born, who should have stayed behind as surety, is by-passed, probably because he had earlier acted as Joseph's would-be deliverer in the E tradition (Genesis 37:22, 29).[16] After returning home, Reuben acts again to save a brother (Simeon is doomed unless the brothers bring Benjamin back) by pledging the lives of his own sons as surety against Benjamin's safe return. But Jacob refuses.

Some Questions for Discussion: Why does Jacob send his sons into Egypt? How does Joseph greet his brothers and of what does he accuse them? Explain how Joseph modifies his order after three days. What might have been Joseph's motive in putting his brothers through these "tests"? Do you think the "tests" are justified? Why, or why not?

What do the brothers consider the cause of their present distress? Why do they not realize that Joseph understands their conversation? What discovery do the brothers make when they arrive home with the sacks of corn? Why do you think Jacob is especially anxious about the welfare of young Benjamin?

Is Jacob's refusal to send Benjamin to Egypt so that Simeon can be released understandable from a psychological point of view, or is it a literary device used by the narrator to create the appropriate mood for the next episode? Or is it both? or neither? Explain your answer.

The Second Journey of the Brothers (Genesis 43–44 J)

Because of the prolonged famine, the family of Jacob must consider returning to Egypt. It is noteworthy that the sole reason for going to Egypt is to secure more grain—not to release the imprisoned Simeon. This is most likely because of the switch in the narrative from the E to the J version. By comparing Genesis 42:30–34 (E) and Genesis 43:3–7 (J), one sees that the spy accusation and the detention of Simeon are omitted from J. The J version described the brothers receiving grain from Egypt, where they were told by the vizier that they could not return again without Benjamin (Genesis 43:3, 5).[17]

Judah plays an important role in the J version (as does Reuben in E). He had saved Joseph's life by suggesting that he be sold into slavery in Egypt (Genesis 37:26f); now he persuades Jacob to send Benjamin by pledging his own life if Benjamin does not return safely. The narrator is pointing out a gradual growth in the brothers' characters through this crisis which Joseph has brought about; they demonstrate a new willingness to give themselves for one another.[18] Age has not robbed Jacob of his cleverness. Having acknowledged that Benjamin must go, he resolves to make the best of a bad situation by sending gifts and a double payment of money.

When Joseph sees that Benjamin has come, he sends his steward to bring the brothers to his private quarters for dinner. The brothers, already uneasy, become increasingly nervous at this strange request. This growing fear is indicated by the defense which the brothers attempt before Joseph's steward. His reply raises even more suspicion and uneasiness in the brothers. He has received their payment; God must have put that money into their grain sacks.

At dinner, however, the brothers soon forget their fears and relax, enjoying the food and wine. The focus is now on Joseph, who is struggling to retain his composure as he sits facing his brothers at the feast.[19] Surely he will now reveal himself. Neither brothers nor readers are prepared for the dramatic reversal which Joseph has planned.

The brothers' sacks are filled with grain in preparation for their return to Canaan. At Joseph's instructions, however, his silver divining cup is placed in Benjamin's sack.[20] This cup was no ordinary utensil; it had power which enabled Joseph to divine the future. Ancient Near Eastern law consistently imposes harsh penalties, usually death, for the theft of sacred objects. Thus the brothers were in an extremely serious situation. Adhering to the customary judicial procedure, they assert their innocence by suggesting the penalty if they are found guilty: death to the thief and slavery for the others. The steward, doubtless on Joseph's instructions, changes the sentence. Only the guilty person will be taken, not to die, but into slavery.

Completely baffled, the brothers return before the vizier, admitting that justice has caught up with them for a deed done long ago. They offer to be his slaves, but Joseph insists that Benjamin alone be held. Joseph has been successful in Egypt; his family is humbled before him by petitioning him for food; his brothers have debased themselves by admitting their sin. But still he does not relent.

A clue to Joseph's behavior is perhaps given by his intentionally changing the punishment suggested by the brothers so that the whole punishment would fall on Benjamin.[21] Joseph was attempting to recreate the earlier situation as nearly as he could. He wanted to see if the brothers had changed. Would they, given the chance, save themselves and leave the other son of Rachel to the same fate of slavery in Egypt? Judah's moving speech (Genesis 44:18–34) shows that the years, and these trials, have indeed produced a change in the brothers. This scene, showing that reconciliation is now possible, is the climax of the entire narrative.[22]

Some Questions for Discussion: What consistent characterization has the narrator used for both Reuben and Judah?

Can you account for Jacob's apparent unconcern for Joseph's hostage, Simeon? Why does Jacob order the brothers to take double money on this second journey? Do the brothers have reason to fear the unwarranted kindness of Joseph's servants? Is there a hint of poetic justice in such fear? What is especially ironic about the brothers' behavior in front of Joseph? Why? Why is Joseph so moved at the sight of Benjamin?

How serious for Jacob's sons is the ruse of the stolen silver cup? What dramatic suspense has been built into the search for this cup? What symbolism lies behind the brothers' action as "they rent their clothes"?

Contriving schemes to bewilder and try subjects was a common practice among legendary epic heroes. Consider the answers to the following questions as illustrative of such a literary device. What does Joseph's steward put in Benjamin's sack? On its discovery, with what penalty is Benjamin threatened? In this scene of mounting suspense, what are the brothers' feelings? What, primarily, do you think causes them to feel this way? (Consider what you know of their past, their present situation, and what they must face in the future.)

Consider the plight of Benjamin in Genesis 44 and compare it with that of Joseph in Genesis 37. Why do you think Joseph had the silver cup placed in Benjamin's sack? Do you think Joseph was attempting to recreate the situation he had once been in? Explain your answer. What does this trick tell you about Joseph? What changes in the brothers are indicated by their response in behalf of Benjamin?

Why is it appropriate that Judah's role becomes prominent

in Genesis 44:18? What parallel or contrast becomes apparent as Judah tries to protect Benjamin? What does Judah's pledge of surety indicate to Joseph? What words and images in Judah's plea to Joseph are especially effective uses of language to convey emotional, dramatic tension? Does the dramatic irony also help involve the reader more sympathetically? Explain.

Joseph's Self-Disclosure (Genesis 45:1–28 JE)

Judah's offer to be enslaved in place of Benjamin, quickly followed by Joseph's disclosure of his real identity, brings the Joseph story to a close. At this point the narrator's theological intent becomes clear. Joseph's being sent to Egypt was not simply an act of his brothers' cruelty; it was also within God's plan, so that his promises and purposes concerning the descendants of Abraham might not be thwarted.

Joseph directs the brothers to return to Canaan, tell their father the good news, and since the famine is to last another five years, bring the entire family and its possessions down into Egypt. Goshen, the place where Joseph would have them live, is most likely a fertile valley in the eastern part of the Nile Delta, not far from where the Hyksos capital of Avaris was located. Laden with gifts from Pharaoh, Joseph's brothers return to report and confess to their father.

Some Questions for Discussion: Does the Judah-Joseph dialogue account for Joseph's climactic self-disclosure? Why does Joseph's revelation at first dismay his brothers? What, then, makes Joseph seem magnanimous? Does the ultimate reason that Joseph gives for his sojourn in Egypt support such a characterization? For what reasons might we consider this event the climax of the entire Joseph saga? It is, essentially, a turning point for whom? Why?

Suggested Activities: An editor of a leading magazine has asked you to write a contemporary version of the Joseph story.

Write a plan for your modern account in which you consider questions like these:

Could you tell essentially the same story—or at least make the same major points—if Joseph became, say, Josephine? Why, or why not?

Who will narrate your story? Why?

Where will your contemporary story occur? Why did you choose that setting?

How many characters will you include in your story? Who will be your major characters? Why?

What events from the entire saga will you include in your contemporary story? Why? Why will you leave out some events?

Why write a modern version of the Joseph story? What groups of people might read and enjoy your story? Why?

Thomas Mann, the German novelist, set out to write a short novella about Joseph but wrote a tetralogy of more than twelve hundred pages entitled *Joseph and His Brothers.* The individual titles are *The History of Jacob, The Young Joseph, Joseph in Egypt,* and *Joseph the Provider.* If possible, read one of the four books and analyze it carefully, noting how it is based on the Joseph story. How does the book differ from the story? How does Mann interpret the characters? What does he add to the account? What does he leave out? Is the book more than a retelling of the Joseph story? If so, what does it accomplish?

Reread all or parts of the Joseph story. Why do you think Thomas Mann could write four novels based on this story that is recorded in only twenty pages of *The Oxford Annotated Bible*? Does the biblical account contain only the bare bones of a story that can be fleshed out into a much larger one? If so, why do you think the biblical story contains only "the bare bones"? And why do you think the Joseph story is one of the most popular in the Old Testament?

Which incident in the Joseph story is the most dramatic? Why do you think so? How would you dramatize the incident? In two or three paragraphs, explain what you would do if you had access to a stage and all the equipment necessary to dramatize the episode.

Some biblical scholars have said that Genesis 45:7–8 sets forth the central theme of the Joseph story. In one or two sentences, state what you think is the central theme. Then explain why you think the Joseph story with such a theme was included in Genesis.

Judah's speech in Genesis 44:18–34 has been called "a paragon of Hebrew eloquence." Analyze the speech and explain why you think it is eloquent. Is it powerful? If so, what evidence can you offer to show that it is powerful?

Read the speech aloud. What words or phrases do you emphasize in your attempt to dramatize the power of the speech? Listen to someone else read the speech. How does his interpretation differ from yours? Which of the interpretations is the more powerful? Why?

Jacob's Migration (Genesis 46:1–34 JEP)

All three sources, easily recognizable, have contributed to the formation of this chapter. E describes God's appearing to Jacob at Beer-sheba in a dream to assure him that his leaving the Promised Land was part of the divine plan (Genesis 46:2–5). He will be cared for by Joseph at his death, and his descendants, who will become a great nation in Egypt, will eventually be brought from Egypt back to Canaan.

The dry precise literary style of the Priestly source is clearly discernible in verses 6ff. The narrative was apparently interrupted because the Priestly editor felt that it was important to give a list of Jacob's family prior to their entering Egypt and becoming a great nation. His source seems to have been a genealogical listing of the tribes similar to, or identical with, that found in Numbers 26.[23] Note how verse 28 of Genesis 46 continues the narrative of verses 1–5.

The J narrative (Genesis 46:1, 28ff) describes the meeting between Jacob and Joseph and the preparations which Joseph makes in order to secure the region of Goshen from Pharaoh for his family. There is no deception involved because the descendants of Jacob were shepherds. Yet the note that "every shepherd is an abomination to the Egyptians" (Genesis 46:34) is puzzling and cannot be substantiated through other Egyptian sources. In Genesis 47:6, it is acknowledged that the Egyptians did own livestock. It has been recently noted that the Hyksos were known as "shepherd kings," and that this passage may well be a subtle reference to the antagonism which the Egyptians felt toward these foreign invaders.[24] At any rate, Goshen seems to have been an area in which other seminomadic Semitic tribes were periodically allowed to sojourn during times of famine.[25]

Some Questions for Discussion: Describe Jacob when he hears that Joseph is alive in Egypt. Which better reveals Jacob's feelings—the narrator's description, or Jacob's words? Explain your answer.

What is the meaning of "Joseph's hand shall close your eyes" in Genesis 46:4? How do you interpret "I will go down with you to Egypt, and I will also bring you up again"? How are the situations in Genesis 46:3 and Genesis 12:1–2 similar?

Describe the reunion of Jacob and Joseph. Why does Joseph advise his brothers to tell Pharaoh that they are shepherds? What is Joseph's plan for his family?

Jacob Before Pharaoh (Genesis 47 JP)

The interview before Pharaoh, which Joseph had carefully planned in advance, had even better results than anticipated. Joseph first brings in his most presentable brothers, who tell Pharaoh their occupation and humbly petition to be allowed to sojourn in the area of Goshen. Pharaoh not only grants the request, he leaves it to Joseph's discretion to appoint his brothers to high positions tending the royal cattle. Next Jacob is brought before Pharaoh, who is quite impressed with the old man's appearance. Perhaps as a rejoinder to Jacob's blessing ("Long live the king"),[26] Pharaoh asks him how many years he has lived. Jacob's answer, modestly stressing the lack of fulfillment in his life, is quite close to the "wisdom philosophy" which was cultivated in Near Eastern courts.

The theme of Joseph's family being reunited and settling in Goshen is suddenly dropped, then, after verse 12, and the narrator returns to a description of Joseph's economic policy as Egyptian vizier. Some scholars have suggested that verses 13–26 at one time followed chapter 41 and are out of place in their present context. Although this is possible, the section seems quite appropriate where it is—to fill out the time between Jacob's arrival in Egypt and his death and to add to the peaceful conclusion towards which the narrative is moving.

This part of the Joseph story has always been a favorite source for anti-Semitism. It should be stressed, however, that the narrator's intent is not to portray Joseph as a clever tyrant who took advantage of helpless people. The Egyptians were grateful that they had been saved from starvation. "The ancient narrator is honestly amazed and wants the reader also to be amazed at the way an expedient was found to save the people from a gigantic catastrophe. In this respect there pervades the narrative a naive pleasure in the possibilities of human wisdom which can conquer economic difficulties by a venturesome shift of values, money for bread, manpower and land for seed corn, etc."[27] The point is completely missed if we use our own presuppositions and standards for judging Pharaoh's Egypt in the second millennium B.C.

It should also be noted that this new royal agrarian policy reflects actual economic changes which took place in Egypt during and after the Hyksos period. In the early part of the second millennium, the pharaohs of the Middle Kingdom had begun the practice of ceding large tracts of land into the hands of their nobles and high officials. With the land divided into petty princedoms, the pharaohs' position became severely weakened. When the pharaohs reasserted their claim to all the land of Egypt during the Hyksos period and New Kingdom, they were moving toward the consolidation and reunification of Egyptian power.

Some Questions for Discussion: What honor does Pharaoh accord to Jacob? How does the narrator continue to stress the importance of Joseph's position? What ironic reversal has occurred in Joseph's fortunes by Genesis 47:21–22? (Recall Joseph's situation in Genesis 39:1.)

In the years of famine that follow Jacob's arrival in Egypt, how does Joseph contrive to feed the people after they have exhausted their supply of money? property? What, again, does this show about Joseph's talents? How does Joseph's plan affect the people?

The Deaths of Jacob and Joseph (Genesis 49:28–50:26 JEP)

All three sources play a part in closing out the story of Joseph. The Priestly writer is primarily concerned with Jacob's deathbed request that he not be buried in Egypt (Genesis 49:28–33; 50:12–13). Abraham had purchased a cave near Hebron for the burial of his family (Genesis 23), and it was extremely important to Jacob (and to P) that this toehold in the Promised Land be retained. Members of his family and the reader are called on to remember that, despite Joseph's power and their prosperity in Goshen, Egypt is not the final goal toward which the divine promises point.

P describes Jacob's death as his being "gathered to his people" (Genesis 49:33). There is no separation of body and soul in Israelite thought and thus no idea of eternal life.[28] A man lived on through his family, who cared for him at death and preserved his name and memory. As long as his body existed and memory of him remained, a person was thought to maintain a shadowy, weak existence in a subterranean region called *Sheol*. The corpse was placed in a tomb which was usually near where the family lived. It was first stretched out on a bier, but eventually the bones were placed in a corner to make room for succeeding generations. As memory of him gradually faded, the deceased eventually merged into that group of ancestors called "the fathers" from whence the present family is derived.

The J tradition stresses the care which Joseph takes to see that his father is properly buried (Genesis 50:1–11, 14). He commands that Jacob be embalmed—a costly, lengthy process used only for Egyptian nobility and not attested in Canaan. Because of his contact with death, Joseph is unclean (see pp. 111–112) and does not have direct access to Pharaoh. Through intermediaries he requests permission to return his father to Canaan. After a seventy-day period of mourning, which is approximately the time set aside in Egypt for mourning the death of a pharaoh,[29] the funeral procession sets off for Canaan. As it includes high officials from Pharaoh's court, the procession causes great amazement among the Canaanites.[30]

J's final words describe Joseph's return to Egypt. This is a solemn reminder that, although Canaan is ultimately the land of promise, the long, bitter sojourn of the descendants of Abraham in Egypt has just begun.

It is quite possible that the E tradition did not contain Judah's remarkable offer to stay behind as a slave in place of Benjamin (Genesis 44:18–34). Thus, for E the question of the brothers' guilt has not been completely resolved (Genesis 50:15ff). The brothers, fearful that Jacob's death will release Joseph from his earlier restraint, beg for mercy. Joseph replies that God has already punished and preserved them and that he will not undo what God has done. God had used their evil intent to serve his purposes (see 45:5ff).

Joseph lives to be 110 (the ideal life span in Egyptian thought)[31] —long enough to receive his great grandchildren into the family.[32] Following his death, he was embalmed and placed in a coffin (sarcophagus) in Egypt. In the Exodus, Joseph's body is returned to Canaan (compare Exodus 13:19, Joshua 24:32).

Some Questions for Discussion: What is significant about Jacob's deathbed request? Why do the brothers again fear Joseph's reprisals? Why does, or doesn't, Joseph's character remain consistent with his previous portrayal?

How many years did Joseph live? How does the narrator indicate that Joseph's life has been successful? What is Joseph's final request?

Suggested Activity: The name *Genesis,* "beginning," was given to the first of the five books of Moses in the earliest Greek translation. What "beginning(s)" are in Genesis? What are the views about God expressed in this book? What does the book tell us about the nature of man? about his world?

Summarize the book of Genesis for a younger brother or sister or a child in your neighborhood. What are the major points recorded in Genesis that you think this child should be aware of? How would you express these points to him? Would you tell him stories? dramatize the stories? or do something else? Select one method of presentation and then list the points you would include.

CHAPTER 6

Moses and the Exodus

The book of Exodus is one of the most important in the Old Testament, since it not only describes one of the most critical events in the history of Israel but also explains the religious significance of the deliverance from Egypt. The Exodus deliverance and the religion of Moses have been discussed in the section of Israel's historical background. (See pages 13–16.) The following notes on the passages from Exodus are intended to supplement the earlier discussion.

Bondage in Egypt (Exodus 1:1–6:1 JE)

During the age of Joseph, many of the descendants of Abraham, Isaac, and Jacob had migrated to Egypt. At first they prospered greatly because the land was being ruled by the Hyksos, people of the same general Semitic stock and background. Following the expulsion of the Hyksos from Egypt (about 1550 B.C.), however, it seems likely that some of the descendants of the patriarchs were captured and enslaved. The population of the Hebrew community which participated in the Exodus was probably between one and five thousand—judging from the tradition that the group was served by two midwives (Exodus 1:15).*

The story of Moses in the bullrushes is a charming legend, with several ancient Near Eastern parallels. Sargon, the great Akka-

* See Early Israelite History, note 9.

dian king, tells us that, having been born in secret, he was placed by his mother in a reed basket which had been sealed with pitch and set afloat in the Euphrates River.[1] He was reared by the gardener of Akki, the man who found him, and eventually he won the love of Ishtar, the Mesopotamian Venus, who made him a great king. Another parallel is evidenced in the birth legend of the Persian King Cyrus, as told by the Greek historian Herodotus. At his birth, Cyrus was placed in the wilderness by a king who feared him as a future rival. He was miraculously saved, however, and eventually won power over that wicked ruler. One can also cite Herod's slaughtering of the children of Bethlehem following Jesus' birth as another parallel to this motif (Matthew 2:1–18).

One major theme introducing the birth story is the paradoxical juxtaposition of Pharaoh's oppression and the thriving Hebrew multitudes. In fact, the Egyptian bondage is accounted for in this narrative as an attempt to check the rapidly increasing Hebrew population. In verse 10, Pharaoh says, "Come, let us deal shrewdly with them . . ." and the language here is suggesting that the entire resources of wisdom in the great Egyptian court are going to be used against the hapless Hebrews. But paradoxically, this wisdom does not prevail: like Haman in the story of Esther, the Pharaoh emerges as the wise fool who is eventually overthrown by his own connivings. There is virtually no mention of divine guidance and activity here, but it is clearly presupposed as the narrator stresses the mysterious thriving of the Hebrew people in the midst of oppression. The power of the god who stands with the oppressed is already at work, even though the Hebrews in Egypt do not yet know it. On the one hand, the narrator is both relishing and idealizing the Hebrew bondage period; but the balance is restored in 1:13f, where a form of the root "to serve" is used five times. This is not because the writer is dry and unimaginative in his use of language; he is trying to reproduce the effect of the soul-deadening quality of slave labor through the montonous, droning, drum-like repetition.

As a second form of controlling the growing Hebrew population, Pharaoh turns to the midwives, Shiphrah and Puah. But they fail to comply, slyly comparing the vigorous Hebrew women with the pampered Egyptians. This is slave literature, produced by an oppressed people; it is parallel in many ways to the traditions of black Americans during the period of slavery. Note the great relish in this uneven conflict between the effete elite and the crude but shrewd, vital, resourceful oppressed.

Pharaoh ups the ante a third time, commanding that newborn Hebrew boys be thrown into the Nile. Nothing has been said, but both the narrator and his audience are already anticipating the end result of Pharaoh's activity—the death of the Egyptian first-born in the Passover, a child for a child. The theme will be introduced more specifically in 4:22f, where Moses is instructed to demand before Pharaoh that Israel, God's "first-born son," be set free. This reflects the profound Mosaic feeling that history comes back to haunt the oppressor.

The climax of 1:8–2:10 is reached with the discovery of the child in the river. Pharaoh in his wisdom had set about to destroy the Hebrew people, and the result is that the deliverer of Israel is rescued and raised in the court of the oppressors. The final irony is that Moses' mother is paid for nursing her own child— with funds from Pharaoh's treasury. Again this is a common theme in slave literature. Note the important role of women in Pharaoh's undoing: first the clever midwives; then Moses' resourceful mother, first hiding the child then carefully building the ark; then Moses' sister, who watches over the ark and in an instant is by the side of the princess, suggesting a wet-nurse from among the Hebrew women who could care for the child. And finally, Pharaoh's daughter becomes an unwitting accomplice in what the narrator sees as the divine plan to deliver the Hebrews from Egypt. Thus the narrator is affirming that the "foolishness" of God, who works through the wit and compassion of women, is sufficient to overthrow Pharaoh in all his might and "wisdom."

A favorite motif of the foundling child legend—and there are thirty-two examples in ancient Near Eastern lore—is that the nobly born child, raised in obscurity among common folk, finally returns to claim and win the power and riches which are rightfully his. The adaptation of this "rags to riches" motif in the story of Moses' birth beautifully reflects the early Hebrew mentality—the lowly born child is raised in the splendor of Pharaoh's court. Moses does not emerge as the true hero, however, until he has left the court and affirmed his identity with the oppressed Hebrews.

Moses had to flee from Egypt because he had murdered an Egyptian who was beating a Hebrew. He headed east into the Sinai Peninsula.[2] When he acted heroically to save his bride-to-be from a group of rowdy shepherds, he became associated with a wandering clan of Kenite peoples.

We do not know how long Moses remained with the Kenites before Yahweh's revelation at the burning bush moved him to return to Egypt. The importance of this story cannot be over-emphasized, for Moses' experience sets into motion a chain of events which led to the establishment of Israel as a nation.

Yahweh revealed his new name to Moses because, through the Exodus deliverance and covenant at Sinai, he was about to reveal a completely new aspect of his character. "I am who I am" does not convey the precise meaning of the term *Yahweh*. It has been plausibly suggested that his liturgical title originally meant "God who creates,"[3] but it should be emphasized just as strongly that the term connotes the ultimate otherness and unknowability of God. How did Moses learn the name Yahweh? A generally accepted hypothesis is that Yahweh was worshiped by the clan of Jethro, the family into which Moses married. Interestingly, Jethro is referred to as a priest who greets Moses after the Exodus with a sacrifice to Yahweh (Exodus 18:1–12). Would a pagan have been permitted to officiate at a sacrifice to Yahweh?

Moses is understandably reluctant to undertake the commission to which he has been called, for Egypt was a powerful nation. In addition to dealing with the Egyptians, Moses must convince his own people to accept him as their divinely chosen leader and to accept Yahweh as their god. Thus Moses demands and receives the power of Yahweh's presence to authenticate his claims.

The legend of Exodus 4:24–26 had a long prehistory before it was adopted into Israelite literary traditions.[4] In some other cultures the prospective bridegroom was circumcised as a magical rite to protect him from evil spirits on the wedding night. As ancient kings used to claim the privilege of spending the first night with the brides in their realm, it was thought that jealous deities also desired this privilege. On his wedding night, then, the bridegroom was thought to be in danger of attack by demons who wished to possess his bride. Circumcision was regarded as a safeguard against the attack of demons. The original significance was forgotten as this legend became incorporated into Israelite traditions to account for infant circumcision. The attacking demon was transformed into Yahweh, because early Israelite faith could brook no evil deities who might oppose his will. And finally, the circumcision was carried out on Moses' child to bring the story into conformity with standard Israelite ritual procedure.

The literary form of Moses' speech before Pharaoh is that of a messenger who is conveying the message of his Sovereign (Exodus 5:1). Consequent addresses (Exodus 10:3, for example) are couched in the literary form of a suzerain (Yahweh) to his rebellious vassal (Pharaoh). Pharaoh does not acknowledge Yahweh as his suzerain. He refuses to comply with the request, making the lot of the Hebrew slaves even more severe by ordering that they gather their own straw for making brick. The Hebrews, who had at first joyfully received Moses as their deliverer (Exodus 4:31), now turn against him (Exodus 5:21). They are no longer sure that Yahweh is mightier than Pharaoh. Thus the stage is set for a mighty conflict between the two powers.

Some Questions for Discussion: How does the narrator make the transition between Genesis and Exodus? Why does verse 7 seem to be a key transitional passage from Genesis to Exodus? What are some of the stated reasons for the captivity of Israel? What could be some other reasons?

Explain why it was necessary for Moses' mother to put him in a basket in the river. Moses' name is explained by a Hebrew verb meaning "to draw out." What are two symbolic reasons for his receiving this name? What irony do you see in Exodus 2:5–10?

In chapters 2–5 of the narrative, we are told about the birth and upbringing of Moses, how he had to flee from Egypt, and how God called him to deliver his people from slavery. How detailed is the account? Do you see the choice of details as particularly interesting? significant? lacking? misleading? Explain your answer.

What character traits of Moses are shown in his dialogue with the Lord in Exodus 4:1–17? What parallels and differences do you find between the stories of the call of Abraham (Genesis 12) and the call of Moses? Can you see some reasons for God's revealing to Moses a new name for himself? How does Yahweh respond to accommodate Moses' fears and objections concerning his mission? What do you think it is that finally convinces Moses to go? How was Moses to convince the Israelites that Yahweh had spoken to him?

What role was Aaron, Moses' brother, to play in the Exodus? How do the Israelites first react to the promise of deliverance? What causes them to change? How did Pharaoh react when Moses asked him to let the Israelites go into the wilderness to worship? What evidence is there that the Pharaoh's reaction was part of God's plan? In answer to Moses' request, what action was taken toward the Israelites by the Pharaoh?

Judging from Exodus 2:11–4:23, what kind of man do you think Moses is? Do you find a consistent personal character emerging—that is, one who remains recognizable as the same individual through the developing events, or do you perhaps find contradictions? (Look again at the Burning Bush Moses as compared to the earlier passages which show him slaying the Egyptian in defense of a fellow Hebrew and coming to the defense of his future wife at the well.)

Suggested Activities: Moses has been the central figure in several Hollywood movies, and the actors portraying him attempt their particular characterizations. You have been chosen to direct a new movie based on Exodus. After rereading Exodus 1:1–6:1, write instructions to the actor who will play Moses explaining how you think Moses should be portrayed and citing specific passages from Exodus to support your portrayal.

"Let My People Go" is a popular spiritual obviously inspired by Exodus. Bring to class any short stories, novels, plays, copies of paintings, and pictures of statues that you think have been inspired by Moses. Explain why you think that Exodus is the source of inspiration.

The pursuit of freedom has been a dominant theme in literature for centuries. In a short theme, identify contemporary groups of people who use the Exodus as a symbol for expressing their hopes for freedom and explain how they use the symbol. Can the Exodus symbol have other levels of meaning besides a people's being set free from bondage? What meanings can you identify?

The Plagues (Exodus 7:8–12:39 JP)[5]

The Israelites were convinced that Yahweh's powerful intervention had saved them from destruction at the sea and sent them on their way to the Promised Land. They also believed that this event, which was the cornerstone of their faith, had a long prehistory: Yahweh had been guiding and protecting his people since the time of Abraham. Although Israel's bondage in Egypt had been long and bitter, the people now saw that even then Yahweh had been active on their behalf.

Egypt had undoubtedly suffered her share of natural catastrophes during the preceding decades.[6] These events were vividly recalled and discussed throughout the land for many generations, just as Americans still talk of the horrors of the San Francisco earthquake and the great Chicago fire. Thus the plagues upon Egypt, which had probably occurred as isolated events in various parts of the land over a long period of time, were eventually incorporated into a larger narrative structure within Israelite tradition and given a unified interpretation. As the tradition developed, all of these events came to be centered about one figure (Moses) and were compressed into a very short period of time. Furthermore, they were worked into a set narrative pattern: (a) Yahweh instructs Moses to appear before Pharaoh with an ultimatum: Israel must be permitted to journey into the wilderness to serve (worship) her god; (b) Moses makes the request, but Pharaoh refuses to comply; (c) the plague comes upon Egypt; (d) Pharaoh relents; (e) the plague is halted; (f) Pharaoh's heart is hardened and the cycle begins again.

This pattern depicts the plagues as the result of a mighty struggle between Yahweh and Pharaoh over control of Israel's destiny. Pharaoh, of course, loses out each time. He must admit Yahweh's superiority by requesting that Moses intercede to spare the land. But before the next plague can be recounted, Yahweh's wrath must be rekindled. The narrator solved this problem by stating that Pharaoh's heart was hardened, and he refused to let Israel go. A further development of the tradition says that Pharaoh's refusal to comply resulted not from his own stubborn pride, but because Yahweh had hardened his heart. Here the intent is simply to mock Pharaoh's power: the mightiest king on earth, who indeed claimed that he was a god, is actually nothing but a helpless pawn who must play his part in Yahweh's plan for history.

In this episode, the narrator has raised a serious theological question which students will sense: Does God make people bad to further his own purposes? There was a strong element of human freedom in Israel's faith. The terms of the suzerainty covenant insisted upon the vassal's willing obedience. And yet Israel's God was mighty—so mighty that all things could be ultimately attributed to his will. The early stories in Genesis clearly illustrate Israel's belief that evil originates through man's disobedience against God's will. But such rebellion can never overthrow God's control of history; it is always used to accomplish his sovereign purposes.

There are indications in the narrative that the plagues on Egypt were originally attributed to Yahweh's direct action. But as the figure of Moses continued to dominate the folklore of later generations, great magical power was accorded to him by popular imagination. Repeatedly he strides before Pharaoh.[7] He touches the Nile with his rod, and the water turns to blood. His outstretched hand brings on hail, locusts, darkness. The dust which he throws into the air brings skin boils on man and beast; he strikes the dust with his rod, and gnats appear upon the land. It should be stressed, however, that the Israelites did not consider

Moses a grand magician possessing occult powers: his power came exclusively from Yahweh. Israelite faith and law explicitly repudiated magic.

It is interesting to note that Pharaoh's magicians are able to match the first three signs which Moses performs (Exodus 7:8–24). The tension of the contest is thereby increased, and, more importantly, the narrative shows that the actual plagues—deeds which Pharaoh's magicians could not match—far surpassed the power which could be conjured up from the occult world.

The plague traditions were developed and preserved in connection with Israel's annual celebration of the spring Passover festival. The Passover, in which Egypt's first-born were slain, was seen as the final plague through which Israel's bondage was ended and the people were started on their journey to the Promised Land. Each year as the people gathered to relive the Passover by eating unleavened bread, the great story of their deliverance from Egypt was retold. And the plague stories, of course, were an important prologue to the story of deliverance.

The origins of the Passover cannot yet be clearly traced by scholars. The festival itself certainly antedates the escape from Egypt. It could well have been a spring ritual which was commonly practiced by many seminomadic tribes in the Near East.[8] Springtime was an important, although dangerous, season for the herdsmen. The flocks had just foaled, and as the tribes pulled up stakes to search for new pasture lands, the hardships of the coming journey threatened the lives of the newborn. Thus the pre-exodus Passover was probably intended as a ritual to protect the newborn of man and beast, particularly the highly regarded first-born. Sacrificial lamb's blood was sprinkled at the entrance to dwellings to ward off the death angel's nighttime attack on the newborn.

One should note that Moses had attempted to leave Egypt to hold a feast to Yahweh in the wilderness (Exodus 5:1). It could well have been a Passover celebration which was intended. After the deliverance at the sea, however, this ancient ritual for the newborn (first-born) acquired new significance. The death angel now becomes Yahweh's agent for effecting Israel's escape by bringing death to the Egyptian first-born. The Passover meal and the lamb's blood at the entrance are no longer primarily regarded as an annual protection of Israel's newborn. They become the core of the festival by which Israel remembered and celebrated her Exodus from Egypt.

Some Questions for Discussion: Considering the events narrated in 7:8–13 within the "contest" context, what do you think increases the tension? What is indicated about the power of God and the power of Pharaoh in the incident with the rods? How did Pharaoh react to the waters of Egypt being turned to blood? Why?

Structurally, we are able to find a set narrative pattern in the story of the plagues. Examine 7:14–11:10. How would you describe or outline this narrative pattern? Can you see any controversy in the "hardening of Pharaoh's heart" tradition as it affects the theme or central idea of the narrative? Why do you think the narrator included this motif? What was the final plague by which the Israelites' bondage was ended? How has the narrative prepared you for this climax?

What is the meaning and significance of the *Passover?* How does the Passover become a core event in the faith of the people of Israel? Why, do you think, didn't Yahweh free his people immediately instead of allowing them to remain in Egypt for the duration of the plagues? How might natural phenomena, known to have occurred in the history of Egypt, help to account for the plague tradition?

Suggested Activities: Ask a rabbi or Jewish student to explain the Passover feast to your class. After the explanation, make certain you can answer these questions: What does the feast commemorate? What is eaten during the feast? What prayers are part of the ritual? When is Passover celebrated?

Professors J. L. Mihelic and G. E. Wright make these comments on the historicity of the plagues in *The Interpreter's Dictionary of the Bible*:

The concentration of miracles in the period of the Exodus, in the work of Elijah and Elisha, and in the ministry of Jesus is the biblical testimony to God's special and powerful activity acknowledged to have occurred during these events. Time and space, however, together with cultural and mental outlook, so separate us from biblical man that it is impossible to re-create completely the actual situations he faced and interpreted. We are left, in the case of Miracles, very largely to his understanding that mighty deeds were indeed wrought by God, of which unusual occurrences in nature were signs. With regard to the Exodus "signs," however, it can be stated that they are peculiarly Egyptian in type and that the traditions about them must be assumed to have arisen ultimately among a people which had had unusual experiences in that country.

The first nine plagues have been explained as natural scourges known in historical times to have been troublesome in Egypt, perhaps, indeed, occurring with particular severity at the time of the Exodus between late summer and the following spring (cf. Ex. 9:31, which suggests an early spring date in the tradition of the seventh plague). After the Nile reaches the height of its inundation by August, it is said that the water often becomes a dull red from the presence of minute organisms, and at certain times the water can be worse than at others. This would appear to be the setting, at least, of the first plague (water turned to blood; 7:14ff). A plague of frogs, generally in September, has a number of historical witnesses, and quantities of dead frogs would easily give rise to the insect pests (gnats and flies), and probably disease for cattle and human beings (third to sixth plagues). Hail, locusts, and severe sandstorms are also known in plague proportions, the last mentioned being the "thick darkness" which is said to have lasted for three days (10:22). The evidence is such, indeed, that a natural basis for the traditions must be assumed; the severity of the scourges was interpreted as the "sign" of God's power.

Yet it would be a mistake to assume that the present form of the Exodus plague traditions can be easily or entirely rationalized in the light of the above-mentioned evidence. They were so long transmitted by a worshiping people and so commonly employed in a cultic liturgy that they are not related as history for history's sake, but rather as a celebration of God's great victory whereby He is glorified and acknowledged as sole sovereign and savior. Liturgical usage has given form and heightened theological content to the traditions, though in saying this one must beware of the temptation to assume that the cultus invented the traditions that it celebrated and interpreted.

Compare the explanation of the "natural scourges" with the account of the plagues in Exodus and explain why you think the narrator described the plagues as he did. Why do you think the present account in Exodus has greater impact than one that would note the plagues as natural phenomena? What do you think is the purpose of the plague description?

The Escape from Egypt (Exodus 13:17–16:36 JP)

Instead of taking the main highway along the Mediterranean coast into Canaan,[9] the Israelites headed southward through rough terrain toward the lower part of the Sinai Peninsula. It was a necessary detour because the coastal highway was dotted with Egyptian military outposts. The alarm would have been quickly spread and the escaping Israelites easily overtaken by Pharaoh's swift chariots. Another reason for this choice may well have been Moses' desire to bring Israel to Mount Sinai, the holy place where Yahweh had previously revealed himself.[10] Here the people of Israel could appear before him to formally acknowledge themselves as his people.

Exodus 13:21ff states that Yahweh preceded the Israelites through the wilderness in a pillar of cloud by day and a pillar of fire by night. According to the tradition, these "pillars" accompanied the Israelites all the way to the Promised Land.[11] It has been suggested that in the course of their journey the Israelites may have come across several active volcanoes and that Mount Sinai might well have been one of them.[12] The volcanoes could be seen from afar, belching smoke during the day and erupting fire at night. Although the primary means of Yahweh's presence and guidance at this time was thought to be the Ark of the Covenant,[13] it is not surprising (since fire and smoke were traditional symbols of divine presence in ancient thought) that these volcanic eruptions would be viewed as further manifestations of Yahweh's leadership. Only a slight modification of the tradition was required to depict the "pillars" as personifications of Yahweh, moving before the people, accompanying them from Egypt to Canaan. Other scholars, pointing out that there is no evidence of active volcanoes at that time in the Sinai Peninsula, prefer to interpret the pillars of fire and smoke as an expression of Israel's experience of powerful divine guidance during the wilderness period.

Before the Israelites were able to get out of Egypt, they were overtaken by a contingent of Pharaoh's charioteers. They were able to escape, and the Egyptian host was destroyed in the sea. Through a mistranslation of the Hebrew *yam suph,* the Septuagint understood this event to have taken place at the Red Sea. Actually the text should be read *Sea of Reeds*, which was probably located somewhere in the marshy region north of the Gulf of Suez, close to the present Suez Canal. The exact location is uncertain because of the shifting of flow patterns and the silting that have slowly but constantly taken place.

There is no scholarly consensus as to precisely how the Israelites escaped destruction. The task of reconstructing is complicated by two versions of the event: the prose narrative in Exodus 14:21–31 and a poetic account in Exodus 15:1–12.[14] A careful reading of Exodus 15:1–12 indicates that the Egyptians sank *into* the sea when a violent storm came upon them (see Exodus 15:1, 4–5, 8–10). According to this version, they may have been crossing the sea to head off the Israelites when the storm capsized their barges, causing the chariots and heavily armored soldiers to sink. On the other hand, the earliest level of tradition in Exodus 14 (verses 21b, 24–25, 27b, 30–31) indicates that a strong east wind temporarily drove back the shallow waters of the marshland, allowing the Israelites to escape while the heavily armed Egyptian chariots bogged down. The Priestly editor made some significant additions to this prose narrative. Interpreting the storm imagery in Exodus 15:8 literally, he pictured the waters as dividing to form the walls of a passageway for the Israelites (Exodus 14:22).

After entering the wilderness of Sinai, the Israelites had other experiences that came to be interpreted as signs of divine providence. Manna, one of the foods which is said to have sustained them, is thought to be a honeydew substance excreted by scale insects which suck the sap from certain plants and bushes in the wilderness. The substance falls to the ground where it is quickly solidified by the dry desert air. Flocks of quail are also known to migrate over this area in the springtime. When they have become exhausted from the long flight, they can be easily caught.

Some Questions for Discussion: Why did the Israelites not follow the shortest route to the Promised Land? There are several naturalistic explanations for the Israelites escape at the Sea of Reeds. How do you see the event's happening? Compare the two accounts of this event (Exodus 14:21, 22a and Exodus 14:22b, 23, 26–30). How were the Israelites assured of God's presence during the Exodus? How might we explain the "pillar of cloud" and the "pillar of fire"?

What is your interpretation of this statement the narrator attributes to the Lord: "And I will harden Pharaoh's heart, and he will pursue them and I will get glory over Pharaoh and all his hosts; and the Egyptians shall know that I am the Lord." How often does this or a similar statement occur in the Exodus account? What do you think is its purpose? Why do you think the narrator repeats it?

What are some differences between the content and tone as given in the prose narrative (Exodus 14) and poetic song narration (Exodus 15:1–18)? Why did Miriam and the other women dance? What other cultures have used dancing for the same reason? What metamorphosis has the dance undergone in our own culture?

What seems to be the emerging pattern of the Israelites' response to their leader Moses as they proceed through the wilderness? What is Yahweh's response to his people? The Israelites said to Moses and Aaron, "Would that we had died by the hand of the Lord in the land of Egypt, when we sat by the fleshpots and ate bread to the full; for you have brought us out into this wilderness to kill this whole assembly with hunger." Consider the arguments for and against that statement. With which position do you agree? Compare this experience of the Hebrew Exodus with the status of refugees who fled from the Fascists of Italy, the Nazis of Germany, and other oppressive dictatorships.

Suggested Activities: The escape from Egypt could be retold in a powerful short story. In two or three paragraphs, answer the following questions about a short story you would write:

Who would narrate the story? Why? What are the advantages of having this person be the narrator? What are the disadvantages?

What, if anything, from Exodus 13:17–16:36 would have to be left out of your story because of your choice of narrator? Could the thoughts and feelings of the narrator be inserted in the story without distorting it? Explain your answer.

How would you begin your story? What incident would serve as the opening scene? What incident would you use as the conclusion of your story?

How would you describe the crossing of the "sea of reeds"? What information influenced your description?

Consider the statements and actions the narrator attributes to God thus far in the Book of Exodus. Compare them with statements and actions attributed to God in Genesis. Then write a description of God as you perceive him through Genesis and Exodus.

Reread Exodus 15:1–18, comparing verses 13–18 with the first twelve. Then explain why you do or don't think the last six verses were added to the poem at a later date by a different narrator.

The Covenant at Mount Sinai (Exodus 19:1–21:36 JE)

Chapter 19 describes Israel's preparations for receiving the covenant law. The people began with a three-day waiting period in which they were to make themselves ritually clean. The concept of clean and unclean was an extremely important one in all ancient cultures.[15] People believed that hostile powers in the world could harm the community if its members came in contact with "unclean" things. Also, as Yahweh was holy and perfect, it would be dangerous to come into his presence in a tainted condition. How was it determined whether an object, place, or person was unclean? In general, one could be rendered unclean by anything connected with the mysterious forces of sex, birth, and death; anything repulsive or abnormal; anything associated with pagan customs or religion or moral wrongdoing against another member of the community. People with leprosy, running sores, or other bodily discharges were unclean; so was any person who had touched them or had touched a corpse. A person could become unclean through eating certain foods (animals which had died of themselves or had been killed by wild beasts, or animals which did not part the hoof and chew the cud—scavenger birds, rodents, and reptiles). The cleansing rituals, which could be participated in only after the source of contamination had been removed, involved a waiting period, a cleansing ceremony, and a sacrificial offering.

Even ritual purity, however, did not qualify the people to come before Yahweh's holiness at Mount Sinai. His dwelling place was proclaimed sacred territory; death would come to any trespasser.[16]

The gap between Yahweh and man could be bridged only by the covenant mediator, Moses, who relayed messages back and forth between the unapproachable suzerain and his vassals. Yahweh remained secluded on his holy mountain—shrouded behind fire, smoke, and thunderous quakes.[17]

The covenant ceremony was conceptualized as a suzerainty treaty in which Israel was being offered a vassal relationship to Yahweh. It was instituted by Moses at Mount Sinai and was periodically renewed after the Israelites had settled in Canaan. This renewal took place at the climax of the Passover festival.[18] The deliverance from Egypt had established the basis of Yahweh's claim upon Israel. Exodus 19:4–6 states in succinct, poetic terms the entire covenant concept. Yahweh's gracious acts were intended to elicit Israel's obedient response. In striking contrast to the covenant with Abraham, verse 5 emphasizes a conditional element: Israel would be Yahweh's possession only if she remained obedient to his covenant demands. For the Israelites, then, election was not a sign of continuous blessing and favor; it was a constant goad toward obedience. Israel had been called into being to establish a just society which might become a "kingdom of priests" (Exodus 19:6) to mediate Yahweh's will to all other nations.

The covenant stipulations, like the Hittite suzerainty treaties, were stated in absolute terms ("Thou shalt . . .; Thou shalt not . . ."). Only the Ten Commandments (the Decalogue) were given in the actual covenant ceremony.[19] They are the basic principles of the contract by which Israel's behavior was to be regulated. Basically they involved maintaining exclusive loyalty to Yahweh as suzerain Lord and preserving justice in the community of covenant brothers. The third commandment needs some clarification. It is not aimed solely against cursing, but also forbids using Yahweh's name in perjured testimony or in oaths which might later be broken.

Exodus 21:1–23:13 contains early Israelite case laws. For the most part they are stated in conditional form ("If . . ., then . . ."). These laws were not read during the covenant ceremony. Rather, they were decisions which were made by Israelite courts over a considerable period of time.[20] When a specific complaint or crime was brought before the judicial assembly, a decision, based on the principles of the Decalogue, was worked out. This decision then became a precedent upon which other similar cases were settled.

Of course, not all cases could be resolved on the basis of the Decalogue. Israel was heir to a vast, highly developed ancient Near Eastern legal tradition. The Babylonian Code of Hammurabi, which dates around 1700 B.C., is an example of this tradition.[21] Scholars have noted the similarities in content and literary form between the laws of Hammurabi and those in the Old Testament. But it is equally important to point out several significant differences. As was explained in our discussion of the creation stories, Israel had a more exalted concept of man than was held in Mesopotamia. This is also reflected in Israelite law, which places more value on human life and less on property than its Mesopotamian counterpart. Mesopotamian law sometimes punished the murderer by imposing a fine based on the murdered man's social status, whereas a thief was executed when he could not pay his fine. Except in cases involving kidnapping, Israelite law never prescribed the death penalty for stealing. Human life was of infinitely higher value than silver and gold. For the same reason, however, murderers had to be executed in Israel because the life taken was considered too precious to be compensated for with money. Israelite law also shunned the practices of vicarious punishment and maiming, both of which were common in Mesopotamia. Finally, whereas Mesopotamian law sometimes provided that the sentence be commuted if the defendant were forgiven by the offended party, such forgiveness was impossible in Israel, since God, the giver of the law, was regarded as the offended party who would not rest until justice had been reestablished.

Israelite law may appear severe and primitive ("eye for eye, tooth for tooth," Exodus 21:23f), but when the law is viewed in its ancient Near Eastern context, the impression is modified. The *lex talionis* ("eye for eye"), for example, asserts that the punishment must not exceed the crime. It became the basic principle of justice in Israelite law courts. No longer could a person inflict an arbitrary punishment for a wrong which had been done to him or to his family (see Genesis 4:23–24). Furthermore, Israelite law affords far-reaching, unprecedented protection for the dispossessed, the widow, the orphan, the sojourner, the slave. The Israelites remembered only too well their miserable lot in Egypt.

Some Questions for Discussion: In what ways do you think the Israelites' experiences of the deliverance from Egypt and God's guidance through the wilderness were preparation for God's revelation, the making of the covenant, and the giving of the laws? What preparations are made by the Israelites for receiving the covenant law? Describe the scene when the Lord came down upon Mount Sinai.

What are your personal reactions during a violent thunderstorm? Why do you think the storm metaphor was used in the description?

Trace the line of action in 19:3–25. What is Moses' role in the covenant? Explain the conditional element in the Mosaic Covenant. How does the covenant in this narrative contrast with the one God made with Noah in Genesis 9:9? with the one God made with Abraham in Genesis 15?

The religion of Abraham was a religion of faith, whereas the Mosaic religion is based on ethics—a code of behavior. According to the Ten Commandments, what are the two underlying principles upon which Israel must act? The "eye for eye" concept of law became the basic principle of justice in Israelite law courts. What do you think about this form of justice? In what ways does it protect a wrongdoer as well as prosecute him?

Suggested Activity: Write a set of commandments to govern your own conduct. How many do you have? How many are similar to, or the same as, the Ten Commandments? Compare your code of conduct with one of your friends.

The Worship of the Golden Calf (Exodus 32:1–35 JE)

In chapter 32 the scene switches from Moses, who had just received the two tablets of the law on Mount Sinai, to the people at the foot of the mountain, who are already beginning to lose faith in Yahweh. A golden calf is fashioned by Aaron from the gold which had been taken in Egypt (Exodus 11:1–3). Scholars have long recognized that this tradition is related to I Kings 12:25ff, the clue being Aaron's calling the object which he has made "gods" (compare Exodus 32:4 with I Kings 12:28). This later passage tells of events which took place following the death of Solomon, when the ten northern tribes broke away from the house of David to form North Israel. In an effort to keep his people from going to Jerusalem to worship, Jeroboam, the North Israelite king, established rival shrines in Dan and Bethel where the people could worship Yahweh. (This was not condoned in Judah, of course, where Jerusalem was considered the central place of worship.) Jeroboam made the mistake, however, of placing a golden calf in each shrine. Probably the golden calf is an ancient symbol connected with the worship of Yahweh. The animals were not set up as gods to be worshipped by the people. Rather, they were regarded as part of the invisible god's host, which accompanied him or upon which he rode. Furthermore, the Hebrew term *Elohim*, which means literally *gods*, was a legitimate designation for Yahweh in North Israel, where it was felt that Yahweh was the totality of all divine powers.[22] Thus Jeroboam's intentions probably were good; he had instituted sanctuaries where his people could worship Yahweh without the necessity of traveling outside the country to Jerusalem. But people soon realized that the calf was a popular symbol in Canaanite religion. This, plus the tendency to incorporate Canaanite practices into the worship, eventually led to prophetic rebukes against the sanctuaries of Dan and Bethel.

In Judah these rival sanctuaries had always been viewed as attempts to subvert true Yahweh worship by the introduction of pagan ways. A tradition concerning Aaron and the Israelites at Mount Sinai seems to have been reworked, incorporating strong overtones of the polemic against Jeroboam and thus giving this feeling further legitimacy. Note that Aaron, like Jeroboam, is depicted as introducing other *gods* into a festival of Yahweh.

Though we will never know exactly what happened at Mount Sinai to give rise to the golden-calf tradition, the Israelites are pictured as being rebellious and stiff-necked throughout their journey from Egypt to Canaan. Thus it is not impossible that some crisis of decision between Yahweh and other gods was reached at Mount Sinai, where the people were being asked to accept Yahweh as their sole suzerain.

Moses' intercession before Yahweh saved the people from complete destruction. Upon his return to the camp,[23] however, Moses smashed the tablets of the law, indicating that the covenant relationship had been terminated. When a vassal broke a covenant stipulation, the suzerain, if he decided that the offense was grave enough, would break the tablets upon which the agreement had been written. The vassal could humbly sue for reinstatement, but the suzerain was not obligated to show him any mercy.

After burning the pedestal, Moses seized the golden calf and ground it into powder. The powder was stirred into water, which the Israelites were forced to drink. This is an ancient method of determining guilt (see Numbers 5:11–28). A curse was spoken as the dust was poured into the liquid, and it was thought that divine power would bring judgment upon any guilty person who drank the mixture. The story of Exodus 32:20 is continued in verses 30–35.[24] Moses rebuked the people the next day and tried to intercede before Yahweh so that Israel might be spared. He was assured that only the guilty would be punished. A plague came upon them, presumably from the cursed water which had been drunk the preceding day.

Some Questions for Discussion: What is the *sin* of the Israelites while Moses is still up on the mountain? What is Aaron's role in it? How does he later explain it to Moses? Remembering the actions and murmurings of the Israelites during their journey through the wilderness, would you consider their actions here to be characteristic? Explain your answer.

What does Moses do when he comes down from the mountain? What is the significance of his action? What persuaded Yahweh not to destroy the people? How does this relenting relate to other ideas or impressions the Exodus narratives have given?

The narrative has clearly established Moses as a mediator between Yahweh and his people. To what extent is Moses willing to carry out this role? How is the covenant between the Lord and the people of Israel reaffirmed? What characteristics of a great leader do you think have been displayed by Moses in his experiences throughout the book of Exodus? How has Moses changed since we observed him at the burning bush?

Suggested Activities: Select what you think are the most significant scenes in Exodus 1–32. Describe at least six of those scenes so vividly that an artist could paint them from your descriptions.

You have been asked to direct a play based on Exodus. Describe the Moses that you want your actor to portray. Describe the Aaron that you want portrayed. What passages in the text of Exodus support your descriptions of Moses and Aaron?

Read one of the following novels: *Moses* by Sholem Asch; *Moses, Prince of Egypt* by Howard Fast; *Moses, Man of the Mountain* by Zorah Neale Hurston; *The Burning Bush* by Sigrid Undset. How is Moses characterized in the novel you read? Compare that characterization with yours.

CHAPTER 7

The Fall of Jericho

The Israelites secured a base of operations for the invasion of Canaan by conquering territory in the Transjordan (see Numbers 21). Moses died, and the responsibility for carrying out the invasion was given to Joshua, his successor.

Joshua 6:1–27 JE

Jericho was the first city to be attacked after the Israelites had crossed the Jordan River. Archeological excavations of the city have produced extremely disappointing and inconclusive results for this period.[1] Jericho was a flourishing, well-fortified city during much of the first half of the second millennium B.C. But it suffered a violent destruction around 1580 B.C., perhaps in connection with the Hyksos' being expelled from Egypt. Several tombs provide sparse evidence that the city, after remaining uninhabited for a considerable period of time, was briefly reoccupied during the end of the fourteenth century, but not as a major settlement. There is no evidence that these inhabitants built a new wall. Either the old wall continued in use or a new wall, now completely eroded, was built directly over the old one.

It is more likely that Jericho fell to the Israelites about 1250 B.C., but the archeological evidence concerning a thirteenth-century occupation of the city is completely lacking. Is the destruction of Jericho a fiction? We think not. The description of the siege and fall of the city is quite detailed (for example, Joshua 6:22–23). Furthermore, along with the battle at Gibeon (Joshua 10), this event was remembered and celebrated above all others in Israel's traditions of the conquest.

It should be noted that Jericho is situated on a hill and that the city was not resettled for almost four hundred years (I Kings 16:34). During this long period the destroyed remains, subject to the eroding forces of sun, wind, and rain, could well have been washed down the slope.[2] Nevertheless, since absolutely nothing from the thirteenth century has been found, we are forced to the tentative conclusion that Jericho was a rather minor settlement during this period.

Archeology has shown that earthquakes destroyed earlier walls in Jericho. Thus, an earthquake is the most reasonable explanation of the sudden collapse of the wall (Joshua 6:20).

The method of attack used by the Israelites appears strange to us. The inclusion of seven priests blowing trumpets of rams' horns in a procession of armed men who encircled the city once a day for seven days would be incomprehensible to a modern military strategist. The battle between peoples was conceived as a struggle between their gods. The size of the army was unimportant; the outcome was determined by divine power and planning—in the case of Israel by the power and plan of Yahweh. His will was sought through oracles before the battle. Only after being assured that the enemy had been given into her hands would Israel attack. She believed that Yahweh himself, seated invisibly upon the Ark, led the Israelites into battle. Israel's war was Yahweh's war. It was being waged to fulfill his promises concerning possession of the land. The spoil—both human and material—which was taken after victory was also thought to belong exclusively to Yahweh. The Israelites did not deem it proper to profit from the victory which Yahweh had won. Thus all captured items were destroyed and sacrificed to Yahweh. The Israelites also believed that the land belonged to Yahweh, and that such destruction purged it from the abominations inherent in Canaanite society.

Some Questions for Discussion: Before you answer the following questions, read Joshua 1–5 and reread Joshua 6:1–27.

The Old Testament contains many passages that echo previous passages. Compare Joshua 1:6, 7, 9, and 18 with Deuteronomy 31:6, 7, and 23. To whom is the admonition "be strong and of good courage" attributed in each of those verses? Why do you think it is repeated? What does it foreshadow for Joshua? for Israel?

What does Joshua promise the people after his encounter with God? How do the people respond to Joshua? Why do you think Joshua was confident the people would believe he had spoken with God? Why did he not have the same fears that Moses expressed in Exodus 4? Before you answer the last two questions, read Deuteronomy 31.

What characteristics would you attribute to Rahab? What is the significance of the scarlet cord in Joshua 2:18? Compare the scarlet cord with the signal described in Exodus 12:7 and 13.

What is the Ark of the Covenant (see Exodus 25:10–22)? Compare the crossing of the Jordan in Joshua 3:14–17 with the crossing of the Sea of Reeds in Exodus 14:21–29. Why do you think the crossing of the Sea of Reeds is the more celebrated of the two events?

What do the twelve stones from the Jordan signify? Why did Joshua set them up in Gilgal? Is the practice of marking the site of a great event still followed today? Explain your answer.

What instructions does Joshua receive for the siege of Jericho? What repetitious phrases and sentences do you find in Joshua 6? What is the effect of the repetition?

Who in Jericho was saved? What material things were saved? Why? Why was the city destroyed so completely? Explain Joshua's curse on Jericho's restorer.

Suggested Activities: Reread Joshua 1–6 and then write a description of Joshua. Before you write your description, you might want to answer these questions:

What, if anything, do you know about Joshua's appearance? What do you think he looked like? Why? What kind of leader do you think he was? Why? Why would you, or wouldn't you, follow Joshua?

Compare Joshua with Moses. How are they alike? How do they differ?

Using only the information about Jericho that you are given in Joshua 1–6, draw a picture of the city, write a description of it, or build a model of it.

Retell the story of the siege of Jericho from the point of view of a citizen of Jericho. As the narrator of your story, how would that citizen of Jericho describe the procession of priests? What effect would Joshua's strategy have on your narrator? What details of the siege recorded in Joshua 6 would he know? What details could he not know? Why?

CHAPTER 8

The Judges

Deborah (Judges 4–5)

The confrontation between the tribal militia of Israel and the Canaanite armies led by Sisera "at Taanach, by the waters of Megiddo" took place around 1125 B.C.—a century after the initial conquest under Joshua.[1] During these hundred years the Israelites had further established their foothold in the rugged hill country of central Palestine and were becoming an increasing threat to the powerful Canaanite city-states which still controlled the fertile valleys. The Canaanites responded by using their superior weaponry and fortified cities to block access to the strategic Esdraelon valley (Judges 5:6f), which cuts from the Mediterranean Sea deep into the central hill country. Israel thus found herself suddenly split in two. Into this situation comes Deborah, the Israelite Joan of Arc, rallying the tribes to break the Canaanite stranglehold.

Chapters 4 and 5 present two varying accounts of the battle—one in prose, one in poetry. The "song of Deborah" in chapter 5 is one of the most beautiful pieces of biblical literature, and of the two descriptions, it is more likely the work of an eyewitness to the battle.[2] The prose account in chapter 4 reflects a much more complex literary development. The chief protagonist in it is Jabin, king of Hazor, who is mentioned in Joshua 11:1 as a contemporary of Joshua. Furthermore, the only Israelite tribes said to have participated in the battle are Zebulun and Naphtali, who assembled at Kedesh, a city near Hazor far north of the Esdraelon valley (Judges 4:10). The defeat of Sisera, however, took place near the river Kishon in the Esdraelon valley (Judges 4:12f; 5:19ff). We know from recent archeological discoveries that Hazor had been in Israelite hands since the time of Joshua. Thus chapter 4 seems to be a conflation of two battle accounts: one describing the thirteenth-century defeat of Jabin near Hazor, the other describing the twelfth-century destruction of Sisera and his army in the Esdraelon valley. The stories were interwoven by portraying Sisera as Jabin's general, whereas Judges 5:19–20, 28–30 show clearly that Sisera was the leader of a coalition of Canaanite kings.[3]

Early Hebrew poetry has a terse, exciting rhythm which is exceedingly powerful. Its basic structure is the bicola, with each cola containing two or three stressed words.[4] A repetitive parallelism is formed, wherein the second cola will repeat or paraphrase several elements from the first cola, while maintaining the same number of stresses. For example verse 3 begins:

AB:A'B'   Hear / O kings   Give ear / O princes

But the second cola will almost invariably avoid dry repetition by adding a new element which is not in the first. When nothing new is added, as in the bicola cited above, the movement is created by the succeeding bicola. Verse 3 continues:

AB:A'B'   Hear / O kings   Give ear / O princes
CD:C'E   I / to Yahweh   Even I / will sing
ED:D'F   I will sing / to Yahweh   The God / of Israel

Note that the novelty can be achieved within the second cola either by adding a completely new element (as in the second bicola "will sing") or by expanding one of the elements from the first cola (as in the third bicola "the God of Israel"). An example of the first approach is in verse 20:

ABC:A'BD   From heaven / fought / the stars
             From their courses / they fought / against Sisera

An example of the second approach is in verse 19:

ABC:C'AD The kings / came / (and) they fought
Then fought / the kings / of Canaan

Thus the effect of the second cola is to reinforce the first cola through repetition, while at the same time fulfilling the anticipation which it has created. This is often called "climactic parallelism."

There is also a larger structure in Hebrew poetry than the single bicola. Several bicola are often grouped into a larger unit which reaches its climax in a tricola. It is difficult to demonstrate this throughout the song of Deborah because the text is corrupted in some parts—especially verses 8–15. But one example, verses 24–27, should illustrate the tricola.

ABC:BDA Blessed / above women / be Jael
Above women / of the tent / be she blessed

AB:CD He asked / water
She gave / milk

EF:C'D' In a lordly / bowl
She brought him / curds

ABC:A'DC' Her hand / to the tentpeg / she put
Her right hand / to a workman's / mallet

AB:A'C:A'A'C' She struck / Sisera
She crushed / his head
She shattered / and pierced / his temple

ABC:ABC'BC'D At her feet / he sank / he lay flat
At her feet / he sank / he fell down
There he sank / he fell down / dead

Note how the meter changes as the strophe progresses and that the alternation of meter indicates variation in the intensity of emotion during this progression. It begins with a 3:3 bicola, which is the most common meter in Hebrew poetry. Then it moves to a series of 2:2 bicola to point up both the simplicity of the action and the underlying excitement and potential in the situation. As Jael picks up the tentpeg, a 3:3 meter is resumed to stress the calmness and stealth by which she acted. Two successive tricola bring the strophe to its climax. The uneven 2:2:3 meter is charged with the highest emotion as the blow is struck, whereas the measured 3:3:3 cadence indicates the resolution of the action.

If this poem were to be orchestrated, the staccato 2:2's might be set to rolling drums, the 2:2:3 to crashing symbols, and the 3:3:3 would be the soaring finale.

It is worth noting that the poet has used almost the exact same metric structure for the final strophe, which is set in Sisera's court:

ABC:DC′B′	Through / a window / she peered
	Sisera's mother / gazed / through the lattice
AB:CD	"Wherefore / tarries
	His chariot / in coming?
AB′:EC	The wisest / of her ladies / answers
	Yea she returns / words / to her:
AB:CD	"Have they not / found
	Divided / the booty?
EF:GH	A maid / two maids
	For each / warrior?
IJK:IJL:J′LM	Booty / of dyed stuffs / for Sisera
	Booty / of dyed stuffs / embroidered
	Two dyed cloths / embroidered / for his neck?"

The 2:2:3 of the earlier strophe has been replaced by two 2:2's. Otherwise the structure of the two strophes is the same. The 2:2's predominate here, skillfully delineating the atmosphere of agitation and anxiety which pervades the court of the long overdue king.

Verses 2–11c introduce the main action of the poem. The rulers of the nations are summoned to hear the praises to be sung to Yahweh, who has mightily delivered his people from the enemy. The description of his coming in verses 4–5 is more than a general theophany which has been added to enhance the religious nature of an otherwise secular poem. It would seem more likely that this passage is a specific description of God as he appeared for the battle against Sisera. He is conceived as coming up from the south: from Mount Sinai, across Edom (Seir), and into the land of Canaan.

The fact that Sisera's army had iron weapons and nine hundred chariots which controlled the plains (Judges 4:13) was inconsequential; nor was it significant that the Israelite armies had only crude and primitive weapons (Judges 5:8b). The determinative factor was Yahweh, whose entire host was engaged in the battle against Sisera:

> From heaven fought the stars
>   From their courses they fought against Sisera (Judges 5:20).

The preparations for the battle are described in verses 11d–18: the troops gather; Deborah is called to urge them on with a war song; Barak is encouraged through the anticipation of the captured enemy host. Then follows a list of the tribes which did not fight in the battle. Those which participated were for the most part the tribes geographically adjacent to the Esdraelon valley: Ephraim, Benjamin, and Machir (the largest clan of Manasseh) to the south, and Issachar, Zebulun, and Naphtali to the north. Since any war in which Israel was involved was also Yahweh's war, all the tribes were expected to give assistance. Thus those tribes which did not participate are mockingly rebuked. One could say that these tribes were too far distant to feel the threat of Sisera's armies. But it must also be said that these particular tribes were having an extremely difficult time establishing themselves in the land which had been apportioned to them.[5]

We have already discussed the description in verses 4–5 of Yahweh's appearance to lead the Israelite armies into battle. Old Testament theophanies contain almost stereotyped formulae, which include fire, smoke, shaking earth, and violent storms. It appears, however, that a sudden storm did take place during the battle, bogging down the Canaanite chariots and cutting off retreat by turning the little river Kishon into a raging torrent (Judges 5:21).

The village of Meroz has not yet been definitely located. It is most likely an Israelite settlement near the Esdraelon valley. Why is the tribe of Meroz singled out for special cursing, whereas the other tribes which did not participate are merely scornfully rebuked? One should note that the curse, solemnly pronounced by the angel of the Lord—the captain of Yahweh's heavenly armies—comes after the battle was fought. The most likely suggestion is that the fleeing Sisera went through Meroz, but the villagers were fearful of the powerful Canaanites and the possibility of reprisals, and allowed him to escape.[6]

The poet contrasts the response of the inhabitants of Meroz with the courageous action of Jael. In Judges 4:18–21, Jael drove a tentpeg through Sisera's head while the exhausted king lay sleeping. In Judges 5:25–27, she struck him on the head, apparently while he was drinking, so that he fell dead to the ground. It is likely that Judges 4:18–21 is secondary, having arisen from a misunderstanding of the repetitive parallelism characteristic of early Hebrew poetry.[7]

> Her hand / to the tentpeg / she put
> Her right hand / to a workman's / mallet

How many weapons is Jael holding? After our discussion of Hebrew poetry, which shows how the second cola repeats and reinforces elements from the first cola, it should be clear that she has only one weapon. Simply from practical considerations Jael would not attempt to drive a tentpeg through Sisera's skull while he was standing up. Verse 27 shows clearly that Sisera was standing when the blow fell. Note, incidentally, the great skill of the poet in portraying Sisera's gradual collapse following the blow:

> At her feet / he sank / he lay flat
> At her feet / he sank / he fell down
> There he sank / he fell down / dead

The final mark of the poet's superb skill and imagination is the closing scene in Sisera's court, where the queen mother and her retinue anxiously await his return. We know already the gruesome event which they will later discover, and that the "wisdom" of the court ladies—who envision the dividing of the spoils among the victorious Canaanite troops—is but the folly of wishful thought. Yes, we know what they will soon learn; but the denouement is left to our imaginations. The final verse of the chapter ("So perish all thine enemies . . . "), though not a part of the original poem, does warn us against interpreting the court scene as showing compassion for the mother of a fallen enemy. There is no pity here, but rather the glee of revenge. Perhaps an ironic comparison is also being made between the Canaanite ladies, who sit in their palace eagerly anticipating the spoil which will be theirs, and the women of Israel, Deborah and Jael, who dare to act so that their people can be free from the threat of oppression.[8]

This story is unusual in the Old Testament because it centers on women: Deborah, who initiates the action; Jael, who fulfills the action; and the Canaanite mother, who suffers the consequences of the action. Very little is said concerning Barak, the leader who was appointed by Deborah to be Israel's military leader. Deborah must have had such great authority because she was acknowledged as a prophetess who knew the will of God. Her closest parallel is Samuel, the religious leader who anointed Saul to lead Israel's armies. Was Deborah ever a judge over all Israel? In the song she is portrayed as leading the soldiers of Issachar (Judges 5:15a). Perhaps as a result of the victory she gained national fame and moved south into Ephraim to judge all Israel under "the palm of Deborah" (Judges 4:5). However, since this tree marks the place of burial of Rebekah's nurse Deborah (Genesis 35:8), it is also possible that the tradition of Deborah's judging all of Israel from that place is secondary.

Some Questions for Discussion: Judges 4 begins: "And the people of Israel again did what was evil in the sight of the Lord. . . . " To determine what they did, read Judges 2:11–13 and 3:7.

What evidence can you find in Judges 4 to indicate that Deborah was considered a powerful woman? What facts about Deborah are you given in Judges 4? about Jael? about Barak? about Sisera? about the battle? Compare the account of the battle (Judges 4:12–16) with the siege of Jericho (Joshua 6:1–25). Which gives you more details? Which is more vivid? Compare the description of the battle with that of Sisera's murder (Judges 4:18–22).

Chapter 5 is a poetic version of chapter 4. Which do you prefer? Why? What is Deborah called in the poetic version? Why do you think she is given that distinction?

What is the tone of the narrator as he refers to the tribes that did not enter the battle? Compare the tone in verses 15–18 with that in verse 23.

What is the effect of the repetition in the "song of Deborah"? How does the repetition here differ from the use of repetition in other passages you have read so far (for example, Genesis 1)?

What do you thing is the purpose of verses 28–30? What irony do you see in those verses?

What is the role of the women named in Judges 4–5? Compare their roles with those of the women in Exodus 1–2.

Suggested Activities: Using only the facts you are given in Judges 4–5, write an account of the battle for a newspaper.

Plan a choral reading of the "song of Deborah" and present it to the class. For which passages would you use only women's voices? only men's? both? Why?

Gideon (Judges 6:1–8:33)

An entirely new situation faces the Israelite settlers during the time of Gideon. Each year marauding bands of Bedouins came streaming in from the fringes of the Arabian desert in the east. These Midianites[9] were not attempting to settle permanently in the land. Instead, perhaps driven west by an excessively severe drought along the semiarid land which borders the desert, their intent was to gain access to the food supplies in the fertile valleys of Palestine. For Israel, the novelty lay not in the prospect of resorting to warfare in order to maintain her tenuous hold on the land; it was rather the necessity of battling invaders who attacked on camels. As W. F. Albright has shown, this story is our earliest evidence that the camel had been domesticated.[10] An attack waged on camel was difficult to defend against, and it left a desolate land in its wake. R. Kittel cites an eyewitness account of such an attack which occurred around the turn of this century:

> In June and July they (the Bedouins of the Arabian Desert) came northward from the desert half dead with thirst. The

"birke" (pool) is not sufficient to quench their thirst. Then the tens of thousands of camels with half naked riders mounted on their select delules (riding camels) break through the thin ranks of soldiers, and woe unto the fields over which the hungry hordes first scatter! Not a stem, not a blade of grass is left, for what they do not devour is trampled under the broad hoofs of their camels.[11]

Not only was the destruction immense, but the domesticated camel now made possible the perfect getaway into the desert where no man could follow.

Israel's desperate plight is well illustrated in Judges 6:11ff, where Gideon is introduced into the story as he is flailing the wheat by hand—not in the exposed and easy to find threshing floor on the hilltop, but rather in the concealment of the wine press. The enemy would soon attack, and it was hoped that they would pass by when nothing substantial was found. Resistance seemed out of the question; the only recourse was concealing the provisions and hiding in the caves until the invaders had gone.

We can see from Judges 6:25ff that there were several popular traditions concerning Gideon's commission to lead Israel, and that these traditions have been merged by a later editor. Here Gideon is commanded to tear down the Baal altar on his father's land and erect an altar to Yahweh. He had just built an altar to Yahweh on his father's land in verse 24. Apparently both traditions are explanations of the origin of the altar, which "to this day . . . still stands at Ophrah" (Judges 6:24). Judges 6:25ff seems to be a continuation of verses 7-10, in which a prophet admonished the Israelites against worshiping other gods. Gideon secretly tears down the Baal altar, and is almost executed by the men of the town, who are incensed at such sacrilege. Apparently a religious syncretism existed in which Baal worship was tolerated because it was not seen as a threat to Yahweh's supremacy over the gods. Baal, the Canaanite vegetation deity, could be regarded as a subordinate member of Yahweh's host. This would explain Gideon's other name, Jerubbaal ("Let Baal contend [for him]"). The text would indicate that this name was given to Gideon as a result of his having destroyed the Baal altar. But it is far more likely that this was his original name (note that the Baal altar was on his father's land), and that the story's purpose is to explain the name through an event which portrays Gideon and Baal emerging as adversaries rather than allies "Let Baal contend [against him]"). This second tradition of Gideon's commission as a judge apparently concludes with an alternate version of the divine sign of assurance (Judges 6:36–40).

The battle took place in approximately the same region where Deborah had overcome Sisera: the eastern stretch of the Esdraelon plain north of Jezreel. As we have noted, this strategic and fertile plain cuts in from the Mediterranean Sea almost over to the Jordan River. Fording the Jordan from the east, the Midianites would apparently make their annual incursions across the plain all the way to Mount Carmel on the Sea, where the road turns off to Gaza (Judges 6:4). This explains Gideon's summoning Manasseh, Asher, Zebulun, and Naphtali—the tribes most immediately affected by such an invasion route.[12]

The armies of Israel gather; but what hope do they have against enemy troops mounted on camels? Gideon has already received the assurance that Israel will be delivered by divine power. A further good omen is forthcoming when he overhears a Midianite warrior recounting his dream: a cake of barley bread came rolling into camp, toppling the tent so that it lay flat.[13] Whether or not the dream's portent was clear to the talking soldiers it was obvious enough to Gideon: the barley cake represented the farmers of Israel and the crushed tent the nomadic Midianite invaders.

Returning quickly to his camp, Gideon prepared for an immediate attack. Nighttime attacks were unheard of; no one could distinguish friend from foe. But this is precisely what Gideon was counting on. His plan was to encircle the enemy camp, but not to enter it. The sounding horns and shrill war cry[14] would awaken the Midianites, and the crashing pots would simulate the noise of battle.[15] One can picture the panic and confusion which must have resulted. The startled Midianites, running pell-mell from their tents only to find the way to escape barred by armed Israelites holding torches, would wheel around into the camp, meeting other confused comrades whom they mistook for the enemy attacking from the other direction, and the melee would run its course. The Israelites had only to hold their ground.

It should be noted that one of the themes most frequently recurring in the Gideon stories is a theological one: God's power is revealed and his purposes are achieved through human weakness. He chose the youngest son in the smallest clan of a weak tribe; the superfluous troops were sent home so that Israel would never doubt that the victory was Yahweh's. The point is an important one, and it is well made.

It is difficult, however, to interpret this tradition. Some scholars maintain that chapter 7 is describing a skirmish between the Midianites and Gideon's clan (the Abiezrites), and that only later was the tradition expanded to include other Israelite tribes. It must be granted that some legendary elements have entered the tradition. But this confrontation was more than a skirmish; the Midianites are never again mentioned as potential enemies in the Old Testament. They must have met a disastrous reversal so great that "the day of Midian" still epitomized deliverance from the oppressor four hundred years later (Isaiah 9:4; cf. Psalm 83:9-12). It would thus seem more likely that a coalition of tribes did take part in achieving the victory. Could it be that Gideon, preferring not to meet the camel-mounted enemy in open battle on the plain, planned this daring night attack in which three hundred men would be more effective than thousands? But did he send the others home? It seems likely that Gideon, relying on his three hundred to initiate the rout, deployed the rest of his army at the fords of the Jordan to cut down the fleeing enemy. This strategy would help to explain Ephraim's belated participation in the final slaughter. Many Midianites, finding the northern fords of the Jordan blocked, headed for the southern fords near the River Jabbok, where they met the waiting Ephraimites (Judges 7:24-25).

The Ephraimites were angered at having been excluded from the initial summons to battle. Ephraim was the foremost tribe in Israel, where Shechem, Shiloh, and Bethel—the ancient covenant centers—were located. The tribe was offended that its customary leadership had been bypassed; but it was also aggrieved over not receiving a full share of the spoils of victory. Gideon, tactfully minimizing his role in the victory, pacifies their rage by praising them for capturing and slaying the Midianite chieftains, Oreb and Zeeb.

The Ephraimites had crossed the Jordan to meet Gideon, who was continuing the final pursuit of the remnant of Midian in the Transjordan (Judges 7:25). But in Judges 8:4ff Gideon is shown just crossing the Jordan. Now he is chasing after two other Midianite chieftains, Zebah and Zalmunna, and the reason, we soon learn, is to exact blood vengence against them for slaying his brothers. Clearly the editor has switched to a different narrative tradition. It is difficult to determine whether this represents (1) an alternate version of the earlier pursuit story; (2) a continuation of the same event, with the dislocation caused by the misplacement of the Ephraimite confrontation; or (3) a completely separate incident from the battle described in chapter 7. This new narrative must originally have included an account of the death of Gideon's brothers, along with his vow to avenge their blood.

Blood vengeance is an ancient custom in tribal society, designed to protect its members from violence. Any would-be murderer is thus restrained by the knowledge that his victim's family would not rest until his life had been forfeited. The obligation falls primarily on the next of kin, who, in this case, is Gideon. Having captured the two Midianite leaders, he asks his son Jether to slay them. The youth was being invited to assume the responsibilities of an adult by requiting his family's blood. When Jether falters, Gideon slays the captives, who were anxious to avoid the disgrace of dying at the hands of a boy.

The story concludes with Gideon's being offered kingship over the tribes. Israel could very easily have slipped into the Canaanite pattern of hereditary kingship at this time had not Gideon recalled a central tenet of the Mosaic covenant faith: Yahweh alone is ruler over his people. Thus the Israelite system of charismatic leadership was preserved, at least for the time being. So that later generations would recall the memorable victory, Gideon created an ephod (which was perhaps intended as a garment for his deity) from the Midianite spoils and placed it near his home, perhaps next to the Yahweh altar he had built. Eventually this ephod became an object of worship rather than commemoration.

Some Questions for Discussion: Recount the trials of the people of Israel prior to the time of Gideon. How are the Israelites threatened in Judges 6:1–5? According to the narrator, why are the Israelites being punished?

Describe the Lord's call to Gideon and Gideon's initial reaction. Compare the commissioning of Gideon with that of Moses in Exodus 3–4. How do they differ?

What does Gideon ask the Lord to do before he leads the Israelites against the Midianites? Why does Gideon put the Lord through two "trials"?

For what reason does Gideon reduce the size of his fighting force? How does he accomplish the reduction in troops? What is the dream Gideon hears the men discussing? How does Gideon interpret it?

How would you rate Gideon as (a) a leader, (b) a military strategist, (c) a diplomat? Cite passages from Judges 6:1–8:33 to support your conclusions.

What tradition of Israelite leadership is reasserted in the Gideon story? Reread Judges 8:24–27 and explain the irony of this conclusion to the Gideon story.

What personal matter does Gideon have to settle with Zebah and Zalmunna? Recalling what you have learned about blood vengeance in earlier stories, how would you explain Gideon's behavior?

Suggested Activities: Imagine that you were an eyewitness to the battle between the Israelites and Midianites. Give a written or an oral account of the battle.

Consider Moses, Joshua, and Gideon. Before completing the suggested theme assignment below, list the characteristics of the three leaders. What do they have in common? How do they differ?

Write a theme in which you explain which of the three leaders you admire most. Give reasons for your decision.

Thus far you have read about some of the important figures in the Old Testament: Adam, Eve, Cain, Abel, Noah, Abraham, Sarah, Rebekah, Isaac, Jacob, Rachel, Esau, Joseph, Potiphar's wife, Reuben, Judah, Benjamin, Moses, Aaron, Joshua, Rahab, Deborah, Jael, and Gideon. You are the casting director for a major motion picture studio that will produce a panorama of the Old Testament. Select any six of the Old Testament figures listed above. Name the contemporary movie, television, or stage actor or actress you would cast in each of the six roles you have selected. Then give either a written or an oral defense for each choice, explaining the major characteristics of the biblical figure that you think your actor or actress can portray better than any other contemporary performer.

Jephthah (Judges 11:1–12:7)

Israel's next crisis occurs in the Transjordanian land of Gilead. The Ammonites, a seminomadic people related to the Israelites, were challenging Gilead's possession of the land between the Arnon and Jabbok rivers. The Gileadites had searched in vain for a charismatic leader who would be powerful enough to withstand the threatened attack. Finally in desperation they turned to Jephthah, a renegade freebooter who roamed with his band in the land of Tob—far north of the area of contention. Jephthah was, however, a Gileadite: the son of a whore, he had been driven from his father's house by his half brothers and denied a share of the inheritance.[16] This expulsion had apparently been ratified and enforced by the tribal elders (Judges 11:7). But now they are willing to make him their leader if he will deliver them from the enemy. These vows are solemnized before Yahweh in Mizpah, the covenant center of the Transjordanian tribes.

Verses 12–28 are regarded by many scholars as a secondary editorial insertion because they seem to deal with a land dispute with the Ammonites rather than the Moabites. This is indeed a possibility, since Jephthah's story is based primarily on Israel's past relationship with Moab rather than Ammon. He refers to Chemosh, the Moabite god, and Balak, an earlier Moabite king (see Numbers 22–24). But it is also possible that the verses are a part of the original story.[17]

Jephthah is attempting to establish Israel's claim to the land. In so doing he is forced to recall the precedent of the historical involvement of the Moabites rather than the Ammonites, who had not yet arrived on the scene (see Numbers 20–21). When Israel had come out of Egypt, he points out, they had carefully avoided conflict with the Edomites and Moabites. The land of Gilead had been conquered from Sihon the Amorite; it had been given to Israel by Yahweh, just as the land south of the Arnon had been given to Moab by Chemosh (Judges 11:24). Balak, the Moabite king, had never challenged Israel's right to this land.[18] So what legitimate claim could the Ammonites possibly make on it?

This passage might seem to be wordy and the work of an editor who wanted to recall a portion of Israel's earlier history. But we have many records of similar statements by kings who would notify the enemy of the legality of their case, invoking the gods to act so that justice would prevail in the ensuing battle. Jephthah's message was sent to the Ammonite king; but it was directed primarily to "Yahweh the Judge, (who would) decide this day between the people of Israel and the people of Ammon" (Judges 11:27).

The focal point of the story is the tragic vow which Jephthah makes before Yahweh prior to the battle. In an attempt to rally the tribal armies, he had journeyed with his band throughout Gilead and Transjordanian Manasseh until he reached the covenant shrine of Mizpah. Perhaps he was driven to such a desperate vow (the sacrifice of the first human being who would come from his house to welcome him after the victory) because the full support the tribes expected had not materialized. Child sacrifice (usually of the first-born), a custom commonly practiced in Canaan, was banned in Israel (see Leviticus 18:21; 20:2–5). But Jephthah's act does not fit into this category. He is not yielding passively to the demands of a pagan religious custom of the time.

Faced with a crisis where the fate of the nation hangs in the balance (and one cannot help note the parallels between this and Agamemnon's sacrifice of Iphigenia), Jephthah freely offers a part of his family for the sake of his people (see II Kings 3:24–27). The act was voluntary, which makes it at once more heroic, more tragic, and more horrible. But once the vow had been made, it was obligatory. Not to have complied would have been regarded as gross sacrilege.

The encounter between Jephthah and his daughter at the moment of his triumphant return is told with great poignancy. She was among the maidens who had come out to welcome the victorious army with song and dance (see I Samuel 18:6). The celebration becomes a nightmare as he sees her and suddenly recalls the irrevocable vow. Although the nature of the vow has not been spelled out, the girl senses what it is and readily offers herself as the price of victory over the Ammonites. She asks only for a two-month reprieve to mourn that she would be cut off before her life was fulfilled through marriage and bearing children. When she returned, Jephthah "did with her according to the vow which he had made." By avoiding the specific details, the narrator allows the full horror of the event to be built up in the imagination of the hearer.[19]

The story of Jephthah ends with the famous "Shibboleth" incident—an altercation with the Ephraimites similar in many ways to the situation which Gideon faced (Judges 8:1–3). Some scholars have suggested that these are alternate versions of the same event which have been incorporated into both the Gideon and Jephthah traditions. But the differences between the two stories are far more significant than the similarities. The Ephraimites are ready to execute Jephthah and his entire family for failing to notify them about the conflict. Jephthah replies defiantly that they had been summoned[20] and that when no aid was forthcoming he had been forced to go into battle with those troops which had answered his call. The Ephraimites are not placated and the battle takes place—with disastrous consequences for the challengers. The Ephraimite group is routed by the enraged Gileadites,[21] who send them fleeing back toward the Jordan. At the fords, the fugitives are recognized by their northern dialect (which pronounced the *sh* phoneme as *s*) and are executed. We are told in Judges 12:6 that forty-two thousand Ephraimites were slain. This is without doubt a great exaggeration of the small punitive expedition sent by the Ephraimites to deal with Jephthah.

Some Questions for Discussion: What is ironic about the Gileadites' going to the land of Tob to ask Jephthah to be their leader? What is Jephthah's condition for accepting leadership? What does Jephthah's first attempt to settle the land dispute tell you about him?

How does the narrator portray Yahweh in the story of Jephthah? How does Yahweh's role here compare with his role in previous stories of the Judges? How might the choice of Jephthah be viewed as consistent with Israelite emphasis on Yahweh's role in delivering Israel to freedom?

Why might Jephthah's vow be considered rash? As you read his vow, what horror entered your mind? Why do you think you thought something terrible might happen to Jephthah? What clues in other stories might have led you to expect the worst?

Compare Jephthah's reaction to seeing his daughter come out to meet him to Abraham's reaction when he was told to sacrifice his son. Reread the two accounts of sacrifice (Abraham's and Jephthah's). How are they similar in choice of words and details? How do they differ?

Consider what you have learned about Jephthah's character in the various incidents in this story. Do you view him as a tragic figure? simply rash? nobly heroic? Explain your answer. What now familiar complaint do the Ephraimites raise after the battle? How might their actions be accounted for? Do you feel that their annihilation is justified?

Samson (Judges 13:2–16:31)

The Samson stories portray a hero who is quite different from the judges who precede him. The other judges consistently appear as charismatic leaders who rally the tribes and deliver Israel from the enemy threat. Samson, too, is filled with Yahweh's spirit, but he emerges primarily as a heroic individual whose major preoccupation is loving Philistine women and fighting Philistine men. It was his weakness in the hands of women, combined with his prodigious feats of strength against his enemies, that fascinated the storytellers of Israel. Thus the figure of Samson, more than any of the other judges, has been enshrined and shrouded by the process of folklore. Unlike the other judges, who are usually described through their participation in one mighty act of deliverance, Samson is the hero of an entire cycle of traditions. The cycle can be roughly divided into three parts: chapter 13, the story of Samson's birth; chapters 14–15, stories connected with his marriage to a Philistine woman; and chapter 16, other love adventures which culminate in his betrayal, capture, and death.

The tribe of Dan, of which Samson's family was a part, had settled about twenty miles west of Jerusalem in the foothills which bordered the coastal plain. They were not a large tribe, and no sooner had they settled there than a new group of people came storming in from the sea. They were the Philistines; their movement into this area just before 1200 B.C. was a part of the sea-peoples' invasion of the eastern Mediteranean coast. They were a European people who had set sail from islands in the Aegean Sea. Their onslaught against Egypt had been withstood at the Nile Delta, and it was perhaps a remnant of this group that settled along the coast of south Canaan. The Philistines were not large in number; they lived primarily in five cities on the Mediterranean coast (Ashdod, Gaza, Ashkelon, Gath, and Ekron). But their armies were well-trained and well-armed. Unlike the Israelites, they had learned to make iron weapons.

The Samson stories give us an excellent insight into the political situation and everyday life during the middle of the twelfth century B.C. The two peoples, though latently hostile to one another, lived side by side—engaging in frequent skirmishes, but also carrying on trade and establishing enough cultural contact for occasional intermarriages. Even during this early period, however, Philistine superiority was acknowledged in the southern region (Judges 15:11). This power was destined to expand during the next century, until it was challenged by Saul and finally checked by David. In the course of this Philistine expansion, the tribe of Dan was finally forced to give up its claim to the southern foothills and migrate to a region north of the Sea of Galilee (Judges 18).

Samson is the only Israelite judge who is accorded a birth story. It is quite possible that this story was added to the cycle in order to legitimatize his somewhat shaky claim to the title of judge. As we have pointed out, Samson at no time acted as a national deliverer. Only from the perspective of Saul and David could Samson be pointed to as the forerunner who "shall begin to deliver Israel from the hand of the Philistines" (Judges 13:5). The motif of the long-barren woman who is finally enabled to conceive through divine visitation and providence is a familiar one in Hebrew culture.[22] The visitor's not being recognized as the angel of the Lord is also common in this literary genre. Manoah and his wife mistake the angel for a prophet, and only after offering a sacrifice do they realize that they have encountered the deity (see also Judges 6:11–24).

Manoah's wife is instructed to dedicate her son to God at birth as a Nazirite. Even while the child is in the womb she is to prepare herself by abstaining from unclean food and the fruit of the vine. A Nazirite was a holy man, often endowed with charismatic power. He was forbidden to make himself unclean by coming into contact with corpses; nor could he drink wine because of its close association with the degrading influence of Canaanite culture (see Numbers 6:1–12). He could be recognized by his hair, which was not to be cut as long as he remained a Nazirite.[23] Samson seems to have followed only this latter provision, for here, according to legend, lay the secret of his strength. It is possible that his having long hair led secondarily to the tradition of his Nazirite origins.

We first meet Samson as a headstrong young man who is demanding that his parents take action to secure the hand of a young maiden whom he had recently seen in the Philistine village of Timnah. It was customary for the bridegroom's father to initiate the negotiations which would lead to marriage (see also Genesis 34:1–12), but Samson's parents were unwilling to tolerate any kinship with the hated Philistines. Rebelling against parental authority, Samson insisted on having his own way. At this point, the narrator feels compelled to explain Samson's gross disrespect —by apologizing for the parents' ignorance (verse 4). They did not know that their son's impulsive desire had been instigated by Yahweh as a means of provoking conflict with the Philistines. Such an explanatory gloss as we find in verse 4 definitely belongs to the latest stage of the narrative tradition, as the Samson stories were finally being written down. Note that "at the time the Philistines had dominion over Israel" presupposes a time such as the Davidic monarchy when the Philistine threat had been contained.

There is some textual confusion in verses 5–9, which obscures the progression of the story. It is quite certain that Samson's parents were not won over by his arguments and had nothing whatsoever to do with the marriage negotiations and wedding festivities. Samson was forced to give the wedding party in his bride's home, and he was so lacking in friends and family that he had to accept thirty Philistines from Timnah as his groomsmen.[24] Thus "with his father and mother" in verse 5 is the addition of a later redactor who was probably concerned over Samson's blatant disregard of his parents' will. Note that this addition was not carried through consistently—even in the same verse: "Samson went down with his father and mother to Timnah, and *he* came to the vineyards of Timnah" (see also verse 7). Where were Samson's parents? How would they not know that a young lion had attacked him and that he had slain it? (Incidentally, the Asian lions which occasionally roamed through the hills of Palestine were not as large as the African lions with which we are familiar. Therefore, although it would still be a remarkable feat, it would not be impossible for a strong man to kill such a lion.)[25]

The sequence of events becomes confused in verses 7–9 after the slaying of the lion. Samson visits his fiancee in Timnah (verse 7). Then *in returning to Timnah* to marry her he finds honey in the lion's carcass, which he gives *to his parents*. Something is wrong here. Although there are other possible solutions, it would seem best to omit "to take her'" in verse 8 as an intrusive gloss. Samson was not on his way to the wedding. This allows the following sequence: Samson killed the lion while going to Timnah to visit his fiancee. Upon returning home several weeks later (from that visit, or, more likely, from a subsequent visit), he found the honey in the lion's carcass and gave some to his parents. Was it because he had broken his Nazirite vows that he was reluctant to tell his family where he had found the honey? At any rate, this secret becomes the key to the tragic events that follow.

The wedding feast traditionally lasted for a week. With the wine flowing freely, it was an occasion for all to enjoy—filled with jokes, songs, games, contests, and riddles. Samson could not resist demonstrating to the Philistines that, although they may have the superior material culture, they were still no match for the earthy wisdom of the Israelite peasant. The riddle he propounds is both crude and sophisticated and, of course, impossible to solve:

"Out of the eater came something to eat.
Out of the strong came something sweet."

In such a setting one can almost hear the raucous laughter as the Philistines immediately arrive at the obvious answer: vomit.[26] Midway through the week[27] the groomsmen begin to grow uneasy, sensing defeat. There is more at stake in the outcome of this contest than their honor; a wager had been made which would cost the loser dearly. Viciously turning upon Samson's bride, they threaten her with death if she does not help them learn the secret. She succeeds in the nick of time. The delighted Philistines victoriously mock Samson with a riddle of their own:

"What is sweeter than honey?
What is stronger than a lion?"

They have not only solved Samson's riddle, but they have also discovered his fatal flaw. The answer to their riddle is "love," against which Samson's strength is no match.

Enraged at the deceit, Samson storms out and leaves his bride waiting at the tent. He pays the debt incurred by the lost wager through an act which brings him revenge for his humiliation. He slays thirty Philistines in Ashkelon, giving their garments to his former groomsmen. Why do we not hear of any immediate repercussions from such an attack? Undoubtedly there were some. But it should be noted that the Samson cycle in the Bible certainly does not contain all the traditions which were passed down about him. The narrator's main interest at this point is to tell about the repercussions of the interrupted wedding feast. By Judges 15:9ff, Samson finds himself at war with the entire Philistine pentapolis. Undoubtedly his venture in Ashkelon was one of the factors which put such a high price on his head.

Having regained his composure, Samson returns to Timnah for his wife. Note that his purpose is not to bring her to his home, but rather to have sexual intercourse with her in her father's house. Samson had evidently entered into a *sadiqa* marriage arrangement with his wife. In such a marriage the woman remained in her father's house where she would be visited from time to time by her husband. Children born from the marriage would be considered as part of the mother's household. Samson probably thought that such a course was preferable, since his parents had taken a strong stand against his taking a Philistine wife.

At this point a basic question must be raised: was Samson really married? Did his leaving on the evening of the seventh day constitute a forfeiture of his claim to his bride? It had been thought that the marriage was not consummated until the seventh night of the feast, and that the father was within his legal rights in lessening his family's humiliation by finding another groom so that the ceremony could proceed. But Genesis 29:21–28 shows that, although the festivities lasted for a week, the marriage contract was consummated following sexual intercourse on the first night. This is clearly presupposed in the narrative. Samson and the woman are called "wife" and "husband" already on the fourth day (Judges 14:15f). Samson surely does not feel that he has reneged on an agreement which had not yet been fulfilled. He returns to Timnah, saying "I will go in to my wife in the chamber." Thus, from an Israelite viewpoint, the two were married; and the father had done a terrible thing in giving his daughter to another, in effect forcing her to commit adultery. This explains Samson's feeling that he is justified in burning the Philistine wheat fields. It could also explain the father's apologetic and conciliatory attitude toward Samson (Judges 15:2). The father could have known of this marriage custom and deliberately broken it, thinking that Samson would never return. It also explains the Philistines' execution of the father and daughter for adultery, acknowledging the justice of Samson's case (Judges 15:6).

On the other hand it is possible that this conflict arose because of differing marriage traditions. Perhaps the Philistines accepted the Near Eastern custom which allowed the father to give his daughter to another in order to avoid humiliation when the bridegroom deserted her. No Philistine seems to have objected when the best man took the bridegroom's place. The Philistines did not object until they lost their wheat harvest. The father's conciliatory attitude can also be explained in that Samson is who he is: an enraged superman. And finally, one cannot assume that the violent Philistines, who were ready to burn the bride in her father's house if she didn't help them solve Samson's riddle, were carrying out a legal execution. It is just as possible that they were exacting a fire-for-fire retribution for their burned wheat fields.

It is interesting to note that Samson always seeks vengeance for the wrongs he has suffered from one family by indiscriminately punishing the Philistines as a whole. This would support the argument that he felt himself to be a member of his wife's family and thus could do no direct harm to them, and also that Philistine society as a whole was in some way responsible for his having lost a wager and a wife. His second act of vengeance sounds like an adolescent trick, but burned wheat fields at harvest time would be disastrous for the peasants living in that region. It would bring them close to famine. The ingenious means by which the fields were burned adds a grim humor which the Israelite storytellers would enjoy. Three hundred foxes, of course, points up the exaggerative quality of folklore.

The Samson stories are structured on vengeance, where one act of revenge triggers yet another in response. By setting fire to the

Philistine fields, Samson thought that he had evened the score once and for all; he had not intended to provoke wrath against his wife's family. When he discovers that his wife and father-in-law have been burned to death by the Philistines, Samson assumes the next of kin obligation of blood vengeance (yet another proof that he considered himself a part of that family). He leaves, once again feeling that the score is evened; but he has now enraged the Philistines. He must flee his home and hide out in Judah near the village of Bethlehem.

The Philistines attempt to apprehend Samson by threatening to attack Judah, the tribe in which he has found sanctuary. Here we see that the ties of tribal loyalty are stronger than those to the nation. Samson is an outsider—a Danite, and the Judahites feel no obligation to defend him, especially in the light of the acknowledged Philistine political-military superiority. They bind him and hand him over, promising only that they will not kill him themselves. Samson meets his would-be captors at Lehi, bursts his bonds, and routs the enemy—armed only with the fresh jawbone of an ass.

Lehi means *jawbone* in Hebrew, which casts some suspicion upon the details of this story. One might propose that the village was renamed after Samson's prodigious feat. But it seems more likely that the village received its name from the nearby hill Ramath-lehi, which perhaps was shaped like a jawbone. There are at least three possible solutions: (1) the incident took place at Lehi, and the jawbone weapon secondarily entered the tradition; (2) Samson actually used a jawbone to rout the Philistines, and the incident was located secondarily at Lehi in the course of the story's development; or (3) despite the suspicious coincidence, the event happened roughly as it is described in the story. A legend which explains how En-hakkore (the spring at Lehi) received its name concludes this tradition. It is similar in some ways to the story of Moses' bringing water from the rock in Exodus 17:1–7. Verse 20 ("And he judged Israel in the days of the Philistines twenty years") indicates that at one stage in its redaction the Samson cycle ended at this point.

A small incident at the beginning of chapter 16 skillfully prepares us for Samson's finally being trapped by the wiles of Delilah. We find that Samson is still impulsively consorting with Philistine women, and that the Philistines are still chasing after him. He is almost trapped when the Philistines discover that he is with a harlot in Gaza. They close the gates of the city for the night and patiently wait for their prey to be flushed, feeling certain that he cannot escape. But somehow Samson eludes them. According to folklore Samson went to the gates of the city at midnight, pulled them out of the ground—posts and all—and carried them to a hill near Hebron forty miles away. How this could be done without being detected is not of prime importance in folklore, where a "tall story" is occasionally tolerated and often enjoyed. Perhaps he did have a narrow escape in Gaza; and it is possible that there were some ancient city gates lying outside Hebron which caused the tradition to develop in this manner.

The final story depicts Samson's downfall through his affair with Delilah. From previous experience, the rulers of the five Philistine cities were well aware that Samson could be weakened by women. Accordingly they offer a fantastic bribe (about four thousand dollars) to Delilah, his latest amour, if she would betray him into their hands. After three unsuccessful attempts at ascertaining the source of his power, each of which provides Samson (and the narrator) a new opportunity to demonstrate that power, Delilah finally succeeds in learning the secret. Can we say that Samson was weakened by the power of love, or worn down by a woman's nagging? Both are equally powerful, and can be equally destructive. When his hair was clipped, Yahweh's spirit left him, and he became an easy prey. After being blinded, he was taken to Gaza and forced to grind at the prison mill. The irony is well captured here: the man who had shown great courage and strength by withstanding the Philistines armed only with the jawbone of an ass must now perform the work of an ass because of his weakness for women. But Samson is victorious in the end. When his captors gathered to worship Dagon, a Canaanite grain god and the father of Baal, he tore down the supporting pillars, causing the temple to collapse and many who were in it to perish.

Some earlier scholars have attempted to interpret Samson as a mythological figure.[28] His name is based on the Hebrew word for "sun." In Psalms 19:4c–6, the sun is described as coming forth like a bridegroom. Sending the foxes into the wheat fields points out the destructive, withering influence which the sun can have if its power is unchecked. The power of his hair suggests the power in the sun's rays, which are cut off by night (Delilah is somewhat related to the Hebrew word layla, *night*). His blinding and imprisonment, accompanied by the gradual growth of his hair, parallel the sun's annual waning and return. This is all very suggestive, and perhaps minor elements of solar mythology have entered into some details of the tradition. But there can be no doubt that Samson is a real hero of flesh and blood, whose exploits have been glorified and magnified by the process of folklore.

It is to the narrator's great credit that he refrained from passing any moral judgment on Samson. He tells the stories without giving any evaluation. The moral sensitivity and careful reflection of the theologian are lacking. And this is what one expects in genuine folklore, with its rough and tumble humor and its fascination with human weakness as well as strength. But Samson is called a judge who was possessed by the spirit of God. In the Gideon stories the narrator went out of his way to portray Gideon as the least likely candidate for the office of judge. So also with Samson. One might say that in Israelite thought the charismatic was morally neutral—no better or worse than other men.[29] He is "good" only to the extent that he becomes the agent through whom Yahweh delivers his people. Although Samson was impetuous and foolish with women, he exemplified the power which Yahweh could work through his spirit. But Samson's demise also illustrated man's lonely weakness once Yahweh's spirit had departed.

Some Questions for Discussion: What was unusual about Samson's birth? What instructions were given to Samson's mother concerning him? How does Samson approach his parents to request his choice of wife? What is their response? Does this incident reveal anything about Samson's personality or character? Where was the wedding party held? (The wedding was customarily held in the home of the groom.) The thirty groomsmen were Philistines; might this say something about Samson's status in the Israelite community? Give evidence from the narrative to support your answer. After hearing the riddle answered through his wife's trickery, what does Samson immediately do? Why? Is anything new added to Samson's stature?

Where does Samson seek sanctuary when fleeing from the Philistines? Why is he betrayed to the Philistines? How do Samson's experiences compare to those recorded about Gideon and Deborah? Do you find these conflicts the result of a personal, or a national commitment? What is there to be admired in Samson at this point in the story? What weaknesses in his character are evident? Why is the reader able to accept the many "tall tales" in the narrative?

Following each major episode involving a Philistine woman, Samson wreaks havoc indiscriminately on his enemies. What is the impact of the given sequence in describing his punitive actions? What striking image occurs in Judges 15:4–5? In describing Samson's various modes of revenge, does the narrator rely on realistic, or hyperbolic portrayal of Samson?

What motivated Delilah's betrayal? How does her motive immediately characterize her for the reader? How does the riddle incident at Samson's marriage feast foreshadow Samson's downfall at the hands of Delilah? What then, seems to be Samson's tragic flaw? What literary effect is achieved by Samson's "delaying tactics" with Delilah? Why do you think Samson finally told Delilah the secret?

In Judges 16:22, do you see irony in the fact that he is grinding at the mill, which is the work of an ass? Explain. What final request does Samson make to Yahweh? For what reasons? Describe Samson's last great feat of strength. What didactic effect might the narrator intend by the denouement of the Samson tale? Does one view Samson, finally, as a villain, or hero? Has his characterization been consistent with the events described in the prologue to his tale?

If the story of Samson were not a biblical story, how might it be classified in, say, American literature? Which heroes in American literature might be compared with Samson? Why?

Suggested Activities: Compare Samson with these major figures in Judges: Deborah, Gideon, and Jephthah. In your comparison, point out what, if anything, they have in common. How do they differ from one another? How do they differ from other biblical heroes you have read about thus far?

Vengeance is a dominant motive in the Samson story. Consider contemporary American literature. Discuss novels, short stories, and plays in which vengeance is a dominant motive. What happens to the characters motivated by vengeance? Do most of them suffer a similar fate, or does the fate seem to depend on the reason for vengeance? Explain your answer to your classmates.

CHAPTER 9

The Early Monarchy

Only a century had elapsed between the death of Samson and the birth of Samuel. The system of charismatic leadership had more or less successfully withstood the sporadic challenges to Israel's claim to the land. But Israel's position vis-a-vis the Philistines was rapidly changing. By the middle of the eleventh century, these former inhabitants of the Aegean islands, who had arrived in Canaan within a decade or two of the Israelites, were ready to expand. They had maintained a limited control over some of the southern tribes during Samson's time; but now they were ready to move north—and inland—toward a total domination of all Israel. This was the first time since the initial invasion under Joshua that Israel's national existence had been threatened.

The Philistine menace led to one of the most significant turning points in Israelite history: the move from the charismatic judges to the hereditary monarchs. It took four generations for this transition to occur: from Samuel to Solomon. Samuel was in many ways the last judge who, like Deborah, acted as Yahweh's spokes- man to find a military leader and bring deliverance to the nation. Saul, a genuine charismatic of the old tradition, was a transitional figure, tragically torn between the old and the new. Although called *king*, Saul held back from taking the steps which would lead to a permanently established monarchy. David was also a charismatic, who used his popularity, success, and power to establish an empire and to undertake a significant restructuring of Israel's political and religious life. By the time of his death there was no question that one of his sons would succeed him. Set upon the throne by a palace coup, Solomon was not a charismatic. The wealth of the empire enabled him to fulfill the ancient Near Eastern ideal of what a monarch should be.

The Israelites were not unanimous in their appraisal of the institution of monarchy. This can be noted not only in the conflict between Samuel and Saul but also in the sources which describe the conflict. (Compare, for example, Samuel's contradictory attitudes toward kingship in I Samuel 8–12, and the means by which Saul was selected as king.) Scholars almost unanimously agree that an editor has used at least two sources in compiling the books of Samuel; many think that there were more.

Traditionally the two major sources are called the Early Source (where Saul and the institution of kingship are favorably regarded) and the Late Source (where human kingship is viewed as a dethroning of Yahweh, and Samuel is portrayed as the real leader of Israel). This nomenclature, however, is based upon the assumption that there were no misgivings about kingship in Israel until the oppressive rule of Solomon and later. Samuel's rejection of Saul, the two revolts against David, and finally, the secession of the ten northern tribes show that there were misgivings aplenty from the time of Saul's anointment. Through observing their Canaanite neighbors, the Israelites knew how kingship could develop; they also knew that it would necessitate a major adjustment in Mosaic theology, which regarded Yahweh as king. Thus we would argue that these two sources are both "early"; they both are genuine reflections of variant views which were held within the Israelite community during the eleventh century.[1] It seems preferable to follow B. W. Anderson in renaming the "Early" source the Saul source and the "Late" source the Samuel source.[2] It is possible, though not proven, that these two sources may be continuations of the J (Saul) and E (Samuel) traditions from the Pentateuch.

Eli and Samuel

THE BIRTH OF SAMUEL (I SAMUEL 1)

The opening two verses skillfully establish the setting of the story. A man is usually identified by his father (X, son of Y), but

Elkanah's genealogy is traced back four generations. The author is indicating that Elkanah was a man of high rank—a member of one of the best known and respected families in his Ephraimite village. He had enough wealth to afford two wives.[3] But, we are told, one of the wives was childless. Thus we know that the story will involve: (a) a barren woman yearning to conceive and bear a son; (b) jealousy and conflict within the household because one of the wives has fulfilled her role by bearing children and the other has not (see also Genesis 16; 30); and (c) an act of divine intervention resulting in the birth of a child of special destiny.

The opening scene takes place in Shiloh, the central place of worship for the Israelite tribal confederacy. It was customary for all Israelites to come periodically to this place, where the sacred Ark was kept, to reaffirm their covenant relationship with Yahweh. It was also customary for families to celebrate private sacrificial festivals in their own villages at other times of the year (see also I Samuel 20:6). From the story it would seem more likely that Elkanah and his wives were participating in a family, rather than a national, celebration. If this is true, it is a special mark of Elkanah's piety that his family would journey to the central shrine at Shiloh for a festival which could have been celebrated at home.

Hannah's barrenness is the central theme of the scene at Shiloh. Each year the family would come to celebrate, and each year at the feast Hannah would be freshly reminded of her failure as a wife. The Hebrew text of verse 5 is difficult to interpret. It seems to indicate that Elkanah gave Hannah a special portion because she was his favorite wife. This favoritism provoked Peninnah, who taunted Hannah because she was barren. But Hannah's grief does not arise primarily from the derision of her rival or because she has received only one portion. It is rather because she has not been enabled to respond to her husband's special love by bearing him sons. Elkanah attempts to console her: "Am I not more to you than ten sons?" But it is precisely because he does mean so much to her that she grieves. She wants to be instrumental in assuring the continuation of her husband's name by providing him with progeny.

After the feast Hannah enters the sanctuary of Yahweh in great anguish. In desperation she vows that she will give her first-born to Yahweh—not as a human sacrifice, but as a servant in the Shiloh sanctuary. Eli, the ancient priest and judge, whose sons are now the custodians of the shrine, has been observing Hannah as she prays. Apparently it was the custom to pray aloud. Eli, mistaking her internalized monologue and quivering lips for drunkenness gruffly upbraids her. This first picture of Eli is telling: he emerges as the stern guardian of the Mosaic past who frowns upon the use of wine, which is symbolic to him of the degrading Canaanite culture which the Israelites are gradually accepting. On the other hand, his mistaking anguished prayer for frivolous drunkenness reveals his lack of sensitivity. He is an old man who has been worn down by struggling to maintain the traditions of the past. Hannah's response to his rebuke is beautiful: she has not been pouring down wine; she has been pouring out her soul to Yahweh. As soon as Eli perceives the real situation we see the genuine, paternal compassion which lies beneath his gruff, insensitive exterior. He sends her away with the assurance that God will act in her behalf.

After Samuel's birth, Elkanah prepares for the annual pilgrimage to Shiloh, at which time he intends to fulfill *his* vow. The story has told us only of Hannah's vow to give up her first-born son to the service of the Lord. The regulations in Numbers 30:1–15 make it clear that a woman's vows were subject to the veto of her husband. Thus the narrator is stressing the fact that Elkanah not only did not object to his wife's vow but that he had taken it upon himself and was now fulfilling his responsibility by seeing that the vow was carried out.[4] Hannah demurs temporarily; a mother's love has been awakened by this child who needs her. She will see that the vow is fulfilled, but not until after the child is weaned. (Children are nursed in the Near East for at least the first two years.) This artful indication of Hannah's love for Samuel makes the final festive ceremony in which the child is handed over to the Shiloh priesthood even more dramatic and meaningful.

In verse 20, Samuel received his name because he was "asked" from God. The same Hebrew root is used in verse 28 when

Hannah "lends" the child to Yahweh for lifelong service. "Samuel" (meaning "the name of God" in Hebrew) sounds somewhat like this Hebrew root, *sha'al*, but this is actually the root for forming the name "Saul." The passive participle, *sha'ūl*, means "the one who has been asked for." Some scholars would maintain that this entire birth story was originally part of a cycle of Saul traditions, and that at a later time it was incorporated into the Samuel cycle. But this theory is difficult to accept. There are too many particulars which are essential to the development of the narrative that would not be appropriate to Saul's birth. There could well have been a Saul birth story which emphasized that he was so named because he had been "asked" from Yahweh in order that Israel might be delivered. We can only assume that such a story secondarily influenced the Samuel story as the people came increasingly to realize that the genuine deliverer of Israel was Samuel, not Saul.[5]

Some Questions for Discussion: What was the purpose of the journey of Elkanah and his family to Shiloh? How did Hannah feel about her barrenness? Why? (Consider her reputation, her relationship to members of her household, her relationship to her husband, etc.) Explain what you understand by "And her adversary also provoked her sore" (I Samuel 1:16).

Compare and contrast the birth stories of Samson and Samuel. Reread Genesis 16:1–6 and Genesis 30:1–24. What parallels can be drawn between these passages and those details given concerning the birth of Samuel? In each case, what role do we expect the child to assume in the subsequent narrative? What evidence can you find to show Elkanah's feelings toward Hannah?

In the temple, who observes Hannah at prayer? How does he interpret her behavior? Can you justify such an interpretation from a holy old man? Consider his attitude toward wine and why he would have such an attitude. After Hannah's explanation, what is the tone and substance of his blessing, and what does this reveal about his personality or character? Describe the details of Hannah's offering of Samuel in the temple. Why did she do it? What sacrifice accompanied the offering? For what purpose is she offering him? For how long?

ELI'S SONS (I SAMUEL 2:11–26)

The author's purpose in this section is to explain why Samuel eventually replaced the house of Eli as the religious leader of Israel. In rapidly alternating sequence, the piety and charm of the young boy are contrasted with the gross, sinful behavior of Eli's sons, Hophni and Phinehas. Verse 11 is actually the conclusion of the Samuel birth story, which has been cut from chapter 1 by the editor in order to insert the "Song of Hannah" (I Samuel 2:1–10). After giving his son to be a servant at Shiloh, Elkanah returns home. Does this mean that Hannah remained for a while longer at Shiloh, perhaps serving with the other women at the shrine, in order to raise her son until he became somewhat older? The possibility exists, although the text is not clear on this point.[6] At any rate the verse portrays Samuel being trained by Eli to minister before Yahweh. There is no mention of his contact with Hophni and Phinehas. The implication is that Samuel is to be the true successor of the faithful old priest, thus preserving (or restoring) the purity of the Shiloh priesthood.

Verses 12–17 describe the greed of Eli's sons. As priests they were entitled by long-established custom to a certain portion of the sacrifice. But they wanted more and used trickery and force to get it. Verses 13–14 are somewhat difficult to understand, because the author is assuming that his readers know what the correct procedure was. Only the violation is described. Apparently the priest's rightful portion was whatever he brought out of the pot with his three-pronged fork *after* the meat was cooked. Hophni and Phinehas, however, did not wait. While the meat was still boiling they exacted their claim. Why? Not because they were hungry and could not wait, but probably because meat which has been well cooked will not hold to the fork as well as meat which is still raw. Thus the priests were coming early so that they could pull out a larger portion with the fork. But this is not all.

The priests are not only pressing their claims at the expense of the people; they are also putting their claims ahead of the portion which was owed to Yahweh. After the animal had been sacrificed, and before the meat was prepared by the families for their feast, the fat was traditionally removed and offered to Yahweh. But Hophni and Phinehas wanted their portion even before this was done; they were now demanding raw meat. The protests of any pious Israelite were overruled with the threat of force.

Although the major theme of this section is the sin of Hophni and Phinehas, the leitmotif which runs throughout, providing the continuity between chapters 1 and 3, is that of Samuel's growth as he ministers before Yahweh under Eli's tutelage. He is pictured as a young priest, already clothed with a linen ephod which his mother would replace each year. Eli was pleased with the youth. So also, implies the author, was Yahweh, for Samuel's service brought divine blessing upon his family; Hannah bore three more sons and two daughters.

Eli was not so pleased with the activities of his own sons. Although he had been priest at Shiloh and had apparently trained his sons to succeed him, he only learned of their misdeed from the reports of others. This is another indication of Eli's age and of his inability to cope with the situation. To the previously described sins the author adds that Hophni and Phinehas had been consorting with the women who served at the sanctuary. Eli rebukes them, but it is to no avail. They do not heed their father's warning. Their hearts were hardened, for, maintains the author, it was Yahweh's will to slay them.[7] Seen from the perspective of a later age, the deaths of Hophni and Phinehas were necessary so that Yahweh would begin to deliver his people through Samuel.

The section ends: "Now the boy Samuel continued to grow both in stature and in favor with the Lord and with men." The author has been developing a comparison between Samuel and the house of Eli which here reaches its sharpest point of contrast.

Some Questions for Discussion: How does the elaborate account of the sins of Eli's sons contribute to the development of the character of Samuel? What might be the narrator's purpose for including these incidents?

THE CALL OF SAMUEL (I SAMUEL 3:1–4:1a)

Samuel might have been known throughout the area for his service in the sanctuary, but there was no indication that he had been singled out to function as Yahweh's spokesman. As we have noted, it was traditional during the time of the judges for all Israel to gather periodically at the central place of worship to renew the covenant with Yahweh. This ceremony was presided over by a spokesman who delivered the words of the covenant to the people so that they could reaffirm their relationship with Yahweh. Moses performed this function in earliest times (Exodus 19–24); he was succeeded by Joshua (Joshua 24); and Samuel assumed the same role following Eli's death and the capture of the Ark (I Samuel 7). It is impossible to trace the development of this role during the period of the judges; we can only assert that it was maintained by the institution of the central sanctuary. It is most likely that the covenant mediator was the charismatic judge himself, who was not solely a military figure.[8]

Undoubtedly the covenant mediator in Samuel's youth was Eli, who is described as having judged Israel for forty years (I Samuel 4:18). Apparently this office of divine spokesman was conferred and legitimatized by divine visions. The story implies that God had revealed himself in earlier times to Eli, whereas Samuel did not yet recognize the voice which called. Eli was near death; the word of God had become rare in the land; visions were infrequent. Yahweh, in his holy wrath, had withdrawn himself from the corruption of the Shiloh priesthood. Hophni and Phinehas were Eli's sons, but no fit successors to the office of covenant mediator.

The setting of Samuel's call is the Shiloh sanctuary. Because of Eli's blindness, Samuel had been delegated to serve Yahweh at night by sleeping next to the sacred Ark. As a human king had a nighttime attendant to serve him, so also did Yahweh, the divine King, whose presence was mysteriously connected with the Ark of the Covenant. It should be noted that ancient man often sought divine guidance by sleeping near the holy place of the temple where the god was thought to be enthroned, hoping that the resulting dreams would be communications from the deity. Although Samuel may not have recognized the purpose, it is possible that the hope of divine revelation was Eli's motive in placing Samuel beside the Ark.

Samuel's call took place shortly before dawn. The lamp of God, filled with enough oil to burn through the night, had not yet gone out. Three times Samuel was awakened by the twofold calling of his name; and three times he ran to Eli, thinking that he had been summoned. He did not recognize the voice of the one who called. But Eli realized what it might be and told Samuel what to say the next time he was awakened. Finally the divine oracle did come to Samuel. It was a message of complete doom upon the house of Eli because he was unable to restrain his blasphemous sons.

It has been proposed that in one stage of its development this story included a call to Samuel (because strictly speaking there is no "call" in chapter 3). Following the message of doom concerning Eli's family, perhaps Samuel was told that he had been established as Yahweh's new judge and prophet. But such an assumption is unnecessary. The important thing for the people was that Yahweh had once again begun to reveal himself. The oracle concerning Eli's family, especially after its fulfillment, was sufficient authentication of Samuel's "call." The long spiritual drought had ended with the appearance of Samuel, who was acknowledged throughout the land as the new mediator of the divine word. The concluding verses in this story include the phrase that Yahweh let none of Samuel's words fall to the ground. In Israel the "word" was thought to be an extension of the power of the person who had spoken it. Whether words of blessing or words of woe, they were thought to be a powerful (almost magical) influence in bringing about the events which they proclaimed. The best expression of this concept is in Isaiah 55:10-11, where Yahweh speaks:

> "For as the rain and the snow come down from heaven
> and return not thither but water the earth,
> making it bring forth and sprout,
> giving seed to the sower and bread to the eater,

> so shall my word be that goes forth from my mouth;
> it shall not return to me empty,
> but it shall accomplish that which I propose,
> and prosper in the thing for which I sent it."

Some Questions for Discussion: What is the message the Lord delivers to Samuel? What reasons can you give for the Lord appearing to Samuel with a message concerning the house of Eli? What dramatic qualities has the narrator built into this scene? How is the suspense intensified?

Based on the reading of I Samuel 3:20, what would you assume are the locations of Dan and Beer-sheba? How does that assumption help you to infer what is happening to Samuel's reputation? What conditions in Israel's religious life at this time might have contributed to the rise of Samuel's reputation and authority? Why do you think the narrator chose to tell this section of the story in the form of dialogue? What, if anything, would be gained or lost by a strict narration of the events of this chapter? Explain your answer.

ELI'S DEATH (I SAMUEL 4:1b–18)

The focus of the narrative suddenly switches from young Samuel's ministry in Shiloh to the Israelites facing the Philistines in the fields of Aphek. No mention is made of Samuel and his activity. The nation's religious leaders are still Eli's sons, Hophni and Phinehas, whose sinfulness is not referred to.

The abrupt break in the narrative at 4:1b would suggest that the editor is now relying on a different source for his material—a source which has no interest in tracing the rise of Samuel, but whose main concern at this point is to describe the fate of the Ark of the Covenant.[9] However, this passage is useful to the editor because it shows the word of God to Samuel being fulfilled by the death of Eli and his sons. The chapters (4–6) also provide an interlude in the story of Samuel so that the next time he appears he is a mature adult who is the acknowledged religious leader of Israel.

The result of the initial encounter against the Philistines was discouraging for the Israelites. Although not completely routed, the Israelites were unable to withstand an enemy whose superior armaments, which doubtlessly included chariots, gave such great advantage in pitched battle on the open plain. In an attempt to reverse the tide of battle, the elders of Israel met in the evening and decided to send for the sacred Ark of the Covenant in Shiloh. As we have noted before, the Ark was conceived as the shrine upon which Yahweh was invisibly enthroned. Basic to Israel's holy war concept was that Yahweh was leading his people into battle, and that through his power the victory would be won. In earlier times it was customary for the Ark to be carried into battle as visible manifestation of the divine presence, but we cannot determine the extent to which it was used in Israel's wars during the Tribal League period. We know that it was kept at the central place of worship, and from this story it could be inferred that its function was becoming increasingly liturgical rather than military. It is unjustified to assume, however, that because there is no mention of the Ark in other battles it was therefore not in use.[10] It is only mentioned in our story because it was captured by the Philistines, and the narrator is interested in describing the plagues which were visited upon its captors.

When the Ark is brought into the Israelite camp, accompanied by Hophni and Phinehas, it is greeted with a mighty war shout. The author proceeds with a masterful description of the consternation which the Ark's appearance provoked in the Philistine camp. It has been suggested that no Israelite could write about the gods of Israel who smote the Egyptians with plagues in the wilderness. But we would maintain that the author deliberately garbled the information because he was trying to give a realistic account of the confusion which resulted among the Philistines. It would be quite natural for polytheistic peoples to refer to the gods of Israel; and it is quite possible that the Philistines were dimly aware of the plagues through which Israel was delivered out of Egypt. Another indication that the author is trying to create an air of authenticity is the Philistine reference to the enemy as "Hebrews." This term was rarely used as an Israelite self-designation; it was almost exclusively a term which foreigners used in referring to Israelites and which Israelites used in identifying themselves to foreigners.[11] The initial panic in the Philistine camp is transformed into the courage of despair; with calm resolve they take the field. The overconfident Israelites are completely routed. Many are killed; the rest are sent fleeing to thir homes. The Ark, left lying on the field next to its slain bearers (Hophni and Phinehas), is taken home by the triumphant Philistines as a trophy of victory.

In Shiloh the aged Eli was sitting at his familiar place by the door of the sanctuary. Although now completely blind, he was "watching" the road to the west—waiting in great agitation for news of the battle's outcome. His primary concern was that the sanctity of the Ark be maintained. Could it be that he had some premonition that the word of Samuel was about to be fulfilled (I Samuel 3:11–14)? He did not have long to wait. On the same day a fugitive from the battle reached Shiloh. The sanctuary must not have been close to the city's main gate, where the news was first announced: Eli could hear only the sound of mourning. When the messenger finally reached the sanctuary, Eli was so overcome by the news of the Ark's loss that he fell off his seat and died. The loss of the Ark of the Covenant, which symbolized God's presence among his people, was a tremendous blow to the Israelite Tribal League. It was surely a factor in the establishment of monarchical rule in Israel.

Some Questions for Discussion: Recall the significance the Israelites attached to the Ark of the Covenant. Why, then, is it brought to the battlefront? Since the narrator is an Israelite, how can you account for the statements in verses 7–8? What reasons might the narrator have for including those statements? To what does the narrator attribute Eli's death?

Samuel and Saul

SAMUEL ANOINTS SAUL (I SAMUEL 9:1–10:16; 11)

After the death of Eli and his sons, Samuel became the religious leader of Israel. During these years the nation's strength was at an all-time low. The Philistines followed their smashing victory at Aphek by pressing far inland so that almost all of the central mountain territory south of the Esdraelon valley came under their control. The balance of power had definitely tipped in favor of the Philistines, and they preserved it by placing governors and military outposts throughout the country. They further secured their power by maintaining a monopoly on iron. No Israelite was permitted to own an iron weapon; even iron farming implements had to be taken to the Philistines for sharpening and servicing (I Samuel 13:19–22).

During this time of Israel's humiliation, Samuel did not remain in Shiloh, because it had been completely destroyed by the Philistines. It is quite likely that he returned to his home in Ramathaim-Zophim (called Ramah). It was difficult for him to serve as Israel's religious leader when there was no longer an acknowledged central place of worship for the tribes, although by this time the Ark of the Covenant had been returned by the Philistines (see I Samuel 5 and 6). Samuel seems to have solved the problem by traveling on an annual circuit throughout Israel, staying for extended periods at several of the old religious centers (I Samuel 7:15–17). Through these journeys he was able to keep the covenant traditions alive and prevent the total collapse of Israel's sense of nationhood. During this time Samuel had married, for by the time our story begins he has two sons who are already adults.

We have noted earlier that the editor has combined several sources in chapters 8–15, so that we are left with variant versions concerning how Saul became king and of Samuel's attitude toward Saul and the institution of kingship. All of these sources probably reflect some aspect of the historical situation. In chapter 8 (part of the "Samuel source"), the elders of Israel visit Samuel, demanding that he establish a king to rule over them. Samuel is old and, like Eli, has sons not fit to take his place. The Israelites wanted Samuel to anoint a strong warrior who would deliver Israel from the Philistines. Samuel was incensed at this request; he felt that turning to a human king for deliverance was in fact denying that Yahweh was Israel's only king. Furthermore, he warned the elders that putting exclusive power in the hands of one person would ultimately lead to the loss of freedom. But the situation was desperate. Samuel finally acknowledged this fact and acquiesced to the demand. Sending the elders to their houses, he assured them that, although he had many misgivings, he would find a king for Israel.

At this point the "Saul source" breaks in with the charming story of a man who sets out to find his father's lost asses but instead finds himself anointed to rule over Israel. Unlike most biblical narratives, which are filled with action and move rapidly toward their climax, this pastoral idyll proceeds at a very leisurely pace. The author is undoubtedly savoring every detail of the scene which he is creating. Like Samuel, Saul is also portrayed as descending from a powerful and well-established Israelite family. He is a man of unusual appearance—strikingly handsome and a head taller than anyone else. His youth should not be overstressed, for he is the father of several grown sons; he is in the prime of life.

The search for the asses brings Saul and his servant far to the north and west—to the land of Zuph, which is in the hill country facing out on the Philistine plain. (Here also is Samuel's home-town, Ramathaim-Zophim.) Saul is about to give up in discouragement, but the resourceful servant suggests that they try the nearby man of God. Here Samuel is referred to as a "seer" rather than a "prophet" or a "judge." He is not called a prophet, because in pre-monarchical times prophecy was associated with bands of ecstatic dancers. The fact that Samuel is the judge of Israel is not important at this stage of the story. He must also have been well known throughout the land as a clairvoyant, and it is in this role—that of the seer—that he is important to Saul and the servant.

Much has been made over the apparent discrepancy in the sources' views of the position of Samuel. In the Samuel source, he is portrayed as the religious leader of the nation, whereas here in the Saul source, say many scholars, he is merely a local seer whom Saul has never heard of. Admittedly there is some difference in emphasis, but the distinction is not that clear-cut. Saul's uncle, although Benjaminite, knew perfectly well who Samuel was without need of explanation (I Samuel 10:14–16). And finally, the major factor in Saul's later deterioration lies in Samuel's rejection of him. It seems quite certain that both sources acknowledge Samuel as the religious leader of the nation—not a mere local seer—and as instrumental in establishing Saul as king.

As Saul and his servant approach the city, they meet some maidens coming to fetch water from the well. The customary social hour at the well has just assumed new significance with this handsome stranger asking how to find Samuel. The youthful joy and excitement of the maidens is strikingly captured in their staccato-like, eager, polite, newsy, bossy response. Samuel has just returned from his travels as "circuit judge" (I Samuel 8;12; 7:15–17), his return coinciding with a major festival. He will soon be going up to the high place where the festival is ready to begin.

Samuel had been searching for Yahweh's designate who would deliver Israel from the Philistine oppression. Upon seeing Saul, Samuel knew immediately that the deliverer was found. There is no anti-monarchical bias in this narrative. Yahweh has heard the cry of his people, and it is through Saul that the situation will be corrected (see Exodus 3:7–9). Samuel begins by fulfilling his task as clairvoyant, telling Saul that the asses have been found and he need no longer worry. Concluding with a vague statement about the glory which will soon be Saul's, Samuel prepares the way for the more important things to be discussed by inviting Saul and his servant to the festival, where they are treated as guests of honor. Saul is increasingly perplexed by the special treatment which he has received; but perhaps he senses that he is about to receive a commission. He stresses, as Gideon did before him, his inadequacy to accomplish any great task (see Judges 6:15). After the feast, they return to Samuel's home, where accommodations are made for the guests.

It was a common courtesy to escort guests out of the city as they departed. Samuel uses this opportunity to confront Saul with the divine commission, anointing him as prince over Israel. Anointing—pouring oil over a person's head—is an act of consecration whereby the anointed is set apart and divinely authorized to function in a particular capacity. Priests, prophets, and even cultic implements were anointed. In the case of the king, the anointing represented a divine empowering—a bestowal of the spirit so that the king would be made capable of fulfilling, and obediently subject to, Yahweh's demands. It should be noted that Saul was anointed "prince," not king. There were two stages in becoming a king: divine designation and popular acclamation. In order to be accepted as king, Saul's divine designation had to be ratified by the people. Thus the anointing has made Saul a a potential king, but he will not be accepted as such until he has demonstrated his ability as a leader. Thus, Samuel encourages Saul to grasp the first opportunity that comes along after he returns home (I Samuel 10:7).

After giving a divine oracle, prophets would sometimes perform or pronounce a sign in order to authenticate the validity of their message.[12] Saul still has many doubts: could he rally the listless tribes? Would Yahweh indeed act through him to save Israel? Samuel reassures Saul through a sign that has three parts: first, Saul will learn that the asses had been found, which will confirm Samuel's status as a clairvoyant; second, Saul will meet three men on their way up to worship at the high place in Bethel and receive two loaves of bread from them, symbolic of the future tribute he will receive as king; and finally he will be filled with Yahweh's spirit upon meeting a group of prophets, pointing to the charismatic quality of Saul's new office. The narrator goes on to describe the fulfillment of only the third part of the sign. He wants to stress the sudden transformation of Saul into a person willingly receptive to divine promptings. Much to the surprise of those who had known him, Saul joins the band of prophets and is caught up in their ecstatic frenzy.[13] They cannot understand why a man from a respectable family can associate with such a group of fatherless (that is, of unknown family origin) madmen.

Upon returning home, Saul is pressed for details about his journey, especially when it is discovered that he has been with Samuel. Saul does not tell about his being anointed; the secret must be kept until the moment comes when he can prove himself as Israel's new leader.

The opportunity for Saul to receive national recognition came from an unexpected direction. Other nations were taking advantage of the complete Philistine domination over Israel. In the Transjordan, the Ammonites, who had been subdued a century before by Jephthah, were making fresh inroads into Israelite territory with little fear of resistance or reprisal. They had extended their power as far as Jabesh-gilead near the Jordan River.

The scene opens with the Ammonites laying siege to Jabesh-gilead. The inhabitants of the city realized that they were powerless to withstand the assault and sued for peace. They were willing to make a covenant with the Ammonites whereby Nahash would be acknowledged as their overlord and they would be taxed a certain percentage of their annual produce. But Nahash wanted more than such an easy victory; he desired that all Israel be humiliated through the fate of this city. His terms were appalling: the right eyes of all the inhabitants were to be gouged out.

It seems quite surprising at first that Nahash would allow the beleaguered city a seven-day respite in order to seek out help from other tribes. But he was quite sure that the Philistines would never allow an Israelite army to be gathered. He wanted total humiliation for Israel, and he knew that if the tribes were forced to turn down the plea of Jabesh-gilead his purposes would be accomplished. Furthermore, he preferred to have the city handed over to him without loss of life among his men, and a seven-day respite seemed like a cheap price to pay.

The story suddenly skips to Gibeah, Saul's home town. We are not told about the messengers' fruitless journey throughout the rest of Israel. They are appealing to the Gibeahites, who are sympathetic but unable to respond. One sees how shrewd the Philistines were in destroying Israel's central place of meeting. The people were unable to come together, and no individual city (or even tribe) was able to face an entire nation. Saul learned of the crisis as he returned to the city from tilling the fields. Immediately he responded as a true charismatic. Hewing his oxen into pieces, he summoned the tribes by sending out the pieces with a threat of reprisal if they did not come. His bold action elicited a respectable turnout, although the numbers given in verse 8 are greatly exaggerated.[14]

The place for the soldiers to assemble was the village of Bezek, south of the Esdraelon valley. It was chosen for at least two reasons: first, it was directly across the Jordan valley from the besieged city, and second, it was far enough on the eastern side of the Israelite hill country to escape the notice of the Philistines. The good tidings are brought back to the people of Jabesh-gilead, who tell the unsuspecting Ammonites that they would "come out" to them on the morrow. They did not say that they would be coming out for battle. Early in the morning Saul's army, divided into three groups, attacked the Ammonite camp, routing the enemy. After the victory, the jubilant Israelites proceed to the shrine at Gilgal, and Saul is officially made king. But a problem is raised in these final verses. According to the Samuel source in I Samuel 10:17–27, Saul had already been selected by lot to be Israel's king. Following the ceremony, it is noted in I Samuel 10:27 that some "worthless fellows" doubted Saul's ability to deliver Israel. This same group is mentioned again after the victory at Jabesh-gilead (where Saul is once again made king) as they are saved from death by Saul's magnanimity. The almost unanimous scholarly consensus is that these verses (I Samuel 11:12–14) were inserted by the editor to make the two versions of Saul's becoming king more harmonious. Their case is as follows: according to the Saul source, of which the Jabesh-gilead story is a part, only Samuel and Saul know who the future king is to be. When the messengers from Jabesh-gilead arrive in Gibeah, they do not go directly to Saul. Presumably they had made similar appeals in other villages along the way, unaware of the Samuel source tradition that Saul had already been selected king by all Israel.

This interpretation may be correct, but several points should be raised. (1) The text states only that the Jabesh-gilead messengers left their city and arrived in Gibeah, and that finally Saul heard the news as he was returning from the fields. Scholars assume that the messengers had tried to secure help in other villages, and that Saul only heard the news by chance. It is just as possible to assume that the messengers went directly to Gibeah and that its inhabitants were told the news in the process of trying to locate Saul. (2) I Samuel 11:12–14 in no way harmonizes the two accounts of Saul's becoming king. Had the editor been concerned with harmonizing, he would have excised I Samuel 11:15. Verses 12–14 could very well reflect a genuine tradition of Saul's sparing a group of Israelites who, before he had proved himself, had been hostile to his being selected. Furthermore, if these verses are merely the secondary work of an editor, would not one expect I Samuel 10:27 to be more exactly reproduced? (3) I Samuel 11:15 states that Saul was made king at Gilgal after the victory at Jabesh-gilead. How do we account for I Samuel 10:17–27? Is it not possible that Samuel proclaimed Saul as Yahweh's anointed at Mizpah, but that Saul's kingship did not take effect until he proved himself to be a genuine charismatic? Having proved this at Jabesh-gilead, his kingship was ratified by the people. Admittedly there are problems in either interpretation, but it does not seem that the former is an open and shut case.

At any rate Saul is acclaimed as king in the ancient Yahweh sanctuary at Gilgal. This site, located near the Jordan River, was far removed from Philistine surveillance. Now Saul can return home to face Israel's main enemy—not as a lonely voice appealing for reluctant support toward a lost cause, but as the acknowledged charismatic leader of a victorious army which has already proved itself in battle.

Some Questions for Discussion: Why is Samuel so pleased to meet Saul on the road? How does Saul react to Samuel's cordiality? With Saul's anointment, what new phase of Israelite history is being introduced? For what purpose has Saul come to Samuel? How do you learn that Saul's joining the band of roving prophets was out of character for him?

What details of Saul's physical appearance and personality does the narrator include? Do these details show Saul as having the characteristics of a great leader? Do you note any characteristics in Saul which might foreshadow his downfall? Why, after he returns home, does Saul keep his anointment a secret?

Note that he is anointed as *prince*, not king of Israel. How is Saul's reaction to Samuel's pronouncement similar to the reactions of other leaders commissioned by Yahweh about whom you have read previously?

Explore the relationship between Yahweh, Samuel, and Saul. How is the relationship between Saul and Yahweh different from relations between Yahweh and his previous leaders? What two roles, formerly united in the judges, have now been separated?

What is Nahash's condition for making a treaty with the men of Jabesh? How has your previous reading prepared you for such a condition? How did you react to I Samuel 11:3? Why?

What does Saul do when he hears about the plight of the men of Jabesh? Reread I Samuel 11:1, 11:3, and 11:10. How would you characterize the men of Jabesh?

What happened to the Ammonites? How do the people react to Saul's victory? How does Saul calm them?

SAMUEL BREAKS WITH SAUL (I SAMUEL 15)

The story of Saul's rejection is one of the most dramatic, moving, and tragic pieces in the entire Bible. This classic confrontation between man of God and monarch is the prototype of what will become a hallmark of Israelite history after the firm establishment of kingship: the conflict between the absolute demands of Yahweh, as expressed by the prophets, and the secular needs of the state, as personified in the king. Saul had been anointed as king over Israel, and he had been acclaimed as such by the people. He followed his victory at Jabesh-gilead with a series of bold maneuvers which drove the Philistines out of the Israelite hill country. But Samuel had no intention of allowing Saul to use his new power to establish a secular state like the other nations. Samuel felt that Saul should remain subject to his authority because Samuel was Yahweh's spokesman.

The occasion for the final break between the two leaders was a battle against the Amalekites, Israel's most ancient enemy who had attempted to prevent them from entering Canaan after they had fled from Egypt (Exodus 17:8–13; Numbers 14:41–45). The Amalekites were primarily a nomadic people who wandered in the southernmost region of Canaan and in the northern part of the Sinai Peninsula. It is unclear why an expedition would be undertaken against the Amalekites when the Philistine danger was ever-present. Perhaps it is because Samuel's sons in Beersheba had alerted him to the danger of Amalekite incursions into this area. At any rate Samuel commanded that the rules of holy war be carried out against this most hated enemy: everything was to be destroyed—men, women, children, and animals.

Having gathered his army, Saul marched south, found the fortified encampment of Amalek, and surrounded it. The Amalekites were routed; everything captured was put to the sword save for Agag, the Amalekite king, and the choicest of the flocks. These were set aside for a special sacrifice of thanksgiving in the Gilgal sanctuary.

According to the narrative, Samuel discovered that the holy war commandment had been violated even before he met Saul at Gilgal. He further learns that this violation means that Yahweh has rejected Saul as king. The concept of Yahweh presented in this passage is typical of Mosaic theology: He "repents" that he had made Saul king. That is, the God of Israel is not an abstract, unchanging being who is tied down to universal decrees of world order; he is rather conceived as a god of history who constantly changes in response to the course of events. Man has been given his freedom, but the God of Israel is also free to see that his purposes ultimately come to pass. The rejection of Saul is also expressive of Mosaic theology in that man's relationship to God is thought to be contingent upon his obedience to the divine commandments.

Upon meeting Samuel at Gilgal, Saul confidently and joyously greets him, informing him that the Amalekites had been routed in accordance with Yahweh's command. When Samuel rebukes him concerning the Amalekite flocks which have been brought back, Saul replies that they were not taken for personal gain, but for sacrifice to Yahweh in Gilgal. To Saul, this was an act of supreme piety: What could be more appropriate after the victory than a thanksgiving service of sacrifice which had been won through Yahweh's might?

Samuel saw things differently. The Amalekite property had been put under the curse of holy war; it was to be totally destroyed. To bring even the choicest of the flocks to Gilgal was a desecration of Yahweh's sanctuary. To feast on flocks which were to have been devoted entirely to Yahweh through the ban was an act of complete sacrilege. Saul struggles to have his position understood by the severe old man of God, but his words are drowned out by a rebuke which will become a standard theme of classical prophecy: Yahweh takes greater delight in obedience than in sacrifice. The unique element of Israelite faith was its insistence that religion transcended ritual obligation; one's relationship to God was determined far more by one's ethical response. Samuel concludes his oracle with the dread words that Saul has been rejected as king of Israel. He might continue to go through the motions of being king, but he would no longer possess that spirit of God which had been given to him when he was anointed.

Realizing the seriousness of the situation, and perhaps understanding Samuel's point of view, Saul desperately tries to win forgiveness. But it is too late; Samuel had received a word which he felt was irrevocable. As Samuel turns away, the crestfallen king grabs his robe, hoping to maintain his possession of the spirit by keeping the man of God from deserting him. The robe rips, and Samuel sees in this a further sign that Yahweh had ripped the kingdom from Saul's outstretched hand. The torn robe is more than an evil omen; ancient man saw such events as giving added power to the spoken word so that the oracle which had been proclaimed (in this case, the termination of Saul's charisma) would even more surely be brought to pass.

In addition to the choicest of the flocks, Saul and his army had brought the captured Amalekite king, Agag, back to Gilgal. It is misleading to conclude from verse 9 that Saul intended to spare Agag's life. He was being returned to Gilgal to be slain before Yahweh in a ritual which was probably similar to that described in Joshua 10:22–30. Note that Samuel never rebuked Saul because of Agag. Returning with Saul, Samuel completes the ceremonial slaying of the captured king. Agag, seeing the old man of God accompanying Saul, is greatly relieved, thinking that the mercy of old age will help him to escape death; but no mercy is given.

According to this tradition, Samuel and Saul never saw each other again. The rest of the book of I Samuel is the record of the shattering effect which this one event had upon Saul. We see from it how dependent he was upon his sense of divine empowerment. It is incorrect to interpret Saul as a renegade monarch who knowingly opposed Yahweh's will. Saul was as faithful as he knew how to be. But keenly feeling the wrath of divine rejection, the tormented king was driven to ever-increasing acts of despair, which led to his death and the near ruin of Israel. Samuel, having washed his hands of the kingship which he had initiated, remained aloof and secluded the rest of his days. He grieved over the fate of Saul, because surely he loved this noble, tragic hero. But his grief was also caused by the realization that a king who was incapable of conforming to the divine will still ruled over Israel.

Some Questions for Discussion: What is Saul commanded to do following the battle with the Amalekites? Why? What reason does Saul give for not following the command? Why do you think it is, or is not, a good or justified reason? How does Yahweh react to Saul's action? Why? In verse 10, what reasons can you give for Samuel's anger? What has Saul lost by his disobedience? How important was it to him? How might it affect his view of himself?

Examine verse 22. What is the essence of the statement made there? How does Saul react to Samuel's disfavor? What does this tell you about Saul's view of his role as king? Do you see a larger scope of conflict in this story besides the quarreling of Samuel and Saul over the spoils of one battle? Why does Agag come into the presence of Samuel "cheerfully"?

What is symbolic in Saul's tearing of Samuel's robe? How do you know that Samuel and Saul also regarded the gesture as symbolic? Do you feel that Yahweh has dealt justly with Saul?

Why, or why not? Would the Israelites have felt Saul was treated fairly?

Suggested Activity: Write a script to dramatize the break between Samuel and Saul. What instructions will you give your actor for the portrayal of Samuel? of Saul? Why do you want Samuel and Saul portrayed as you suggested to your actors? What do you find in the text to support your portrayals?

What is the most dramatic moment in your script? Why? What can you have your actors do to dramatize the tension without overacting?

Saul and David

DAVID AND GOLIATH (I SAMUEL 17:1–18:16)

The story of David and Goliath raises several perplexing critical problems which need not be discussed at length in this exposition. You should be aware that they exist, however. First, we are told in II Samuel 21:19 that Goliath was slain by a certain Elhanan of Bethlehem. Is Elhanan an earlier name of David, which was changed when he became king?[15] Or was Elhanan's victory later attributed to David to help explain his fast rise from Saul's ranks to the kingship? Or was Goliath, the well-known name of an enemy hero, later used to describe this anonymous Philistine challenger of Saul's ranks?

Another problem is raised by I Samuel 17:55ff, in which King Saul does not seem to know who David is. How did David first come to Saul's attention? As the musician who was brought to the court to soothe the king's troubled spirit (I Samuel 16:14–23)? Or as the daring slayer of Goliath? There were probably different versions in Israel of David's sudden rise to power. Some elements surely regarded him as an illegitimate upstart. The tradition of David's slaying Goliath may well be genuine; here the intent is to present David as the conquering hero who is in every respect suited for future kingship. He is highly regarded by the royal court, is a close friend of the king's son, and is to be rewarded with the hand of a princess for his courage.

The earlier border skirmishes between Israelites and Philistines had now developed into full-fledged warfare. The Philistines had made serious inroads into the Israelite hill country and were threatening to cut the nation in half through control of the Esdraelon valley, which stretches from Mount Carmel to the Jordan River. After Israel's low ebb following the defeat at Ebenezer (I Samuel 4), Saul had managed to rally the tribes and recoup much of what had been lost. The confrontation with Goliath took place in the valley Elah, within a stone's throw of Samson's former stamping grounds. The opposing armies lined up for battle each day on opposite sides of the valley. Neither side seemed willing to press the attack. The great champion of the Philistine lines, here called Goliath, advanced toward the Israelites, demanding that a victory be decided by individual combat, a method of settlement which may have been derived from Greek military practice. Goliath's imposing armor is described in detail by the narrator to convey the impression of invincibility which the champion must have made upon the lightly armed Israelite mountaineers.

Verses 12ff explain why David happened to have been in the Israelite camp. Note that the narrator seems to be introducing David for the first time, unaware of what has preceded in chapter 16. After forty days of fruitless confrontation between Goliath and the Israelite army, David was sent by his father to bring special provisions to his brothers, who were in Saul's army, and to return with news regarding their welfare and the progress of the war. When David arrived at the camp, the army was drawn up in battle line. Consequently he heard Goliath's reproachful challenge and was stunned by the insult against King Saul and Yahweh, the God of Israel.

According to the tenets of Israel's holy warfare, divine might provides the victory, not the number or armor of the army. Trusting Yahweh to give Goliath into his hand, David begins discreet inquiries about the rewards which Saul had offered to the victorious champion. David's father's commission—to deliver bread to his brothers and cheese to their commanding officer—is now inconsequential to both David and the narrator. David finds his brothers and is sternly rebuked for neglecting his responsibilities with the flock so that he might see the battle.

When Saul hears that an Israelite has volunteered to meet Goliath, he has the Israelite summoned. David's bravery and confidence allay Saul's doubts concerning his inexperience as a warrior. David discreetly (and significantly) declines the offer of Saul's armor. He is not yet ready to grasp at the office of kingship. Armed only with his sling and five stones, he strides forward to meet the giant.

The sling was one of the main Israelite weapons of war. Stones measuring two and three inches in diameter could be slung accurately from a considerable distance (see Judges 20:16). They were not shot through the prongs of a forked stick, as is our custom today. The stone was placed in a leather (or woolen) pocket which was attached to two cords. The cords were then whirled around the head, and the stone was released with great force when one of the cords was pulled.[16]

It was customary in both Greek and Near Eastern military practice for warriors to vaunt themselves before engaging in individual combat. Goliath mocks the unarmored youth who appears before him. David replies that he is fighting in behalf of Yahweh, the God of Israel, who will give him the victory. Goliath is stunned by the stone which strikes his forehead and is then killed by his own sword.

Through David's victory over Goliath the emboldened Israelite army routed the Philistines from the battlefield. David was immediately drafted into the king's service, where he developed a particularly close and lasting friendship with Jonathan, Saul's son—a bond which was sealed by an exchange of clothing and armor, symbolizing the giving of the self into the other's possession. David rose quickly in Saul's ranks, stirring no jealousy or rancor—so winning was his way with all whom he encountered.

Soon, however, David's great success and charm led to his undoing. Saul had been dispirited since Samuel had pronounced Yahweh's rejection upon him. Lacking his former charisma, the restless king was haunted by the fear of a rival to the throne. As the young maidens chanted "Saul has slain his thousands, and

David his ten thousands," the tormented king saw who that rival would be. Ironically Saul's demented jealousy turned David into the rival which originally he had no intention of becoming. The young captain was successful in the dangerous missions which Saul had intentionally assigned to him, further increasing his popularity and compounding Saul's anxiety and jealousy.

Some Questions for Discussion: Why are the Israelites fighting in this narrative? Who is their enemy? Describe the physical scene of the opposing camps and the battle area. Does this picture of the battleground tell you anything about the methods of ancient warfare?

What challenge was Goliath issuing? Was it a "fair" challenge? Why, or why not? What effect does this often-repeated challenge and its refusal have on the story? What would be decided by individual combat with Goliath? What do you think of this method of warfare? How do you account for David's being presented as if he had never been introduced before? How does David get into the picture? What is the effect of the narrator's sudden shift from the battle scene to the description of David? Why do you suppose David's circumstances are described so extensively?

What does David's question in verse 26 tell us about what is going on in his mind? What do you think is foremost in David's mind at that moment? Why do you think so? If you were in David's place, what would be foremost in your mind? What does the scolding David receives from his brothers reveal about human relationships in any age? Similarly, how does Saul's statement, "Thou art not able to go against the Philistine to fight with him: for thou art but a youth . . . " reveal a tension that exists in any age? Judging from verses 28 and 29, what, apparently, was the consensus of the camp concerning David's motivation? Consider David's response to Saul in verses 32–39.

Do you think David realized what he was actually volunteering to do? Might he have acted in the same way if the confrontation had not taken place in front of such a large audience? What makes you think so? What reason does David give for refusing

Saul's armor? Does it seem reasonable to you? Do you see any symbolism in his refusal?

In verses 41–47, what purpose does the shouting serve? What effect(s) do you suppose Goliath's defeat had on the Philistines? Would the insult to the Philistines have been as great if David had seemed a more equal match for Goliath? Why? What implications does David's slaying of Goliath in spite of superior size, strength, and armor have for us? What devices has the author of this story used to heighten the climax of David's victory over Goliath?

Why is a story such as this included in the saga of David? Is such a story a common part of a saga? Can you find comparable episodes in the lives of other folk heroes such as Davy Crockett, or men such as John F. Kennedy? Are such stories necessary to the saga of a folk hero? Why, or why not?

DAVID AND JONATHAN (I SAMUEL 20)

Intertwined with the traditions concerning Saul's fall from divine favor and David's accession to control of the kingdom are other themes which seem to be included for their beauty and human interest rather than their importance in political or religious history. Such a theme is the story of David's love for the king's son, Jonathan, and the way in which this friendship made David's rise to power even more complex, more wonderful, and more compelling in its human interest.

Just as a number of traditions exist concerning David's first entrance into Saul's court and favor, so a number of stories tell of the strong friendship that came to hold Jonathan and David together even after David had become an enemy of the king (compare I Samuel 18:1–4; 19:1–7). The friendship is made all the more dramatic by the increasing enmity between Saul and David. Jonathan is torn between love for his friend and loyalty to his father. Shakespeare has used the same motif in portraying the romance between Romeo and Juliet.

In I Samuel 20, the ancient storyteller presents an independent tradition involving themes which are present in other narratives of the David and Jonathan cycle: David's fleeing in fear from Saul; Jonathan's bewildered reaction to the enmity between the two men; Jonathan's attempts to protect David and to mediate with Saul in his friend's behalf; the impossible union between the warring houses represented by David and Jonathan's friendship.

> The Lord shall be between me and you, and between my descendants and your descendants, for ever. (20:42)

The occasion for the rift between David and Saul, which becomes irreparable, is the early Hebrew custom of feasting and sacrifices at the time of the new moon's appearance (I Samuel 20:1–29). The king apparently expects all of his courtiers to be present at the banquet, but David is hiding out in fear. Jonathan promises to sound out the king in David's behalf, and to offer an excuse for his absence. The result is an outburst of rage against Jonathan (I Samuel 20:30–31). Saul's cursing takes the form of an attack on Jonathan's mother and reveals that he knows very well that Jonathan's loyalty is now divided. The king, astute enough in spite of his apparent insanity, knows also that Jonathan is throwing away his own chance to succeed to the throne.

> "As long as the son of Jesse lives upon the earth, neither you nor your kingdom shall be established. Therefore send and fetch him to me, for he shall surely die." (20:31)

Jonathan, in his idealism and loyalty, refuses to do as Saul commands. The scene closes with the maddened king trying to kill his own son rather than see the kingdom go to David. Jonathan, the storyteller relates, withdrew from his father's presence in fierce anger to fast and to grieve over his friend's disgrace.

Now all that remains is to give the prearranged signal to David so that he may know of the king's anger. Jonathan hunts in the rolling hills near his home and shouts after his page, "Is not the arrow beyond you? Hurry! Make haste! Do not wait!" The words, of course, are really intended for David, who is hiding nearby.

Instead of returning to his home, however, Jonathan sends the page away with his weapons and has a last meeting with his friend. In a scene of emotional intensity not common in biblical narratives, the friends say good-bye to each other and swear their loyalty. They do not meet again. Saul and Jonathan later die in battle, and David laments them in one of the most beautiful poems of the Old Testament (II Samuel 1:17–27).

> Saul and Jonathan, beloved and lovely!
> In life and in death they were not divided;
> > they were swifter than eagles,
> > they were stronger than lions. . . .
>
> Jonathan lies slain upon thy high places.
> I am distressed for you my brother Jonathan;
> > very pleasant have you been to me;
> > your love to me was wonderful;
> > passing the love of women.
> > How are the mighty fallen,
> > and the weapons of war perished!

Some Questions for Discussion: Why is the use of "knit" especially appropriate for the description of David and Jonathan's friendship? What evidence do we have of a mutual response to this friendship? What are the implications and the results of David's behaving "wisely" in Saul's court? What is Saul's reaction to the praise of the women for himself and David? What character traits are revealed by Saul's reaction to their praise both in attitude and in subsequent action?

What motivation might Saul have for making David "captain over thousands"? What purpose might the author have in mind for establishing very close relationship between David and Jonathan? What forces are in conflict within Saul?

In I Samuel 20, we are given one specific incident of Jonathan's helping David. As the scene opens, what is David asking Jonathan? Why doesn't David know why Saul wants to kill him? Why does Saul want to kill David? Why doesn't Jonathan believe his father wants to kill David? Do you think he is rationalizing? Why? What counter point does David offer to Jonathan's answer? Do you think he is rationalizing? Why? What agreement do the two men come to? What do you suppose the new moon has to do with sitting at the king's table? Why would David be missed? What set of signals do they agree upon? Why do they need a set of signals?

David hides in the woods. And he *is* missed at dinner. What rationalization does Saul make to account for the fact that David is missing? What does he mean "he is not clean"? What, in effect, is Saul saying to Jonathan in verse 30? What prompts a father to say "you're just like your mother," or a mother to say "you're just like your father"? What reasons does Saul give Jonathan for wanting David dead in verse 31? How does the interview between father and son end? The next day Jonathan keeps his rendezvous with David. After making sure no one is around, Jonathan dismisses the page and tells David what has transpired. They pledge a vow to one another. What is the meaning of this vow?

David wrote a poem in which he mourned for Saul and Jonathan (II Samuel 1). Compare David's memorial to Tennyson's "In Memoriam"—a frequently quoted love song, yet the product of one man's love for another. When David asks Jonathan to slay him if he (David) has done any wrong, what insight into David's character is revealed?

What two settings are used in this story? How might this contrast in settings be significant? What have you learned about David and Jonathan's characters? How have you learned it?

DAVID AND ABIGAIL (I SAMUEL 25)

Here both the scene and the mood of the storyteller have shifted abruptly. In place of the tenderness of the Jonathan and David narrative, we encounter rude humor and the celebration of a country woman's shrewdness. The new scene is the barren, craggy wilderness of Judah along the western shore of the Dead Sea and the scarcely less barren hill country of Judah further west.

David has come here to hide out with his band of outlaws, living off the country and profiting from "protection money" extorted, more or less gently, from landholders in the area. David demands that one of these stock raisers, a wealthy man named

Nabal, reward him and his men for the protection they have furnished from other outlaw bands. Nabal rudely (and foolishly) refuses; David's men arm themselves and prepare for a fight.

As in the story of Deborah's defeat of Sisera, a woman's shrewdness now replaces the pugnacity of the menfolk. Nabal's wife, Abigail, hears of the impasse and journeys to meet David with gifts. Her speech to David is a masterpiece of cunning and humor; she excuses her husband's folly by pointing out that the name Nabal means "a fool," and Nabal has simply been living up to his name.

David blesses Abigail for her discretion and does not hesitate to form a treaty with her. The clever woman returns home to find Nabal feasting and drinking. When she tells of her successful meeting with David behind her husband's back, "Nabal's heart died within him." Apparently he suffers a stroke or heart attack—and within ten days he is dead.

The denouement comes with the not unexpected marriage of David to Abigail and to another woman of the area, Ahinoam. The result is a much stronger political position for David and the control of considerable wealth as well. These marriages mean that David can command a following in the southern area where Saul's control is weak or nonexistent. As we shall see, David makes good use of this foothold as he continues his climb to power.

Some Questions for Discussion: Does the phrase "down to the wilderness" have any special significance in this story? What does the narrator's description of Abigail and Nabal foreshadow? Why does Abigail speak evil about her husband?

Why did David think he had a right to ask Nabal for food for his men? (Look at verses 7 and 8.) Do you think David had a right to this "protection money"? Why, or why not? What reason does Nabal give for refusing to send David anything? How does he "add insult to injury" in his refusal? What effect does Nabal's answer have on David? Do you think Nabal expected David to react the way he did? To what can you compare David's action in verse 3?

How does Abigail find out what has happened? What does she do to save her household? Why doesn't she tell Nabal what she's going to do? In what ways does Abigail's action substantiate the earlier statement that she is intelligent? When David and Abigail meet, to what character trait in David does she appeal?

Do you think the story of Abigail is a welcome addition to the saga of David? Why? What does David's wanting a wife like Abigail say about him? Compare the character of Abigail to that of Katherine in *The Taming of the Shrew*.

SAUL PURSUES DAVID (I SAMUEL 26)

This graphically vivid story has the flavor of an eyewitness account. The setting is the desolate wilderness country to the west of the Dead Sea, as in the account just studied. The tradition has even recorded the exact place names as part of the substance of the story. We might imagine an author who had actually been with David and his men in David's outlaw days in Judah.

As might be expected from such a source, the story idealizes David's magnanimity and reverence for Yahweh's anointed king when he spares the life of Saul. While Saul is sleeping with his men in their encampment—and in the midst of an expedition designed to eliminate David and his band of outlaws—David sneaks into Saul's camp and departs without harming the slumbering king. But to demonstrate his loyalty (and to show up the laxness of the king's guard), David steals the king's water jar and spear.

As elsewhere in these early traditions, the presence and activity of God is taken for granted as a force to be reckoned with in human events. David refuses to kill Saul on the grounds that Yahweh may eventually smite him, but more importantly because Yahweh has chosen and empowered this man as his agent through the sacred ritual of anointing. The narrator even believes that Saul's camp slept because "a deep sleep from the Lord had fallen upon them" (verse 12). The matter-of-fact manner of this remark points up the distance between our world-view and that of the ancient Hebrew, for we would doubtless conclude instead that the deep sleep of Saul's men was the result of fatigue and of their not knowing that David was anywhere in the vicinity.

Our way of explaining events, however, presumes a clear separation between the secular and the sacred. We do not expect God to act within ordinary affairs. But for the Hebrew narrator, God does not act only in the miraculous event, with a sensational display of his power. He does not limit himself, either, to the sacred —the sphere of worship, the lives of holy men, the ecclesiastical structure. Yahweh works in those areas surely. But for our Hebrew narrator, Yahweh's most mysterious and meaningful acts take place right within the midst of everyday human affairs, making use of the actions and decisions of men who are not consciously pursuing the aims of God at all. Such is the outlook of the J narrator and of this court historian as well. And this is what allows these authors to tell stories which are so humanly compelling and understandable, and at the same time to depict the activity of Israel's God in behalf of his people.[17]

After David puts a safe distance between himself and Saul's camp, he shouts back and awakens the king, not neglecting to taunt Saul's guard as well. David then pleads for the king to restore their old friendly relationship and to allow David to return to his home and people. Even here, the religious structure which undergirds the community is evident (verses 19–20): for David to be forced to leave his people and flee in the wilderness is for him to be alienated from Yahweh himself. Thus he pleads, "Let not my blood fall to the earth away from the presence of the Lord; for the king of Israel has come out to seek my life, like one who hunts a partridge in the mountains." It is the pain of being cut off from the community of Yahweh's people which is here expressed, rather than any notion that Yahweh's sovereignty is geographically limited to a particular part of the world.

As before, when directly reminded of David's old loyalty and friendship, Saul is remorseful and apologetic. He offers his blessing to David and promises no further harm. David may well have realized that the king in his madness was not to be trusted, for there is no indication that David ever saw Saul again or that he was safe to come out of hiding before Saul's death.

Some Questions for Discussion: What do you think the author intends to point out about David in this episode? Why does he wish to emphasize this point? What did David do between the time Jonathan sent him away and the death of Saul? What common term might we use to describe his "occupation"? In what way was his band of followers anything like the outlaw gangs of the last century in the American Southwest? Might he better be compared to Robin Hood and his merry men? Why, or why not? Do you think these "David Outcast" stories carry the same amount of truth as the Robin Hood stories? Why, or why not?

How do David and Abishai get into the heart of Saul's camp and into his tent without anyone in the camp knowing it? For what reason does David take Saul's spear and water jug? When David calls across the valley, whom does he taunt and for what reason? Why, when Saul admits his error and asks David to return, does David ask for a young man to come get Saul's spear and then go on his way instead of rejoining Saul?

What is God like as he is presented in this story? Do you think Saul can be blamed for what he is doing to David? Why, or why not? Do his actions seem logical (remember that the Philistines are invading the country)? How might we explain his illogical actions? Do you think it is unfair of Yahweh to keep picking on Saul the way he does? Why, or why not?

THE WITCH AT ENDOR (I SAMUEL 28:3–25)
AND THE DEATH OF SAUL (I SAMUEL 31)

The death of Saul in battle with the Philistines brings an end to the tragic career of Israel's first king. But before that end comes, one more moving scene must be played out by the king as he attempts, in a mood of desperation, to evade or at least to understand his destiny.

Samuel has died and David is in exile; only Saul remains to lead Israel. The Philistines have extended their control up the coastal plain and into the strategic valley of Jezreel, which links the plain to Transjordan and to the essential trade routes to Syria and beyond. All that is left for Saul to control is the central hill country, and even here he is hard pressed because he has lost the religious and popular support once extended to him through Samuel's anointing. The lines are drawn for a hard battle between the Philistines encamped at Shunem, overlooking the fertile Jezreel valley, and Saul's forces on Mount Gilboa, across the valley to the south.

Bereft of Samuel's guidance and even of Yahweh's presence, perhaps sensing his approaching doom, Saul seeks to contact the spirit of Samuel by consulting a witch, or necromancer, at the nearby village of Endor. The narrator suggests the pathetic plight of Saul when he remarks that "Yahweh did not answer him, either by dreams, or by Urim, or by prophets." Saul, that is to say, had exhausted all the ordinary and approved means by which the will of God might be known—dreams; the priestly casting of lots, called Urim and Thummin (see I Samuel 14:41–42; 23:6–14; Exodus 28:30); and the prophetic word. Yahweh remains silent, for he has withdrawn his presence from Saul.

The ancient Hebrew who had exhausted the legitimate means of determining God's will had only one recourse left—some variety of magic or necromancy. Saul himself, faithful worshiper of Yahweh that he was, had banned such practices in his kingdom, for the Israelite prophets and lawgivers characteristically declared that such pagan practices had no place in Israel's faith. God revealed to man what he needed to know; the rest was hidden in the mystery of God and was not to be inquired into. "The secret things belong to the Lord our God; but the things that are revealed belong to us and to our children for ever, that we may do all the words of this law" (Deuteronomy 29:29).

And yet, just as modern people retain their superstitions in the face of their own belief in a rationally explicable world, the ancient Hebrews, surrounded by pagan magic, continually slipped back into these practices. Saul's use of the necromancy which he himself has banned is ironic, but even more it is pathetic. He faces the battle with the Philistines with dread and feels himself utterly alone, so he begs the witch to raise up the spirit of his old mentor Samuel from the realm of the dead.

The narrative is charged with tension. The woman is terrified when she recognizes the king (in verse 12, read "When the woman saw *Saul,* she cried out with a loud voice . . . "), and then, perhaps in a trance-like state, she mutters, "I see a god coming up out of the earth." The word *god* is used here in exactly the same way as in Babylonian necromancy texts;[18] it means a spirit called up from the netherworld in which the dead resided in both Mesopotamian and Hebrew belief.[19] Saul recognizes Samuel and prostrates himself on the floor of the witch's hut.

Trembling, Saul asks his question: " . . . God has turned away from me and answers me no more, either by prophets or by dreams; therefore, I have summoned you to tell me what I shall do" (I Samuel 28:15). The answer of doom which Samuel gives has probably been expanded by a later editor. The earliest tradition must be the brief oracle in verse 19.

Yahweh will give Israel also with you into the hand of the Philistines; and tomorrow you and your sons shall be with me. . . .

Thus, instead of being told what to do, as though the tragic ending of Saul's life could be averted, Samuel simply tells what must be: Saul cannot avoid the battle, and he cannot avoid his death and the death of his sons.

The king lies motionless on the earthen floor after hearing this oracle. The excitement and dread of his meeting with Samuel's spirit, coming at the end of a day and night of fasting, have robbed him of his strength. He does finally arise, however, and is fed by the witch. He then goes out to battle.

The brief and poignant account of Saul's death in I Samuel 31 follows directly upon the narrative just discussed; the intervening chapters contain a misplaced story concerning David's adventures in the Judean area. The Philistines attack the Israelite encampment on Mount Gilboa and completely vanquish the forces of Saul. Saul's three sons are killed and the king himself is badly wounded. Fearing that he will be captured and possibly tortured or mutilated by the Philistines, the dying king begs his armor-bearer to kill him. The same reverence which David expressed for the person of the king as God's chosen ruler prevails even here; the armor-bearer refuses to kill Saul. The king then falls upon his own sword. The armor-bearer himself then follows the king in suicide.

The story of Saul is indeed tragic in the classic sense. Forced by circumstances which he did not create to take a role of leadership which had no structure as yet in Israelite society, deprived of the sole support which was meaningful—that provided by Samuel—and challenged by a popular young military hero in the person of David, Saul would inevitably meet his downfall. And yet, like the hero in a Greek tragedy, Saul did not stop, but pressed on toward his tragic destiny.

Some Questions for Discussion: Reread I Samuel 28:3–7. What is ironic about Saul's order to his servants in verse 7? According to verse 6, the Lord did not answer Saul. What does his failure to answer Saul tell you about their relationship at this point?

In verse 12, why does the witch at Endor cry out "with a loud voice"? How do you interpret the word *god* in verse 13 when the woman says: "I see a god coming up out of the earth"?

According to Samuel, why has the Lord become Saul's enemy? What does Samuel predict? How does Saul react?

What do you know about the battle referred to in chapter 31? Why do you think the narrator gave you no details of the battle but focused on Saul's suicide and the treatment given his body by the Philistines?

Suggested Activities: Compare Saul to King Lear, the Mayor of Casterbridge, or Oedipus Rex. Why could those four be called tragic figures? Give a written or an oral explanation of why you think Saul could be called a tragic figure in the classical sense of the term *tragedy*.

Describe the witch at Endor. Why do, or don't, you envision her as the kind of witch you find in *Macbeth?* Explain how you would have the witch at Endor portrayed in a play.

Saul and David have been the subjects of poems, plays, short stories, and novels. Read Robert Browning's "Saul," which some critics call "possibly the greatest short poem in the [English] language." How does Browning depict Saul and David? How do you respond to his version of these biblical figures?

Or read Stephen Vincent Benet's "King David," or James Barrie's *The Boy David*, or D. H. Lawrence's *David*, or Gladys Schmidt's *David the King*, or Frank Slaughter's *David, Warrior and King* and answer the questions in the above paragraph.

David the King

DAVID MOURNS FOR SAUL AND JONATHAN (II SAMUEL 1)

The materials which comprise the Second Book of Samuel are largely drawn from the same tradition circle that produced the "Saul source." These are early and highly authentic traditions, which must first have circulated among the folk and particularly among the military men who followed David. As we have noticed earlier, these stories frequently convey the impression of being drawn from eyewitness accounts. This tradition circle looks upon monarchy as God's gift to his people. Saul is not deprecated, as in the "Samuel source," and David is viewed with high admiration.

With the deaths of Saul and his sons in battle, tragic as the event may have been in itself, the way is open for David to advance toward the royal position which seems to be his destiny. Yet David does not gloat over the opportunity now open to him. He is in fact enraged at the Amalekite messenger who claims (falsely, if we are to believe I Samuel 31) that he administered the *coup de grace* to Saul. The messenger doubtless thought he would ingratiate himself with David by claiming that he put Saul to death, but he knew neither of David's reverence for the Lord's anointed nor of his persistent affection for the king.

It may be noted without cynicism that David here, as elsewhere, manages, through natural genius for doing the politic thing, to benefit from other's misfortune without seeming to be responsible. Here as in the death of Abner (II Samuel 3), David is placed in a much stronger position by the elimination of rivals or enemies—and yet he sincerely and publically grieves the departed. He is angry over the terrible results of war and the wicked behavior of men, and yet he moves an important step closer to becoming Israel's king.

We have already mentioned the touching lament which David sings for Saul and Jonathan. The antiquity of the poem gives support to the popular tradition that David was a musician and poet; because of this tradition, many Psalms were attributed to him, as well as other poems in the Old Testament (for example, II Samuel 23:1–7, the "last words of David"). The text of this lament has been corrupted in the centuries of transmission, but the basic meaning still shines through. In it David hopes that the news will not reach the Philistine cities of Ashkelon and Gath so that the enemy will not exult in Saul's death. He calls for Gilboa, the site of death, to be struck with drought, receiving neither dew nor rain nor "upsurging of the deep"—the water that was believed to flow from the great deep under the earth into the springs and rivers (see Genesis 2:6, Revised Standard Version alternative reading, "flood"). The singer weeps for the fallen heroes and touchingly concludes with a final address to the beloved Jonathan.

Some Questions for Discussion: According to the Amalekite, how did Saul die? Why do you think the Amalekite told David that story? How does it differ from the account in I Samuel 31? What might have motivated the Amalekite to tell his version of Saul's death? How has the messenger misjudged David? What is the Amalekite's fate? Why?

How did David feel about Saul and Jonathan? How do you know? How might David's lament in II Samuel 1 have given rise to the tradition that he also wrote the Psalms? What type of literature is David's lament? Discuss its characteristics.

DAVID AND BATHSHEBA (II SAMUEL 11)

The narrative has reached a point where the external affairs of the kingdom are almost under control. Only the Syrians remain a threat. The internal affairs of David's kingdom, and especially of the royal family, now move into focus.

Before considering these stories of family intrigue in the palace, let us review the steps by which David has reached this position of power. As a youth he became a member of Saul's court and was thus close to the king and the affairs of the kingdom. He was forced to flee to Judah when Saul became jealous of his military successes and popular acclamation, but even there he used time and circumstances to his own profit by marrying into a wealthy family of Judah.

After the deaths of Saul and three of his sons in battle and after the unplanned death of Saul's army commander Abner, David became king of Judah, with his seat of power at Hebron (II Samuel 2:4). Later, after a period of bitter fighting between the supporters of David and those still loyal to Saul's family, David was accepted as king over the northern area also (II Samuel 5:1-5).

David, with his customary political genius, then chose the city of Jerusalem, still a Canaanite enclave, for the capital of his new kingdom (II Samuel 5:6-10). He managed to focus the loyalty of the people on his capital by bringing to Jerusalem the Ark, which had been their symbol of unity in Tribal League days and as far back as the time of Moses.

We are not told in detail about David's elimination of the military threat posed by the Philistines, but it is clear that from David's time on these old enemies were limited to a few cities on the southern coastal plain (II Samuel 5:17-25). Almost equally important for the future of the kingdom were David's brilliant military victories in campaigns against Moab and Edom to the southeast and against the small Syrian city-states to the north (II Samuel 8). The end result was that Israel had been catapulted, in scarcely more than two generations, from the status of a moribund tribal league, facing extinction at the hand of the Philistines, to a small empire and a major power in the Near East. There is no escaping the fact that this was largely David's personal achievement, and it is a very remarkable achievement viewed against the backdrop of the centuries of political division and weakness that Palestine knew both before and after David.[20]

Now our attention is turned to affairs within David's own life and family, and we see that folly and tragedy plagued this outwardly successful man like an evil nemesis. The wars within the Transjordanian city-state of Ammon provide the framework for the sordid opening episode. David has sent his army into battle against Ammon while he remains in Jerusalem. The winter rains have ceased and the brilliant sunshine of a Palestinian spring floods the city. David watches a young woman bathing on a flat roof-top and lusts for her. He has her brought to the palace, sleeps with her, and sends her home again.

The irony of the situation could scarcely be greater, for the young woman, Bathsheba, is the wife of one of David's own officers, serving with David's army in the field. The news that Bathsheba is pregnant creates a terrible predicament for the king, however, for their relationship can no longer be kept secret. David attempts to resolve the predicament by summoning the husband home so that the pregnancy can be attributed to him. But Uriah, faithful to the holy-war rules which forbade contact with women during the soldier's period of duty, refuses to go to his wife. He sleeps instead with David's servants in the palace.

In the classic instance of making a bad thing worse, David sends Uriah back to battle with a secret note to Joab, David's general, to see to it that Uriah does not return. Uriah is put in the front of the fighting and then his support is withdrawn. As a consequence he is killed. When David is informed of Uriah's death, he replies with a terrible nonchalance, "Do not let this matter trouble you, for the sword devours now one and now another" (verse 25).

The period of Bathsheba's mourning for her husband soon ends, and David marries her. But the narrator concludes with a note of doom: "But the thing that David had done displeased the Lord."

It would be wrong to try in any way to diminish or gloss over David's crime. By our standards or by the standards of the Old Testament, he has committed both adultery and murder. His crime is compounded by the innocence and faithfulness of Uriah and by the king's role as the agent and representative of Yahweh toward the people.

It is remarkable that the narrator, who must surely have been a member of David's court, depicts so frankly and unhesitatingly the crime of the king. In the narrator's view, we must understand, a full knowledge of these events is essential if we are to grasp the import of the events which follow and which turn David's later life into a twisted tragedy. There is just a hint in the concluding remark of the chapter that the events which followed were not just chance, but the judgment of Yahweh on David's crime.[21] This hint is broadened in the next chapter into a full certainty.

Some Questions for Discussion: What contrasts of character can you draw between David and Uriah? Of what two crimes is David guilty? What elements of irony are involved in his crimes? What is David's reaction to the news of Uriah's death? How does the outcome of the story foreshadow future tragedy? How is David characterized in this story? Why would an Israelite narrator include such a damning story about an Israelite king?

DAVID AND NATHAN (II SAMUEL 12)

We must understand first of all the role of the prophet in relation to the king. Long before David's time, prophets had been employed by Near Eastern kings to give oracles before battle and to give advice concerning the propitious times for undertaking other important enterprises.[22] The prophets were believed to be messengers of the gods, whose favor it was necessary to obtain.

In the time of Samuel, as we have seen, a good deal of prophet activity was present in Israel, especially of the ecstatic or dervish-like variety. Samuel himself was called a prophet, and appears to have drawn bands of prophets together and to have made them subservient to the Hebrew faith and to the needs of the community for leadership. Samuel must have intended for the king to be subservient to the prophetic declaration of Yahweh's will, and there was, of course, a continual struggle on the part of the prophets to make the king carry out his duties in a reverent and obedient fashion. Saul had rebelled against Samuel's prophetic leadership and had been disowned. Now, as a result of his crimes, David must face the same judgment.

The messenger of Yahweh's judgment on David is the prophet Nathan, himself a member of the royal entourage. In a very clever way, Nathan approaches David on the matter indirectly, by the use of a parable-like story. In the story a rich and powerful man has deprived a poor man of the one possession he loved, his pet lamb. He has even killed the lamb and served it at a banquet. David hotly interrupts, " . . . The man who has done this thing deserves to die." Nathan responds with the famous words, "You are the man." And then he details his knowledge of David's guilt and declares the sentence which Yahweh has passed: "The sword shall never depart from your house." He adds that David's own wives will be taken by others, just as David took Bathsheba from Uriah, and that the child to be born to Bathsheba will die.

The courage of Nathan in thus confronting the king is remarkable. Among all the nations of the Near East, such a confrontation was possible only in Israel, where in the last analysis the king was subject to the rule of God no less than was the meanest peasant. The ancient Hebrew knew as well as we do that the rich and the powerful may be oppressive and arrogant and ruthless toward the weak. But the Hebrew was convinced that Yahweh and his demand for justice and mercy stood above every man, and that Yahweh's judgment could mysteriously reach into a man's life and shake it or destroy it, even if the man seemed at first glance to have gotten off scot-free. The remainder of the so-called "Court History of David" (II Samuel 9–20; I Kings 1–2) intends to show us how David's life and the lives of his family were terribly damaged by the judgment which he brought upon himself through the Bathsheba incident.

There is another theme running through the Court History of David, and its beginning is also in this chapter. After Nathan's visit, the author relates, the child born to Bathsheba became sick and died, in accordance with the prophet's warning. But then another child was born and his birth was greeted with a favorable oracle from Nathan (II Samuel 12:24–25). This child, Solomon, although rather far down the line of succession to the throne, eventually became king after David's death. The author of the Court History takes pains to show how the other claimants to the throne were eliminated by death—the deaths being viewed as God's judgment on David—and Solomon alone was left to take the throne. Thus German scholars quite correctly refer to this piece of writing as "the History of the Succession to the Throne of David," for the story reaches its natural goal when Solomon's accession is assured (I Kings 1:38–40).

Some Questions for Discussion: Why does Nathan appear before David? What is Nathan's role? Why do you think he recited the parable? What is its purpose?

What is ironic about David's reaction to Nathan's parable? What did Nathan prophesy? How did David react to the death of Bathsheba's child? How do you know that David married Bathsheba?

Suggested Activities: Compare Nathan's parable with those that Jesus tells in the New Testament. Discuss the function of parables and their effectiveness.

Consider a problem that you are having—perhaps a difference of opinion that has caused trouble with a friend. Or consider how you might criticize or praise a friend for his actions or mannerisms by writing a parable. Then read the parable to a friend who does not know about your problem. Does he understand the parable? Why, or why not?

Dramatize the encounter between David and Nathan. How will you or a classmate you designate portray Nathan? David? What are the reasons for your portrayals?

DAVID AND ABSALOM (II SAMUEL 13–18)

Now begins the tragic account of events within David's household which explains the elimination of most of the natural successors to David. The first story concerns David's eldest son Amnon. Like his father, Amnon was consumed by lust for a young woman, his half-sister Tamar, and he could not wait for a legitimate marriage (if such were possible according to current custom).[23] He seduced Tamar but then refused to have anything further to do with her. She was thus worthless, having been deprived of her virginity, and she could only withdraw into seclusion (II Samuel 13:10–22).

Amnon's crime was found out by her full brother Absalom, David's third son.[24] He carefully plotted and carried out revenge for the crime, and Amnon was killed (II Samuel 13:23–29). Then Absalom himself had to flee and live in exile, even though he continued to feel that his actions had been morally justified (II Samuel 13: 37–39).

The relationship that now develops between Absalom and his father is exceedingly complex. Absalom feels that his father holds him guilty for Amnon's death, so that his exile is at least partly voluntary. David, on his part, longs for Absalom's return (II Samuel 13:39), but he makes no move toward reconciliation, probably because he, too, is shocked by Absalom's murder of Amnon. Not only sentiment is involved, however, for an ancient Israelite belief was that the guilt generated by the shedding of blood hung over a community until the murderer was punished. David does not want to avenge Amnon's blood by killing Absalom, nor does anyone else, and yet it would be natural to fear sharing the guilt which hangs over the culprit.

Joab, David's clever old army commander, circumvents the impasse by sending an old peasant woman to the king with an indirect message. The message, like Nathan's condemnation of David, is cast in the form of a parable-like story. She says that two of her sons fought as the result of an argument in the open field, and one killed the other. Now she is trying to protect the surviving son from the rest of her family, who are bent on avenging the bloodguilt which adheres to him. "Thus," she concludes, "they would quench the one coal which is left, and leave to my husband neither name nor remnant upon the face of the earth."

David is moved by the story and condemns those who seek blood revenge, and he promises protection for the guilty boy. Then the woman reminds him that the situation is much like his own. Why, she asks, do you not bring your banished son home? David has no answer.

And so Absalom returned home. But a full reconciliation still did not take place; Absalom did not see David for two full years. This may have been a grievous political error on David's part, however understandable it may be, for during this period the alienated Absalom must have gathered around himself a body of followers who were also alienated from the life of the kingdom under David's rule. Joab finally brought about a meeting between Absalom and David, but by this time Absalom's ambitions were growing fast. Already the heir-apparent, he now wanted the throne of his father immediately.

A conspiracy began with Absalom at its center, and many discontented citizens were drawn toward him like iron filings around a magnet. Absalom capitalized on one weakness in his father's administration of the kingdom—the poor judicial system—and set himself up as an arbitrator for those wronged in the courts. The narrator succinctly remarks, " . . . so Absalom stole the hearts of the men of Israel" (II Samuel 15:6).

Absalom laid his plans and gathered his forces for four years. Then he journeyed to Hebron, the Judean city where David had first become king, and had himself proclaimed king there. Undoubtedly he picked Hebron carefully as a center of disaffection;

the Hebronites may have been disgruntled after David's moving of the capital to Jerusalem. At any rate, Absalom was proclaimed king and rebellion spread throughout the land (II Samuel 15:7–12). David ordered his men to prepare to evacuate Jerusalem.

Pursued by forces of discontent and rebellion which he himself unleashed in the kingdom, and having become the victim of the same lust and urge for power he knew so well, the old king departs from Jerusalem as the people weep (II Samuel 15:23). But in all the haste and emotion of his departure, David did not forget his cunning. He left faithful advisors behind—Zadok, Abiathar, and Hushai. These men were prepared to act as spies for David while pretending to work for Absalom (II Samuel 15:24–37).

It was the operation of these spy-advisors within the captured capital city which enabled David to overthrow the rebellion. David had fled across the Jordan to Mahanaim, where he gathered his troops around him and awaited word from the city. The sons of Abiathar and Zadok brought word concerning advice which had been given to Absalom by his military experts, including David's man, Hushai. Absalom followed Hushai's deliberately poor advice and advanced on David in the jungle-like Jordan valley, intending to engage the foe in classic formal combat. Doubtless this form of combat was entirely unsuited to the terrain, with its heavy thickets and dense woods; furthermore, David was the experienced master at such fighting. The attack fell apart; Absalom's army was crushed as the men attempted to form ranks in the thick swampy woods.

David, torn between his role as father and his role as general, had ordered his men to crush the rebellion but to spare Absalom's life. Absalom, however, was caught by his head in the branches of a tree as he attempted to ride through, and was deliberately stabbed to death at Joab's command.

The news of Absalom's death broke on David like a flood, drowning out the welcome news that the rebels had been cut to pieces in the battle. In one of the most moving scenes in all literature, the king receives the news and stumbles off with the words, "O my son Absalom, my son, my son Absalom! Would I had died instead of you, O Absalom, my son, my son!"

Some Questions for Discussion: Why has Absalom left home? How did Joab get David to bring Absalom back? How does Absalom begin his conspiracy against David? How did Absalom "steal the hearts" of the people of Israel? Were Absalom's acts predictable from his character as revealed in the early part of the story? What incidents foreshadow possible disunity in the house of David?

In what ways are David and Absalom alike? unlike? Consider appearance, ambition, integrity, values, methods of achieving goals, etc. In describing Saul and Absalom particularly, the narrator has pointed out their physical attractiveness. What reason(s) might he have for doing so? Consider the effect of the "handsome" person in today's society. What characteristics are often attributed to him because of his appearance?

In Mark Antony's funeral oration in *Julius Caesar,* he questions the ambitious motives of Caesar: "Did this in Caesar seem ambitious?" As Absalom gained popularity with the people, many of his actions could also be considered ambitious. What are the differences and similarities between Caesar's ambitions and those of Absalom? When do you think we can justify ambitious actions?

How would you use the theme of the David-Absalom story as a basis for a story on today's youth? How does the narrator give a sense of reality to the story? Do you see changes in the characters over time? Does the story emphasize any kind of universal human experience? Are any value judgments implied in the story? Compare the "human" qualities of David and Absalom as presented by the narrator to those of Jacob and his father, for example. Do you notice changes in the style of the narrative? Which is more enjoyable to read? Why? What might account for these differences?

How do we know the agony in David's lament? What device is used? Why didn't David restrain Absalom when he first began his seditious and arrogant acts? What does the rebellion imply about the union of Israel and Judah? Why did the narrator record that the common soldier wouldn't slay Absalom?

Trace and describe the role of Joab in David's affairs. Can you think of other literary figures whose role parallels that of Joab's? Why didn't Joab obey David's request to spare Absalom?

Why do you suppose David became "the" king in the minds of later Israelites? Why do you think David became such a popular figure for writers, painters, and sculptors? Consider the point of view of the writer. Overall, what do you think he was trying to say about David and Absalom? What strategy did David use to deceive Absalom? How did he keep himself informed of the progress of the rebellion? Why do you think David fled Jerusalem? Why didn't he stay and fight? What does David's attitude toward Shimei, both before and after Absalom's defeat, show about David's character?

Solomon

THE ACCESSION OF SOLOMON (I KINGS 1–2)

As a result of Absalom's death, only two sons are left to David, Solomon and Adonijah, and only one can succeed to the king's throne. The author of the Court History of David concludes his story with an account of the intrigue-laden accession of Solomon.

The old king seems now more the subject of his courtiers' intrigues than the ruler of his followers. On the side of Adonijah we see Joab, the one-time army commander (he had been replaced after the killing of Absalom), and Abiathar the priest. Arrayed against Adonijah are Zadok the priest, Nathan the prophet, and some other younger followers of David, as well as the palace guard (I Kings 1:5–8).

The aged king is informed of Adonijah's pretensions to the throne by Bathsheba, mother of Solomon, and then by Nathan. David is forced by the two to make an open decision concerning his successor. He swiftly arranges with his remaining supporters to have Solomon declared king in a great public display (I Kings

1:32–40). But it is ironic that the shouts of "Long live King Solomon" seem to be generated more by careful staging and clever behind-the-scenes intrigue than by genuine popular support. It is also a very dangerous thing for Solomon and for the monarchy that the forces of discontent are glossed over rather than openly and honestly confronted and dealt with.

The account ends with the trembling departure of Adonijah from the center of the stage. He is promised by Solomon himself that no harm shall come to him. This promise, like many another in the dark final days of David's life, was not kept. And of the legacy of revenge which David passed on to Solomon, the less said the better. According to I Kings 2, David did not depart this life without leaving instruction for Solomon to punish Joab, his old army commander, and Shimei, who had cursed David as he fled Jerusalem in the Absalom revolt. Shimei had supposedly been forgiven, but David here recalls the fine print: he had said, "I will not put you to death with the sword." Therefore it is considered legitimate for David to have Solomon kill him. With this legacy, and with a good deal else, both good and bad, David leaves Solomon. "So Solomon sat upon the throne of David his father; and his kingdom was firmly established" (I Kings 2:12). It remains only for the narrator to dispose of the other characters in this tragic drama. Adonijah is killed after impertinently requesting David's latest concubine for a wife. Abiathar, who has supported Adonijah, is expelled from his priesthood. Joab fled for refuge to the Tabernacle or tent-shrine in which the Ark was housed, but was there struck down and killed. Shimei, who had cursed David, was allowed to live in the confines of Jerusalem, but warned that he must never leave the city. After three years, Shimei broke the agreement and was put to death.

"And so the kingdom was established in the hand of Solomon." Solomon brought the little kingdom to the peak of its military and economic power. He established trading fleets, which brought rare objects from as far away as the coast of Africa. He built lavish buildings, including the great Jerusalem Temple for which he is especially remembered. He brought in sages and authors and composers from other Near Eastern countries and thus helped make possible the first great flourishing of Israelite literature (both the Yahwist or J epic and the Court History of David were probably written during his reign). But the forces of discontent within his kingdom were strong, and they burst forth to destroy the nation at his death.

Before considering that turn of events, let us look more closely into Solomon's most enduring trait in the popular mind, his skill as a man of wisdom.

SOLOMON'S WISDOM (I KINGS 3:16–28; 4:29–34; 10:1–13)

There was a long tradition of "wisdom literature" in the ancient Near East, stretching back centuries before the birth of Israel. In both Egypt and Mesopotamia, wise men produced a considerable written deposit and probably a much larger oral tradition of "wisdom." This "wisdom" actually encompassed many different kinds of speculation and observation. Some of it was a type of primitive natural science, and represented an attempt to understand and classify the varied forms of animal and plant life observed by ancient man. It is this kind which is alluded to in I Kings 4:33, when it is said that Solomon spoke of trees, beasts, birds, reptiles, and fish.

Then there was the speculative wisdom which dealt with ultimate problems in human existence: pain, sickness, death, the apparent unfairness of life in the apportioning of riches and health. In the Bible this type of wisdom is most clearly represented by the books of Job and Ecclesiastes. Ecclesiastes is in fact attributed to Solomon (Ecclesiastes 1:1, 12), but most scholars are convinced that this attribution is not to be taken literally. Ecclesiastes was written much later than the time of Solomon, and came to be attributed to him only because his name was synonymous with wisdom. In any case, I Kings does not attribute to Solomon any examples of this "speculative wisdom."

There is, thirdly, the type of wisdom represented by the Book of Proverbs and by many other collections of wise sayings and aphorisms found in the ancient Near Eastern world. This empirical wisdom is concerned with giving good advice as to the prudent course of action which a sensible man should take. Proverbs abound which warn of the folly of drinking, revelry, and other unseemly behavior, and advocate conduct which is sober, pious, and reasonable. This type of wisdom is attributed to Solomon by Old Testament traditions, both in the present account (I Kings 4:32) and in the Book of Proverbs (Proverbs 1:1). Again, most scholars do not accept the proposition that Solomon is the actual author of the Book of Proverbs, which is a collection of smaller groups of proverbs and sayings spanning centuries in Israelite wisdom. That Solomon is named as the source of the book is simply a reflection of his traditional connection with all phases of wisdom. The same can be said of Solomon's connection with the Song of Songs, a collection of love poems tangential to the central wisdom tradition, probably attributed to him because of the record in I Kings that "his songs were a thousand and five" (I Kings 4:32).

What then is the real basis for Solomon's fabled connection with wisdom? If he wrote neither Ecclesiastes, the Song of Songs, nor the Book of Proverbs, how did his reputation for wisdom first arise?

The historical reasons for Solomon's reputation as the source of all later "wisdom" must be two-fold: first, his patronage of the wisdom movement, and secondly, his actual ability to make wise decisions which resolved knotty problems of everyday life.

With respect to the first proposition it can be remarked that Solomon's reign marked a significant opening up of Israel to the outside world. The formerly provincial capital city of Jerusalem quickly became a minor cosmopolitan center, flocking with foreigners from the more ancient cultural centers of surrounding nations. The critical account given of Solomon's many foreign wives bears this out (I Kings 11:1–8), as do the account of the building of the Temple with the aid of Phoenician craftsmen and the famous story of the visit of the queen of Sheba (South Arabia). We should add also the references to Solomon's trading expeditions (I Kings 9:26) and the joint trading venture with Hiram, the king of Tyre (I Kings 10:11–12). It is surmised that Solomon at the same time imported and patronized foreign wise men, for wisdom was not primarily an Israelite phenomenon prior to Solomon's era. Thus Solomon was known for his wisdom because of his creation and patronage of a group or school of wisdom writers and thinkers in Israel.

Secondly (and here we must draw upon the accounts in I Kings 3:16–28), Solomon was capable of very wise decisions concerning problems which arose between his subjects, and he was sought as the final arbiter in cases which appeared to have no solution. Such was the memorable case of the two women, each of whom claimed a baby boy as her own. Solomon's perceptive solution was very simple: divide the baby in half with a sword and give one half to each woman. Of course the woman who was the child's real mother would rather give up the baby than have it killed, while the false mother was willing to let it happen.

It is most unfortunate that the Old Testament tradition has preserved only this single story of Solomon's own wisdom. Apart from this one narrative, the connection of Solomon with wisdom appears to be a derivative and secondary phenomenon. And in fact his administration of the kingdom does not reflect much wisdom in matters of politics and statecraft. The rise in economic power and cosmopolitan contacts was paralleled by a decline in national morale and the beginning of a process of attrition by which the kingdom was reduced to a smaller and smaller size and ultimately torn apart by internal dissension. But this is the story that will be taken up later. Suffice it to say now that the tradition of Solomonic wisdom is like a huge pyramid resting upside down on a very small point. The small point on which it rests is Solomon's wisdom in household matters and his patronage of wisdom schools. In the larger affairs of the kingdom, one can see that wiser courses of action could have been followed.

We are left, rather disappointingly, with a picture of Solomon which is both flat and obscure. While the Court History of David and the so-called Early Source or Saul Source in I-II Samuel enable us to project a full three-dimensional portrait of David, this type of authentic and humanly compelling narrative is not available for Solomon. In its place we find a series of highly stylized editorial summaries which give us a fascinating impression of cultural and economic developments, but scarcely any glimpses of Solomon as a man. Doubtless the theological purposes of the Deuteronomic editors were well served by this depiction of Solomon, concentrating as it does on his central achievement—the building of the Temple. But from a strictly literary point of view it is of markedly inferior quality when compared with the brilliant David narratives.

Some Questions for Discussion: How had Saul and David been chosen as kings? What does the existence of the conflict over succession in this story tell you about the evolution of monarchy in Israel? Upon whom did Adonijah depend for support in his bid for the thone? Why might these men be considered strong support for Adonijah's cause?

Without knowing the laws governing Adonijah's grabbing the horns of the altar, can you conclude what this act means from your reading? Explain. When David cautioned Solomon against Joab, what reasons did he have for apparently turning against the man who had served him for so many years?

Adonijah must have been aware of the court reaction to his brother Absalom's grievous actions toward David's harem. Do you feel that Adonijah would knowingly court death in the same manner? Explain. How did Joab meet his death? What about the death of Joab would have offended the religious people of Israel? What element of poetic justice can be found in the unlawful manner in which he was killed? Should we overlook the manner in which he was killed because of the kind of person he had been during his lifetime? Explain.

What situation brought the two women into the court of Solomon? Does the writer make the women and the circumstances of their quarrel credible to you? Explain. What do you think was the writer's purpose in I Kings 4:20–34? Why did the queen of Sheba make her famous visit to Solomon?

Considering what you have read about Solomon's reign and what you know about the tradition of Israel as God's chosen people, how would you evaluate Solomon's success as king? Support your arguments.

Compare the characters of David and Solomon. On what do you base your character analysis of David? of Solomon? Compare the narrator's skill in developing the characters of David and Solomon with regard to personal attitudes, the "humanness" of each character, the motivating forces within each man, etc. What can you conclude about the skill of character development in each story?

Give several examples of Solomon's wisdom. Is Solomon always wise? Cite passages from I Kings to support your answer.

In *The Interpreter's One-Volume Commentary on the Bible,* John William Wevers writes this about I Kings 10:23–25: "This exaggerated summary of Solomon's riches and wisdom finds parallel in ancient oriental inscription. A later age made Solomon the wisest man of all times, a judgment contradicted by ch. 11." Read I Kings 10:23–25 and 11. Do you agree with Professor Wevers' phrase, "a judgment contradicted by ch. 11"? Why, or why not?

CHAPTER 10

The Divided Monarchy and the Rise of Prophecy

Following Solomon's death, the forces of discontent and division that had simmered since David's time, or even longer, finally boiled to the surface. The result was a division of the nation into a northern kingdom and a southern kingdom, called Israel and Judah. The boundary between the sister kingdoms ran from east to west just a few miles north of Jerusalem. The capital of Judah remained at Jerusalem, the site selected by David. The capital of Israel was first Shechem, followed briefly by Tirzah and then Samaria.

Modern scholars date the beginning of David's reign over the United Kingdom at approximately 1000 B.C. It appears that both he and his son Solomon reigned for about forty years, as claimed in the biblical traditions, and that Solomon's death and the division of the kingdom occurred around 922 B.C. From this point on, the Kingdom of Judah was ruled continuously by descendants of David, until the kingdom fell to the armies of the neo-Babylonian Empire in 587 B.C.

The life of the Northern Kingdom was both shorter and more turbulent. The dynasty of the first king, Jeroboam I, lasted only through the reign of his son Nadab, who was assassinated around the year 900 B.C. His successor, Baasha, took the throne and was followed by his son Elah, who was in turn assassinated in 876 B.C. by Zimri, who committed suicide while under attack. Zimri was succeeded by Omri. The powerful Omri dynasty lasted for less than forty years, from 876 B.C. to 842 B.C. It was overthrown by Jehu, whose dynasty lasted for nearly one hundred years, ending shortly after the brilliant reign of Jeroboam II (786–746 B.C.). Just a quarter of a century after the death of Jeroboam II, the Kingdom of Israel fell to the Assyrians (722 B.C.). In that last twenty-five years of its existence, the nation saw four of its monarchs assassinated. The concentration of political chaos in this period was unusual, but the occurrences themselves were not surprising for any who knew the bloody earlier history of this doomed nation.

It was in the Northern Kingdom that the institution of prophecy, uniquely important in the development of Israelite literature and religion, had its beginnings. Elijah and Elisha lived in the Northern Kingdom in the ninth century, and Amos and Hosea spoke there a century later. Not until the last years of the existence of the Northern Kingdom did great prophets arise in the Southern Kingdom as well.

The institution of prophecy had its origin, as we have seen, in the activities of holy men who gave oracles while in ecstatic or trance-like conditions. We do not know the ways in which these ecstatic states were achieved, although the use of music to induce a trance is recorded more than once (I Samuel 10:5–6; II Kings 3:14–15). Through the work of men like Samuel, the activities of the prophets were shaped in accordance with the faith of Israel, and the prophets became messengers of Yahweh, demanding of king and commoner alike utter obedience to his will.

We have seen also that the prophets were, from the time of Samuel on, quite closely related to the monarchy. In some cases, as with Nathan, for example, the prophets were actually members of the royal court. In other cases they spurned such attachments, living and working independently. But even the independent prophets were political figures of considerable power, deeply involving themselves in political and economic affairs.

The prophets characteristically viewed the political life of their nation from the standpoint of *theocracy*. The true ruler of Israel was, they believed, Yahweh of Hosts. All aspects of the life of the kingdom lay under the sovereignty of Yahweh and were subject to his demands of absolute justice.[1] Thus the prophets could become the enemies of an arrogant monarch or of a greedy upper-class citizenry that devoured the poor with their great estates and businesses. They could also, from their theocratic point of view, attack the religious life of the nation and excoriate both priests and worshipers for the hollowness of their devotion to Yahweh.

In the light of Yahweh's demands and the nation's performance, the prophets even ventured to depict the destiny of the kingdom. It is with this element of prediction in their message that modern people are best acquainted, so that "prophecy" has become synonymous with "prediction." But it must be remembered that the prophets were not just seers who gazed into the mysterious future. They spoke of the future only as it impinged upon the present life of the people. They spoke of the future in order to warn, to threaten, to cajole, and to reform. The real center of the prophets' message was the present and the immediate future that flowed out of the decisions the king and the people made in their current crises.

Indeed, crisis was the classic context of prophecy. The most remarkable prophetic figures are those who are seen against the backdrop of terrible social and political events, such as the glare of burning cities, as first Israel and then Judah fell to their conquerors. The prophets were aroused to speak, it would seem, only by potentially lethal threats to the national life. These men who made themselves Israel's counselors in times of crisis faced head-on what one writer calls "the terror of history," and they demanded that the whole nation face this terror with them.[2] They even dared to assert that it was Yahweh himself who controlled all the forces of history and nature, and that if these forces had turned upon Israel it was because Israel had failed to live up to her destiny as the people of God. The prophetic God is a terrible god, because the events that moved the prophets to speak were terrible events. As messengers of this terrible god, the prophets themselves were viewed by their contemporaries as either terrifying or ridiculous, depending upon how seriously their words were taken. They were lonely men, but their courage, faith, and clarity of vision will cause them to be remembered as long as men care about human responsibility in the face of historical challenges.

The Division of the Kingdom (I Kings 11–12)

At the beginning of the Northern Kingdom, prophetic activity was a potent force. Jeroboam, whom Solomon had put in charge of his forced labor, was designated by a prophet named Ahijah to become king in Solomon's place (I Kings 11:26–40). The prophetic hostility to Solomon's rule had been aroused by Solomon's introduction of pagan cults to please his foreign wives (I Kings 11:1–8) and by his pretensions to a mode of monarchic rule that aped both the splendor and the oppression practiced by other Near Eastern sovereigns. Solomon had built the economy and culture of his kingdom by sacrificing the old way of life in Israel, with its tribal orientation and religious zeal. He had divided the kingdom into twelve administrative districts for the purpose of taxation; the new boundaries shattered the older tribal structure (I Kings 4:7–19). In order to carry out his extensive building projects, Solomon had resorted to conscripting forced labor from his own people (I Kings 5:13–18). Thus even the erecting of the Temple, pious work that it was, was carried out at the expense of the old freedom of Israel's citizens.

It is not hard to see that prophetic and popular discontent with Solomonic practices and policies would coalesce. Older divisions already existed, especially the separateness of Judah from the rest of the tribes, which may go back into the generations before monarchy arose. Discontent with the policies of David, who had certainly begun organizing the kingdom along the lines Solomon had followed, was evident in the revolt of Absalom and in a later revolt led by Sheba (II Samuel 20). All that was needed in Solomon's time to fan the sparks of revolt into open flames of rebellion was an event and a leader. The leader was already at hand, thanks to Ahijah's designation of Jeroboam as future king; the event was provided by the death of Solomon.

The man who would succeed Solomon on the throne was his son Rehoboam. The succession to kingship over Judah appears to have been automatic, but Rehoboam had to travel to the ancient northern shrine of Shechem in order to be accepted as ruler of the northern portion of the kingdom. And, not unexpectedly, trouble developed at Shechem, for the northern elders demanded a relaxation of the Solomonic burden of taxation (I Kings 12:1–5). A wise king would have sensed the potential for revolt in the northern area and perhaps would have negotiated with the elders at Shechem. Unfortunately, neither Rehoboam nor his younger counselors, whom he depended upon in this decision, exercised much wisdom. As a result, the heavy yoke borne by the people under Solomon became heavier (I Kings 12:8–15). Rehoboam tried to enforce his iron rule by sending Adoram, taskmaster of the forced labor, to the northern representatives. In the end, Adoram was stoned to death, and Rehoboam had to flee for his life to Jerusalem. The kingdom, so painfully pulled into the shape of unity by Samuel, Saul, and David, was thus torn apart without even a battle.

The story concludes with an account of Jeroboam's attempt to set up the machinery of government for his new kingdom. Essential as a part of such machinery was a temple or shrine to be associated with the royal house. Intending to rival the Jerusalem Temple at least in antiquity as a cult center, Jeroboam picked Bethel for his shrine. To supplement the Bethel shrine, Jeroboam set up another at the far northern end of his territory in Dan.

Jeroboam had nothing to match the Ark of the Covenant as a cult object, so he constructed golden bulls or calves, which were very ancient symbols of deity in Canaan. He also appointed a priesthood and arranged a calendar of sacred events (I Kings 12:25–33).

The editor of the Deuteronomic history, of which I Kings is a part, is convinced that Jeroboam's setting up the golden bull images was a terrible act of rebellion against Yahweh. An allusion to Aaron's golden calf of Exodus 32 is certainly intended, and the allusion is entirely in Jeroboam's disfavor. Modern scholars tend to doubt that Jeroboam intended the calves themselves to be worshiped. They were probably intended as pedestals upon which Yahweh was invisibly enthroned, just as in the Jerusalem Temple he was enthroned above the cherubim, which were composite animals of Hebrew mythology, perhaps winged lions or the like.[3] It is quite possible, of course, that worshipers at Bethel and Dan might worship the calves themselves. But what was most serious, in the view of Israelite prophets, was that Jeroboam had shattered the religious unity of Israel by spurning the Jerusalem Temple with its ancient Ark of the Covenant, setting up his own royal sanctuary as a substitute. In any event, the Deuteronomic historian views Jeroboam's sin as the worst of a series of royal sins committed by the Kingdom of Israel, and he attributes the final downfall of the nation to Yahweh's judgment upon Jeroboam.

Some Questions for Discussion: In what two ways did King Solomon disobey the word of the Lord? In I Kings 11:5 and 7, what does the phrase *abomination of* mean when it is used to refer to Milcom, Chemosh, and Molech? Why do you think the narrator used that phrase? What does the use of the phrase tell you about the narrator's religious belief?

According to the narrator, how will the Lord punish Solomon? Why won't the Lord destroy the entire kingdom? What mercy did God show in his punishment of Solomon? Why do you think God did these things "for David's sake" and "for Jerusalem's sake"? What might have happened if Solomon had obeyed God?

How do Hadad, Rezon, and Jeroboam contribute to the punishment of Solomon? What do you think are the most significant prophecies that Ahijah makes to Jeroboam? Why do you think that some scholars refer to I Kings 11:41–43 as Solomon's obituary notice?

Seeing the discontent of the people under the "heavy yoke" of Solomon and sensing the potential for revolt in the northern area, what might a wise king have done? What advice did the elder counselors give Rehoboam? What advice did the young men give? Why do you think Rehoboam followed the advice that he did?

Jeroboam became king over Israel. How did his attempt at setting up the machinery of government work out? How did he fail as king? What caused the kingdom to divide? What action of Jeroboam's caused the actual division?

Elijah (I Kings 17–19, 21–22)

Elijah is introduced into the recital of the fates and fortunes of Israel's kings with a suddenness that may very well be intentional. Certainly the prophet's whole career, as glimpsed in the vivid narratives of I Kings, has about it the qualities of unexpectedness and rapid movement. This impression is confirmed by the words of Elijah's friend, Obadiah, in I Kings 18:12: "As soon as I have gone from you, the Spirit of the Lord will carry you whither I know not. . . ."

These stories are set in the framework of narratives about the Aramean wars of the ninth century. During the period between Omri's accession (876 B.C.) and Jeroboam II's accession (786 B.C.), the Northern Kingdom was engaged in almost steady warfare with her vigorous Aramean neighbor to the north, the Kingdom of Damascus. At times—especially during the reign of the Aramean king Ben-Hadad II—Israel was almost wholly occupied by Syrian troops.[4] Certainly the military threat posed by the Arameans was the most serious external problem which Omri had to face when he took the throne.

It is not hard to understand, therefore, why both the Elijah and the Elisha narratives, spanning the years between about 850 B.C. and about 800 B.C., constantly refer to the wars with Syria.

The other great enemy of Israel, at least in the view of the prophets whom Elijah represented, was the cult of Baal, the Canaanite deity of storm and rain. The worship of this ancient deity was officially encouraged by Omri's son Ahab, whose wife, Jezebel, was a Phoenician princess from the city-state of Sidon, to whom the worship of Baal would be natural. Just as Solomon had provided for the religious needs of his foreign wives by introducing the worship of their gods in the heart of Jerusalem, so Ahab provided a temple of Baal in Samaria, the new capital city of Israel (I Kings 16:31–32).

Both the marriage to Jezebel and the provision for her worship of Baal might have been sensible political moves had it not been for the opposition which these moves aroused in Elijah and his followers. But Elijah found such rebellion against the God of Israel intolerable. He could doubtless picture the already divided kingdom splitting apart again or disintegrating into merely another third-rate Canaanite state. In any case, the God who spoke to Moses on Sinai had not created Israel for the worship of Baal.

In addition to the framework provided by the Aramean wars and by the Baalism threat, there is therefore one more recurrent motif in the Elijah narratives: the constant struggle for leadership between king and prophet, with the prophet standing for the old order of theocracy.

The opening narrative of I Kings 17 fits perfectly into this context. Elijah has announced an all-out attack on the worship of Baal by the king and his followers. The chosen battleground is the sphere that Baal was believed to control above all else, the sphere of the earth's fertility, brought about by the life-giving winter rains and year-round dew of Palestine.[5] Elijah declares that Yahweh will bring about a long drought, thus proving that he alone controls the powers supposedly held by Baal. But the storyteller assures us that Elijah himself was miraculously fed, just as Yahweh preserved the life of his people in the wilderness by means of quails, manna, and water from the rock. This is but the first of many allusions to the Moses narratives.[6] The implication of these allusions is that Elijah is a second Moses, called to hold Israel together in a time of crisis. Just as Moses had battled the gods of the Egyptians and the wicked Pharaoh, so Elijah struggles against Baal and Ahab.

In the second narrative of I Kings 17, Elijah is commanded to leave Ahab's domains and travel to the Phoenician town of Zarephath. The implication is that the king sees the land suffering from the drought and would like to reach some agreement with Elijah, but the prophet makes himself unavailable. While staying in Zarephath, the prophet is cared for by a widow to whom he miraculously provides oil and meal that never run out. Elijah also restores the life of her son after he has stopped breathing.

Both elements in this story—the relationship with the common people and the occurrence of miracles—are typical of the Elijah stories. The prophet is shown moving among the pious poor of Israel, who are faithful to their god, in contrast to the wicked king and his wife. Elijah and his successor Elisha are also credited with a number of miracles—again reminiscent of the Moses narratives—which demonstrate both their faithfulness and Yahweh's power.

It is difficult for the modern reader to understand these stories as they were intended to be understood. We are inclined to make a sharp division between the possible and the impossible, the natural and the unnatural. But for the ancient Hebrew, all things were possible to God, and there was no strict order of nature which had to be "broken" for a miracle to occur. A "miracle" was simply a wonderful event that Yahweh brought about within the events of history at some critical point where the life of his people was at stake—hence the clustering of Old Testament miracles in two crisis periods, the time of Moses and the time of Elijah and Elisha. In addition, the miracle attributed to Elijah in the present story confirms, like his announcement of the drought, his role as Yahweh's true representative.[7]

> And the woman said to Elijah, "Now I know that you are a man of God, and that the word of Yahweh in your mouth is truth." (I Kings 17:24)

The drought was now hard upon the land, and it was time for Elijah to make his most stunning display of the power of Yahweh. The narrator introduces the great scene that follows in a laconic style that is typically Hebraic.

> After many days the word of Yahweh came to Elijah, in the third year, saying, "Go, show yourself to Ahab; and I will send rain upon the earth."

Elijah first contacts his follower, Obadiah, a member of the royal court, and tries to use him as a messenger to Ahab. But the king's hostility to Elijah is so intense that Obadiah is afraid of being caught in the crossfire between the two enemies. His speech also reveals the situation of Israel's prophets, who have been driven into hiding by Ahab (I Kings 18:7–14). Elijah assures Obadiah of divine protection as he faces the enraged Ahab, so Obadiah carries the message.

The king meets Elijah with sarcasm and perhaps fear: "Is it you, you troubler of Israel?" Elijah responds with a proposal. The prophets or devotees of Baal are to attempt to end the drought through prayer to Baal. If they fail, Elijah will intercede with Yahweh on the people's behalf.

In the following scene, the worshipers of Baal are caricatured as they engage in a ritual intended to arouse the storm god to activity. Elijah, with deep sarcasm, mocks their attempts:

> Cry aloud, for he is a god; either he is musing, or he has gone aside, or he is on a journey, or perhaps he is asleep and must be awakened. (I Kings 18:27)

But there is no response, even after hours of prayer and self-mutilation by Baal's worshipers (I Kings 18:28–29). Elijah then takes charge and prepares for a ceremony which will, in a sense, renew the covenant between Yahweh and Israel, and will demonstrate Yahweh's sovereignty over the whole range of natural activities. A bull is laid ready for sacrifice, the wood under it is drenched with water, and Elijah prays. Lightning falls and sets fire to the wood, devouring the sacrificed bull in the flames. The people confess their renewed faith:

> "Yahweh, he is God; Yahweh, he is God." (I Kings 18:39)

It is as though the grip of the drought was broken by that confession. With tremendous rapidity and intensity, the storm arises out over the Mediterranean and sweeps inland. Ahab must hasten in his chariot to his summer residence of Jezreel before the road becomes impassable. Elijah, in a state of ecstasy ("the hand was upon him") dashes ahead of the king and runs before the chariot as the rain pours down (I Kings 18:45–46).

Even so, the prophets of Yahweh are not in the royal favor. In fact the next narrative has its setting in a persecution of the prophets by Jezebel, the queen (I Kings 19:1–3). Fearing for his life, Elijah flees through the wilderness to Mount Sinai, the place where Israel was born as a sacred community. Like Israel in the desert, his life is miraculously supported on his journey (I Kings 19:4–8). The struggle that now takes place is not a struggle with the king and people, nor yet with the prophets of Baal. Elijah now struggles with himself and with the God who thrusts him into the life of a frightened fugitive. He even prays, in profound discouragement, that he be allowed to die, but Yahweh gently pushes him forward to Moses' meeting place at Sinai (I Kings 19:4–5, 7).

At Sinai, Elijah is confronted with the presence of Yahweh himself. In an enigmatic narrative, that nevertheless powerfully conveys the Israelite understanding of God, Elijah is exposed to phenomena in which Yahweh was thought to dwell—a great wind, a shattering earthquake, and fire. Elijah is told, however, that Yahweh is not in these phenomena (I Kings 19:9–12). Then comes, according to the traditional translation, "a still small voice." Now Elijah goes forth and receives his command from Yahweh. He is told to return, and is given two tasks: he must anoint Hazael as king over Syria and Jehu as king over Israel. He then is instructed to designate Elisha as his own successor in the prophetic role.

Scholars continue to puzzle over the meaning of the "still small voice." Even the translation is in question, for the Hebrew could mean "utter silence," or a silence so absolute that it seems palpable or audible.[8] If so, then the narrative seems to be saying that Yahweh is not found (as earlier Hebrews, like the Canaanites, had expected) in storm, wind, and lightning. Elijah looked there for him and found nothing. Then came a long and pregnant silence, and out of that silence Yahweh spoke. He demanded that Elijah live up to his responsibility as an historical figure, and he asserted his own control over the kings and prophets of history. The whole narrative thus conveys paradigmatically the contrast between the Israelite understanding of God as the Lord of history, and the Canaanite conception which ties the deity to the cycles of natural events.

Elijah returns and passes his mantle, symbolic of the prophetic office, to Elisha (I Kings 19:19–21). There remains for Elijah one final confrontation with the king, one final championing of the oppressed.

The narrative of this encounter is found in I Kings 21, and concerns the ancient right of Israelite landowners to retain their land as a family holding from generation to generation. Naboth, owner of a plot of land near Ahab's summer palace in Jezreel, is approached by the king and offered a good price for his land. A deep and ancient principle is involved, however, for in Israelite belief the land of Canaan had been won by holy war under Yahweh's kingship and generalship; the land was therefore a sacred inheritance given to each family. It is typical of Ahab's disregard for Israel's ancient beliefs and customs that this principle means nothing to him. Frustrated by Naboth's refusal to sell his vineyard and goaded and taunted by his wife, Ahab consents to having Naboth put to death (I Kings 21:5–14).

The king then proceeds to take possession of the land. As he surveys his new vineyard, however, an old enemy appears with characteristic suddenness and utters a chilling oracle. Elijah announces that Ahab and his whole dynasty will be swept away into bloody ruin and that Queen Jezebel herself will be eaten by the dogs that scour the countryside for carrion. The oracle hangs over Ahab and his family like a nemesis from this point on; the narratives that follow are held together by suspense as we await the oracle's fulfillment.

The actualizing of the doom of Ahab himself is rapid. I Kings 22 relates the death of Ahab, as if by chance (". . . a certain man drew his bow at a venture, and struck the king of Israel between the scale armor and the breastplate" I Kings 22:34), in the heat of a battle with the Syrians. Every bloody prediction made by Elijah is carried out as Ahab's blood is licked up by the dogs when his battle chariot is cleaned (I Kings 22:37–38).

Inserted into the middle of the story of Ahab's well-deserved death is a striking narrative that portrays a further struggle in Israel—the struggle between the false and the true prophet. Many prophets were supported, as we have seen, by royal funds. While some of these may have been men of great integrity, many simply fabricated oracles that pleased the king. This at least is the implication of the present narrative. Here the king of Judah, Jehoshaphat, joins with Ahab in a campaign against the Syrians. They arrange for a pre-battle oracle from the royal prophets and are told to launch their attack, since Yahweh favors them.

One prophet, however, is yet to be heard from. Micaiah, son of Imlah, is reluctantly summoned by the king, who fears a negative (and honest?) oracle from this man, apparently an old opponent of Ahab's. Micaiah first gives—completely in sarcasm— a favorable oracle. Ahab senses the sarcasm and demands the truth. The truth, when Micaiah tells it, is as chilling as Ahab feared it would be:

> I saw all Israel scattered upon the mountains, as sheep that have no shepherd; and the Lord said, "These have no master; let each return to his home in peace."

When Micaiah is challenged by the false prophets, he gives a response that is most illuminating. He replies that in his vision he saw himself in the presence of Yahweh and his heavenly court, and he heard Yahweh send a lying spirit to speak through Ahab's prophets and thus entice the king toward his death (I Kings 22: 19–23). The true prophet, we may understand from this, is the man who sees and hears the proceedings within Yahweh's heavenly court. Yahweh is even able to use false prophets to bring about his will; so the prophets themselves can be deceived.[9] The final test, however, is the outcome of the events themselves. Micaiah concludes sarcastically, when Ahab speaks of his return to camp after battle, "If you return in peace, Yahweh has not spoken by me!" (I Kings 22:28). The king does not return, and Micaiah's courageous words of denunciation are upheld.

Some Questions for Discussion: After telling Ahab that there will be a drought, why does Elijah "hide" by the brook Cherith? How does he survive? How does he provide for the widow and her household? What does Elijah do for the widow's son? What might be the narrator's purpose for telling these three stories— Elijah at the brook of Cherith, the jar of meal and the cruse of oil, and the revival of the widow's son?

How do you know that Obadiah revered the Lord? What are Ahab's instructions to Obadiah? Why do you think Elijah sees Obadiah before showing himself to Ahab as the Lord had instructed the prophet to do? Describe Elijah's showing himself to Ahab. What impression of Elijah do you get from I Kings 18:18–19?

Describe the contest between Elijah and the prophets of Baal. Why might this contest remind you of Moses before the Pharaoh?

Why did Elijah fear Jezebel? How does Elijah receive the strength to journey to Horeb? What does Elijah's response to the Lord's question, "What are you doing here, Elijah?" tell you about Elijah? Reread I Kings 19:18 before answering this question: How does the Lord indicate to Elijah that the prophet is not the sole surviving worshiper of the Lord? What is Elijah's three-fold mission? What part of it are you certain that Elijah fulfilled?

After reading I Kings 21:2–29, how would you describe Ahab? How would you characterize Jezebel?

What is to be the fate of Ahab? How does he try to avoid it? How is he killed? What happens to Ahab's kingdom after his death?

Suggested Activities: If you were writing an account of a modern-day prophet, explain why you might use the technique employed by the narrator in I Kings 17. Describe three incidents that illustrate the powers of your modern-day prophet.

Dramatize Obadiah's meeting with Elijah and Elijah's confrontation with Ahab in I Kings 18:17. What instructions for portraying characters will you give to the actor who is playing the part of Obadiah? Elijah? Ahab? Defend your instructions with references to biblical passages.

Reread Exodus before writing a comparison of Moses and Elijah. Be certain to indicate what characteristics they have in common as well as showing how they differ.

Elisha Succeeds Elijah (II Kings 2:1–18)

There is a complex and somewhat enigmatic relationship between the figure of Elijah and that of his successor, Elisha. For example, the commands to anoint Hazael king of Syria and Jehu king of Israel (I Kings 19:15–18) were never carried out by Elijah at all, but by his successor. Yet the circles in which the story of Elijah's commission was told must have believed that Elijah followed his orders. Furthermore, Elisha is credited with providing a miraculous supply of oil for a widow and restoring a boy to life (II Kings 4:1–7, 8–37). These stories are very similar to the ones told of Elijah in I Kings 17, and some scholars think the stories originally concerned only Elijah but were later told of Elisha as well.[10] Similarly, there are two different stories of the passing of Elijah's mantle to Elisha: I Kings 19:19–21 and II Kings 2:1–18.

The historical reasons for these phenomena could be the following: We have good reason to think, first of all, that the Elijah and Elisha stories actually date from a time shortly after the events. Many scholars date them in the ninth century, making the stories almost contemporaneous with Elijah and Elisha. But the stories appear to have gone through a period of oral transmission, during which they were told as sagas in prophetic circles in which Elijah and Elisha were revered. The sagas would have somewhat different forms in the different circles, and this would account for variant traditions about the anointing of Hazael and Jehu and about the passing of the prophetic mantle. It would also account for the same stories being told of both prophets, for it would be natural for stories current in prophetic circles to be attached first to one of the main figures and then to the other.

This means, of course, that we cannot be certain about the precise facts of many of the stories told of Elijah and Elisha, and in this respect the stories are not "historical" in any absolute sense. In another sense, however, the stories are profoundly historical because of the insight they give us into the beliefs and practices of the ninth-century prophetic circles who told the stories, and the light they throw on the life of the common Israelite, as well as of the aristocracy, in this period. And doubtless some of the glimpses of Elijah and Elisha which the stories afford are absolutely authentic. This is particularly true of stories which tie these men in with the military and political history of the period. Through such stories, Elijah appears as a towering figure of courageous faith who sought to reconstitute Israel as the people of the covenant in opposition to the paganism and oppressive tactics of the monarchy. The narrators suggest that he is a second Moses, and Elijah certainly appears worthy of this accolade.

Elisha emerges as a leader who is much more closely bound up with the life of the prophetic guilds. Many more miraculous events are associated with him than with Elijah, but at the same time he does not emerge as a religious leader who equals Elijah. Elisha's involvement in political events is deep and significant, however. It is he who carries out the order to anoint a new king over Syria, and he also foments revolution in Israel by arranging to have Jehu anointed king (II Kings 8:13; 9:1–13). It might be said that if Elijah is almost another Moses, Elisha worthily fills the role of a second Joshua.

Let us now look at the narrative that tells of Elisha's succession to the chief prophetic role played by Elijah (II Kings 2:1–18). As is typical of many narratives in the Elisha cycle, the bands of prophets or prophetic guilds (called in Hebrew "the sons of the prophets") play a prominent part. Elijah and Elisha journey together toward Transjordan, where Elijah will make his destined departure. Elijah continually requests that he be allowed to go on alone, but Elisha will not leave him. As they pass through towns where bands of prophets reside, these prophets come out and remind Elisha that his master is soon to depart (II Kings 2:1–7). Finally the two arrive at the Jordan, and Elijah, in his role as a second Moses, parts the waters with his mantle. He asks

Elisha what last request he has to make, and Elisha replies, "Let me inherit a double share of your spirit."

The "spirit" of Elijah would actually mean the divine power by which he is able to exercise leadership and perform wonders. A double share would not represent a greedy request, but simply the share of an estate that Hebrew law set for the first-born son (Deuteronomy 21:15–17). Elisha asks to be, in the fullest possible sense, Elijah's successor as prophet.

Suddenly Elijah is separated from Elisha by chariots and horsemen that appear to be made of fire. Elisha cries out, "My father, my father! The chariots of Israel and its horsemen." That is to say, Elijah has been worth armies to Israel as her prophetic leader.[11] A whirlwind then appears (perhaps one of the "dust devils" frequent in the desert), and Elijah is gone.

Elisha picks up the fallen mantle of Elijah and begins the journey home. That he is the true successor to Elijah is proved when he used the mantle to part the waters of the Jordan (compare the crossing into Canaan under Joshua, Joshua 3:1–17), and he is accepted as such by the prophetic band at Jericho. The story concludes with a narrative that confirms Elijah's mysterious disappearance. Like Moses, the place of his death was never found (Deuteronomy 34:6). Indeed, both Christian and Jewish tradition reflect the belief that Elijah never actually died, but was taken directly into heaven, not to appear again until the end of the age (see Malachi 4:5, Matthew 17:9–13). So great was the impression that this towering figure left on his followers!

Some Questions for Discussion: People to this day refer to the event called "the ascension of Elijah." To what are they referring? Why do you suppose a vacant seat is still kept ready for Elijah at the Jewish observance of Passover? How was Elijah regarded by his people? by the rulers of his country? What evidence do you have to support your answers? Why was it imperative for the author to stress the search for Elijah's body? Why does Elisha persist in going with Elijah even though he was urged to "tarry" more than once? What is the significance of the encounters with several groups of men with respect to the future status of Elisha as a prophet? What effect would Elijah's total disappearance have created among the people of the area? (What were some of the speculations at the time of Bishop Pike's disappearance?)

Does the reader know how this story will end after reading verse 1? Does the information you get in verse 1 spoil the remainder of the story for you? Why, or why not? Why would a narrator insert such a passage into the beginning of a story?

In I Kings 3:5–14, another young man is about to assume tremendous responsibility. Compare and contrast the requests made by both Elisha and Solomon. How are both requests answered?

Suggested Activities: Using I Kings 3:5–14 or II Kings 2:9–12, prepare a dialogue between Solomon and Yahweh or between Elijah and Elisha. Imagine the feelings of each character in each set of circumstances and develop the conversation from there. Was Solomon more humble than Elisha? Consider their later use of their gifts in answering the above.

Jehu's Purge (II Kings 9:1–10:27)

The ghastly oracle uttered against Ahab and Jezebel and against the entire dynasty they represent had not yet been fulfilled. True enough, Ahab himself had died in battle in a manner that seemed to indicate divine intervention (I Kings 22:29–36). Jezebel, however, remained alive and lived in the royal palace as the queen mother. Her son Joram had succeeded his father to the throne.

The external affairs of the kingdom were unchanged. Close relations with Phoenicia continued because of Jezebel's relation to the royal family of Sidon. Judah was also brought into friendly relations with the Northern Kingdom through intermarriage of the two royal families (II Kings 8:18, 26). The Syrians to the north continued to be a threat, but with Judah and Phoenicia as allies, Israel could withstand them.

The only cloud on the horizon was generated by that fanatic

band of prophets now under the leadership of Elisha. To them the external strength of Israel merely covered over her internal rottenness. The paganism and oppression practiced by the ruling house were intolerable in the eyes of Yahweh, and therefore that house must fall. It was only a question of waiting until the right moment to instigate a revolt against Joram and Jezebel and all the worshipers of Baal.

That moment came in the judgment of Elisha, some time in the year 842 BC. King Joram and Jezebel were at the royal residence in Jezreel, scene of the infamous incident involving Naboth's vineyard. Joram was there recovering from a wound suffered in the perennial wars with the Syrians. The king of Judah was also at the Jezreel palace on a visit. The army of Israel was in the field in Transjordan, near the town of Ramoth-gilead, standing guard against Syrian invasion.

If Elisha judged that the situation was right for a combined prophetic and military *coup d'etat,* he was right. His emissary, one of "the sons of the prophets," traveled secretly to the army camp and there, still in secret, he anointed Jehu king. When Jehu's officers learned of the anointing as he emerged from meeting with the prophet, they fell in behind the revolt and proclaimed him king.

The narrative that follows tells in striking and gory detail of the death of all of the royal family and their followers at the hands of Jehu. He first rode to the Jezreel palace on his chariot, and was met near Naboth's vineyard by both the kings who were staying there, Joram of Israel and Ahaziah of Judah. Joram was killed immediately and his body thrown into Naboth's vineyard. Ahaziah was mortally wounded, but managed to escape to Megiddo, where he died.

Now for Jezebel. That seemingly indestructible woman, whose very name was anathema to the prophetic groups, was not yet aware that Jehu represented a threat which she could not charm into submission. The narrator tells us that she adorned her head and painted her eyes and spoke to Jehu from an upper window as he approached. Yet even her own household was not loyal, for when Jehu commanded two of her servants to throw Jezebel out into the courtyard, they did so. Jehu mercilessly crushed her with his chariot and left her body for the dogs to devour. He himself went in—and perhaps this tells us something of his personality—to eat and drink, as though nothing unusual had taken place that day.[12]

The rest of the narrative is equally bloody. Jehu next dealt with the royal family who lived in Samaria, the capital city. At his order, the ruling elders of the city delivered to him the severed heads of seventy males of Ahab's descendants. Jehu piled the heads at the entrance to the Jezreel palace, then fell upon the entire body of Joram's counselors and supporters and slaughtered them to a man. A group of royal kinsmen of Ahaziah from Judah were also slain nearby.

Now Jehu must advance on the capital city itself and continue his extermination of the supporters of the extinct dynasty of Ahab. As he drove there in his chariot, he was met by Jonadab, the son of Rechab, who pledged full support to Jehu in his bloody purge. Jonadab's support was significant, for he represented the Rechabite order, an extremely conservative ascetic group that adhered strictly to the desert ideals and customs of early Yahwism. The Rechabites were noted for their disdain for Canaanite culture and religion; they even spurned the use of wine, which symbolized the settled (and corrupted) life of Israel in Canaan (see Jeremiah 35).

That the Rechabites opposed Ahab and Jezebel and their descendants is not hard to understand, notorious as that dynasty was for its treaties with pagans and its assimilation of the Canaanite worship of Baal. Rechabite ideas in many respects paralleled the beliefs of the prophetic groups that instigated the Jehu revolt. Thus, whether Jehu's personal aims were primarily religious or not, he found himself supported by two respected and powerful religious groups among the people of Israel.

Once he had arrived at Samaria, Jehu set about exterminating the worshipers of Baal in the capital. He invited one and all to a great festival of worship to be held in the temple of Baal which Ahab had erected. When the worshippers thronged the building, Jehu had the exits sealed and ordered his men to fall on the crowd with swords. As a result of this massacre, the narrator tells us, "Jehu wiped out Baal from Israel."

How may we assess the significance and effect of the Jehu revolt? Certainly it has considerable religious significance, in that Jehu found his most solid backing among the prophetic and Rechabite groups. The military element also played a strong part, for Jehu himself was a high general, and his earliest allies, in addition to Elisha's band, were the soldiers who followed him.

Jehu must also have profited from the resentment that had built up against new social and economic patterns in Israel. As we have seen, the early Israelite farmers were small freeholders who held their plots of land as a perpetual and inalienable gift from Yahweh. In the ninth century, however, as seen in Ahab's seizure of Naboth's vineyard, the small farmers were being deprived of their land, and large estates began to be amassed by the wealthy. Whether the land was taken as collateral for loans during times of drought or simply seized, as in the Naboth affair, the result was the same, and the populace must have joined with the prophets in protesting this development.

It is difficult to ascertain whether Jehu himself deeply believed in the ancient tenets of Israel's faith, as did the prophets, and whether he was indignant as they were over the oppressive tactics of the ruling house and aristocracy. It may be that his personal ambitions for power just happened to coincide with the aims of more religiously oriented groups.

One thing is certain: later prophetic opinion turned against Jehu and condemned him for the bloodbath generated by his revolt (Hosea 1:4–5; cf. II Kings 10:28–31). And we might add that even from a more purely political and military point of view his assassination of Jezebel, and of the king and princes of Judah as well, brought a bitter aftermath for Israel, for the nation now had to face her enemies alone. No longer protected by the treaties with Phoenicia and Judah, Israel suffered serious territorial losses to the Syrians throughout the ninth century. By the end of the twenty-eight year reign of Jehu, all of Israel's possessions in Transjordan were lost, putting the Syrians within an easy march of Israel's capital. It was only the increasing might of Assyria that saved Israel, for Assyria attacked the Arameans and thus furnished Israel some relief. Nevertheless, a price had to be paid for this safety: the famous Black Obelisk of the Assyrian king Shalmaneser III shows Jehu bowing down as he offers ransom to preserve his kingdom.[13]

In the last analysis, then, the Jehu revolt was certainly successful in the punitive sense, and this was the prophetic aim. The dynasty of Ahab, including all of his supporters, was exterminated. Judging from attacks against Baal worship by later prophets, we think Baalism itself was not exterminated. The external affairs of Israel were in much worse condition at the end of Jehu's reign than before. The relatively minor force of the Syrians had been replaced by the vast threat of the Assyrian Empire, and the actual extinction of Israel as a nation was now for the first time a possibility. We shall see how that terrible possibility became a reality in the next century.

Some Questions for Discussion: What does Elisha tells his emissary to say to Jehu? Reread I Kings 21:21–24 and compare those verses with II Kings 9:6–10. Why do you think the narrator has the emissary repeat the verses from I Kings 21?

From what you already know about the prophets, why do you think the servants of Jehu referred to Elisha's emissary as a "mad fellow"? How do the servants react when Jehu tells them what the emissary said? Why were you, or weren't you, surprised by their hasty action?

How does the narrator build suspense in II Kings 9:17–22? Compare Jehu's slaying of Joram, and the description of actions leading to the actual death, with other accounts of slayings, for example, that of Jezebel in II Kings 9:30–33. How do the accounts differ?

What do Jezebel's actions in verse 30 reveal about her character? If a woman is called a Jezebel, what is implied about her? What is the lexical definition of Jezebel?

Why does Jehu write a second letter to the men of Samaria? What does he demand? To whom does Jehu attribute the slaughter of the king's sons? Why does he slay the kinsmen of

Ahaziah? What is the significance of Jehu's meeting with Jehonadab? How does Jehu trick the prophets and priests of Baal? Why does he slay them?

Suggested Activities: Compare Jehu with Joshua, Deborah, and Jephthah. What characteristics do they have in common? How do they differ? Which of the four leaders do you admire the most? the least? Why?

You are a writer for a weekly news magazine. Summarize Jehu's activities in II Kings 9:17–37 and 10:1–27. Which details will you include? Why? Why did you leave some out?

After you have written your summary, give it to someone who is not familiar with Jehu. How does your reader react to Jehu? How has your account influenced your readers' reactions?

CHAPTER 11

The Prophetic Movement

The prophetic movement is one of the most remarkable phenomena in Israel's history, and it is given extensive treatment in the Old Testament. The oracles of early prophets like Samuel, Elijah, and Elisha were preserved only to a very limited degree within the context of historical narratives. Beginning in the middle of the eighth century B.C. and continuing for the next three hundred years, however, written collections were made which preserved many of the oracles of the leading prophetic spokesmen of this later period.

Scholars are still debating how the sayings of these prophets came to be set down in writing. Some scholars maintain that the prophetic books were not written until the Exile in the sixth century. They believe that the sayings of the eighth and seventh century prophets were kept in oral form for a long period by later generations of disciples before finally being written down. This is an extreme view, but it is useful as a corrective against the popularly held misconception that the prophets delivered their messages in written form or that they were speaking from a "prepared text." The prophets reached their fellow Israelites almost exclusively through the spoken word. Of course it is possible that on occasion a prophet would write down some of the oracles he had delivered (for example, Isaiah 8:16ff); but, with the possible exception of Ezekiel, the prophets do not seem to have been responsible for the writing or the final editing of their books.

Before we study Amos, the first prophet whose oracles were

collected and preserved in writing, it is necessary to give a brief description of the nature of Israelite prophecy. The prophetic literature is much more approachable if one has some understanding of the conceptual background out of which the prophets were operating. Archeology has uncovered texts that show us that prophecy did not originate within Israelite culture. Several texts from the Mesopotamian city of Mari (about 1700 B.C.) describe prophets appearing before governors and princes with messages from their god demanding that certain actions be taken. Another text tells of a youth's epileptic seizure in the Canaanite city of Byblos (about 1060 B.C.) being interpreted as an oracle from the local deity. Israelite prophecy—more than other Near Eastern prophecies—was deeply concerned with the ethical issues in the social and political problems of the nation.

Earlier scholarship had gone so far as to credit the prophets with being the true founders of Old Testament religion. Through their ethical teachings and their doctrine of monotheism, it was maintained, Israel had been able to transcend her primitive origins and develop one of the great religions of the world. But more recent scholars are becoming increasingly convinced that the norms of Israelite faith upon which the prophets are drawing were formulated at an earlier period—during the time from Moses to Samuel. Thus, without detracting from their uniqueness, the Israelite prophets are not to be understood as the great religious innovators of the Old Testament. They stand much more in that conservative tradition that tried to maintain the Mosaic heritage in the face of the threat of Israel's being totally assimilated into Canaanite culture during the period of the monarchy.

Since the monarchy itself was one of the greatest factors contributing to the assimilation process, it is not surprising that we find the prophets in constant controversy with the kings (as we saw in the two preceding sections). Israel had been able to keep her traditions nearly intact until the advent of kingship. But when David conquered the Canaanite enclaves in the land and incorporated them into his kingdom, easy access between the two cultures was made possible. One of these Canaanite enclaves was

Jerusalem, where the religious traditions of the past were reformulated into a new covenant tradition which, in good Canaanite fashion, gave divine sanction to the monarchy's establishing permanent political control over a people who, until very recently, had had no other king but Yahweh (see page 21). One further inevitable result of the empire of David and Solomon was that as Israel became increasingly wealthy, the power gradually shifted away from the Israelite peasant, who had lived in the small villages in the hill country, toward the larger cities that were still basically Canaanite in their orientation and that were now becoming the commercial and administrative centers of the realm.

Prophecy arose as a conservative movement of protest against the changes that were radically affecting Israelite society; it was supported by the Israelite peasant, who felt threatened and disenfranchised by the forces of urbanization, assimilation, and centralization that had been set loose by the coming of the monarchy. The goal of prophecy was a return to the Mosaic and Tribal League ways of the earlier period, when no king save Yahweh ruled as absolute lord and when the military leader remained subservient to both the divine and the popular will as it was expressed in the central place of worship.

The prophets felt empowered to intervene in the affairs of state because they regarded themselves as *messengers* who had been commissioned by Yahweh to communicate his will to his people. There are other literary forms in the prophetic books, but by far the most common is the speech form of the messenger which begins "Thus says the Lord: . . ." Although letters are quite often used for diplomatic correspondence in the ancient Near East, a major means of communication was the spoken word, which was entrusted to the messenger and which was to be repeated *verbatim* to the recipient. Such a message was spoken in a fixed, traditional form as is indicated by these two passages:

And Jacob sent messengers before him to Esau his brother in the land of Seir, the country of Edom, instructing them, "Thus you shall say to my lord Esau: Thus says your servant Jacob, 'I have sojourned with Laban, and stayed until now; and I have oxen, asses, flocks, menservants, and maidservants; and I have sent to

tell my lord, in order that I may find favor in your sight.' "
(Genesis 32:3–5)

"And you shall say to Pharaoh, 'Thus says the Lord, Israel is my
first-born son, and I say to you, "Let my son go that he may serve
me"; if you refuse to let him go, behold, I will slay your first-born
son.' " (Exodus 4:22–23)

Note that there are three parts: (a) the messenger is told to
whom the message is addressed; (b) the message is introduced
by "Thus says . . . ," indicating the identity of the sender; and
(c) the content of the message is given, with the sender speaking
in the first person, addressing the recipient in the second person.
The message was repeated verbatim to the recipient, preserving
the first person-second person distinction, as we see in Exodus 10:3.

So Moses and Aaron went into Pharaoh, and said to him, "Thus
says the Lord, the God of the Hebrews, 'How long will you refuse
to humble yourself before me? Let my people go that they may
serve me. . . .' "

The same pattern carried over into prophecy:

The word of the Lord came to me, saying, "Go and proclaim in
the hearing of Jerusalem; Thus says the Lord, 'I remember the
devotion of your youth. . . .' " (Jeremiah 2:1–2)

This is not only important from the literary point of view; it
also gives us some insight into the nature of prophecy. The
prophets have been variously portrayed as teachers, reformers,
political commentators, religious leaders, and social revolution-
aries. But they understood themselves as messengers—men who
had been called to bridge the gap between God and man, having
been entrusted with words that they had to speak regardless of
the public response or the personal consequences. Preserving the
suzerain-vassal relationship presupposed in the Mosaic covenant
(see pages 14–16), the prophets saw themselves as servants who
had been sent from the court of the great king to accost the insub-
ordinate vassal with warnings, demands, threats, and pronounce-

ments of doom—just as envoys would be sent regularly by the Hittite or Egyptian kings with similar demands to vassals within their empires.

What was Yahweh's court, and how did the prophet conceive himself as being part of it? We see from passages such as I Kings 22:19ff and Isaiah 6—to note the two most obvious examples— that the prophet, having envisioned Yahweh deliberating with his heavenly host, felt compelled to make known and bring about on earth the divine decision which he had heard pronounced in the heavens. As did any human king, Yahweh was thought to have a court—the angelic host (for example, Job 1). In this setting, Yahweh ruled over his subjects. He would reach decisions regarding all the important matters pertaining to Israel, such as her foreign policy, domestic rule, and social conduct. Through their call, the prophets felt "tuned in" on these divine proceedings and commissioned to report, and to help bring about, that which had been determined in the divine council.

The divine council is an important concept that Israel borrowed from her ancient Near Eastern environment in order to affirm Yahweh as the supreme king. Although the imagery was originally polytheistic, Israel adapted it to express Yahweh's absolute uniqueness and supremacy over all creation. The nations worship other gods, Israel maintained, only because these deities are subservient members in the divine council whom Yahweh has appointed as his vice-regents to rule in his behalf (Deuteronomy 32:8–9)[1]—just as a king would name various princes in his court to serve as governors of the outlying districts in his kingdom. Psalm 82 claims that these patron deities, who have no existence apart from the extent to which they fulfill God's will, have indeed corrupted the earth by failing to enforce God's plan for social justice among the nations over which they had been placed. Therefore, the psalm asserts, the gods will be replaced by Yahweh's direct, personal rule over all the nations of the world. The king has banished his worthless governors. But there are other members in a royal court besides district administrators; there is an entire entourage of advisers and servants. In fact, the larger the court, the greater the prestige and power of the king. Thus the divine council concept was also used by Israel to ascribe greater majesty to its god.

The background of the divine council is confusing to students who wonder how it can be reconciled with the biblical belief in one god.[2] This motif occurs quite frequently in the Old Testament, and some of the most important of these passages are in the prophetic literature.[3] It is certainly legitimate to raise the question—as some students undoubtedly will do—concerning how the prophets apprehended the divine word, but no final answer can be given. We are coming close to the issue of divine inspiration, the exact solution to which no two scholars or religious groups would agree upon. But since this question will probably be brought up in the classroom, we feel that a brief and very tentative discussion might be helpful.

Were the prophets perceptive, rational men who used the divine council vision and the "Thus says Yahweh" formula resulting from these visions as devices for enhancing the authority of their oracles? Was this literary style of the messenger demanded by long-standing custom, so that any man who felt prompted to speak out on a certain issue would automatically begin with "Thus says Yahweh" in order to assure a proper understanding and reception of his message? There is a great temptation to interpret the prophets as rational men who felt strongly about certain political, social, and religious issues, but who, because of the age in which they lived, phrased their messages as if they were in direct communication with God himself. On the other hand, one could say that just as God walked and spoke with Abraham, so also he appeared directly to the prophets, and the prophets are simply recording the words they heard and the visions they saw in a direct experience of God.

Our interpretation lies somewhere between these two positions. It is difficult to generalize about all the prophets, because each one undoubtedly had a unique experience in apprehending the divine word. Amos saw a basket of summer fruit and realized that the end was fast hastening upon Israel (Amos 8:1ff). Jeremiah perceived that Israel had proven to be a worthless vessel and was about to be smashed as he observed a potter working his clay (Jeremiah 18–19). Isaiah (Isaiah 6) and Ezekiel (Ezekiel 1–3) were overwhelmed by visions of the transcendent, holy God: one in the precincts of the Jerusalem Temple, the other on the banks of a river as he was in Babylonian captivity.

Despite this great variety, an ecstatic experience seems to have been shared by nearly all of the prophets. Of course "ecstasy" can cover a wide range of psychological experience: from deep mental absorption and concentration to psychic unconsciousness. Sometimes this experience can be visual, sometimes auditory, and sometimes it can be both.[4] In a society where it was thought that God presided over his host in the heavens, it is not surprising that the ecstatic experiences were portrayed as visions of the divine council. Earlier scholars had noted that ecstasy was a particularly common phenomenon during the time of Samuel, when prophecy was just beginning in Israel. They correctly pointed out that ecstasy was an ordinary feature of other pagan religions, and then went on to conclude that as Israelite prophecy evolved out of its pagan environment, the ecstatic element was gradually replaced by higher religious and ethical teaching—as if there were some inherent contradiction between ecstasy and "true" (that is, rational) religion. But this generalization does not hold true for the Old Testament. Late prophetic figures like Ezekiel demonstrate that ecstasy was an important element throughout Israelite prophecy.

There were surely many sensitive individuals in Israel who were aware of the social deterioration and of the need for change. But apparently it was felt necessary to be confronted by the living God through an ecstatic experience before one could consider oneself called to be a prophet. Such a confrontation did not give the prophet specific knowledge of the far-distant future. Although certain passages from the prophets were reinterpreted by later generations as having been fulfilled in later times, the prophet is in no sense a crystal ball gazer. His concern was with the present and the realization of God's will in that moment.

Neither were the prophets glorified Walter Lippmanns with their eyes trained on the far-distant horizon, possessed with an uncanny sense of the effects that the movements of nations would soon bring down upon Israel. Amos, for example, could not have foreseen the swiftly approaching end of Israel by observing the growing strength of her enemies. Amos preached doom in a time of unprecedented peace and prosperity. He could not have known that Tiglath-pileser III would rule over Assyria within the decade, bringing about a renaissance of Assyrian power that would result in the destruction of North Israel.

How did Amos know that doom was coming? The answer to this question might tell us something about the nature of Israelite prophecy. Amos did not have his eye trained on some occult crystal ball; nor was he aware of the forces at work that would soon make Assyria the dominant power in the Near East. It seems much more likely that Amos worked out his message on the basis of the Mosaic covenant traditions that had been a part of Israel's heritage for almost five hundred years. At the heart of the Mosaic covenant is the demand for Israel to preserve justice in the land, accompanied by the threat of divine wrath if this demand is not realized. Thus Amos knew what God required; he also knew that Israel was not measuring up. He was not deluded by the peace and prosperity that surrounded him. He did not need to know that the Assyrians were coming in order to realize that doom was inevitable. Assured of his new calling by divine visions that confirmed his fears that judgment was coming, he went forth to prophesy this message in the name of Yahweh.

Amos (Amos 1:1–3:8; 5:18–27; 7)

The prophets had instigated and supported Jehu's purge of the house of Ahab in the hope that the influence of Canaanite culture would be reduced in Israel. It was a naïve hope, and the results were quite disastrous for Israel. Jehu was a weak, ineffective king. His purge had virtually wiped out the political leadership of the country, and he did not have the wherewithal to replace it. Consequently, Israel was unable to withstand the aggressive policies of her ancient enemy, the Syrians, who, under their new King Hazael, were intent on reopening the trade routes to the south which had long been blocked off by Israel. The rest of the ninth century witnessed a rapid decline in Israelite power, so that by 802 B.C. almost half of the land (the Transjordan and the area northwest of the Sea of Galilee) was under Syrian control.

A dramatic reversal in Israel's fortunes occurred at the end of the ninth century. The Assyrians had periodically crossed the Euphrates River in an attempt to incorporate new land into their empire. In 802 B.C., they swept as far south as Damascus, virtually annihilating the Syrian power. But before the Assyrians had the opportunity to move farther south, they were forced to withdraw their troops because of troubles which were developing in the northern part of their empire—troubles which diverted their attention from Syria and Palestine for the next sixty years.

With Syria demolished, Assyria preoccupied, and Egypt still too weak to venture northward, Israel and Judah were both granted the opportunity to regain the power which had been slipping away since the death of Solomon. Under their two great rulers, Jeroboam II of Israel (786–746 B.C.) and Uzziah of Judah (783–742 B.C.), the glorious age of David and Solomon was recreated. Edom, with its rich copper mines, was reconquered, and peace between Israel and Judah allowed the trade routes to run the entire length of the land once again. As in the days of David and Solomon, Israel became the commercial middleman of the Near East, and an unprecedented era of prosperity ensued.

But peace and prosperity were a mixed blessing for Israel. The wealth that had begun to pour into the land was by no means spread evenly among all the people. The main recipients, of course, were the large urban commercial centers. This led to an increased polarization between rich and poor, because the greatly augmented money supply caused a high-soaring inflation that further impoverished the poor. The effects seem to have been especially detrimental to the small Israelite peasant who fell under the power of the urban moneylenders after the first severe crop failure. The inflation caused exorbitant interest rates, and the peasant was quite often unable to get out from under his debt. To satisfy the claim, the peasant was often forced to sell his land and even to sell himself and his family into slavery. The ancient Mosaic injunctions prohibiting the charging of interest, the removal of a man from his land, and the permanent enslavement of any Israelite were no longer enforced in a society that had largely adapted itself to Canaanite norms.

Into this setting steps Amos, the champion of the poor. His background is quite obscure (Amos 1:1); it is very unusual that he is not more specifically identified by the naming of his father ("Amos son of ——"). If his father is unknown, this suggests either that Amos was illegitimate or, more likely, that he had separated himself from the rest of his family and clan. The Hebrew for "who was among the shepherds of Tekoa" denotes remaining for a specific time, again underlining the transitory character of Amos' stay in Tekoa.[5]

Amos was a migrant worker. In the summer dry season, when the flocks would have to do a good deal of moving around to find the sparse pasture land, he hired himself out as a shepherd. In the winter and spring, however, when abundant rainfall made it unnecessary for the flocks to journey from one place to another so that very few shepherds were needed, Amos would hire himself out as a migrant farm laborer. His job was pruning sycamore trees (Amos 7:14). Since the buds would first form in the southern part of the land, Amos would begin his work far south in Judah and gradually work his way through Israel. Such a job, being the lowest rung in Israelite society next to slavery, allowed him to observe and experience the plight of the poor throughout the land.

Although Amos is from Judah, the oracles that have been preserved are directed primarily against North Israel and are spoken at Bethel, which is the major cultic center of the north. Bethel was an ancient Hebrew shrine dating back to the patriarchal age (Genesis 28:10ff; 35:1ff). When the Northern Kingdom was founded after the death of Solomon, Jeroboam I, the first king of North Israel, established Bethel as one of the two major sanctuaries of the land so that the people would no longer make pilgrimages to Jerusalem and come under the influence of the Davidic monarchy in Judah (I Kings 12:25ff). We can see how successful this move was in the confrontation between Amos and Amaziah, the high priest of Bethel, in which the sanctuary is

defined by Amaziah in terms of serving the interests of the state
(Amos 7:10ff). Religion is no longer seen as finding and conforming to the will of Yahweh; rather, the will of Yahweh is identified
with preserving the security and well-being of his people. Yahweh
seems no longer to be understood as the god who is only condi-
tionally related to Israel, who stands against king and people with
covenant stipulations that must be fulfilled in order that security
and well-being be assured. Instead, he is seen as the cosmic
creator who has chosen Israel to be his people so that all the
world will know his glory and power through the dominion
which Israel attains among the nations.

The Israelites felt that they were fulfilling their mission through
the prestigious reign of Jeroboam II. Israel's religious response
was one of thanksgiving through cultic ritual rather than a reformation of society. "Religion" was thriving in the midst of a com-
fortably prosperous nation. Amos came to Bethel with the
disquieting news that God had turned against his people because
the real requirements of Yahwistic religion were not being met.

Amos seems to have reached this conclusion in a series of
visions, three of which are described in Amos 7:1–9.[6] They reflect
a growing premonition of the doom that is coming upon Israel,
and they are apparently interpreted by Amos as his call to
become a prophet (Amos 7:15). The first vision is concerned with
a locust plague about to hit the land. The incident took place in
the springtime, just after the winter harvest had been completed.
If we are interpreting the text correctly, the entire winter harvest
was given over as tax for use by the royal court. It is the lesser
of the two harvests in Palestine, but still a good sign of the
oppressive conditions under which the Israelite peasants suffered
at the hands of the monarchy. There is a question to be answered
in interpreting these verses: Is this a real plague that hit Israel?
Verse 2 indicates that the locusts had devastated the land. On the
other hand, verse 3 indicates that Amos is successful in his entreaty that Yahweh not bring the plague upon Israel. It seems
more likely that the entire event is a visionary experience: Amos
envisioned a desolate land having been consumed by locusts, but
he is assured by Yahweh that such a plague will not come to

pass. Or it is possible that Amos saw some locusts at work right after the spring planting and envisioned this as an impending sign of God's wrath against Israel and that only divine mercy and patience were keeping such a plague from being realized.

The second vision, the severe summer drought, is almost exactly in the same literary form as the first: "Thus the Lord God showed me: behold . . ." (description of the vision); Amos' response: "O Lord God, cease . . . . He is so small!" Yahweh's decision to hold back the plague: " 'This also shall not be,' said the Lord God." Such a stereotyped style would suggest that the visions were written down after they had all taken place, and Amos had had the chance to think about them and work them into the same literary form.

It is noteworthy that Amos uses mythological language to describe the drought. In Near Eastern mythology, fire was a traditional weapon in the divine arsenal.[7] It is one aspect of God's holiness, usually associated with the lightning bolt in Near Eastern mythology, but here it is related to the consuming rays of the sun. So severe was the drought in Amos' vision that it was devouring not only Israel but also the "great deep." Although he seems to be referring to the drying up of the underwater streams, the "deep" is actually the chaos enemy in several Near Eastern creation stories.[8] Amos seems to be using this mythological language to indicate that Israel is now one of God's enemies just as much as the forces of chaos. In fact, because of the rapid deterioration of her society, Israel now is one of these forces of chaos undermining the divine order.

The first two plagues were turned back through Amos' intercession. Why did Amos dare to intervene? Perhaps because these first two plagues would have most severely affected the very group that he cared most deeply about—the impoverished Israelite peasant. The locusts would have destroyed the summer crop, on which the peasant depended for his livelihood. The drought would have further increased the plight of the farmer. If a judgment on the land were to come, it should fall on the whole land—especially upon those groups which were most guilty in Amos' eyes.

The third vision describes this judgment. Notice that the literary sequence of the first two visions is broken. As in 8:1–3, Amos is shown an object and then Yahweh asks him what he sees. Immediately after Amos answers, Yahweh interprets the meaning of the vision in terms of the coming judgment on Israel. Amos is not given the opportunity to intercede; the judgment can no longer be turned back. The vision that Amos sees is of Yahweh assaying the straightness of a wall with a plumb line. The implication is that the wall (a figure for the house of Israel) is warped beyond repair and is about to be destroyed.

"I will never again pass by them" in verse 8 is somewhat enigmatic, but the imagery seems to refer to Yahweh, enshrined in the Ark, proceeding before his people. The Ark was the symbol of God's presence as he went before his people to lead them to their land and to give them victory over their enemies.[9] Amos maintains that Yahweh will never do this again; he will, in fact, march against his own people, just as he had earlier led them against the Canaanites. Israel's justification for conquering the land under Joshua was that the Canaanites had been unable to establish a just society. Now Amos is using this same rationalization against Israel, saying that God will drive her off the land because she also has failed to maintain a just society. Yahweh's sword, which earlier had been drawn against the Canaanites (Joshua 5:13–15), is now to be directed against Israel—especially against the monarchy, which was most responsible for creating the breach in Israelite society, and against the places of worship, where organized religion, by failing to maintain the Mosaic norms, had done nothing to heal the rift.

It is possible that 7:10ff was placed at this point by a later editor because of the references in verses 9 and 11 to Jeroboam II. But it also seems quite likely that Amaziah, the high priest of Bethel, would have challenged Amos when he gave an oracle which threatened the life of the king. We have no way of knowing the sequence of events, or how much of what is recorded in the Book of Amos was spoken by the prophet during this confrontation at Bethel. It should be noted that the message that Amaziah sends to Jeroboam (Amos 7:11) contains quotes from 5:27 and

7:9. We would suggest that the passages from Amos which we are studying are most reasonable if they are interpreted as hinging upon the abrasive meeting between Amos and Amaziah which is described in 7:10ff.

Amaziah sends a message to Jeroboam II, giving a synopsis of the seditious statements that Amos had made against the king and his kingdom. He prefaces the quote by calling Amos a "conspirator" and saying that "the land is not able to bear all his words." In the Near East, the spoken word was thought to have an inherent power that would help to bring about that which had been spoken. The greater the power of the speaker, the more capable were his words of becoming reality. Of course the most feared and respected words were those of the men of God, who claimed to be delivering words from the deity. And so with Amos. It was bad enough when a man would pronounce ill upon his fellow men; but when this denunciation was spoken as the word of God, the occasion was made all the more threatening.

Amaziah tells Amos to return to his homeland in Judah, where what he had to say regarding Israel would be more favorably received. There must have been a deep-seated animosity between North Israel and Judah that all the foreign diplomacy of Jeroboam II and Uzziah had not been able to overcome. Amos is being cast in the role of an enemy agent who has been sent from the south to foment trouble. He is being told to go back home where he belongs. Notice Amaziah's conception of prophecy: Amos should earn his living by going to a place where his message would be popular. Either Amaziah is showing his scorn for the prophets, who had sold out by becoming subservient supporters of the interests of the state, or more likely, he genuinely believes that a man of God should not be supported at public expense in the sanctuaries of the land unless his oracles give support and encouragement to the people of God. This attitude seems to indicate what has happened to prophecy since the purge of Jehu almost a century earlier. The prophets must have concluded that Yahwism had been victorious over Canaanite influence (and Baal worship) and thus they must have become loyal and uncritical supporters of the interests of the state. The only prophet between

Elisha and Amos mentioned by the Bible is Jonah ben-Amittai, who reinforced Jeroboam II's ambitions to reconquer Syria and Palestine with oracles indicating divine approval (II Kings 14:23–27).

Amos had already described the visions that he had had in order to authenticate his claim to speak as one of God's prophets. He now develops this point further in response to Amaziah's challenge. His point in 7:14f is that he does not need to rely on giving prophetic oracles to earn a living; he has other occupations that sustain him. The Revised Standard Version translation of verse 14 ("I *am* no prophet . . .") seems to indicate that Amos is denying that he is a prophet, implying that the office of prophecy has been so sullied by selling out that he is deliberately disassociating himself from this group. This is one commonly held interpretation. But there is no sure way of distinguishing "I *am* no prophet" from "I *was* no prophet" in Hebrew, so we would prefer to follow the Jewish Publication Society translation "I was no prophet. . . ." Amos is not disassociating himself from the office of prophecy: he is maintaining that he had not always been a prophet since his youth, not having grown up in a prophetic guild ("son of a prophet" means a member of a prophetic guild) at one of the sanctuaries. These, he is implying, are the popular prophets who enter the prophetic guild just as one would choose to enter any other profession. Amos is claiming that his oracles should be taken more seriously than those of the lifelong professionals because, unlike them, he had not become a prophet through his own choice but rather through a divine call which compelled him to speak harsh things in God's name. He concludes by pronouncing a horrible judgment against the house of Amaziah because the high priest has tried to use his office to undermine what Amos felt to be a genuine message from God.

Looking at chapter 7 as a whole, we see the portrait of a man who is struggling with the compulsion to prophesy. The development of the three visions shows us Amos' desperate attempts to ward off his forebodings that Israel was doomed. He did not want the judgment to be realized; he did not want to be the instrument through whom the dread news would be made known.

But he was finally overwhelmed; the forebodings became a terrible certainty, and he was compelled to turn away from the harsh pastoral life to one that was perhaps even more severe. This is a rather consistent theme in the Bible: man's unwillingness to speak and act being overcome by a compulsion that he can only interpret as being divine constraint.

The overwhelming sense of the necessity to prophesy once a person feels that he has been addressed by God is beautifully illustrated in 3:3–8, where Amos likens it to a cause and effect relationship. In a series of telling illustrations, most of which refer to the sign which precedes and announces a calamitous event, the prophet shows that when the word of Yahweh is spoken in the divine council, two things must happen: (a) the prophet to whom that word has been revealed must speak it to those to whom it is addressed, and (b) that word will inevitably come to pass. Verse 3 refers to a meeting of two parties in the desert wilderness; Amos is saying that they would never meet there had they not made an agreement. It is most likely that he is referring to the covenant made between Yahweh and Israel in the wilderness at Sinai—a covenant which, although it was ultimately intended for the salvation of the world, could also, Amos maintains, have fateful implications for a recalcitrant Israel. A lion roaring just as he is about to spring upon his cornered prey, a cub lion growling over the catch as he gnaws on it, the trapped bird, the springing snare, the blowing trumpet—all of these images are used with great effectiveness to catch the sense of doom that is hanging over Israel. The lion is about to spring; Israel cannot but be destroyed. Yahweh has addressed his prophet; Amos must speak out.

We have gone into great detail on the visions that led to Amos' prophetic ministry and on the manner in which he defined and defended this calling in order to convey some feeling of the nature of the man and of his understanding of the prophetic office. What was it he said which aroused such antipathy and which necessitated such a forceful defense? We will examine two examples of Amos' oracles, 1:1–3:2 and 5:18–27. Amos 1:1, the essence of which has already been discussed, is a formula which is intended to introduce the entire book. Verse 2 is likewise an editorial introduction, showing perhaps that the book was ultimately edited in Jerusalem. There is no question that chapters 1–2 were delivered in North Israel, so Yahweh's speaking forth from Jerusalem would be an irrelevant introduction for Amos to have used. The address really begins with verse 3, where we find a series of indictments and judgments against Israel's neighbors that culminates with the announcement that Israel herself will receive the most severe judgment of all.

Notice that each oracle begins with a stereotyped formula: Thus says the Lord: "For three transgressions of X, and for four, I will not revoke the punishment." (Amos had not tallied seven offenses against each of the nations. He is expressing himself in poetry, and "number parallelism," in which the second cola both balances and heightens the effect of the first cola by going one number higher, is a favorite literary device in ancient Near Eastern poetry.)[10] In the great majority of cases, this introductory formula is followed by a one-line (bicola) indictment introduced by "because" and a three-line sentence of judgment introduced by "so." This structure is quite precisely worked out, and the fact that it is not found in the oracles against Tyre, Edom, and Judah would probably indicate that our present text in these three cases does not exactly reproduce what Amos said. Some scholars have suggested that these three oracles are secondary additions by later editors who were not aware of the precision in the strophic structure with which they were tampering. This theory seems plausible in regard to the Judah oracle, in which the tone and language are quite different from the others. But it seems far more likely that the oracles against Tyre and Edom are genuine and that we are dealing with occasional insertions and accidental scribal omissions in the text rather than with original editorial additions.

In general, the nations are indicted for crimes they have commited against Israel. The Syrians (Damascus) are condemned for executing prisoners by running threshing sledges over them. The Philistines (Gaza) are accused of engaging in slave trade—not of selling prisoners of war, which was an accepted practice, but of raiding villages (most likely in Judah) and carrying their entire populations off to be sold into slavery.[11]

As we have noted, the oracles against Tyre and Edom are no longer perfectly clear. The indictment of the Phoenicians (Tyre) seems to have been confused with the preceding one, for slave trading with the Edomites is again the issue. The Phoenicians' not remembering the "covenant of brotherhood" could be a reference to the treaty which was made between Solomon and Hiram of Tyre two hundred years earlier (I Kings 9:10–14). The charge against Edom has been expanded beyond its original one-bicola structure, perhaps because of the atrocities which were committed by the Edomites against the Jews when Jerusalem was destroyed in 587 B.C. (see also Obadiah 10–14). However, the accusation is not specific enough to determine what event Amos was originally referring to. Like the Syrians, the Ammonites are also condemned for savage acts against Israelites living in the region of Gilead.

Amos begins a new task in his oracle against the Moabites. The indictments in chapter 1 had described atrocities which Israel had suffered at the hands of her neighbors. But Moab is condemned for a crime against the king of Edom—apparently the desecration of the royal tomb, which was thought to dishonor and disturb the spirit of the dead.[12] Israel and Moab had had a long and bloody coexistence; instances of barbarous actions wrought by Moab against Israel would not have been lacking. By condemning Moab for crimes against Edom, Amos is emphasizing Yahweh's universal sovereignty. Israel had of course been given a specific body of law through Moses at Sinai. But Amos seems to be implying that there is an unwritten universal law to which Yahweh holds all people accountable. Amos is deliberately moving beyond the role of the nationalistic prophet who shakes his fist at the enemies and cries, "Our god is going to punish you for what you have done to us."

Moving from northeast (Damascus) to southwest (Gaza) to northwest (Tyre) to southeast (Edom) and on to the Transjordan (Ammon and Moab), Amos has raked Israel's neighbors with a devastating barrage of divine judgment. Why has he done this? If he is speaking at Bethel, those upon whom the condemnation has been pronounced are certainly not there to hear about it. It seems most likely that although Amos was speaking the oracles against foreign nations, the real audience he had in mind was Israel. He was an unknown in the north; he was playing the role of the popular, nationalistic "prophet" to gain a hearing for the one point he had come to make: judgment was to fall on Israel. Amos' delivering these oracles against enemy nations would have been understood and accepted by the people of Israel. It was customary to hire a man of God whose words were especially filled with power to bring doom upon one's enemies (Numbers 22–24). The spoken word, as we have remarked, did not have to be heard by its recipients to bring into reality that which had been proclaimed. The power lies within the word to fulfill itself—especially since it is Yahweh's word. Thus Amos would have been regarded as a man of God who was stepping forward at Bethel in order to enhance the glory of Yahweh and Israel by weakening the common enemies with Yahweh's terrible wrath. Using the solemn indictment-sentence language of the lawcourt, Amos claims to be relaying the judgment which had been spoken against the nations in the divine council: Yahweh has declared holy war. His holy fire will soon consume the enemies of his people.

In order for his message to be most telling, it is quite likely that Amos chose one of the large festival days. In 5:18ff, the festival is called "the day of Yahweh." Although the meaning of this term and the nature of this festivial are very problematical and still the subject of widespread disagreement among scholars, it seems to us that the major theme of the festival was the celebration of Yahweh's appearance to rule over creation. He became king of the world by subduing all of the cosmic and historical forces that threatened to undermine its right ordering. Included among those who threatened Yahweh's kingship were the enemies of Israel, who must be weakened and held in check if Yahweh's rule over the world was to be realized through his people. The major purpose of this festival was the assertion of Yahweh's universal sovereignty. In the popular understanding, however, such a celebration was very nationalistic, because it was equated with expanding Israel's power and prestige, since Yahweh was now thought to be so closely tied to his people. Thus this "day of Yahweh," as it was traditionally celebrated, was characterized by rejoicing and the anticipation that the blessings which had been brought upon Israel through the festival would be even more fully realized in the coming year.

There is no doubt that 2:6ff was completely unanticipated by the people at Bethel:

> "For three transgressions of *Israel,* and for four, I will not revoke the punishment."

Jaws must have dropped. Amos is saying that the realization of the events which are being celebrated in the festival is going to be much different than anticipated. Yahweh's wrath is going to be directed especially against Israel because she has neglected the Mosaic covenant stipulations which demand a just society. In rapid-fire succession, the prophet gives five dramatic images of the social abuses that are running rampant through the land: the needy sold for a pair of shoes (in complete violation of the Mosaic principle that human life cannot be measured in economic terms);[13] the head of the poor being trampled into the dust; father and son taking sexual advantage of servant girls who are regarded as pieces of property; worshipers seeking dream visions of God by spending the night at shrines in garments which should have been returned to debtors at sundown (see also Exodus 22:25–27); and the using of wine, which had been secured through misuse of the law's power, in worship services.

The stern indictment language of the lawcourt (Amos 2:6–8) is replaced by the pleading, and yet ominous, language of the suzerain addressing his rebellious vassal (2:9ff). Israel is reminded of the gracious acts through which she had been established as a nation.[14] She had been delivered from injustice in Egypt, but she had not prevented injustice from flourishing in her own land. Therefore, Amos proclaims, Yahweh has declared holy war against his own people. Israel will perish.

The oracle against Israel ends with 2:16. A new passage begins with 3:3. Thus it is a problem to know how 3:1–2 fits in. It is possible that this is a completely independent saying of Amos which was inserted by the editor at this point. On the other hand, we would like to raise the possibility that 3:1–2 is related to the preceding oracle against Israel. As pointed out in the introduction to prophecy, the prophets by and large did not write their oracles prior to delivery; they were delivered orally before groups of people. Prophets might come before the crowds with a prepared oracle, but quite often the direction the speech would take depended upon the response of the audience. Questions might be raised; challenges or threats might be hurled at the spokesman. Generally the prophetic books do not preserve the crowd's reaction. We can only guess at the questions raised by the audience, which would elicit an on-the-spot further development of the oracle by the prophet. It is tempting to suggest that such a response was made by the stunned Israelites after Amos had finished his oracle in chapter 2. The crowd had just been told that Yahweh had turned against Israel and that destruction was imminent. The natural response would be: "But we are Yahweh's people. He has chosen us above all the peoples of the world. Therefore, he loves us and would never turn against us." Amos' reply is that Israel's election was indeed a special privilege, but it also involved special responsibilities. Israel had been given much more, and from her much more was expected.

In 5:18ff, Amos continues to develop the theme that the day of Yahweh will bring doom upon the Israelites rather than the rejoicing which they had anticipated in their festivals. This fate is inescapable: one can flee the lion, but a bear will overtake him; one can seek refuge in his home, but there the serpent waits. These festivals and sacrificial rituals are repugnant to Yahweh, Amos maintains, because they create a false sense of security and well-being which undercuts the motivation for maintaining justice in society. So we are left with the irony of religious institutions and celebrations that reinforced rather than corrected the injustice which prevailed. According to Amos, the essence of biblical religion is social justice rather than sacrificial ritual. Not through cultic activity but through establishing and maintaining a just society is man related to Yahweh, the God of Israel. This radical understanding of religion—a unique contribution of Israelite faith—had been undermined by the gradual assimilation of Canaanite culture.

In trying to sustain his polemic against sacrifices, Amos turns to the Israelite religion of an earlier period. During the Mosaic era, as the people wandered through the desert wilderness on their way from Egypt to Cannan, there was no sacrificial system in Israel. Whether this assertion is historically accurate or not is beside the point. Amos regards the wilderness period as the ideal time, when Israel truly knew who Yahweh was and what he demanded. Suddenly the sure knowledge strikes Amos of how Israel's doom is to be realized. Israel will return to the wilderness. The text of verse 26 is quite corrupt (the reference to Sakkuth and Kaiwan, Assyrian astral deities, is probably the result of later scribes misinterpreting the text), but the general sense is that Israel is to be removed from the land—not back to Egypt, from whence she came, but to the region "beyond Damascus."

There is no certain answer as to whether Amos had any hope for Israel's future. Was the exile beyond Damascus supposed to be a purifying experience so that the relationship between Yahweh and Israel could be restored? Perhaps. There is some small indication in 5:15 that Amos thought Yahweh might forgive the remnant which survived the judgment (9:11–15, the other passage of hope, is most likely the work of a scribe during the exilic period or later). But it seems to us that the evidence is too slight to build a case on. Amos appears to have held little or no hope for Israel's future. He knew well that the Mosaic covenant presupposed a conditional relationship with the covenant demands. If we are correct, then, the exile was not going to lead to a new beginning; it was the end of Israel as the people of God.

"Then the Lord said to me, 'The end has come upon my people Israel; I will never again pass by them.'" (8:2)

Some Questions for Discussion: What is Amos' everyday occupation? Where does that occupation place him on the social scale in Israel? How might that profession have helped him get a better view of Israelite life?

The messages of Amos are filled with figurative language. Find examples of metaphor, simile, and personification in chapters 2 and 5 and explain how this use of figurative language adds to, or detracts from, the messages.

If God wished to bring his message to Judah and Israel, why does Amos first allude to punishments meted out to other nations? Each transgression enumerated in chapters 1 and 2 begins identically, "for three transgressions . . . and for four," and continues "I will send a fire . . . it shall devour." What rhetorical effect is achieved by this repetition? Why do you think the speaker first says "three" and then "four"? Is he undecided? Do you think he is trying to create some special effect? Explain your answer.

Why do you think the speaker mentions the Amorites (2:8) and the Exodus (2:8; 3:1), when they seem to have little to do with the charges being lodged? What is the significance of "family and families" in 3:1?

Sentence 3:2 begins a series of theoretical questions, all of which are structured alike. What is achieved by this repetitive structuring? These questions have no apparent connection with God's warning—can you determine the relationship? What do the questions mean? As a consequence of their "special status" (3:1, 2), what corresponding obligations did all of Israel assume? To what extent are the metaphoric references to a lion and a bird (3:4, 5) effective?

Explain the paradox in 5:18. What visions are described in chapter 7? Explain the significance of these visions. What is the apparent contradiction in 7:1 and 2? Can you explain it?

What appears to be a repetitive sequence in 7:1–6 is broken in 7 and 8. Of what significance is this thematically? rhetorically? What is the central theme(s) of Amos? What relationship between man and God does Amos espouse?

Characterize God as portrayed in the opening chapters. Find passages in Amos that characterize God's powers. What are the nature and extent of his powers? Identify and discuss the various symobls used here. Do you note a symbolic patterning? Are they consistent with each other? To what extent are they appropriate? How effective are they?

The social-religious structure which Amos condemns may indeed have parallels throughout history, including contemporary society. Point out and discuss such parallels and their similarities. Analyze the prophecies made by Amos in 1:1–5. Is the imagery complementary to the content? Relate the imagery to the life experiences of Amos.

What is Amos' view of ritual? What explicit remarks does Amos make about the role of the prophet? What ideas about the role of the prophet are implicit in his statements and actions? How could anyone in Israel know he was hearing a *true* prophet? How can you know when *you* are hearing a true prophet?

Suggested Activities: Imagine that Amos were living in the United States today. Rewrite chapter 1, making it applicable to the situation he would find in this country.

In *You Shall Be As Gods,* Erich Fromm says that Amos was a "radical humanist," a person who "emphasizes the oneness of the human race, the capacity of man to develop his own powers. . . . " Consider this designation carefully and discuss or write about the extent to which you believe that this characterization is valid. Draw examples from the text.

It has been said that man continually ignores the lessons of history. Consider the truth of this statement and react as Amos might have. To what extent is this statement true today? Who and what are the contemporary Amoses trying to warn us about? How successful do you think they will be?

Can you think of any person in the present century who might be called a modern Amos? Discuss that person, indicating why he may be so designated.

Hosea (Hosea 1:1–8; 3:1–5; 5:15–6:6; 11:1–11 2:14–23)

Hosea, a younger contemporary of Amos, lived in North Israel and was an active prophet during the last twenty years of his nation's existence. He witnessed the rise of the mighty Assyrian empire following the accession of Tiglath-pileser III. He also witnessed the rapid deterioration of North Israel which, although unrivaled in power several decades earlier, responded to the Assyrian menace with a political extremism that led to four royal assassinations in fifteen years and created a state of total anarchy.

Hosea condemns the utter dissolution of Israelite society:

> . . . there is swearing, lying, killing,
>   stealing, and committing adultery;
> they break all bounds and murder
>   follows murder. (4:2)

Here he sounds very much like Amos, lashing out against flagrant abuses in the land. In fact, much of the Book of Hosea sounds like Amos, since both men addressed themselves to the problems in North Israelite society within a decade or two of each other. But there is a fundamental difference between the two prophets: whereas Amos described and denounced the social ills that plagued the country, Hosea probed beyond the symptoms of the disease to determine the cause. He saw more and more that external obedience to a specific agreement actually depended upon the quality and vitality of the internal relationship. Increasingly, he found that Israel's troubles were due to a fundamental breakdown in her relationship with God.

> There is no faithfulness or kindness,
>   and no knowledge of God in the land. . . . (4:1b)

How do we account for the difference between Amos and Hosea? The answer to this question hinges on 1:2–9 and 3:1–5, and scholars are by no means in agreement on the interpretation. Chapter 1, describing Hosea in the third person, tells of the prophet's being commanded by God to marry a harlot and have children by her. Hosea does this; three children are born of the union, each of whom receives a symbolic name bearing an ominous portent for the future of Israel.[15] In the third chapter, Hosea, writing in the first person, is told by Yahweh to go out and love an adulteress. He bought her, ostensibly from a slave market, and brought her to his home so that she could prepare herself to be his wife.

There are many problems involved in interpreting these two chapters. Is it a symbolic story, or did the prophet really marry a harlot? Are chapters 1 and 3 alternate descriptions of the same event, or are they to be interpreted sequentially? Is the woman mentioned in chapter 3 the same woman as in chapter 1? Was the woman already a harlot, or did the prophet make discoveries about her past after the marriage? There are seemingly an infinite number of theories on these two chapters, but, in general, there are three major interpretations.[16]

(1) One position maintains that the events described in chapters 1 and 3 did not really happen to Hosea. The prophet had a vision that he tells as a parable, because he saw a parallel with the relationship between Yahweh and Israel. If Hosea had really committed such acts, his oracles would never have been included in the Old Testament, since there was such a high view of marriage in Israel. These scholars also point out that the birth of the children would take at least three years. If one assumed that the prophet married the harlot to make a symbolically striking appeal to the nation, the long time span would cause the action to lose its dramatic impact. The prophet has compressed many years into one symbolic story to make his point. Note that even the children have symbolic names.

(2) Many scholars maintain that the best interpretation is the literal one. Gomer was a well-known harlot, and Hosea deliberately married her in the hope that such scandalous behavior would demonstrate Israel's constant violation of her covenant relationship with Yahweh. Such an interpretation stresses the syncretistic character of Israelite religion, wherein

it is assumed that Canaanite thought and fertility practices had deeply penetrated the fabric of Israelite life. We can point to the Jewish colony at Elephantine in Upper Egypt, which seems to have been composed mainly of refugees from the fall of North Israel. Yahweh is still worshiped there; but he also has a wife and son—both of whom were Canaanite deities.[17]

How does this assimilation of the Canaanite fertility cult relate to Hosea's marriage? Many scholars maintain that Hosea's dramatic action is an attempt to reinterpret the fertility imagery in terms that would be acceptable to normative Yahwistic religion. Certainly Yahweh is married, Hosea is saying through his action, but his consort is not one of the Canaanite fertility goddesses. He married himself to an historical people through his covenant with Israel. This marriage is in no way related to the sexual practices that had become common in the cultic centers. Yahweh did not enter into this relationship in order to bring fertility to the land; he called Israel out of Egypt and into covenant in order to establish justice in the land. Thus Hosea is drastically reinterpreting the fertility imagery of pagan religion by using it to dramatize Yahweh's covenant love for his people. But in his marrying Gomer, Hosea is not only saying something about God, he is also telling Israel that she is a whore. Israel had worshiped other gods prior to the forming of the covenant (see Genesis 35:2–4; Joshua 24:14–15); and even afterwards she had remained a harlot, still given to pagan ways—just as Gomer had been unable to remain faithful to Hosea.

(3) This interpretation advances the idea that Hosea only gradually discovered after his marriage that Gomer was unfaithful to him. In naming the third child "not my people," he could be claiming that he is not the father of the child as well as maintaining that there was now an absolute separation between Yahweh and Israel. Looking back, he perceived that it had been Yahweh's will from the beginning that he marry someone who would turn out to be a harlot. Such a shattering experience shaped the content of his prophecy, for he was led to see the parallel between his humiliation and suffering and

that which Yahweh was enduring. Because of his experience with Gomer, Hosea came to understand how Yahweh was deeply hurt because the people whom he loved had violated the relationship at every opportunity. This understanding caused Hosea to express Yahweh's activity and Israel's dilemma in terms of the establishing and the breaking down of the love-marriage-covenant relationship. It forced the prophet to go beyond denouncing social abuses to probe the nature of an alienated relationship. According to this theory, Hosea also came to realize that love does not necessarily reciprocally die when one of the parties violates the relationship. He still loved Gomer even after she was gone from his household, and he came to see that perhaps Yahweh still loved Israel. Chapter 3 is interpreted as the prophet's seeking out his estranged wife and bringing her back home. He is doing this as a symbolic affirmation that Yahweh will somehow also restore the relationship between himself and Israel.

Hosea 5:15–6:6 is an important passage that subtly and effectively dramatizes Israel's predicament. It is the key stanza in a larger poem which begins with 5:8. In verses 8–14, the prophet condemns the unstable foreign policies of North Israel (Ephraim) and Judah in response to the rapid rise of Assyrian power. In quick succession, Israel would vacillate from a frantic search for allies to resist the Assyrian menace to an abject capitulation brought about by a new group that had come to power through assassination. Resistance is the only hope; submission is the only hope—an unbroken cycle of indecision. In no case did Israel affirm Yahweh as her only hope, and for this she is rebuked. Hosea states that Yahweh is weary of seeking out Israel and finding no response. He will bring down destruction upon his people through the very policies they had hoped would be their salvation (verses 13–14). The image of the lion destroying his prey and withdrawing to his lair causes Hosea to declare that Yahweh will also depart from Israel in the midst of her destruction. This withdrawal is not to be interpreted spatially, but existentially. Yahweh is going to remove himself from his people in the hope that they will be brought back to their senses when they experience his absence. In order for the relationship to be restored, it is Israel who must now seek out Yahweh.

In verses 1–3, Hosea cites a repentance liturgy through which Israel would attempt to regain Yahweh's favor. From the introduction in verse 15,[18] it appears that Yahweh is hoping for such a response, and that it would suffice to heal the estranged relationship. But we see from Yahweh's reaction in verses 4–6 that this liturgy in no way fulfilled his expectations. What makes this repentance unacceptable? Scholars are not unanimous in their interpretations of these verses,[19] but we would maintain that Israel is being condemned because, although the Israelites still call their god *Yahweh,* they no longer understand his real nature. In these verses he is being worshiped as one would worship a Canaanite deity.

The section is full of allusions to Canaanite fertility rituals. Verse 2 describes the restoration of Israel in the death and resurrection imagery common in pagan fertility religions. Each year the storm god, the bringer of rains, was thought to have succumbed as a result of the long summer dry spell. But in a ritual that preceded the rainy season, the people would search for him, lamenting his death. At the last moment he would be found—alive again—snatched from the jaws of death within three days and brought to the Temple amidst great rejoicing that abundant rainfall was assured for another year. The purpose of this ceremony was to produce fertility in the land through the sympathetic magic of a dramatized ritual. The king would play the role of the storm god, and it was thought that what man acted out in rituals on earth was a reflection of what the gods were doing in heaven. It was essential that the storm god revive, and the rituals were thought to help bring this about. Rain was needed, but also the earth must be impregnated with seed. In mythological terms, this impregnation was brought about through sexual relations between the storm god and the earth goddess. Thus, as the storm god (king) was brought alive again to the Temple, the culmination of the festivities would be rites of sexual intercourse between the king and a sacred priestess. It is extremely doubtful whether such rituals were ever performed by the official cults in Israel. Some scholars think so, but we think not. However, it does seem that the fertility imagery from Canaanite culture was so all-pervasive in Israel that it heavily influenced the popular patterns of thought.

Students will probably raise the question of the relationship between 6:2 and the Christian belief in the death and resurrection of Jesus. Although a new significance was undoubtedly seen in this verse by the early Christian church, it is difficult to conceive of this verse's being responsible for the New Testament resurrection concept. It does not refer to the resurrection of an individual, but of an entire people. How can such a concept apply to a nation? Certainly Israel is not literally dead. *Life* and *death*, however, were relative terms in ancient Near Eastern thought. There was abundance of life, which was experienced through material possessions: a large and happy family, peace, and so forth. And there were various gradations of death, such as one's being diseased, oppressed, conquered, barren, and so on. Any condition of weakness was, in fact, a form of death, and this was the condition in which the Israelites found themselves due to their political instability and the growing Assyrian threat. Just as vegetation (and the vegetation deity) returns when all appears lost after the long summer months, the Israelites were hoping that Yahweh would restore them to fullness of life. They were sure that Yahweh had caused their affliction only so that he could show them his mercy and win their deeper gratitude (verse 1). There seems to be no awareness that the nation, through neglect of the covenant demands, could perhaps be responsible for its plight.

The third verse also contains allusions to Canaanite fertility imagery. The verb translated *let us press on* is used in 2:7 to refer to Gomer/Israel pursuing her other lovers. The verb *to know*, which is twice used here, can denote a sexual knowing. Of course it does not in this context, since the object is Yahweh, but the connotation is there. Hosea, it seems, is using a very subtle irony to suggest that the traditional Israelite piety that describes the revitalization of the nation and that claims to have easy access to the knowledge of God has in fact been shaped by imagery drawn out of the pagan fertility cult. Yes, Hosea concludes sarcastically, God's return to his people is a sure thing—as sure as the return of the spring rains. The essence of pagan religion is the use of ritual to coerce the powers that be to conform to man's will: to make "a sure thing" of the gods. Yahwistic religion maintains that the God of Israel was never a sure thing apart from the covenant relationship being maintained and its demands fulfilled. Israel's dilemma, according to Hosea, is that her "faith" is so secure that she has made "a sure thing" of Yahweh. This taking of the other for granted is a certain sign of an alienated relationship.

Yahweh's response to this enthusiastic but misbegotten attempt at repentance reminds one of a father dealing with his wayward son: "What shall I do with you, O Ephraim? . . ." Through sacrifices and cultic rituals, Israel is outwardly trying to please Yahweh, but she no longer understands what he demands. Ritual actions cannot revitalize a dead relationship. Hosea is driven to the realization that Israel's case is hopeless: she cannot return to Yahweh, because she has become so alienated from him by the spirit of Canaanite culture that she no longer knows who he is (5:4). This is a much more serious problem than that which Joshua (Joshua 24:14–15) and Elijah (I Kings 18:21) faced when they had to make a choice between Yahweh and other specific gods. Hosea's Israel has ostensibly chosen Yahweh, but her attempts at repentance (such as the one which Hosea mimics in 6:1–3) are doomed to failure because popular Yahwism has been reformulated in alien Canaanite terms. Perhaps out of his own personal experience Hosea has come to the insight that when love is gone one can continue to go through the motions, but it is impossible to stoke the cold coals of a dead relationship. Israel is, according to Hosea, incapable of returning to God. If we are correct in our interpretation of Hosea, this belief brings him into conflict with one of the most fundamental precepts of Mosaic religion—that man is free to choose whether he will obey or

disobey God. He is saying, we think, that the spirit of harlotry/
alienation has robbed Israel of this freedom.

In this context, Hosea interprets Israel's ritualized worship as
merely going through the motions—external, formalized actions
that provide a religious aura but conceal a broken relationship
(6:6). "Steadfast love" and "the knowledge of God"—both relational terms—are what the prophet demands instead. "Steadfast love" (Hebrew *hesed*) denotes that bond of affection that
exists between two parties through which loyalty, obedience, and
service are no longer regarded as a duty but are rather rendered as
a freely given response to the love of the other. This term is basic
to Mosaic religion, wherein Israel's adherence to the covenant
stipulations was regarded as a grateful response to having been
delivered from Egyptian bondage. "The knowledge of God" is
not a mystical term referring to closer communion with God. It
expresses the other side of the paradox of biblical religion. On the
one hand it means the specific knowledge of the demands of the
covenant (see 4:6); but at a deeper level it also is a relational
term. It refers to the acknowledging of God as absolute suzerain
to whom total loyalty is due. The term's connotation is of the
vassal knowing his place—that is his fearful position against a
demanding suzerain who holds him strictly accountable. Steadfast love and the knowledge of God were lacking in Israel; Hosea
has come to see that they could not be regenerated from within
by exhortations to repentance and reformation.

Just as Hosea had perhaps faced a wife who could not change,
now he had been called to confront a nation that could not alter
its course toward destruction. The end appeared certain; the
Assyrian onslaught was imminent, aimed at a people incapable of
regenerating their national spirit. The dire threats of Amos were
about to be realized—Israel taken off into Exile, rejected by her
God because she had not been faithful. In chapter 11, Hosea
ponders the meaning of this relationship, and in so doing creates
a poem of great beauty. Turning to the father-son imagery to
dramatize the close bonds of the covenant relationship, the
prophet reviews the past history of God's dealing with his people.

When Israel was a child, I loved him,
and out of Egypt I called my son. (11:1)

The Old Testament is quite often characterized as a book of law, and Israelite faith as a strict legalism centered around a god who is regarded as a stern, wrathful judge. This is certainly one aspect of Old Testament religion, but it should be stressed that this aspect is quite secondary to the view that love was the primary cause of God's acting in Israel's behalf and placing his claim upon her. Certainly Yahweh is often portrayed as being angry with Israel, but this is only one of a wide range of emotions which the two parties felt toward one another. There is rage and disappointment as well as joy and fulfillment in all close personal relationships; but all of these emotions are derived out of the context of love. This is why Hosea is coming extremely close to the heart of Israelite religion when he uses both the husband-wife and the father-son imagery to express the relationship between Yahweh and Israel.

What does a rebellious son deserve? A severe chastisement, which is the surest sign of a father's love. God cares so much about Israel that she will be punished—returned to the yoke of oppression, whether it be in Egypt or Assyria, ". . . and none shall remove it" (verse 7c). At this point it appears as if the Exile will be permanent. The picture is almost the same as Amos' ending scene (Amos 5:25–27)—the Israelites in Exile, having been rejected by Yahweh because they no longer served his purposes.

But Hosea seems to know more of what love is all about than Amos. He realizes that in the love relationship—whether it be husband-wife or father-son—punishment is never meted out for its own sake. Wrath does not mean the end of the relationship; it is rather a sign that one party cares deeply that a proper relationship be restored and maintained. Hosea saw, perhaps from his own experience, that love does not necessarily die when one of the parties does not take its demands seriously.

"How can I give you up, O Ephraim!" (11:8a). This is the turning point in the Book of Hosea. Hosea realizes that although destruction and Exile are imminent and unavoidable, God still cannot make a permanent end of his people, as he did with Admah and Zeboiim (Sodom and Gomorrah, Genesis 19). The bonds of love transcend the requirements of the law, especially since God is the plaintiff and not man.

The poem ends in verses 10–11 with the promise that Israel will ultimately be returned from exile. Note the sudden transition from the compassionate God, who will not reject, to the holy God, who roars like a lion so that his people shudderingly return from far-distant lands. This illustrates the point we made earlier that God's holiness is understood as being one aspect of his love. Perhaps Hosea shifted his images here so that one would not sentimentalize over the love of God. Some scholars have maintained that verses 10–11 were not an original part of the poem, because they presuppose the later hope of the return from the Exile after the fall of Jerusalem in 587 B.C. But it has been correctly, we think, pointed out that Hosea was living during a time of exile, as the Assyrians conquered North Israel between 732 and 722 B.C.[20] It is this exile—the removal of North Israelites from their land by the Assyrians—to which he is referring.

The final verses of this poem depict Israel returning to her land and to her god. Hosea is not referring only to a geographical return; he is also describing a religious return—a restoration of the faith relationship between God and his people. As we have already seen from 5:15–6:6, the *return motif* is one of the dominant concerns in Hosea (see also 5:4, 14:1–7). Earlier the prophet had concluded that Israel was unable to return of her own volition. If any change in the relationship were to occur, it would have to be affected by Yahweh, not Israel. How has the relationship been renewed so that Israel is now able to return? The answer, we think, can be found in 2:14–23. After describing the punishment that will come upon Yahweh's wife/people for her adultery, Hosea depicts what will happen in the wilderness of exile. Yahweh will woo her all over again in the wilderness; he will "allure" her and "speak tenderly" to his people—and *Israel will respond*. She will answer Yahweh's call as she did when she first went into the wilderness under Moses. The faith relationship will be restored; Israel will respond to Yahweh out of love as a wife to her husband; and she will be betrothed to Yahweh forever in righteousness and steadfast love.

Amos recalled the wilderness experience under Moses and looked forward to the Exile as a return to the wilderness that would terminate the relationship between Yahweh and Israel. Hosea also knew that Israel deserved such a fate and that she could do nothing to return to her God. But he also knew that God's love was such that he would not let his people go. The return to the wilderness would result in a restoration of the relationship, not in its termination. Israel would be purified through her suffering, and Yahweh would once again be able to speak and act so that she would respond. The return to the wilderness would be almost a repetition of Israel's earlier sacred history—except this time it would work out right. Israel would respond, and the conditional relationship presupposed in the Mosaic covenant would be transformed into a permanent bond between God and his people. This concept makes Hosea one of the important watersheds in the history of Israel's religion. Having lost hope in Israel's capability to reform, yet having kept faith in Yahweh's capacity for a love which is so strong that it can overcome the alienated relationship, Hosea has initiated the hope for a new age that will arise beyond the violence and destruction of the Exile. The imagery he uses for conceptualizing this age is based on the Mosaic traditions of the past.

Some Questions for Discussion: In chapters 1–3 of Hosea, the image of the faithless wife was equated with Israel and the forgiving husband with God's love for his people. What instructions does God give Hosea in 3:1? In view of earlier reference to Hosea's wife, do you find anything puzzling in the reference made to the woman in this verse? Regardless of the identity of the woman, under what circumstances will husband and wife continue their life together? How does the relationship of Hosea to the woman reflect God's relationship with Israel?

What will be the ultimate result of God's action toward Israel? What appears to be the attitude of the people toward God's actions as they express themselves in 6:1–3? According to the narrator, how does God respond in verse 4 to the confidence uttered in verses 1–3? What is the tone you detect in the first two lines of verse 4?

According to the narrator, how does God describe the loyalty of Israel to him? If you had a friend whose friendship could be described in similar terms, how much confidence would you have in his friendship? What is meant by the statement, "For I desire steadfast love and not sacrifice"? What have the prophets had to say about the sacrifices of the people? Find some examples from your previous studies of the prophets. What does Hosea mean when he speaks of "knowledge of God"?

The husband-wife image is replaced by the father-son reference again in 11:4. What references to God's care of his people are used in this passage?

What tone change do you detect as the passage indicating God's anger progresses? According to the narrator, what is God's ultimate promise to the people in verse 11? What is your reaction to trying to understand God through human qualities of man? Is Hosea's reasoning out of God's love a logical view? Explain.

Hosea speaks about several kinds of love. Identify them. Do you accept the descriptions Hosea gives to the different kinds of love he discusses? Why, or why not? How many levels of meaning do you see in the story of Hosea's life? What are they? (Who does Hosea represent? What does Gomer represent?) Why do you think God told Hosea to "Go, take to yourself a wife of harlotry and have children of harlotry . . ."? Why do you think Hosea obeyed?

The name Ephraim is used 37 times in this book. Why? Who is Ephraim? What kind of picture does Hosea draw of the relationship between God and Israel? How is Israel like a child? How is God like a parent?

Why do you think Hosea uses the imagery of a father-son and a husband-wife? Why must a father chastise his children? What do you think is his motivation? How does God deal with his rebellious children, according to 11:4?

What attributes of God's character do you think Hosea is

showing us in this book? What main themes do you see recurring in Hosea? What truths might Hosea be wishing to convey in these themes? What is the tone of Hosea's last words (chapter 14)?

Suggested Activities: Write a short paper in which you compare the structure of Hosea's verses with those of Amos. Explain, for a reader your own age, how the verses differ and why you think each is or is not effective.

Consider both Amos and Hosea, and then write a short paper in which you compare one or more contemporary critics of society to one or both of the prophets.

Read the entire Book of Hosea and then summarize his messages in as few sentences as you can. Compare your summary with those of several classmates. How are they similar? How do they differ? How do you account for the difference?

Isaiah

With Isaiah of Jerusalem[21] and the succeeding prophets, the focus shifts away from North Israel back to Judah and Jerusalem. Isaiah's prophetic career spanned the time from the rise of Assyria under Tiglath-pileser III (745 B.C.) through the Syro-Ephraimite War (734–732 B.C.) and the fall of North Israel (722 B.C.) down to the Assyrian invasions against Judah and Jerusalem (701 and 687 B.C.). He played a key role in the crucial decisions involving Judah's foreign policy and seems to have been in a position of power greater than any other canonical prophet. He probably came from a leading Jerusalem family, and many scholars surmise that he was connected with the Temple priesthood.

THE PROPHET'S CALL (ISAIAH 6)

Isaiah's call to be a prophet, described in chapter 6, is one of the best known passages in the Bible. It is the classic paradigm of the biblical conception of what constitutes an encounter with God: (1) the overwhelming experience of God's glory and holiness (verses 1–4), which causes (2) a strong sense of personal inadequacy and unworthiness (verse 5). Man's realization of his precarious position against the holiness of God is followed by (3) a feeling that the weight of sin has been removed by divine forgiveness (verses 6–7). (4) Only at this point is one able to communicate with God: Isaiah hears that there is a job to be done, and (5) the overpowering nature of this encounter elicits a positive response (verse 8). Communion with God is never sought as an end in itself in the Old Testament; it always results in a commission being given to which man must respond (see I Kings 19:8ff).

Isaiah's vision took place "in the year that King Uzziah died." Note that the prophet does not say "thirty-seven years ago" or "when I was twenty-three years old." Such expressions reveal an abstract, spatial view in which time is seen as running out in evenly measured periods in lives that stretch out on either side of the present. But for the people of the ancient Near East, time is identical with the events that take place in it.[22] One cannot distinguish between time and its content. Although an event may have receded into the past, it is still felt to be vitally related to the conditions of life in the present. Such an event was the death of Uzziah, the great ruler of Judah's golden age. In the minds of later generations, it was this event that presaged the final end of Israelite hopes and claims to empire. Thus the connotation of Isaiah's statement is that his prophetic career encompassed a threatening period of continuing crises in Israelite/Judahite history.

It seems most likely that Isaiah's vision took place in the Jerusalem Temple. The innermost room in that tripartite building was the holy of holies, which contained the Ark of the Covenant on which Yahweh was thought to be invisibly enthroned.[23] Suspended above the Ark in the holy of holies were representations of the cherubim, which were most likely personifications of the wind and clouds upon whom Yahweh was thought to ride (Psalm 18:10). They are pictured as winged lions having human faces, similar to the winged sphinx. From Genesis 3:24, we see that the cherubim also stood ready to perform other services at Yahweh's command.

The larger room adjoining the holy of holies contained several cultic implements, including an incense altar. But the Temple was a very small building (the three rooms measured a total of 105 feet long by 30 feet wide), so many of the cultic objects—including the altar for sacrifices—were located outside in the Temple courtyard, where most of the ceremonies were conducted. No one except the priests was permitted to enter the Temple building itself, and the holy of holies was entered only by select personnel on rare occasions.

Although some scholars maintain that the building referred to in verse 1 is the heavenly temple of God, it seems possible to propose that Isaiah's vision took place as he was officiating at a ceremony in the Jerusalem Temple. For him the Ark of the Covenant was suddenly transformed into the reality that it represented: the throne of the living God. To convey the mystery and awe of the event, Isaiah is very reticent in describing God's appearance. We are told only that his long flowing robe billowed out and filled the temple (which is described in Psalm 132:7 as the footstool of Yahweh). He is more specific in his description of the seraphim, which replace the cherubim in his vision. Each has three sets of wings: with one set they covered their eyes, for no one—not even an angelic being—can see God and live; with one set they covered their sexual parts, as a mark of modesty before the holiness of God (see Genesis 3:10); and with the third set of wings they kept themselves in flight like hummingbirds, poised to dart off at Yahweh's command. We do not know why Isaiah envisioned seraphim rather than the more traditional cherubim. The Hebrew word seraphim (literally meaning *burning ones*) is mentioned in only one other passage of the Old Testament. In Numbers 21:6ff, it refers to serpents who attacked the Israelites in the wilderness; Moses is reputed to have made the bronze serpent in order to protect his people from this attack. This object was preserved in the Jerusalem Temple for many years before it was finally removed by King Hezekiah (715–687 B.C.) for having too many pagan associations (II Kings 18:4). Thus one could suggest that the seraphim were conceived of as fiery serpents who were part of God's angelic host. Smoke and fire were the two traditional ways of depicting Yahweh's presence. Just as the cherubim are associated with the clouds, the seraphim may have been personifications of the fire of God's holiness.[24]

In his visionary state, Isaiah now sees the smoke from the incense altar as a further representation of God's presence, both hiding and revealing his glory. Similarly it is possible that the *Sanctus* refrain of verse 3 was being sung antiphonally by the Temple choirs in the service, but it came through to Isaiah as being sung back and forth among the seraphim in the host of heaven. The dominant stress in the first four verses is on God's holiness (the threefold repetition of "holy" in verse 3 is a way of conveying the superlative "most holy" in Hebrew). Most people have little idea of the wide range of meaning and feeling which the word *holy* had for ancient man. Rudolf Otto has written an entire book on this subject, from which we will try to summarize the five major characteristics.[25] First, there is a feeling of God's awefulness and absolute unapproachability. There is an uncanny, weird quality to the holy, that elicits shuddering and dread—not a natural fear, but more the creeping flesh sense of mystical awe as one finds oneself both enticed and cowering before the mysterious object being confronted. Second, there is the sense of God's majesty—his might and power—before which one finds oneself reduced to nothingness in the face of his transcendent power. The third characteristic of holiness is God's energy, vitality, passion, will, movement—all that lies behind the idea of the living God. There is a certain unpredictable, irrational quality in the experience of holiness which forced ancient man to ascribe personality to the power which he was encountering. The fourth characteristic of holiness is what Otto calls the "wholly other." The only response is a dumb stupor as one realizes that the object being experienced is completely beyond one's comprehension because it is of a nature which has no place in one's scheme of reality. Finally, there is the element of fascination. Divine objects evoke feelings of horror and dread; but there is also a certain charm which captivates. Cowering man is drawn forward (for example, Moses with the burning bush): he cannot run away from it.

Isaiah's response to the Holy is one of dread and self-deprecation. "Woe is me" means "I'm a dead man" for having looked upon the living God. Note that his sense of sin is localized on his lips; perhaps he is already anticipating a call to prophesy and is seeking to fend off such a call by pointing out his inadequacy. But Yahweh is not put off so easily. Isaiah's sin is removed, and he now stands ready to act as Yahweh's prophet. Note that the imagery Isaiah uses to express his sense of forgiveness is still derived from the Temple. One of the seraphim touches his mouth with a burning coal from the incense altar. There is no sentimentality here; the purging experience of forgiveness seems to have been a painful one for the prophet to undergo.

At this point, Isaiah perceives that Yahweh is in the process of deliberating with his divine council. A decision has apparently been reached regarding an important matter. All that remained to be settled was the means through which the decision was to be communicated. Isaiah responds immediately, "Here am I! Send me." Only then does he learn the dreadful nature of his prophetic ministry. Through his words and deeds, Isaiah is to deliberately delude the nation so that it would not repent, because the deterioration of society had progressed to the extent where repentance would be useless. Judgment was imminent and unavoidable, and Isaiah is to be the means through which it is realized. Only when cities lie in waste without inhabitants can the prophet say that his mission has been accomplished.

Of course there is a problem in interpreting verses 9–13. Can it really be that Isaiah entered into his prophetic ministry with the express purpose of deluding Judah so that the nation's destruction would come all the more rapidly? Was Isaiah to be a "false prophet," giving the people words of comfort when what was needed was a call to repentance in the face of impending doom? Can a prophet lie in the name of God? Although we feel that this is the correct interpretation—that Isaiah felt the purpose of his ministry was to further Yahweh's will of overthrowing the nation

—very few scholars agree. Most scholars believe that verses 9–13 represent the *result,* rather than the *purpose,* of Isaiah's prophetic career. That is, Isaiah set out in 742 B.C. with the highest hopes of reforming the nation, and only in retrospect did he see that it must have been Yahweh's will from the beginning that he fail. A variation of this latter interpretation is that the prophet sensed already at his call that, try as he might to bring the nation back to Yahweh, his efforts were doomed to failure. The process of deterioration was too deep-set, and he would not be able to turn back the tide. Isaiah knew in advance that he had been called on to attempt the impossible.

Some Questions for Discussion: Contrast Isaiah 6:1–8 with 6:9–13. Why do you think the two devices used here are, or are not, appropriate for what is being described in each part?

What is the effect of the seraphim's saying *holy* three times? Where else besides Isaiah 6:3 have you seen these words: "Holy, holy, holy is the Lord of hosts; the whole earth is full of his glory" (or a paraphrase of them)?

Why does Isaiah say "Woe is me! For I am lost . . ."? (See Exodus 33:20.) How does verse 5 foreshadow verses 6 and 7? Why is Isaiah concerned about being unclean? What all might *uncleanliness* include?

How do you interpret verses 9 and 10? What is Isaiah's commission? How will the people of Judah respond to his message? What do you think is the message of God in verses 9–13?

Suggested Activities: Carefully reread Isaiah 6 and then describe the "calling" to a person younger than you. Assess his reactions to your description. Why did you, or didn't you, succeed in giving a graphic description?

If you are an artist, draw the "calling of Isaiah."

THE SIN OF JUDAH (ISAIAH 1:1–20; 5:1–7)

We can see from this first group of oracles in chapter 1 that Isaiah definitely tried at some stage in his ministry to exhort his people to return to their God. The prophet uses literary forms derived from the setting of the lawcourt in order to make his point. Verse 2 begins with a call to the heavens and earth, personified as they are summoned to hear the testimony which Yahweh, the plaintiff, wishes to make against Judah, the defendant (see Deuteronomy 32:1ff; Micah 6:1ff; Psalm 50:3ff). The heavens and earth had witnessed the original covenant agreement made between Yahweh and Israel through Moses at Sinai. They had also witnessed the affirmation of that covenant in ceremonies since that time. Furthermore they had observed the repeated violations of this agreement which had taken place in the land. It was common procedure in Israel for legal agreements to be made between parties at the gate of the city. The agreement was made binding by the presence of witnesses, comprising the free, adult male population of the village. When one party felt that an agreement had been violated, he could summon the men of the town to a legal assembly. They had witnessed the precise details of the earlier agreement, and the plaintiff hoped that they had observed the violation of the agreement and would be able to substantiate his claims against the defendant. Isaiah is transposing the village assembly to the cosmic level by calling the heavens and earth to hear Yahweh's complaint.

Yahweh summarizes his indictment in verses 1b–2. He uses the same analogy as found in Hosea 11. Israel is compared to a son whose response to the loving care and protection of his father is rebellion. Whereas animals, once they have been trained, will always recognize and acknowledge their master, Israel is unwilling to do so. Isaiah is demanding the same knowledge of God that Hosea spoke of (Hosea 6:6), a reference to the vassal's knowing what is demanded of him and to his fearful position if these demands are not carried out; or, as Isaiah puts it even more directly, the vassal's knowing to whom he belongs. God's people had been brought into a covenant relationship through their deliverance out of Egypt and had received careful instruction and training through the gift of the Law at Sinai; but now they were "utterly estranged," having turned their backs upon the loving power which created them as a people (Isaiah 1:4).

In verses 5–8, the plaintiff now addresses the defendant directly: Israel is compared to a patient whose internal illness has resulted in external physical manifestations. The spiritual alienation from Yahweh has led to the land's desolation, bringing it close to the ruin which was visited upon Sodom and Gomorrah for their sins. Scholars are uncertain as to whether Isaiah is referring to the destruction of North Israel by the Assyrians between 734–722 B.C., or to the Assyrian invasion of Judah under Sennacherib in 701 B.C. (see II Kings 18:13ff). It seems to us that the former is more likely.

The reference to Sodom and Gomorrah in verse 9 serves as a transition to the oracle in verses 10–17, in which Isaiah denounces the "rulers of Sodom and Gomorrah" (Israel and Judah) for their definition of the service of God in terms of sacrifices and ritualized religion rather than social justice. The thought expressed in these verses is quite close to passages in Amos (5:21–24) and Hosea (6:6). But there does seem to be a difference. Isaiah is not absolutely rejecting the value of all ritualized religion. "I cannot endure iniquity *and* solemn assembly" (1:13c) and "even though you make many prayers, I will not listen; your hands are full of blood" (1:15b) indicate that Isaiah is denying the efficacy of ritualized religion when it is not accompanied by social justice. We can infer that if Israel undertook the corrective action specified in verses 16–17, the new moons and sabbaths and solemn assemblies would once again be acceptable in Yahweh's eyes.

Verses 16–17 comprise a series of imperative verbs intended to form a counterbalance to the Israelite/Judahite stress on ritualized religion. Israel and Judah would not find their salvation through blood sacrifices to appease a wrathful deity; rather, they were to find salvation through delivering the oppressed classes within their society from injustice. The messages from suzerains to vassals that have been uncovered by archeology can be roughly grouped into two categories: (1) those messages which, after enumerating the specific covenant violations in the indictment, end with a specific sentence of doom (for example, "now I will destroy your cities and their inhabitants"); and (2) those messages which conclude with a series of imperative demands of corrective action which the vassal might undertake in order to preserve the covenant relationship. In the former case, the covenant bond has been terminated already by the vassal's insubordination; there is no further recourse save his annihilation at the hands of the suzerain. In the latter case, the covenant has been threatened and may yet be terminated if the vassal does not act quickly; but the vassal still has a chance. We see from verses 16–17 that Israel and Judah fall in this latter category in Isaiah's eyes.

Verses 18–20 state in succinct terms the choice that lies before the people. The understanding of their situation is clearly derived from the Mosaic covenant: if they return and obey, they will be blessed; if they continue in their rebellion, they will feel the curse of Yahweh's continued wrath. However, the meaning of this punch line in verses 19–20 has been obscured by an incorrect translation of verse 18 which is still preserved in several modern translations. The verse should read:

> "Come now, let us reason together,
>   says the Lord:
> though your sins are like scarlet,
>   *shall they be white as snow?*
> though they are red like crimson,
>   *shall they become like wool?*

The Hebrew text clearly indicates that Isaiah is challenging rather than affirming the assumption that God's mercy is so all-encompassing and all-powerful that he will overlook the iniquity of the most flagrant sinner. Isaiah is returning to the theme which he had developed in verses 11–17: sacrifice and ritualized religion will not suffice as an expiation for the sin of Israel and Judah. The sins of violence and oppression cannot be removed through sacrifice, repentance, and prayer; ritualized religion is meaningful only if it activates the popular conscience and quickens the impulse to undertake the needed social reforms.

If we could posit a development in Isaiah's thought, the "Song of the Vineyard" in 5:1–7 would seem to come from a period in his career later than the passage in chapter 1 which we have just discussed. In chapter 1, the prophet concluded with a clear-cut choice which he felt the people were still capable of making for themselves. Now in 5:1-7, he seems much more bitter and disillusioned, certain that the right choice is not going to be forthcoming.

It seems quite possible that this song was sung at a vintage festival in the fall—an ancient Canaanite celebration which had been adapted by the Israelites and incorporated into the feast of booths (tabernacles). Although the building of booths out of branches may have originated among the Canaanites and had something to do with the celebration of the land's fertility, the Israelites reinterpreted it as a commemoration of the period when the nation wandered forty years in the wilderness after escaping from Egypt. During this festival they camped out in makeshift shelters, just as they imagined their ancestors had done before them. It was a time of great rejoicing and merrymaking, when everyone took part in the singing and dancing.

In this setting, Isaiah steps forward as a balladeer, ready to address the farmers of Judah in imagery which they would readily understand. Apparently Isaiah is adapting his approach to the mood of the festival—romantic, sentimental, pastoral—which had been created by the other songs and stories before it. The opening line of verse 1 creates a note of anticipation. It will be a song of praise to his beloved, perhaps similar in tone to the Song of Solomon.[26] But the love song is about his beloved's vineyard. This creates a heightened interest and expectation, as the listeners prepare themselves to interpret the vineyard as a metaphor of the love relationship which Isaiah is attempting to convey. Verse 2 describes all the acts of tender loving care which the beloved performed in behalf of his vineyard. The end result: the vineyard did not respond; it yielded wild grapes.

In verses 3-4, the pronouns are switched. Suddenly it is Isaiah who seems to be the enraged farmer pouring out his frustration over the failure of his vineyard. And the startled people find that they are no longer wistful listeners to a plaintive love song; they have been summoned into the lawcourt as witnesses and judges to decide between Isaiah and his vineyard. The prophet is relying upon an old ploy of his profession—artfully contriving the situation so that the accused will pronounce judgment on themselves (see II Samuel 12; I Kings 20:35–43). The obvious response of the crowd would be that the vineyard must be destroyed.

Isaiah responds by describing the desolation which he will bring down upon his worthless vineyard: the hedge will be removed, the wall trampled down, and thorns and briers will spring up in the resulting wasteland. All very well. But "I will also command the clouds, that they rain no rain upon it." What do we have here? Isaiah commanding the clouds? The denouement follows in verse 7; but we need not be told, as we realize along with the stunned hearers, that all along Isaiah has been talking about rebellious Israel, the vineyard of the Lord of hosts (see Psalms 80:8ff). Yahweh had patiently tended her in the hope that she would produce. And Israel did produce; but it was bloodshed *(miśpāh)* rather than justice *(mishpāt),* an oppressed person's cry for help *(saʿāqā)* rather than righteousness *(sedāqā).*

Some Questions for Discussion: What is the purpose of Isaiah 1:1? What is the message of the Lord in verses 2 and 3? What tone is conveyed in verses 2–20? What kind of God is portrayed in chapter 1? Is this the first time in your reading of the Old Testament that God has been pictured like this? If not, where else have you read a similar portrayal?

What is being described in verses 5 and 6? Why do you think the comparison is, or isn't, effective? What other metaphorical comparisons do you find in verses 7–20?

What is the fate of Judah? How does Judah's fate differ from that of Sodom and Gomorrah? Why does Isaiah refer to the rulers of Judah as the rulers of Sodom and Gomorrah?

According to the prophet, what does the Lord think about ceremonies and sacrifices? What does the Lord command the people to do in verses 15–17? What is promised in verses 18–20? What further warning is given?

What is the setting of Isaiah 5? To whom is Isaiah speaking? Explain the meaning of the parable in Isaiah 5:1–7. Why could you call the song of the vineyard a parable?

What does the vineyard symbolize? What do the wild grapes symbolize? What will be done to the vineyard? Why?

ISAIAH'S ROLE IN JUDAH'S FOREIGN POLICY (ISAIAH 7:1–17)

As we have noted before, Isaiah was more deeply involved in the foreign policy of his nation than any other canonical prophet. There were several crises late in Isaiah's career when Hezekiah, the king of Judah, considered joining anti-Assyrian alliances, and —after he joined them—when the Assyrian troops invaded the land. Basing his position on the ancient principle of holy war, Isaiah consistently advised against relying upon other nations and their gods instead of on Yahweh alone. But Isaiah supported Hezekiah when he rebelled against the Assyrians, because exclusive reliance was now being placed in Yahweh.[27]

The events described in 7:1–17 took place relatively early in Isaiah's prophetic ministry. The background of this passage is the so-called Syro-Ephraimite war. It was becoming increasingly apparent to the small states of Syria and Palestine that the long-dormant Assyrian power had now become, under Tiglath-pileser III, a threat to their existence. Their only hope was to set aside their petty bickering and rivalries and join together to face the common foe. Despite urgings and threats from Syria and North Israel, the two nations leading the coalition, Ahaz, the king of Judah, would not join. Judah was the southernmost country in Palestine, away from the main trade routes stretching between Egypt and Mesopotamia. The land was the last point of conquest the Assyrians would be interested in. Ahaz saw only the danger of antagonizing the Assyrian giant by joining such a coalition. His refusal to unite with his brothers to the north brought about the Syro-Ephraimite war, in which Syria and North Israel (Ephraim) invaded Judah in an effort to replace Ahaz with a ruler ("the son of Tabeel," v. 6) who would take up arms against the Assyrians.

Chapter 7 opens with Ahaz examining the water supply, trying to determine how long Jerusalem could withstand a sustained siege. The enemy has apparently already surrounded the city, and Ahaz is weighing the alternatives. Isaiah meets Ahaz at the water pool to urge him not to capitulate. If he will stand firm, Yahweh will deliver the city from the Syro-Ephraimite enemy. What makes Isaiah so sure? It would seem that Isaiah is basing his position on two well-established traditions: (1) the principle of holy war, which demands that exclusive reliance be placed in Yahweh; and (2) the tenets within the Davidic covenant which affirm that the line of David will forever rule over God's people and that Jerusalem is an inviolable city (see Psalms 132:11–18).[28] Through the enemy attack, Ahaz is being confronted with the existential question of whether he really believes the dogma which he had been affirming in ritual celebration to assure stability and permanency for the house of David in Jerusalem. Isaiah comes to assure the king that the enemy who is threatening him today will soon perish. But, says the prophet, if Ahaz does not believe in the covenant promises from Yahweh, they will no longer be effective for him (7:9b).

A second meeting takes place at the royal court (7:10ff). Perhaps several days had elapsed since the first confrontation between prophet and king. Apparently Ahaz is still wavering: the prospects of weathering the siege do not appear favorable to him. The only way he can see of maintaining himself on the throne is to send to the Assyrians for help.

Isaiah appears before the court to warn against such a course of action and to make one final appeal that the king trust in Yahweh. He is so certain of his cause that he offers to perform a sign for the king. (Signs—indications of supernatural power or knowledge—were sometimes given by prophets to authenticate the validity of their message [see I Samuel 10:1ff].) Ahaz piously declines the offer; it is not right, he correctly asserts, to put Yahweh to the test. One can never coerce the most holy God. This makes Isaiah furious; Ahaz will receive a sign anyhow. That young woman, says Isaiah, pointing to one of the king's wives, is already pregnant and will bear a son who will be called Immanuel ("God with us"). The presence and support of God is one of the central affirmations of the Davidic covenant (see II Samuel 23:5), and Isaiah is assuring the king that it is still in effect and will be even after he is gone. But Ahaz's irresolute behavior would have fateful repercussions for his country: before Immanuel comes of age, Syria and North Israel will lie desolate, but Judah also will suffer terribly under the scourge of the Assyrian power.

There has been a long-raging controversy over the word translated "young woman" in 7:14 because it has come into the New Testament as "virgin" (Matthew 1:23). First, the correct translation is "that young woman"; Isaiah is definitely singling out someone in the Jerusalem court. Secondly, the Hebrew word 'almā is merely the female form for a sexually mature young person. The masculine form, 'elem, is used in I Samuel 17:56 and 20:22. The words do not specify virginity one way or the other. Hebrew has a separate word, bᵉtūlā, to indicate virginity. How do we account for this confusion? About five hundred years after Isaiah, when the Bible was translated into Greek (Septuagint), the word *virgin* was used. Later ages came to look upon this passage as the prediction of a future event, rather than as a sign which Isaiah saw being fulfilled in 734 B.C.

Some Questions for Discussion: What is the political situation as revealed in 7:1? What is Ahaz's feeling toward the situation? How do you know? For what reason does Isaiah go to King Ahaz? What is Isaiah's advice? Does the beginning of verse 10, "*Again* the Lord spoke to Ahaz . . ." tell you more about Ahaz? What kind of comment is being made here about faith? What is a "sign of the Lord"? What reasons might Ahaz have for refusing Isaiah's offer of a sign? What is the tone of Isaiah's response to Ahaz's refusal of a sign from the Lord? Why? What does Isaiah predict for the future for the house of David? What device does Isaiah use to tell his prediction? What is told in addition to *what* will happen?

THE LUCIFER MYTH (ISAIAH 14:3–23)

These verses comprise a taunt song, which in its present form is directed against the king of Babylonia. The great enemy of Israel and Judah during Isaiah's time was Assyria, not Babylonia.

The Babylonians became involved in the history of Judah about one hundred years later, when Jerusalem fell to Nebuchadnezzar and one half of the population was carried away to Exile in Babylonia (587 B.C.). About fifty years later the Babylonian empire collapsed as the Persians became the dominant power. Thus the final form of 14:3–23 seems to come from the sixth century, when the exiled Jews would be eagerly anticipating and greatly rejoicing over the final fall of Babylonia. If Isaiah was the creator of this poem (and we have no reason to suspect that he was not), it was most likely originally directed against Assyrians and then changed by a later editor to fit the different circumstances.

Verses 4b–11 describe the rejoicing of both the earth and the underworld at the demise of a mighty ruler who has terrorized the surrounding nations with his power. The form used by the prophet is the standard 3:2 pattern of the Hebrew lament:

> How / the oppressor / has ceased
> the insolent fury / ceased!
> The Lord / has broken / the staff of the wicked
> the scepter / of rulers

Thus the tone that Isaiah is trying to express is bitter irony: the lament is a song of joy. Even the shades in mournful Sheol will rejoice at the oppressor's coming. They will rise up to "honor" him as he makes his last grand entance; but this will not be the kind of victory procession he had been accustomed to. Sheol has been victorious over him.

Using the same 3:2 meter, the prophet proceeds to raise another "lament" over the deceased king. His fall from power is compared to the fall of Day Star (Lucifer) from the heavens after his unsuccessful rebellion. Isaiah is here referring to a common ancient Near Eastern motif, variant forms of which have been found in Hittite, Canaanite, and Greek mythology. The myth is based upon ancient man's observation that the morning star shines especially brightly just before the dawn. Personifying these forces of nature, ancient man interpreted this phenomenon as an attempt of one of the subordinate deities in the divine pantheon to win sovereignty over the other gods.[29] At first he was successful, but eventually he is overwhelmed and cast down by the greater power of the ruling deity, who is the personified sun.

We see from verses 13–14 that the dominant theme in the story is Day Star's pride and misdirected ambition. Had he succeeded in his goal, he would have caused disorder and chaos throughout the universe, just as the proud king had brought tumult and destruction to all his surroundings (verses 16–17). But the Day Star has been cast down; so also has Yahweh crushed this proud pretender to world dominion.

Isaiah is using this myth as an illustrative analogy to an historical event. It was only in much later times that the Day Star myth became fused into the story of Satan so that it was interpreted as describing the way in which Satan became the enemy of God. We find this interpretation in Milton, where Satan is cast out of heaven for his rebellion and in turn becomes the agent through whom man is tempted to disobey God. The Old Testament makes no connection between Satan and the serpent in Genesis 3. The Old Testament never says that man was corrupted by divine powers that he could not overcome; in biblical thought, Satan never became an active power in the world until *after* man had disobeyed God.

Some Questions for Discussion: To whom is Isaiah speaking? To whom is the song addressed? After reading the entire chapter, can you tell why?

What is to be the fate of the Babylonian king? Of what sin is the king being accused by the prophet? How would you describe the tone of this passage? Could you call this passage a lament? a song of joy? Why is the earth singing and why are the cypresses rejoicing?

What is Sheol? What is the Pit? To whom does Day Star, son of Dawn, refer? What is his sin? How is he punished? Why is his story part of this song?

What is the effect of the structure of this passage on its

content? Is it more, or less, effective than third person prose description of the Babylonian king's fate might have been? Why?

MESSIANIC ORACLES (ISAIAH 9:2–7; 11:1–9; 2:2–4)

Three passages from Isaiah—two referring to a perfect king from the line of David who will bring peace and justice to the world, and the third describing the time in which all the nations of the world will come to Jerusalem to learn the law of God, leading to an era of universal peace—have been grouped together under the category "messianic oracles." Technically the word *messianic* refers only to passages that describe the role the king (Messiah) is supposed to play according to the ideals of the Davidic covenant.[30] But in a looser sense, the term can denote the general hope for the future that began to develop in Israelite thought in the eighth century.

Isaiah 9:2–7 describes the coming of the Messiah-king, who will deliver his people from oppression and chaos. The passage is given a cosmic setting in verse 2 with the imagery of the light shining in the darkness (see Genesis 1:2–4). It is almost as if through the Messiah-king Yahweh intends to re-create the world. Isaiah seems to be so certain that God will deliver Judah from her enemies through this Messiah that he speaks of the coming triumphs and the popular rejoicing as accomplished feats. He compares the dramatic reversal that is about to take place with the victory Gideon won over the Midianites against overwhelming odds (Judges 6–8).

Verses 6–7 give us an idea of the oracle's setting. It could have been given by the prophet at the birth of the heir apparent, expressing the hope that the young prince will one day be enabled to restore the fortunes of Judah. But maybe we are being misled by the phrase "For to us a child is born, to us a son is given" in verse 6a. It was common to refer to the Davidic king as the "son of God" at the moment he was anointed.[31] In this sense, the son is "born" when he accedes to the throne. Thus it seems more likely to us that the oracle was given at the accession of a new king like Hezekiah (715 B.C.), giving assurance that the disastrous reign of Ahaz was about to be replaced by a new era for Judah.

An important part of the coronation ceremony that may have been borrowed from the Egyptian court was the giving of royal titles, such as we find in verse 6c. "Wonderful Counselor" points out the quality of wisdom, a divine gift that was thought to be essential for a prosperous reign (see I Kings 3:16–28; 4:29–34). The second title is misleading when translated "Mighty God." Although the Davidic king did assume a special role in the community as the intermediary between God and his people, he was never *identified* with God himself. The term refers to the divine strength with which the king is endowed, enabling him to be victorious over his enemies. The other two titles depict the effects that the divine gifts of wisdom and strength have on the king's reign: he will be enabled to rule over and provide for his kingdom as a father does his household, protecting it from all enemies without. This will lead to unparalleled bounty and peace "from this time forth and for evermore."

In 11:1–9, Isaiah again describes the ideal Messiah-king who will arise from the Davidic line (stem of Jesse). Verse 2 parallels the giving of royal titles in 9:6c. Again we see that the king is to be divinely endowed with wisdom and strength so that he can properly fulfill one of the ancient Near Eastern monarch's most important functions. He was to protect those helpless members of society—the widow, the orphan, the poor—who had no power to secure justice for themselves save through an appeal to the king, who regarded himself as the divinely appointed shepherd of his flock.

The result of the king's wise and just use of his power is described in the famous verses 6–9. The prophet seems to be envisioning a return of the entire creation to that mythical time prior to the existence of evil. Once again we have the motif of cosmic renewal wrought by the advent of the Messiah-king.

There is widespread disagreement as to how these two passages are to be interpreted. The Christian community looks to Jesus as the figure through whom these prophecies will be fulfilled. While some groups within the Jewish community are still looking for a savior from the line of David, many Jews have interpreted these and other messianic passages as describing the role that each Jew is to fulfill in working toward peace on earth and good will among men.

But the debate among biblical scholars is focused at a different point, and basically there are three main lines of interpretation:

(1) Since the passages anticipate the return of the line of David, which had been cut off during the Exile, and since the picture of the Messiah in these passages does not square with the concept of the Messiah elsewhere in Isaiah, these passages were not written by the eighth-century prophet but come from a time during or after the Exile in order to assure the Jewish community that God would raise up a man from the line of David who would save his people and restore the kingdom in perfect peace and harmony.

(2) The passages were composed by Isaiah of Jerusalem, but they are not concerned with a figure in the far-distant future. These oracles were given by Isaiah at the accession of one of the Davidic kings during the eighth century as a customary part of the coronation ceremony. They express the prophet's hope for the improvement of Judah's lot in the immediate future.

(3) The passages were composed by Isaiah of Jerusalem, but they are not related to any specific Davidic king of the eighth or seventh century. The oracles reflect Isaiah's bitter disillusionment that the Davidic kings did not measure up to the ideal figure which is spelled out in the Davidic covenant passages. Some day, Isaiah hoped, such an ideal king will arise.

The final "messianic" passage (2:2–4) concludes with the famous description of universal peace:

> . . . and they shall beat their swords into plowshares,
> and their spears into pruning hooks;
> nation shall not lift up sword against nation,
>   neither shall they learn war any more.

Once again the prophet is using mythological imagery that seems to be derived from the Davidic covenant traditions. Mount Zion in Jerusalem, with the temple of God on top, will be raised up above all the other mountains, and all the nations will come to Jerusalem—no longer in an attempt to overthrow it, but in order to learn Yahweh's teaching (Torah) so that they might become the people of God.

Hosea began the hope for Israel's restoration in imagery drawn primarily from the Mosaic covenant: a new Exodus, a new wilderness wandering, a new covenant, and so forth. Isaiah adds new content to this hope for the future with imagery from the Davidic covenant. In this new age the people of God will be ruled over by the perfect Messiah from the line of David. Furthermore, we have a new universalism in Isaiah, which is also a by-product of the Davidic covenant. Whereas Hosea had seen the new age in terms of the restored relationship between Israel and Yahweh, Isaiah envisions all the nations of the world transformed into the people of God as they seek and find his will in Jerusalem.

Some Questions for Discussion: What does the phrase "a branch shall grow out of his roots" mean? What is being compared to a tree? Why? What does the word *stump* suggest about the house of David? What six ideal qualities (11:3, 4) will the Messiah-king have as judge? What is the prophet trying to indicate in verses 6–8 about the kingdom that will come? Why might Isaiah have used this completely figurative passage to describe the Messiah-king, rather than a more explicative form?

How would you picture Isaiah delivering these prophecies? Why do you think Isaiah speaks in such figurative language? Is this kind of language characteristic of all Old Testament prophecy? What would you say is the essence of Isaiah's prophecy to Israel? What kind of God does Isaiah essentially describe to the Israelites? How does he describe the Israelite people? How do you reconcile the prophecy of peace with the various descriptions of God's annihilation of his enemies and his characterization as mighty, powerful, etc.?

How is the message Isaiah delivers here essentially different from the messages prophets have delivered to Israel previously? How has 2:2–4 figured in the philosophy of the United Nations? Today's peace movement has adopted 2:4 as part of its philosophy; but since we no longer live in an agriculturally oriented society, what would you suggest be substituted for the words *plowshares* and *pruning hooks?*

Micah (Micah 6:1–8)

Micah was a contemporary of Isaiah who lived in Moresheth-gath, twenty-two miles southwest of Jerusalem. Whereas Isaiah seems to have been closely associated with the Jerusalem nobility and priesthood, Micah is much more a rural rustic like Amos. He sees the Mosaic covenant values, which had been preserved for centuries by the people of the land, rapidly deteriorating in the syncretistic atmosphere of Jerusalem. Thus he bitterly denounces the sinful city, maintaining that it will soon be a heap of ruins (3:12). This shocking prophecy, that runs counter to the entire Davidic covenant theology, must have made a deep impression on the people of Judah, since it was used as a precedent to save Jeremiah's life when he prophesied the same thing almost a century later (see Jeremiah 26:18).

The setting of Micah 6:1–8 is very similar to the setting of Isaiah 1:1–20. (See pages 234–235 for a fuller discussion of the divine lawcourt setting and its relationship to Israelite judicial procedure.) Here the prophet is commanded to lay God's case before the mountains that are to serve as witnesses and judges against Judah for her breach of the covenant agreement. Yahweh is the plaintiff, but there is no indictment in the strict sense in this passage. Where one would expect a listing of specific covenant violations in verses 3ff, we have instead a recalling of the acts through which Yahweh delivered Israel out of Egypt and claimed her as his people. (For the interesting story of Balaam and Balak, see Numbers 22–24.) "From Shittim to Gilgal" is a reference to Israel's crossing the Jordan River and entering the Promised Land (see Joshua 3:1–4:19). This period from the Exodus to the

Conquest was regarded as the most sacred period in Israel's history. In referring to Yahweh's acts of the past rather than Judah's sins of the present, Micah is trying to confront the people with the fact that a violated relationship is far more serious than any specific ethical demands. "O my people, what have I done to you? In what have I wearied you? Answer me!" Yahweh sounds more like a spurned lover who is seeking to understand and to be understood than a holy God who coldly metes out punishment.

Verses 6–8 presuppose a repentant people who would restore the broken relationship but who are not quite sure how this is to be accomplished. The literary form that the prophet is using seems to be derived from a liturgy where a worshiper is seeking to be admitted before the presence of God. As in Psalm 24:3ff, questions are raised by the worshiper concerning what Yahweh requires. In the regular liturgy, a priest would probably speak the conditions of admission: "He who has clean hands and a pure heart . . . " (Psalm 24:4a). Micah enumerates the deeds which were generally thought to make man acceptable to the deity in ancient Near Eastern culture. They all relate to propitiating the deity with various gifts. Once again the extent to which the Israelites had been influenced by the culture which surrounded them is indicated. In verse 8, Micah sums up the Israelite religion. The cultic response to God is always secondary to the ethical life which a man follows in relation to his fellowman. If one "loves kindness" (maintains *ḥesed;* see p. 261), he will do justice in society. Note that the image Micah uses for the ethical life is "to walk humbly with your God." Israel knew that the ethical life was ultimately involved in maintaining relationships: a man with his fellowman; a community with their God. She knew that these relationships could be safeguarded through laws, but that there was a dynamic quality to life that could never be permanently captured by codified, eternal verities. Thus the ultimate image for biblical ethics is walking, following God wherever the course of history leads; it is derived from the Exodus experience, when Israel followed God—away from slavery towards freedom.[32]

Some Questions for Discussion: These eight verses are considered to be among the most beautifully poetic of the entire Bible. Bearing in mind the qualities of poetry (see *Sound and Sense* and similar texts), discuss the poetic quality of this excerpt. Who is "I" of 1:8? If it is Micah, explain and justify his behavior. Analyze the logical development of chapter 3. Is he consistent within this chapter? Is the overall sequence of chapters logically consistent?

Why does Micah denounce the leaders of Israel and Judah and not the people? What is the concept of landownership that Micah is thinking about in 2:4, 5? Relate this concept to the "Promised Land" idea. What is Micah's comment on false prophets?

Why is there a statue of a man beating a sword into a plowshare in the lobby of the United Nations building? Compare Micah 4:3 with Isaiah 2:4.

What are the specific sins Micah accuses Israel and Judah of? What ethical-religious standard does Micah say God requires of his people? In addition to protecting his people, what other function(s) does Micah say or imply God performs for his people?

Compare and contrast Micah's comments about ritual to those made by Isaiah 1:10–16; Luke 11:4–42; Matthew 7:21; John 4:21–24. Why doesn't Micah describe his "call"? According to Micah, what will God finally do to his people? What does this say about Micah's concept of God?

Considering the prophecies made by most biblical prophets, explain why a prophet is without honor in his own land. What did the Greeks seem to think of prophets (for example, Cassandra, Tieresias)? Compare the biblical prophets to characters like jesters or fools in medieval courts and in Shakespearean drama.

Suggested Activities: Write a one-act play in which you have either Isaiah or Micah appear on earth today. How will your chosen prophet respond to the behavior of contemporary man? What will he say? What will he do?

As you write your play, make certain that Isaiah's or Micah's language is similar to that found in the Bible. How will their use of "biblical" language heighten the drama?

Produce the one-act play. What directions will you give to your actors? to your set designer? to your costume designer?

Pretend that one of the prophets visited earth today. Write a letter to the editor of the local daily newspaper that you think the prophets might write as a comment on contemporary society.

Josiah's Reform (II Kings 22:1–23:30; Deuteronomy 6:4–25)

The seventh century B.C., which began midway through Hezekiah's powerful reign (715–687 B.C.), was to see a staggering series of events on the international scene and within Judah. The mighty Assyrian Empire reached its zenith and then, in less than fifty years, collapsed into ruins. The ruins were quickly rebuilt by the Babylonians, who then extended their control over the entire Near East.

Judah's fortunes were the obverse of these enormous power shifts. First, she was totally subservient as Assyrian power stretched toward its zenith. Then, as Assyrian power waned, Judah became more powerful and independent. Finally, with the ascendancy of Babylonian power, Judah became smaller and weaker until, in 587 B.C., she was conquered and destroyed, with her officials and leaders dragged off to exile in Babylonia.

The story must begin with the reign of the reforming king Hezekiah. Moved by Isaiah's and Micah's visions of a strong and free Judah faithfully worshiping Yahweh under a king who was David's descendant, Hezekiah had broken ties with Assyria and refused tribute (II Kings 18:7). Political independence and religious reform went hand in hand in ancient Judah, for to refuse tribute to the Assyrian king was also to spurn the Assyrian gods who stood over the treaties with satellite kingdoms. Hezekiah's reform, detailed in II Kings 18:1–6, included purifying the Temple worship by removing foreign and pagan cult objects and demolishing local shrines ("high places"), where pagan practices were often rampant.

Hezekiah's courageous rebellion against his Assyrian overlord was punished by one and possibly two highly destructive expeditions of Sennacherib, the new Assyrian ruler. Sennacherib advanced on Jerusalem in 701 B.C. and exacted tribute by choking Judah into submission with his armies (II Kings 18:13–16).[33] This punitive expedition was probably followed by another similar campaign in about 688 B.C. He again surrounded the city of Jerusalem, but this time, owing to some event that the biblical writers considered a direct miracle of Yahweh, Sennacherib and his armies departed without even receiving tribute (II Kings 18:17–19:37). Isaiah's faith that Yahweh would not allow his king and holy city to be overthrown surely was sustained by these events.[34]

Nevertheless, the position of Judah was only temporarily secure. With the advent of the Assyrian Empire, the day of the independent small state in Western Asia was over. Only as a tributary kingdom could a nation like Judah survive, except when the empire was beset with temporary internal difficulties.[35]

During the reign of Hezekiah's successor, Manasseh (687–642 B.C.), Judah's policy toward Assyria, and therefore her internal religious and national policy as well, underwent a complete reversal. Where Hezekiah had tried to withhold tribute payments, Manasseh paid in full. Where Hezekiah had eliminated pagan cult objects from the temple, Manasseh introduced them in abundance. Even the horrible pagan practice of child sacrifice was revived, and Manasseh was said to have burned his own son as an offering (II Kings 21:1–9). The Deuteronomic historian of II Kings reflects the shock which Manasseh's religious policies must have generated in prophetic circles. As a consequence of his actions, Manasseh is rated by the historian as the most evil king ever to sit upon the throne of Judah (II Kings 21:10–16). The destruction which fell upon Judah in 587 B.C.— just one hundred years after Manasseh began his reign—was seen as Yahweh's punishment of the nation for Manasseh's sins.

Yet it is difficult to see what other courses of action Manasseh could have followed with regard to his international policy. During his reign, the Assyrians came to control all of Syria-Palestine and even Egypt. The conquest of Egypt was in itself an amazing military and political achievement; one can count on the fingers of one hand the successful conquests of Egypt during historical time. If even this great and ancient power could not stand against the Assyrian tide, what chance did little Judah have? This may have been Manasseh's opinion, and from the practical point of view, it is sensible. But Manasseh clearly went beyond the demands of prudence in his corrupt religious practices and in his cruelty toward his own people, for the historian records that "he shed very much innocent blood, till he had filled Jerusalem from one end to another . . . " (II Kings 21:16). In his determination to preserve the life of his nation at all costs, Manasseh seems to have sacrificed the very integrity of that nation and the life and safety of its citizens.

Manasseh's son, Amon, reigned for just two years (642–640 B.C.) and did nothing to change the pro-Assyrian policy of his father. He was assassinated in the course of a popular revolt in 640 B.C., and replaced by his eight-year-old son, Josiah (II Kings 21:19–26). Under Josiah, Judah was to experience her last flourishing as an independent nation and then, with Josiah's death in 609 B.C., to plunge forward into the destruction which many a prophet had foretold.

Josiah's Reform—We are now in a position to understand the narrative of II Kings 22–23. Josiah had come to the throne under the aegis of a reform movement much like Hezekiah's. The young king's advisers, and doubtless also the popular following that had placed him on the throne, insisted on a reversal of Manasseh's policies. Tribute was not to be paid to Assyria; the Temple was to be cleansed of Assyrian and other pagan cult objects. Concommitant social reforms were doubtless needed as well, for the people had suffered many injustices and even massacres under the evil Manasseh.

By 622 B.C., the eighteenth year of his reign, these reform measures were well under way. Josiah was even dreaming of restoring the ancient boundaries of David's kingdom. This restoration now was made possible, just as Judah's very independence was made possible, by the extreme weakness and internal disruption into which Assyria had fallen. The most serious threat to Assyria was the internal revolt of Babylonia, once a subject kingdom. Together with Assyria's external enemies—the Medes, the Elamites, the Cimmerians, and the Scythians—the Babylonians were soon able to bring Assyria to her knees. In 612 B.C., Ninevah, the Assyrian capital city, was taken. Obviously the revolt of the distant Kingdom of Judah was but a tiny shadow compared to the great night that was swiftly enveloping the empire of Assyria.

In the year 622 B.C., with his independence and reform movement safely under way, Josiah made a significant discovery. While workmen were engaged in cleansing and renovating the Jerusalem Temple, they found a document that was brought to the king himself in great haste (II Kings 22:3–10). With many officials of his kingdom listening, Josiah commanded that the scroll be read. When he heard the words of this mysterious scroll, described as "the book of the law" and "the book of the covenant" (22:11; 23:2), the king tore his garments in repentance and grief. He then launched a series of new reforms in accordance with demands made in the scroll (23:4–25), and he held a great convocation in which "the book of the covenant" was read and accepted as Yahweh's law for his kingdom.

What was the origin of this scroll? What were its contents? The opinion of modern scholars is almost unanimous on this point. The scroll was doubtless the core of our Book of Deuteronomy. Its discovery or promulgation at this time marked a significant turning point in Judah's religious history, for in this book the ancient Mosaic covenant, with its stark power and simplicity, was set before a people who knew only of Yahweh's covenant with David and Zion. Judah suddenly was given a new vision—in reality a very ancient vision—of herself as standing at every moment under the judgment of the God who had rescued his people out of Egypt and led them through the wilderness to Sinai, where they formed into his covenant people. Judah was suddenly swept back through the centuries to the Tribal League period, in which the Deuteronomic traditions had their origin, to a period in which the issues that confronted Israel were clear-cut and the decision that must be made terrifyingly simple: either turn in obedience to Yahweh, or rebel against him. Loyalty and obedience would mean blessing; rebellion would mean destruction. Now, in the chaos of the seventh century B.C., Israel was again called, through this ancient scroll, to make this decision. No wonder Josiah tore his robes! It was as if Moses himself stood before the Israelites in uncompromising judgment on the whole life and history of the nation.

The immediate and practical effects of the finding of Deuteronomy are detailed in II Kings 23. The elimination of all pagan idols and practices was thorough-going and pitiless. The recital of the number of objects and buildings that were thus removed is a long one, marking the extent to which the religious life of the Temple itself had become corrupted (23:4–12). Most significantly, the local shrines outside Jerusalem were razed—some of these doubtless had histories going back into pre-Israelite times—and their priests were dispossessed and brought to Jerusalem. The ancient northern shrine of Bethel was razed and its priests killed.

From this point on, only the Jerusalem Temple was recognized as a legitimate place of worship. This demand for absolute centralization of worship is in fact the only unique demand of Deuteronomy, when compared with other Old Testament legal codes, and was the feature that first led scholars to identify Josiah's scroll as Deuteronomy. The centralization of worship meant on the one hand that worship would be more tightly controlled by the king. When the king was a man of Josiah's ideals, this was certainly a step forward. But it also meant that when the Jews were deprived of their Temple, as they soon were through the Babylonian conquest, entirely new and non-sacrificial modes of worship would have to be evolved.

For the remainder of Josiah's reign, the reform took the center of the stage. The Jerusalem Temple was exalted into new prominence; the boundaries of the kingdom were expanded; the paganism of centuries was replaced by a new zeal for Yahweh's law and covenant. But the storms of history were gathering to the east. The Babylonian Empire was rising out of the ruins of Assyria. Josiah himself met his death in 609 B.C. as the storm gathered. The Babylonians had overwhelmed Nineveh and had driven the Assyrian king and his supporters to Haran, in northwest Mesopotamia. Egypt, again under a strong ruler, planned to go to the aid of the Assyrian king, perhaps to keep the Babylonian Empire from achieving control over so much territory as to be a threat to Egypt herself. Josiah, in a suicidal mission, met the Egyptian king at Megiddo, in the valley of Jezreel, and tried to halt this advance. Josiah was killed in this encounter with the pharaoh, and there is no question that his passing was sincerely mourned by his people. Even though his actions may have come too late, he had managed to restore the integrity and self-respect, as well as the external power, of his kingdom. The historian of II Kings praises Josiah without qualification, and his praise appears to be justified.

> Before him there was no king like him, who turned to the Lord with all his heart and with all his soul and with all his might, according to all the law of Moses; nor did any like him arise after him (II Kings 23:25).

Deuteronomy 6:4–25—The Book of Deuteronomy, the central part of which was the scroll found during Josiah's reforming reign, has a long and complex history. The book is cast in the form of farewell addresses of Moses to the people just before their entry into Canaan. Most scholars do not believe that Moses actually wrote these words, but it is now thought that the basic traditions in Deuteronomy go back as far as the period of the Judges.[36]

The central theme of Deuteronomy is the covenant, and the book itself can be seen as an anthology of sermons preached in covenant renewal ceremonies in Northern Israel from very ancient times. This body of speeches must have been treasured among Levites and prophetic circles in the Northern Kingdom and then, after the kingdom fell to the Assyrians, brought to Judah. Somewhat adapted to the religious and political situation of Judah, the work was put forward during Josiah's reign.

In Deuteronomy, we hear the authentic voice of ancient Israelite religion speaking, and chapter 6 is a perfect example of the style and emphases of that compelling voice. The characteristic themes are these:

The personal address—Israel is spoken to directly on Yahweh's behalf by Moses himself. The community that is formed out of this dialogue is a community of persons, not a machine-like bureaucracy. But this personal dialogue means personal responsibility. Certain demands for justice and integrity and concern are laid upon the people. By their response to these demands, the people shape their own destiny, for good and for ill (verses 10–15).

The demand for love—Verses 4–9 begin the passage known to Judaism as the *Shema* (from the first word, "Hear"). This very passage was cited by Jesus as "the first and great commandment" (Matthew 22:34–40 and parallels). What is demanded under the title of "love" is utter obedience to Yahweh in every aspect of everyday life—an obedience that comes from the heart and is the very antithesis of mere legalism or external conformity.

The givenness of life—Israel is to understand her very existence in the land of Canaan as the gift of Yahweh (verses 10–12). Everything that makes her life possible there was created for her by God, and everything that she possesses can also be withdrawn if she breaks the covenant. This characteristic Deuteronomic theme introduced a note of conditionality that was healthy for a kingdom that had come to believe that Yahweh's protection depended on no conditions whatever. Israel is made responsible before God and history for her own destiny.

The appeal to history—As Deuteronomy continues to reiterate, Israel must understand herself and her identity on the basis of her past history. Her history is seen as the interplay between Yahweh and his covenant people, beginning with the gracious act by which Yahweh rescued the Hebrews from Egypt and made them his people (verses 20–25).

The most striking characteristic of Deuteronomy, however, cannot be captured in such a listing of propositional statements. The real key to the power of Deuteronomy is the style, with its direct address and sense of urgency, and the earthy reality of its content. Behind this work there stands a long line of powerful speakers who overwhelm the listener with the crystal clarity of their conceptions: Israel is Yahweh's people; the structure of her relation to Yahweh is the covenant of Moses; the substance of her life must be obedience to his demand for integrity, justice, and love.

Some Questions for Discussion: How has the author of II Kings 22–23 characterized Josiah as a king? Identify the passage in II Kings 22–23 to support this characterization. Judging from his actions, do you think the high opinion of Josiah is justified? How did the finding of the ancient scrolls come about? What, then, did Josiah systematically set out to accomplish immediately after the scroll was publicly read? Why did these scrolls move Josiah to such action?

Why did Josiah consult a prophetess before beginning his mission? What was her message? Scholars sometimes refer to this period of Josiah's reign as the *Götterdämmerung* (twilight of the gods). Using specific examples from II Kings 23 and 24, explain what you think scholars may mean by attaching this symbolic name to this period of Jewish history. Aside from the destruction of pagan worship areas, what was Josiah trying to accomplish with regard to the reestablishment of Yahweh worship?

Compare Deuteronomy 6:4–25 with Deuteronomy 5:6–21. Do you think Deuteronomy 6:4–5 is an adequate summary? Why, or why not? What is the general tone of the entire passage? Can people be *commanded* to love God? Can *love* (verse 5) and *fear* (verse 13) of God exist side by side? Think of a human relationship which, in your opinion, would serve as a good comparison to the relationship of God and his people presented here (for example, parent/child). Discuss the similarities and differences that exist between the two relationships. How is God portrayed here? How might this picture of God differ from the God that those living during Josiah's reign recognized?

Why do you think 6:10–12 is recited twice daily by devout Jews throughout the world?

Suggested Activities: The message in Deuteronomy 6 is, indeed, powerfully stated. Study Deuteronomy 6:4–25 carefully, before writing a theme in which you compare the style of this chapter with the style of a chapter in Exodus or Genesis. In your comparison, you will want to answer questions like these: What gives the writing in Deuteronomy its force? What technique(s) sets it apart from some other books in the Old Testament? Why is the message in Deuteronomy 6 so readable?

Compare the style and vocabulary of a chapter in Deuteronomy with a chapter in Joshua, Judges, Samuel, or Kings. Why do you think some scholars think the style and vocabulary are similar in those five books?

Select any ruler of any country of the world who can be compared with Josiah and then write a paper in which you compare the two.

Read the entire book of Deuteronomy and then write a set of laws you think necessary for people to govern themselves today. Will you keep some of the laws included in Deuteronomy? Which ones? Why?

Jeremiah

Jeremiah was a contemporary of the reforming Josiah. Unlike Josiah, however, Jeremiah lived on through the terrible years in which the storm of military destruction finally broke upon Judah.

After Josiah's death at Megiddo in 609 B.C., the throne was taken by his son Jehoahaz. This unfortunate young man reigned for only three months before the Egyptians, now in control following Pharaoh Neco's expedition through Palestine, removed him from the throne and took him captive in Egypt. In his place, the Egyptian overlords installed another son of Josiah as king, giving him the throne-name Jehoiakim.

Jehoiakim seems to have been utterly lacking in the religious zeal and seriousness of intent that had made Josiah remarkable. With his country approaching its death throes, Jehoiakim undertook to redecorate his palace, using forced labor from among his own countrymen. Jeremiah scornfully declared in one of his most scathing oracles that Jehoiakim would most fittingly be given an ass's burial, with appropriate lack of lamentation (Jeremiah 22:13–19).

With a king like Jehoiakim on the throne, the government-sponsored reform of religious and social life became a hollow mockery. But worse trouble was coming. In 605 B.C. Nebuchadnezzar, the great military commander of Babylonia, advanced against the Egyptians into Syria and decisively defeated them. Shortly afterwards, Nebuchadnezzar himself became king of Babylonia, and in the following years undertook extensive campaigns into Palestine. By 603 B.C., Judah was forced to shift her allegiance away from the defeated Egyptians and to become a vassal of Babylonia.

If Jehoiakim ever conceived a more foolish idea than his plan to redecorate the palace during a national emergency, it was his decision to revolt against the Babylonians in 601 B.C. by refusing to pay the annual tribute to Babylonia and then looking to Egypt for aid. As the Babylonians prepared to act, raiders from Ammon and Edom fell upon Judah. Shortly after, Jehoiakim himself died, leaving the task of presiding over the nation's demise to his eighteen-year-old son, Jehoiachin. Within two years (598–597 B.C.) the Babylonians were at the gates of Jerusalem. Jehoiachin had no choice but to surrender, though there were some ardent nationalists in the city who were ready to fight to the death, and some religious enthusiasts who believed that Yahweh would intervene to save his holy city. Jeremiah, incidentally, was not a member of either group, for he was convinced that Yahweh intended for his people to fall as punishment for their sins.

Jehoiachin was led into exile in Babylonia, along with other leading personages of the community, and his uncle Mattaniah, youngest son of Josiah, was placed on the throne as Babylonia's vassal. To symbolize their control of the new king, the Babylonians changed his name to Zedekiah.

For ten years Judah lived on as a conquered kingdom within the Babylonian Empire. But the fires of Jewish nationalism still smoldered under the surface of Judah's life; the belief that Yahweh would not allow his holy nation to be destroyed was a belief that some could not give up. Perhaps also there was in some Jews a desperate feeling that things could not be worse—that anything was better than their impoverished and constricted existence as a conquered people. Revolt broke out again, fanned by hopes that a new and powerful pharaoh in Egypt could successfully fight the Babylonians. In 594 B.C. such a revolt began but was quickly quenched. In 589 B.C., however, a final rebellion broke out in Judah. By January, 588 B.C., Babylonian troops arrived and surrounded Jerusalem. The city held out under siege until July, 587 B.C. By that time the rest of Judah lay under Babylonian control. Just as the food supplies of the besieged capital ran out, the walls were breached and the Babylonian soldiers poured into the city.

The devastation that now fell upon Jerusalem fulfilled the worst prophecies of Jeremiah and others. Public buildings, including the palace and Temple, were razed; the city's defense walls were broken down. King Zedekiah, always a rather pathetic figure in his indecisive attempts to govern a doomed nation, was reduced to the most pitiful degradation. He was forced to watch as his sons were put to death, then was blinded and led off in chains to Babylonia to die. Many other leaders and potential leaders were taken into exile; the nation itself was left to die, like the king, in blindness and grief. That the Hebrew people and their stubborn faith did not die is one of the most remarkable facts in human history. From the exiles in Babylonia, a new people and a new religious community were formed out of the shattered fragments of the past. This new life was to a large extent made possible by the faithfulness and courage of such lonely figures as the prophet Jeremiah, whose lifetime spanned all the transitions in Judah's life from Josiah's reform to the final extinction of the kingdom in 587 B.C.

JEREMIAH'S CALL TO BE A PROPHET (JEREMIAH 1:1–10)

The editor of the Book of Jeremiah sets his prophetic hero in the context of Judah's national history in the first four verses, listing the three main rulers during Jeremiah's lifetime: Josiah (640–609 B.C.), Jehoiakim (609–598 B.C.), and Zedekiah (598–587 B.C.). These verses remind us of the political character of prophetic careers. Jeremiah's involvement in the public events of his lifetime was especially profound and frequently painful to him, for his opposition to royal policies and popular movements made him hated and ostracized by nearly every citizen of the distraught kingdom.

Something of the personal cost of such lonely opposition is reflected in the words with which Jeremiah recounts his call (verses 4–10). In these words, Jeremiah hints at the agony of the double identification that he feels: he is torn between being Yahweh's spokesman and being simply another member of the suffering community of Judah. He needs comfort, courage, and support from Yahweh, for he will be afraid. He would rather not undertake the task, offering the excuse that he is "only a youth." This was probably literally true; we should picture Jeremiah at this time (about 627 B.C.) as a boy in his late teens. But Yahweh commands him, and he must speak. He is told that his authority extends

> over nations and over kingdoms
> to pluck up and to break down,
> to destroy and to overthrow,
> to build and to plant.

Hesitant, conscious of his youth, and not knowing what the future will bring, Jeremiah nevertheless accepts his call. He does it in the spirit of a man accepting a painful, but inescapable, destiny (verse 5).

Some Questions for Discussion: What political events were occurring during the time of Jeremiah's prophecy (see II Kings 23, 24)? How does Jeremiah respond to God's call? How is his response characteristic of the responses of other prophets before him? How does Jeremiah's reaction help to characterize him for us? How does Jeremiah come to realize the inescapable nature of his destiny? Can the election of Jeremiah be compared with the election of Israel? Is Jeremiah (Israel) free to choose? How does 1:10 emphasize the dual nature of Jeremiah's mission? Why must the prophet break down and build up?

EARLY PROPHECY (JEREMIAH 2:1–3:5)

This selection of Jeremiah's early oracles probably spans the last years of Josiah and the early years of Jehoiakim. Through these bursts of poetry we gain an impression of the life of Judah that is strikingly powerful. As is frequently done by Hebrew poets, Jeremiah expresses himself through an amazing profusion of images that adds up to a portrait of a people impressionistically blurred but unmistakable in its central themes. The people are likened, in quick succession, to a fool who abandons a clear spring in favor of the stagnant waters of a cistern (2:13), a slave (verse 14), a small animal trying to escape a lion (verse 15), a thirsty man traveling far to drink from a river (verses 18–19), a sex-crazed harlot (verses 20–23); a vine, a young camel, a wild ass in heat (verses 21–25), a thief caught red-handed (verse 26), and recurrently, a bride deserting her husband (2:1–2; 2:32–3:5). The image of the bride, together with the profusion of images drawn especially from agricultural life, suggests an indebtedness to the prophet Hosea.

The portrait of the people that emerges suggests a hollowness, devoid of sense and meaning. Judah appears bent on self-destruction, when her salvation lies close at hand. She is driven by lusts, like a rutting animal or a nymphomaniacal harlot. The nation thus loses her true identity and her destiny. Judah merely goes through the motions of living, serving first one master and then another, like a man suffering under insane compulsions.

The facts that lie behind the poetry are not difficult to imagine. Judah has attached herself vainly to first one kingdom and then another ("the waters of the Nile" and "the waters of the Euphrates'" in verse 18). She has gained no safety by this mad search for allies. Instead, she has lost her reason for being—her devotion to Yahweh, whose people she is. The pagan religious practices that have become rampant in Judah point up the shallowness of her existence. She has undertaken these corrupting cults to gain favor with the nations whom she courts, but as a result she has become to the nations and to Yahweh simply another prostitute offering her favors to any passing stranger (verse 20).

The hollow senselessness that Jeremiah diagnoses as the national illness has not been cured by Josiah's stringent reforms. The priests are still ignorant of Yahweh's law, and the rulers themselves transgress it. Even the prophets cannot be counted on to speak the truth (verse 8). The resulting social crimes are blatant, for only Yahweh's covenant law protected the poor (verse 34). And yet the people cannot even see these crimes. Judah protests her innocence and foresees no trouble in the future.

At this point Jeremiah only hints at the judgment that must overtake his people. Elsewhere he speaks of military destruction by a "foe from the north" (4:5–8; 6:22–26), and tries to communicate the stark terror that Judah so blankly faces (4:23–26; 5:14–18). Only as events progressed would this foe from the north take on a concrete form as the armies of Babylonia advanced.

Perhaps the most significant element in Jeremiah's oracles is the total mood conveyed. The poetry communicates a sense of nervous excitement and a high degree of personal sensitivity that must have been authentic aspects of Jeremiah's personality. Throughout these oracles, there is also a sense of bewilderment, as though the prophet observes the insensitivity and complacency of his countrymen but cannot believe what he is seeing. The question form predominates, as though Jeremiah's whole life had become an experience of utter dismay at the folly of his people (for example, 2:5, 6, 8, 11, 14, 17, 18, 21, 23, 24, 28, 29, 31). Jeremiah is frustrated as he attempts to understand something that is ultimately without sense, and his images convey this frustrated anguish over the failure of all common sense and rationality.

Some Questions for Discussion: How do Yahweh's words in 2:2–3 and 6–7 emphasize the two parts of the covenant relationship? What "two evils" are represented by the imagery of 2:13? What images in chapter 2 are used to depict Judah? Note particularly the recurring image of a marriage. How is it introduced? How does the relationship change? Do you think this is an appropriate image? Why, or why not? Would it be an effective metaphor for the Israelites? Why, or why not?

What does Jeremiah say has been Israel's reaction to her sins? What seems to be Jeremiah's attitude toward Israel's "blindness"? What is the characterization of Judah that emerges from this passage? What effect does Jeremiah's technique of questions and answers have on this passage? What does the use of questions suggest about Jeremiah's attitude toward his people?

THE TEMPLE SERMON (JEREMIAH 7:1–15)

In sharp contrast to the lyric poetry of his oracles, the writings ascribed to Jeremiah contain a number of prose sermons. Stylistically, these sermons are very similar to the Book of Deuteronomy, which was promulgated early in Jeremiah's prophetic ministry, but the contents and emphases are uniquely Jeremiah's.

The Temple sermon is passed on to us in two accounts (see also Jeremiah 26), indicating the importance and controversial nature of its contents. The account in Jeremiah 26 informs us that the sermon was delivered in 609 B.C., at the beginning of Jehoiakim's reign, and adds that Jeremiah was arrested immediately after the sermon, having just barely escaped being put to death for his words.

What is there in this sermon to arouse such rage and hostility in the listeners? Jeremiah had dared to attack the center of the religious life of the kingdom—the Jerusalem Temple. The Temple had always been highly sacred and highly important, both religiously and politically, in the life of Judah. There Yahweh himself made his presence dwell above the Ark of the Covenant in the innermost sanctuary. Together with the Davidic dynasty, the Temple was the central expression of Yahweh's covenant as it had been understood since David's time.

If the Deuteronomic reform had shifted attention away from the Davidic dynasty ever so slightly, it had made the Temple all the more important. In obedience to the unique and forceful demand of Deuteronomy that worship be centralized in the place that Yahweh should choose, all other places of worship had been prohibited or destroyed. Surely this exaltation of the Temple had been a pious act with which God was well pleased.

So must Jeremiah's countrymen have thought. But to Jeremiah the new emphasis on Temple worship made the fundamental rottenness of the kingdom all the more intolerable to Yahweh. Saying to themselves "the temple of Yahweh, the temple of Yahweh, the temple of Yahweh," the people continued in the old paths of oppression and injustice, as if the words would cover their acts. Jeremiah insists that the words about the Temple are deceptive, for Judah's heart is no different than before. "Has this house," he asks in dismay, "which is called in my name, become a den of robbers in your eyes?" (verse 11).

Jeremiah concludes with a terrible pronouncement, and one which nearly brought a swift end to his prophetic career: Yahweh will not allow his people to live on his land and worship at his temple unless they truly respond to his demands. Just as Shiloh was long ago destroyed by the Philistines and even the Ark taken away, so can the Jerusalem Temple be destroyed. And just as the Northern Kingdom ("Ephraim," verse 15) could be overwhelmed by conquerers, so Judah also could fall.

From our vantage point in history, Jeremiah's threats seem sane and perceptive, for in fact both the Temple and the nation were destroyed. But Jeremiah's contemporaries refused to look at either the present or the immediate future. Like a sleepwalker who stumbles ahead and refuses to be awakened to reality, Judah moved inexorably forward toward destruction, pausing only to knock aside any who had the temerity to warn of the chasm that lay ahead.

Some Questions for Discussion: A sermon reveals values. What values does the prophet revere? Why does Jeremiah attack the center of religious life—the Jerusalem Temple? Why does Jeremiah mention Shiloh? What is implied in the comparison of Shiloh and the Jerusalem Temple?

What hypocrisy is Jeremiah condemning here? How does his rhetoric emphasize the hypocrisy? What form does Jeremiah say that repentance should take? Why do you suppose he suggests that form of repentance rather than a change in the manner of worship? What kind of change is he telling the people is needed? What would be your reaction if you received a sermon like Jeremiah gave the Israelites? What do you think a sermon like Jeremiah gave would discuss if it were delivered in America today?

Suggested Activity: Taking the position of a "Jeremiah prophet," write a sermon to be delivered today in a church in your hometown.

A PERSONAL LAMENT (JEREMIAH 20:7–18)

The most fascinating feature of the Book of Jeremiah for modern readers is the glimpse we are given of the inner life of this sensitive and lonely man. Included among his oracles and sermons are a number of poems in which Jeremiah speaks directly and intimately to God of the heartbreaking task that is his. Often called "the confessions of Jeremiah," these poems reveal the torments of a man who can clearly foresee the destiny of his people but whose own role and destiny and relation to God remain a baffling mystery.

The outer events of the prophet's life had continued to follow the pattern seen in his Temple sermon. He continually attacked the monarchy, the religious leadership, and the people themselves for their blind and complacent wickedness. He regularly threatened a coming destruction that would make all past disasters appear minor. Just as regularly, Jeremiah was rebuffed, ostracized, mocked, threatened with death, and sometimes imprisoned and beaten. (See Jeremiah 20:1-6, which provides the context for the present poem.)

This treatment by his countrymen was bitter enough, for Jeremiah loved his people and nation and always projected himself into the future suffering that he believed was inevitable (see Jeremiah 4:19-22). But far more bitter was the feeling that Yahweh himself had deserted his prophet. The promise "I am with you to deliver you" (1:8) seemed deceptive, for all that Jeremiah knew as a result of his prophesying was loneliness and suffering.

In this mood of abandonment, Jeremiah wrote the poem of lamentation in Jeremiah 20. He insists that Yahweh deceived him in promising support and protection. We might better translate verse 7 as "You seduced me, you took advantage of my innocence." The prophet speaks movingly of the derision and reproach that his oracles earn for him. He cannot keep silent, for he feels compelled to speak (verses 8-10).

The mood shifts suddenly as Jeremiah imagines with some relish the destruction and dishonor that will fall upon his adversaries in the end. Yahweh will punish them and vindicate his prophet! He even sings a hymn of thanks for his imagined deliverance (verse 13).

But the mood does not last. Jeremiah was not actually the sort of man who enjoys seeing his enemies suffer; and in any case his own suffering continues unabated, and Yahweh seems as far away as ever. Like a starving man who dreams of food and then awakens again to the reality of his hunger, Jeremiah concludes in a statement of despair that is unsurpassed in Old Testament literature (see Job's lament, Job 3). Like a witch or a necromancer, he tries to cast a curse upon his whole existence by cursing the very day of his birth. He concludes, typically, with a question:

> Why did I come forth from the womb
> to see toil and sorrow,
> and spend my days in shame?

We do not know that this tortured man ever found his question answered.

Some Questions for Discussion: What is the tone that Jeremiah uses in this passage? What are the changing moods in this passage and how do you account for them? What reasons does he give for his despair? What does his attitude here tell you about Jeremiah as a person? What does it tell you of Jeremiah's relationship with the Lord? with the people of Judah? How does Jeremiah's use of the birth motif in verses 14–18 convey his despair in a way especially meaningful to his contemporaries?

Do you think it is possible for a person to continue to pursue his "mission," as did Jeremiah, despite a pervading sense of despair and defeat? Explain your opinion, citing, if possible, contemporary persons and situations which substantiate your viewpoint.

JEREMIAH'S ROLE IN JERUSALEM'S LAST DAYS (JEREMIAH 36:1–40:6)

Together with the oracles, sermons, and personal laments of Jeremiah, we have a series of detailed and unquestionably authentic third-person narratives that set forth the prophet's life in the context of Judah's history. Some of these narratives were written by Baruch, Jeremiah's personal secretary and friend; as a result we know more of the personal life of this prophet than of any other Old Testament figure, with the possible exception of David.

The narrative of chapter 36 is set in 605 B.C., the fourth year of Jehoiakim. In this year the Egyptian overlords of Judah suffered a significant defeat at the hands of Babylonia's armies. The predicted foe from the north was suddenly identified in Jeremiah's mind as Babylonia, and the nation's vain trust in Egypt was exposed for what it was. No longer able to keep silent, even though he was barred from entering the Temple to speak to the people in person, Jeremiah had his oracles against Judah recorded in a scroll (36:1–8).

The appropriate time for the scroll to be publicly read was provided by the king himself, who declared a day of fasting in the midst of the growing national crisis. The scroll was read to the people and then again presented before royal officials (36:9–18). Alarmed at the king's probable reaction but perhaps somewhat convinced by Jeremiah's forthright attack on national policy, the officials advised Jeremiah and Baruch to go into hiding immediately (verse 19).

Jehoiakim did hear of the scroll, however, and quickly lived up to Jeremiah's earlier analysis of his character (22:13–19). He had the scroll read to him as he sat before a burning brazier in his chilly palace, then scornfully cut the scroll to pieces and fed it to the flames (36:20–26). As before, both king and people (though some officials did not agree, verses 25–26) refused to be wakened from their dream. Their belief that all would be well if only the words of Jeremiah could be erased would be pathetic if it were not so dangerously irresponsible.

Jeremiah, however, could not be silenced so easily. The narrator records that he went into hiding and quickly produced a copy of the first scroll, adding even more similar oracles. Scholars believe that this second scroll forms the substance of chapters 1–25 of our present Book of Jeremiah.

In Jeremiah 37, the narrative leaps ahead some twenty years to the time of Zedekiah. The year is 588 B.C. Jehoiachin ("Coniah," 37:1) lives in exile in Babylonia, along with many other leaders of Judah. Zedekiah reigns in his place as Babylonia's puppet, but has now dared to lead a rebellion against his overlord, with the futile hope of Egyptian intervention (verses 2–5). As a result, Jerusalem is under siege, and Jeremiah sees her prophesied end approaching.

Perennially courageous, Jeremiah speaks out against the rebellion. If Yahweh has planned the destruction of his people, Jeremiah argues, it is far better to give up the battle now before more lives are lost. This surrender was Jeremiah's insistent message, even when the Babylonian troops had to lift the siege of the city temporarily.

In the eyes of the city's defenders, such words and such an attitude branded Jeremiah as a traitor. For his pains, therefore, Jeremiah found himself again in prison. But the king, Hamlet-like in his vacillation, is not sure. He sends for Jeremiah and asks if there is any new word from Yahweh. "There is," Jeremiah boldly replies, and then proceeds to predict the king's own capture by the Babylonians. But he also pleads to be released from his miserable dungeon and provided with food. This the king does.

The following chapters portray in graphic detail the vacillation of the king, torn between his war-prone advisers and the unshakable confidence of Jeremiah that all resistance is hopeless. It is as if the king almost awakes from the national dream, but, sleepwalker that he is, cannot bear the light of Jeremiah's sane predictions. First the king is prevailed upon by Jeremiah's enemies, and allows them to place the prophet at the miry bottom of a disused cistern (38:1–6). Then Jeremiah is rescued from the cistern by a foreigner, an Ethiopian official in the court (38:7–13). The king again sends for the prophet, pledging him to secrecy, and begs for an oracle. The word from Yahweh's spokesman is the same, perhaps worse: the city, the royal family, and the king himself will all be seized by the Babylonians. Jeremiah is again imprisoned (38:14–28).

In July, 587 B.C., the end came for Judah. Jeremiah's insistent and anguished message was vindicated to the full. In the wake of the nation's destruction, we catch a glimpse of the courageous prophet receiving better treatment from the Babylonians than he ever had from his fellow Hebrews. Jeremiah was released from prison, assigned a food allowance (a necessity in the starving occupied territory of Judah), and allowed to remain among his people in the custody of Gedaliah, the newly appointed Jewish governor (39:1–40:6). Little was left of the nation and her population. The leaders of the community were deported and the land left in the hands of "some of the poor people who owned nothing" (39:10). We do know that another revolt did take place and that Jeremiah's protector, Gedaliah, was murdered by the rebels (Jeremiah 41). Jeremiah himself fled to Egypt with a group of Judeans who exiled themselves for fear of Babylonian reprisals after Gedaliah's murder (Jeremiah 42–43). In the midst of the insane continuation of Judah's rebellion, however, Jeremiah was able to see beyond the immediate destruction into a new future that Yahweh would bring about.

Some Questions for Discussion: Why does Jeremiah use a scroll to deliver his message? How does Jehoiakim unwittingly co-operate with Jeremiah's plan to proclaim his oracles publicly? What is the irony in the king's destruction of Jeremiah's scroll? Jeremiah 37–41 chronicles more of Jeremiah's warnings to Israel and the inevitable outcome of her deafness. Considering the characterization of Jeremiah already drawn, discuss his prob-able reactions as the prophecies come true. What impression do we get of the Babylonian conquerors from their treatment of Jeremiah?

Beginning with chapter 37, Zedekiah is the King of Judah. How has he become king? After reading verse 2, can you speculate on the type of person he might be? What sort of person is Zedekiah described as? What more do you learn about him through his encounters with Jeremiah?

Suggested Activity: Study the narrative in 37:1–39:7. Assume that you are a close friend of the king or you are the king him-self. Rewrite the narrative as a story or script expressing your view of Zedekiah's situation. How do you feel toward Jeremiah? Will you express your opinions/attitudes in dialogue? soliloquy? narrative? Can you justify Zedekiah's change of heart toward Jeremiah? Could/does Zedekiah's attitude toward God affect his behavior? How might the court's political advisers influence Zedekiah? What is Zedekiah's attitude toward Babylonia? What emotions motivate Zedekiah's behavior? How can those emo-tions best be conveyed? actions? dialogue? gestures? narrative?

Consider the setting for your story or drama. Does the action take place at night, or during the day? How does the inside of the palace look? How might the setting contribute to what you are trying to say about Zedekiah?

JEREMIAH'S HOPE FOR THE FUTURE (JEREMIAH 31:31–34)

If the term *jeremiad* has become a byword for gloomy lamentations over a threatening future, it is because Jeremiah's later readers have not taken seriously the many passages in which the prophet sets forth his stubborn hope for Israel's future. Precisely when the whole world seemed to fall upon his nation and his own worst predictions found fulfillment in years of heartbreaking suffering, Jeremiah was looking beyond the darkness of the present into a future of security and meaning.

Unlike some Old Testament prophets and apocalyptic writers, Jeremiah paints a picture of the coming good age in very restrained colors: Israel and Judah will dwell together in peace and be repopulated. They shall plant vineyards and live to enjoy their fruit. They shall once again rejoice with dancing at the harvest festivals. (See the whole of Jeremiah 31.) That Jeremiah should look above the smoking ruins of Jerusalem, amidst a people dying of famine and sickness, to see such homely scenes of rejoicing in the future is poignant. It is a mark also of his realism and of his solid identification with his people, for the new Israel will be no heavenly existence but simply the fulfillment of what Israel should have been from the beginning—a secure nation whose ground of existence is the faithfulness and love of a just God.

And yet Jeremiah's new covenant prophecy in 31:31–34 contains something that is absolutely new in prophetic hope. The new people who shall be Yahweh's people in the future will be bound to Yahweh with a new covenant. Whereas the old covenant could be broken, and was tragically broken by Israel's disobedience and thus exists no more, the new covenant will be unbreakable, because it is a covenant directly "within them" and "upon their hearts." The factor that makes disobedience a possibility—the confrontation of man's will with an alien will—is thus eliminated.

We can understand Jeremiah's new conception as the result of his own baffled struggles with Yahweh, with his blind countrymen, and with his own heart. He had declared in desperation once:

> The heart is deceitful above all things,
> and desperately corrupt;
> who can understand it? (17:9)

As he struggled to understand his own motives and emotions and to awaken his contemporaries to reality, Jeremiah must have come to believe that what was needed was not just a new covenant or a new set of laws—for man would break these again—but a new man. It is this new man, with the new heart that is not estranged from God, who inhabits Jeremiah's new Israel. If his own anguished self-understanding is here reflected, even more remarkable is the courage with which he retains his stubborn faith in Israel's God.[37]

Some Questions for Discussion: What tone permeates the message of Jeremiah 31:27–49? What words and phrases help you to establish the tone? Explain the relationship between the tone and the content of the message. What is your feeling after reading this passage? Do you think the tone, or the message itself, has a greater impact on you? Why?

What is the distinguishing element between the old and the new covenants? How does Jeremiah view the Lord here? Why does Jeremiah use the poetic description of the Lord in verses 35–36? Does it seem possible that the ever-misbehaving Israelites could function according to the new covenant any better than according to the old? What, according to Jeremiah, will enable Israel to once again gain God's favor?

CHAPTER 12

The Fall of Judah

EXILE AND RESTORATION

The Fall of Jerusalem (II Kings 24–25)

As we have already seen from Jeremiah 36–40, the last days of Judah were turbulent, dramatic, and tragic beyond measure. The great King Josiah, rebuilding his land religiously in the wake of the Deuteronomic reform and politically at the expense of the collapsing Assyrian Empire, was killed in battle at Megiddo as he attempted to prevent the Egyptians from marching north to help the Assyrians against the onrushing Babylonians. Josiah was forced to fight. He knew that if the Egyptians got through, all his work of political consolidation (rejoining Judah and North Israel) would come to naught, and he would once again be reduced to a vassal king, subservient to either the Assyrians or the Egyptians. But his death put a sudden end to the Deuteronomic reform, undercutting the notion that Yahweh blesses the righteous and punishes the wicked.

Jehoiakim, the successor placed on the throne by the Egyptians to maintain their tenuous hold on Palestine, forsook all of his father's ways. Although the people were living on a shoestring because of the heavy foreign tributes that had been imposed, Jehoiakim squandered the little that was left on his own private indulgences. When the Egyptians arrived too late to help the crushed Assyrians and were in turn overwhelmingly defeated by the Babylonians under Nebuchadnezzar at Carchemish in 605 B.C., Jehoiakim quickly transferred his half-hearted allegiance to the Babylonian king. But no sooner were the Babylonians out of Palestine consolidating other parts of their empire to the east than Jehoiakim rebelled, doubtlessly hoping for the protection of Egyptian arms. Several years elapsed before Nebuchadnezzar was able to return to Palestine, but when he arrived, Jehoiakim "died" just as his troops reached the gates of the city. Most likely he was assassinated by people who hoped that the Babylonians would be less vindictive. Jehoiachin, the eighteen-year-old son of Jehoiakim, surrendered to the Babylonians, who spared the city and its population. To quell any further nationalistic ardor, the Babylonians exiled some eight to ten thousand of the leading citizens of Judah —priests, civil officers, and nobles, including the royal family.

Zedekiah, an uncle of the deposed king, was placed on the throne, although Jehoiachin was still regarded by both Jews and Babylonians as the real king of Judah. Zedekiah was a pathetic figure. He knew that subservience to the Babylonians was the only feasible course of action, but being only a regent, he apparently did not have the authority to enforce his will upon his rebellious nobles and advisers. Rebellion was in the air. Emissaries were constantly being sent from the surrounding nations, urging Judah to join in. Zedekiah valiantly held the line for almost a decade, but eventually he capitulated. The tragic events that followed are well recounted in the biblical narrative: the eighteen-month siege of the city and the resulting famine; the thwarted escape of Zedekiah and his men, leading to his being blinded after he was forced to witness the execution of his sons; the total destruction of Jerusalem after the treasures from the palace and the Temple had been removed and sent off to Babylon; the execution of the leading citizens of Judah and the deportation of half the entire population of Judah into exile; and, finally, the needless assassination of Gedaliah, the Jewish leader whom the Babylonians had appointed as governor over Judah and who was attempting to help the remaining population face reality by reconciling itself to Babylonian sovereignty.

These chapters were written by the Deuteronomic editor, who was responsible for the final form of Israel's history from the time of the Conquest through the Exile (Joshua—II Kings). One can note his formulaic hand at work, especially in 24:5–9, in which he makes a cursory judgment of each king's reign according to whether that king had obeyed the law of God. Very few kings receive a passing grade. The Deuteronomist is trying to show that history is determined by the extent to which man is subservient to God's will. An especially good example of this is II Kings 17, in which the Deuteronomist accounts for the fall of North Israel. It is interesting that the fall of Jerusalem is not accompanied by such a long peroration. Perhaps the events are still too immediate and the shock still too great. He certainly cannot blame Josiah for the collapse, since Josiah had done all he could to bring about an effective reform. The Deuteronomist can only account for the tragedy by alluding to the sins of Manasseh, who had reigned the generation prior to Josiah (24:3–5). But no major theological rationale is worked out. Perhaps the Deuteronomist has lost hope. He ends his great history on a bleak note in these chapters and only in the final passage hints that Judah's history may not be totally ended.

Some Questions for Discussion: What evidence do we have that the writer of II Kings had earlier written records of this period to refer to (24:5)? Having been placed on the throne by the Egyptians, Jehoiakim taxed the people of Judah heavily during the early years of his reign. What changes in Jehoiakim's foreign policy are reflected in 24:1? How does Judah fare under this policy?

Why might Jehoiachin fear the return of Nebuchadnezzar? What foreign policy does Jehoiachin adopt and what are the immediate results of it? What group of Israelites are left in Judah? Who succeeds Jehoiachin as king? What is Zedekiah's foreign policy and how does Judah fare under it?

What personal tragedies befall Zedekiah? By what device does the author indicate that the fall of Jerusalem was God's punishment for the sins of the leaders (23:32, 37; 24:3, 9, 19)? Whom does Nebuchadnezzar appoint as governor over those who remain in Judah?

What advice does Gedaliah give to the people? In light of

that advice, what irony do you see in Gedaliah's fate? How does the end of II Kings suggest some faint hope for the future of Judah?

How does the direct, factual style of II Kings 24, 25 reinforce the bleakness of the Judean history being recounted? What is the significance of II Kings 25:28, 29? To what degree does the symbolism reflect the actual Judean situation? How does this passage serve as a catharsis in the tragedy of this phase of Judean history?

Ezekiel

CALL TO BE A PROPHET (EZEKIEL 1–4)

Although some scholars have doubted the authenticity of a sixth century Ezekiel because the thought and the literary style are so completely different from other writings of this period (e.g., Jeremiah), it seems certain that Ezekiel did have an active prophetic ministry in the early Exilic period, being one of the leading citizens who was deported to Babylonia in 597 B.C. It is quite certain that Ezekiel was one of the high priests connected with the Jerusalem Temple; his literary imagery and theology reflect the viewpoint of the Jerusalem priesthood.

Ezekiel's prophetic career did not begin until after he had been in Babylonia for four years, when he was confronted with a vision of God while he was sitting on the banks of the Chebar Canal. This vision, which constitutes Ezekiel's first and most important call to prophesy, is described in chapter 1 and is one of the most striking pieces of literature in the entire Bible. God is depicted as coming out of the far north (a traditional site of theophanic appearances in Syro-Palestinian mythology [see Psalm 48:2]), surrounded by storm, wind, cloud, and fire, as when he appeared before Israel at Mount Sinai (Exodus 19). Ezekiel seems to have conceived of God as appearing enthroned on the Ark of the Covenant, which was conveyed by four cherubim who moved according to his command. In many ways this vision is related to the call of Isaiah (see our discussion of Isaiah 6). But Ezekiel's description is much more specific: the cherubim have four wings and four faces and are propelled upon wheels that enable them to move quickly in any direction at Yahweh's slightest whim. The Ark in Ezekiel's vision is described as made of a crystalline substance through which shines the fiery presence of the one who is enthroned on high. Notice the change in the narrative when the prophet describes the presence of God. Suddenly his language is full of qualifications such as "the likeness of," "like," "as it were," "that had the appearance of," and so forth—as if mortal terms were incapable of describing the overwhelming nature of the divine reality that he had experienced. As in Isaiah 6, the vision of God's presence culminates with a commission impelling Ezekiel to prophesy. He is warned in advance that he is being sent to address a nation that will receive his words with scorn, but he feels he must go anyway so that the people can never claim they had not been warned before disaster strikes.

Isaiah was cleansed and enabled to prophesy when his lips were touched by a burning altar coal held in a tong by the outstretched arm of a seraph (Isaiah 6:6f); Jeremiah is empowered to speak the divine word when Yahweh stretches out his hand and touches the prophet's mouth, proclaiming that the words of God had been placed in his mouth (Jeremiah 1:9); Ezekiel undergoes a similar experience when he is commanded to consume a scroll upon which was written oracles proclaiming Judah's fate. Ezekiel has now internalized the word of God; it is literally a part of him so that he can do no other than speak it. One is reminded of two verses from the confessions of Jeremiah:

> "Thy words were found, and I ate them,
>   and thy words became to me a joy
>   and the delight of my heart;
> for I am called by thy name,
>   O Lord, God of hosts." (Jer. 15:16)

> "If I say, 'I will not mention him
>   or speak any more in his name,'
> there is in my heart as it were a burning fire
>   shut up in my bones,
> and I am weary with holding it in,
>   and I cannot." (Jer. 20:9)

Through the image of the consumed scroll, Ezekiel is also expressing his compulsion (and authority) to prophesy as a response to his vision of God. One should be careful in interpreting Ezekiel's image of the consumed scroll as pure metaphor. Since other prophets perform strange symbolic actions, and since Ezekiel describes other actions even more bizarre in nature, one should consider the possibility that these descriptions are more than metaphorical.

Ezekiel is addressed throughout the book as "son of man," the same title Jesus used to describe himself. A great change in the term's meaning occurred during the six hundred years between Ezekiel and Jesus. As we see from Daniel 7:9–14, the "son of man" described the messianic-apocalyptic figure who was to bring in the new age—the Kingdom of God.[1] During Ezekiel's time, the title had almost the opposite meaning. It stresses Ezekiel's sense of his finitude and insignificance against this vision of God's glory. "Sons of Israel" is generally translated "Israelites"; "sons of Moab" are "Moabites"; so "son of man" stresses Ezekiel's feeling that he is merely one lowly piece of mankind.

A second vision relating to Ezekiel's call is recorded in 3:16–27. Verses 16–21 may be secondary in this context, but they are integrally related to Ezekiel's concept of individual responsibility that we will discuss later. Here he applies this concept to his call to prophesy. If the wicked perish because they have not been confronted with God's word, the guilt for their blood will be on Ezekiel's hands. Not only does he have the authority to speak because he has internalized the word of God, and not only will he have the compulsion to speak because that word will be in him like a burning fire, but he also has the fearful obligation to speak lest the blame for the impending judgment be laid at his doorstep.

Verses 22ff are an extremely strange sequel to the admonition to speak out. Here we see that Ezekiel is not to go out onto the highways and byways to bring the word of God to his people; instead, he is to lock himself in his house, remaining totally dumb except to utter the divine oracles that come to him. We see from 24:25–27 and 33:21–22 that Ezekiel fulfilled this commission, staying in his house for six years. On the day he heard that Jerusalem had fallen, he left the house, for apparently his task had been accomplished.

What was the prophet trying to do? It seems most likely, especially in the light of chapter 4, that Ezekiel was symbolically dramatizing the siege and fall of Jerusalem. In this action, the walls of his house became the walls of the city, and his being constrained to remain within paralleled the fate of the citizens of a city under siege. Further, Ezekiel felt that his actions in far-off Babylonia were helping to bring about the events that he was symbolically portraying. We have discussed this concept before: symbolical actions were never thought of as illustrative in the ancient Near East; they were rather conceived of as magically helping to bring about the events being dramatized. It seems apparent that Ezekiel felt that the first part of his commission as a prophet called upon him to do everything in his power to bring about the fall of Jerusalem so that God's judgment could be complete.

Ezekiel undertakes two further symbolic actions in chapter 4. In verses 1–3, he takes a brick (which archeology has shown to be common in Babylonia but not in Palestine) and draws a map of Jerusalem on it. Like a child playing with toy soldiers, the prophet presses the siege against the beleaguered brick. He moves against the "city" with an iron plate, symbolizing God's presence that will turn back the weapons of the defenders and enable the Babylonians to take the city. Ezekiel, however, is not indulging in child's play; he is engaged in the heartrending process of bringing about the destruction of a people of which he is a part.

Finally, Ezekiel is commanded to lie on his left side for 390 days, indicating the number of years that North Israel will spend in the Exile that had begun in 722 B.C. The words *left* and *north* are related in Hebrew, as are the words *right* and *south*. Following this, he is to remain on his right side for 40 days for the years of Judah's Exile. The entire time he is to remain bound down so that he cannot move and lessen the years of punishment. He is to eat bread that had been prepared from a mixed assortment of grains, once again miming the behavior of people who were enduring a siege in which the grain supply would be so short that the people would have to make do by mixing together whatever is at hand. When Yahweh commands that this mixture be baked over human dung (inhabitants of a besieged city would be cut off from the normal fuel supply), Ezekiel protests. Human dung was ritually unclean (Deuteronomy 23:12–14), and Ezekiel's sensitivities as a priest, let alone as a human being, could not bear such an ordeal. Yahweh relents, and cow's dung is substituted as the fuel.

We may well question whether Ezekiel actually carried out such bizarre actions (see also 5:1ff). But when we dig deeply into the book, we are overwhelmed by the untold agony that this prophet endures. We are not studying a whimsical teller of stories and player of games; we are reading the words of a genius who suffered intensely. Jeremiah and Ezekiel endured the most cataclysmic event that struck the Jewish community until the modern era. Jeremiah was able to persevere through pouring out his grief in his confessional confrontations with God. Ezekiel internalized his agony and was thus pushed to the borderline of insanity.

Some Questions for Discussion: Who is the narrator of Ezekiel 1:1? of 1:2–3? How might you account for the change in narrators, considering what you have studied about the Old Testament thus far?

According to Ezekiel, what did he see in the whirlwind that came out of the north? Prior to your reading of Ezekiel, where have you heard or seen the phrase "wheel in a wheel"? According to Ezekiel, why do the wheels have such great mobility?

Reread Ezekiel 1:26–28, noting the use of the phrases "the likeness of" and "the appearance of" or "appearance like." How many times are those phrases used in 1:26–28? Who is being described in 1:26–28? How does the description in 1:26–28 differ from the description in 1:4–14 and 1:15–24?

According to Ezekiel, what is the Lord's message to him? What does the Lord call Ezekiel? Why? According to Ezekiel, what does the Lord think of the people of Israel? What does the Lord tell Ezekiel to do in 3:1–3? What is the significance of Ezekiel's eating the scroll?

According to Ezekiel, what reason does the Lord give him for the house of Israel's not listening to the prophet? What changes in Ezekiel has the Lord made to help him cope with the people of Israel? What is Ezekiel's commission in 3:17–21?

Why will cords "be placed upon" Ezekiel? What is the significance of the Lord's instructions in 4:1–3? Why must Ezekiel lie first on his left side and then on his right? What will happen to him during this period of punishment? What does Ezekiel's punishment symbolize?

Suggested Activities: Reread Ezekiel 1:1–28 before writing your own description of Ezekiel's vision. Make your description as detailed as possible, and use your own words—not Ezekiel's. Compare your description with that of a classmate. How do the descriptions differ? Why do you think they differ?

Write a theme in which you compare Ezekiel's calling with Jeremiah's and Isaiah's. How are the callings similar? How do they differ? Compare the language of each description. Which account do you prefer? Why? How does the use of language influence your description?

Write a short theme in which you explain why you think the descriptions of the callings of prophets like Ezekiel, Jeremiah, and Isaiah were included in the books of the Old Testament.

You are the editor of a series of childrens' books, and your task is to select only one description of a calling to be a prophet to be included in one of the books for children between the ages of six and nine. Which "calling" will you include? Why? Explain why you would, or would not, change the language of the description in the Bible you are reading. If you would change it, write your description and also a defense of it.

THE GLORY OF GOD DEPARTS (EZEKIEL 8–10)

Chapter 8 is an extremely interesting one in the study of the history of religions, for it describes some of the syncretistic practices taking place in Jerusalem that the prophets had been condemning. As Ezekiel is sitting in his house in Babylonia, surrounded by a group of elders who have apparently come to him for consultation, he suddenly falls into an ecstatic state and is transported in his vision to the Temple in Jerusalem. At the gateway of the inner court facing north, Ezekiel sees the "seat of the image of jealousy." From parallels unearthed in other parts of Syria and Mesopotamia, it seems most likely that he is referring to a niche in the wall near the gate where a slab containing carved cultic and mythological scenes was kept.[2] In verses 14–15, women are seen weeping for the god Tammuz, so the carved slab may have contained a figure of the god relating to this ritual. Tammuz was originally a Sumerian deity, who was probably brought into Palestine through Assyrian influence. He is closely related in type to Baal, Osiris, and other gods who died annually as the crops would wither with the late summer dry spell. Devotees would cultically mourn the death of the fallen god, search for him, and finally find him—thus assuring rainfall and fertility for the coming year.

Ezekiel then proceeds in his vision to a room in the Temple, where he beholds seventy elders from Jerusalem participating in strange rites involving reptile and serpent worship, which is ultimately Egyptian in its origin. In Egypt, such rites were aimed at assuring devotees a blessed existence beyond the grave.[3]

The final abomination witnessed by the prophet is the sun worship which took place in the eastward-facing entrance of the Temple itself. Such rites had flourished on Canaanite soil for several millennia, being too deeply rooted to be totally obliterated during the Israelite occupation. It is also possible that these rites reflect the strengthening of ties with the sun-oriented Egyptian culture as a response to the anti-Babylonian feeling developing in the Jewish community.

Such practices are interesting data for the historian of religion, but for Ezekiel the priest-prophet, they constituted an abomination that could only lead to the destruction of that most holy place—the Temple of Jerusalem. The vision continues in chapter 9 with a summons to the divine executioners to move against the city. Six "men" (angels from the divine host) appear with outstretched swords in hand; they follow the divine scribe, who proceeds through the city marking the foreheads of the righteous whose names are recorded on his scroll (that is, Book of Life). This mark of protection, similar to the mark put upon Cain, turned aside the wrath of the executioners, but none other in the city was to be spared.

It is interesting to compare this passage with the introduction to the destruction of Sodom and Gomorrah in Genesis 18:16–33. In the earlier story, the entire city will be saved if there are fifty righteous found in it, and Abraham succeeds in getting Yahweh to reduce the prerequisite number to ten. In that story we find a corporate sense of guilt and righteousness, where an entire group is found to be one or the other *as a whole*, based on the predominant quality of its component parts. This view of a people as one "corporate personality" is typical of early Israelite thought.[4]

In Ezekiel's time the situation is different. One cannot say that we now find a greater sense of individual responsibility, because in earlier times each individual felt himself to be totally responsible to his corporate unit. One finds instead a more particularized sense of individual accountability—each individual within the community is punished or blessed in accordance with his own guilt or righteousness. We will explore the reasons for this change in our discussion of chapter 18 below.

After the angelic executioners had completed their task, the divine scribe was commanded to reach under the throne of God's presence and take some of the burning coals that moved like torches to and fro among the cherubim (see 1:13). These were to be strewn over the city, and Jerusalem would be reduced to rubble. Thus the holy city was to be destroyed by the very consuming fire that had represented the glory of God in Ezekiel's vision.

The final part of the vision must have been the hardest of all for the priestly prophet to endure: he saw the glory of God—described in the same vivid terms as the overpowering vision he experienced at the River Chebar in chapter 1—depart from the city. Ezekiel had grown up and been trained as part of the Jerusalem Temple personnel. And one of the central dogmas of the Jerusalem liturgy was the inviolability of Mount Zion, the dwelling place of the Most High.[5] But Ezekiel had reached the same conclusion as Jeremiah (see Jeremiah 7): the holy city, beginning with the Temple itself, must be destroyed. It is typical of the two prophets that they give quite different reasons for the necessity of the destruction. For Jeremiah, the Temple was providing a false sense of security, thus undercutting any move toward social reform. The people felt assured of God's presence through the Temple without the necessity of an ethical response. Thus the Temple was being cast down for the good of the people, so that they would be forced to seek God in the right way. Ezekiel tended to see things much more from God's point of view. He could only regard Jerusalem as a city of blood, where violence, oppression, and impurity had become normative among a people who had been called to be so much more. The glory of God was departing—leaving the people to their ruin—for his own sake, not for theirs. For Ezekiel, the pure holiness of God could not tolerate such painful proximity to his sinful people.

Some Questions for Discussion: Compare Ezekiel 8:1 with 1:1–3. Why might the giving of the precise date have been important to early listeners? What effect does this preciseness have? Ezekiel says in 8:1 that the "elders of Judah" were "sitting before me." What does this indicate about his acceptance as a prophet?

What "abominations" does Ezekiel see in his vision? Why might they be called abominations? According to Ezekiel, how does the Lord react to the abominations? Why must Jerusalem be destroyed? Who is to be spared? How will they be identified? Where else in the Old Testament have you read about someone receiving a mark that would signal his salvation?

Compare the description in chapter 10 with that of chapter 1.

What is the effect of the repeated description? What effect might Ezekiel's recounting this description have had on his listeners?

INDIVIDUAL ACCOUNTABILITY IN THE EXILIC COMMUNITY (EZEKIEL 18)

A basic tenet of Mosaic theology is that God acts in history, judging the wicked and blessing those who obey him so that his will is ultimately fulfilled. And yet the men of the Mosaic era were realistic enough to acknowledge that man's actions did not always produce instantaneous repercussions. Sometimes the judgment for man's folly would be visited upon him during his lifetime. But often the judgmental character of the historical process was not realized for several generations. Thus, although early Israel affirmed a God active in history, several generations were allowed for him to respond to the obedience and disobedience of man. Yahweh is one who visits ". . . the iniquity of the fathers upon the children and the children's children, to the third and fourth generation" (Exodus 34:7b). Furthermore, as we pointed out above, divine judgment and blessing were understood as being corporate in nature; individuals were rarely singled out for special treatment.

Ezekiel 18 presupposes such an attitude among the exilic community. A proverb was making the rounds: "The fathers have eaten sour grapes, and the children's teeth are set on edge" (Ezekiel 18:2b; Jeremiah 31:29–30). This is an apt paraphrase of the Mosaic concept of divine retribution. But it was being used by Ezekiel's contemporaries as a way to avoid facing responsibility for their situation. The exiles felt that they were whiling away their lives in Babylonian captivity through no fault of their own. Their fate had been predetermined by the folly of the preceding generation. There was nothing they could do to change their destiny; they could only hope and work for a better lot for their children and their children's children.

Ezekiel stands against the frustration and hopelessness so pervasive in the Jewish community by maintaining that each individual is free to shape his own destiny, and that it is determined by the extent to which he fulfills God's will. The Jews should not be blaming God for the injustice of the fate they were suffering. The Exile was a result of actions for which they themselves had been responsible. But the person who obeys God, as outlined in verses 5–9, shall have the blessing restored to him. Ezekiel is constantly saying that the "soul" that sins or obeys shall "die" or "live." The meaning would be clearer if the word *soul* were translated *person*. Ezekiel is not talking about an immortal soul that will be blessed or punished beyond the grave. He is saying that the person who obeys God will "live"—that is, have a life of prosperity, abundant progeny, and peace. There are gradations of life and death in Hebrew thought. The person who turns away from God will "die"—that is, suffer disease, defeat, humiliation, crop failure and so on.

A summary statement of Ezekiel's concept of individual accountability can be found in 18:19–24. His basic point is that each generation—and indeed each individual within that generation—will determine its own destiny by its own actions. The son will not be judged for the sins of the father. And, indeed, Ezekiel takes this concept of discontinuity between the generations one step further by insisting that it applies also to the lifetime of one individual (verses 21–24). If a righteous man turns away from God, his past will no longer be remembered and he will be judged for his iniquity. The opposite applies to a sinner who becomes righteous. In maintaining this doctrine so strictly, Ezekiel seems to be fulfilling a pastoral role—exhorting the discouraged to keep the faith and encouraging those who have been overly enamored of Babylonian culture to return before it is too late.

Ezekiel's doctrine of individual accountability was to some extent caused and furthered by the loosening of family ties and the waning of national identity that were caused by the expansion of the Assyrian and Babylonian empires into Palestine and by the traumatic, uprooting experience of the Exile. But there is no doubt that Ezekiel's thought at this point was partially responsible in helping Judaism to survive and adapt itself to the Diaspora experience. Jews were now scattered throughout the Near East from Egypt to Mesopotamia. Ezekiel made it possible for the Jew to relate directly as an individual to his God apart from the normal givens of an established monarchy, Temple ritual, and a geographically defined national identity.

Some Questions for Discussion: What meaning do you give to the proverb in Ezekiel 18:2? Why do you think this chapter begins with the Lord's quoting the proverb? Why is it central to the chapter?

What must a righteous man do? What is his fate? What will be the fate of a righteous man who has an evil son? What, in brief, is the message of chapter 18? How does this message differ from the Temple teachings before the Exile? (See Exodus 34:7b.)

What is the effect of the repetition in 18:10–13 and 18:15–17? Why do you think those sins were repeated?

According to 18:25–29, why is the way of the Lord just? Who is unjust? How will the "house of Israel" be judged? Why was the message of chapter 18 important to the exiled Jews?

VISIONS OF THE RESTORED COMMUNITY (EZEKIEL 36:16–37:14)

We have already discussed the eschatological hope for the future begun by Hosea and further developed by Isaiah and Jeremiah. Basic to this hope was the idea that the Jewish community would be brought back into a right relationship with God on the other side of the inevitable judgment. In Ezekiel (chapters 34–48), we find the most thoroughly spelled out eschatological program in the entire Bible. In 33:21–22, a fugitive who had escaped the fallen city brought news to the prophet that Jerusalem was in ruins. This marks a turning point in Ezekiel's prophetic career. When he learns that his task has been accomplished, he immediately leaves his house and begins to proclaim the hope of a future restoration. He envisions a purified Jewish community, brought back to her land and brought into a new covenant relationship with her God. All enemies—both cosmic and historical —will be destroyed so that Israel will be enabled to live in peace and fulfill God's righteous demands. The grand finale of this program is the building of the new Temple and the return to it of the glory of God. Now that both land and people have been cleansed of their sin, God will again tabernacle in their midst.

Ezekiel 36:16ff describes the new exodus that the prophet believes is about to take place. A prolegomena tells why the Exile was necessary: the land had become "unclean" because of Israel's sin.[6] Note how Ezekiel the prophet still sees Israel's alienation through the eyes of a priest. Israel's conduct is compared to a woman's menstrual uncleanness—quite a far cry from Amos' image of the needy being sold for a pair of shoes (Amos 2:6).

According to Ezekiel, Yahweh's purposes were not served through the Exile of Israel. The earlier prophets had hoped that the judgment of the Exile would be a sobering and purifying experience for God's people; they would acknowledge their sin and their need, and the right relationship between God and Israel could be restored. But Yahweh's name had been further profaned through the Exile of his people, because the Gentiles had mocked the helpless plight of the Jews and implied that this reflected on the weakness of their God, who was seen as unable to prevent the suffering of his people. The Gentiles were unable to understand a god who would turn against his own people if they did not fulfill his righteous demands. Thus Ezekiel proclaims that Israel is about to be returned to her land, not because of any new righteousness she had accomplished during the suffering of the Exile, but because Yahweh's reputation was at stake.

The imagery that Ezekiel uses to describe the new age that Israel will soon be entering is a perfect mixture of Temple priesthood and Mosaic covenant traditions. The Jews will be brought back to the Promised Land, from the nations among which they had been scattered, in a new exodus that will far supersede the old. But prior to their entering the land, they will be sprinkled with water, cleansed of their sins. The water imagery is no longer that of passing through the waters to initiate the exodus; rather, it is a priestly ritual that will purify the people of their uncleanness from having lived among the Gentiles.

As the climax of this new exodus and return to the land, the covenant relationship between God and his people will be restored. And this time Israel will be enabled to obey the divine demands because Yahweh will act to revitalize his people. Their heart of stone will be replaced by a heart of flesh. (The heart is the locus of intelligence and will in Hebraic thought.) Furthermore, the people will be given a new spirit—the Spirit of God. This is a hearkening back to the ancient Tribal League period, when Yahweh ruled over his people through his Spirit by endowing certain leaders (Judges) with charismatic power to confront the crisis at hand. Now, however, The Spirit of God is no longer conceived of as enabling Israel to overcome the onslaught of an enemy through the divine power bestowed upon its leader; instead, the Spirit becomes the possession of each individual within the community, enabling him to obey the Torah of his God.

This vision of a restored relation between Yahweh and Israel enables Ezekiel to express the ancient Mosaic covenant formulation in a new way; the conditionality implied in Exodus 19:4–6 no longer exists. Israel *will* obey, and thus she will be brought into a permanent relationship with her God (Ezekiel 36:28). The newly created harmony between God and his people will also have repercussions for the natural order; the land will prosper and cities will be restored, so that Israel need never again be taunted by her neighbors. The end result will be that all men will acknowledge that Yahweh is God through the great new acts he will perform through his people.

The vision of the "dry bones" described in 37:1–14 is a dramatic presentation of Ezekiel's concept of the restoration of the Jewish community. The Jews of the Exilic period had intensely experienced the absence of God. They felt cut off from his presence, and this experience was robbing the community of its vitality. They were like dead men, forsaken by the empowering presence of their God. (Remember that there are gradations of life and death in Hebraic thought, with any experience of oppression, captivity, sterility, famine, sickness, and so forth being regarded as a form of death.)

The vision is introduced by an ecstatic seizure reminiscent of the experiences which Ezekiel interpreted in chapters 1–3 as constituting his call to prophesy. Once again he is brought to a plain (see also 3:22) and confronted with the vision of a community where there was no hope for revival. The flesh had rotted; all that remained were dry bones. What follows is a concrete image of the promise expressed in 36:27 that the Jewish community will be brought back to life by the Spirit of God. Ezekiel is told to address the dry bones, commanding them to revive. "Hear the word of the Lord": the divine word is so powerful that it brings into being that which is spoken. Thus, by speaking the word of Yahweh, the prophet initiates the restoration that he is proclaiming. The bones are joined together, assuming form through sinews and flesh. The final act of re-creation is the bestowal of the spirit (Hebrew *rūah*, translated as *spirit, wind*, or *breath*), which is regarded as the energizing force of man.[7] One is reminded of the Garden of Eden story in which Adam is given life when Yahweh breathes his *rūah* into him. Such an anthropomorphic image of God actually blowing his spirit into man is too crude for Ezekiel's priestly instincts. Instead, as in the priestly story of creation (Genesis 1:1–2:4a), the creative process is accomplished by divine-prophetic fiat.

Apparently the imagery through which Ezekiel expressed his hope for national restoration was derived from a popular proverb: "Our bones are dried up, and our hope is lost; we are clean cut off" (37:11b). The pun is in the dry bones having been picked clean—clean cut off from God's presence. This passage has been interpreted as a prophecy of life after death or resurrection from the dead. In the strict sense that is not what the prophet is talking about; Daniel 12:1ff is the only Old Testament passage which expresses the fully developed concept of resurrection from the dead. In Ezekiel 37, the prophet is using the image of the revival of the dry bones to express his confidence that the Jewish community will be brought back from the death of the Exile.

Some Questions for Discussion: According to Ezekiel 36:22, what is the reason for the Lord's actions? What picture of the Lord do you get from Ezekiel 36:21–23?

According to Ezekiel 36:17–18, why did the Lord punish the

people of Israel? What was their fate? What promises are made to the Israelites in chapters 36 and 37?

What is the message of 37:1–14? Why is the metaphor of the "dry bones" effective? Where else have you heard about Ezekiel and the "dry bones"?

Second Isaiah (Isaiah 40:1–44:8; 52:13–53:12; 55)

The prophetic books of the Old Testament regularly contain individual oracles or whole sections that were not actually written by the prophet whose name is attached to the book. The reason for this inaccuracy is quite understandable. The prophets were surrounded by circles of followers or disciples who remembered and sometimes committed to writing the sayings of their masters. The existence of such a circle of disciples is mentioned especially in connection with the eighth-century prophet Isaiah (Isaiah 8:16), while in Jeremiah's case we know that his words and deeds were recorded by his scribe, Baruch (Jeremiah 36:4–32; 45:1–5).

In the course of the decades and even centuries during which prophetic oracles were treasured by such groups of followers, other oracles and narratives that were valued by the group would find their way into the body of traditions, even though the original prophet whom they revered had not spoken these words himself. As a result, prophetic books were built up which were actually anthologies of prophetic narratives and oracles deriving from extended periods. Scholars now attempt, through literary and historical criticism, to sort out the original oracles found among later additions and to determine the date and situation of each piece of material so that it may be better understood.

It has long been noticed by both scholars and common readers of the Bible that there was a striking difference between the style and tone of the first thirty-nine chapters of Isaiah and the remainder of the book. It is now very widely believed that Isaiah 40–66 comes from an entirely different period and author than the eighth-century prophecies of Isaiah. Chapters 40–66, in turn, have been ascribed by most scholars to two different authors or circles—chapters 40–55 being ascribed to "Second Isaiah" or "Deutero-Isaiah," and chapters 56–66 to "Third Isaiah" or "Trito-Isaiah."

The reasons for the identification of Second Isaiah as a prophet distinct from eighth-century Isaiah are weighty: the historical circumstances reflected are those of the Jews in exile in the sixth century B.C.; the vocabulary and style of chapters 40–55 are utterly different from the language of chapters 1–39; the theological emphases of chapters 40–55 are similarly distinctive. In fact both the style and the theology of "Second Isaiah" are unique and unparalleled in the whole of Old Testament literature.[8]

Let us assume, then, that these chapters of magnificent poetry, so distinctive in style and emphasis, were written by an unknown prophet of the Exile, whom we can refer to as "Second Isaiah." Not only is his name lost, we know nothing of his life or personality, and no narratives throw any light upon the course of his life. Only his poetry exists, and even there the prophet has so fused himself with his work and with the God whose spokesman he is that as an individual he simply vanishes behind his poetry.

The poetry of Second Isaiah makes use of a literary style that has no clear precedent in earlier prophetic literature. Typically, the pre-Exilic prophets expressed themselves in brief, staccato oracles ordinarily directed to a particular and clearly defined set of circumstances. For example, one can recall Amos's oracles against the nations or his attack upon the rich men of Samaria (Amos 1:3–2:8; 6:4–7), or Isaiah's Immanuel oracle (Isaiah 7:13–17). In each of these instances the situation is quite clear; we know who is addressed and we know the specific circumstances. In each of these instances, furthermore, the oracles were first delivered orally, and only subsequently written down. As is appropriate for on-the-spot oral communication, the style is terse and direct.

Second Isaiah, in contrast to these earlier prophetic communications, expresses himself in complex strophic poems of considerable length. No specific situation can be determined for each poem; we can only determine that the general historical circumstances of the exiled Jews in the sixth century B.C. lie behind the whole work.

There seems to be no question of the strictly literary character of Second Isaiah; the poems were composed in writing, even if they were then read aloud to groups of exiles. Moreover, the whole work appears to have been put together by the anonymous prophet himself, with the intention that the reader would approach the total composition as a unity.

Many of the specific poetic devices of Second Isaiah, such as meter, alliteration, onomatopoeia, and rhyming, can only be properly examined in the original Hebrew.[9] Even in translation, however, certain features can be noticed. The prophet uses the parallel construction typical of Hebrew poetry, but in a very flexible and imaginative way so that the most significant ideas are given the fullest possible elaboration. Note, for example, the complex structure of 41:2–4, announcing Yahweh's intervention through the conquests of Cyrus of Persia:

> Who stirred up one from the east /
>   whom victory meets at every step?
> He gives up nations before him /
>   so that he tramples kings under foot.
> He makes them like dust with his sword /
>   like driven stubble with his bow.
> He pursues them and passes on safely /
>   by paths his feet have not trod.
> Who has performed and done this /
>   calling the generations from the beginning?
> I, Yahweh, the first /
>   and with the last; I am He.

At each point the depiction of Cyrus's conquests is reinforced with a parallel phrase, yet the whole idea is put within the realm of Yahweh's sovereignty by beginning and ending the whole strophe with Yahweh's deed and identity. The strophe is simply a question ("Who stirred up one from the east?") and the answer to that question ("I, Yahweh, the first, and with the last; I am He"). Inserted within the question-answer structure is the extended parallelistic description of Cyrus, continuing through 41:3. At that point the question is renewed and restated, then given its dramatic answer.

The use of the triad, or unit of three lines, is another type of parallel structure very common in Second Isaiah. For example:

> Let them approach / then let them speak
> Let us draw near together for judgment (41:1)

and also,

> He was oppressed, / and he was afflicted
> Yet he opened not his mouth.
> Like a lamb that is led to the slaughter /
> and like a sheep that before its shearer is dumb,
> So he opened not his mouth. (53:7)

The combination of the two triads is frequent, as in the example from 53:7; in this instance the two triads are joined together by the reiterated line, "he opened not his mouth."

The study of the complex parallelistic structure of Second Isaiah's poetry can be fascinating, and can be pursued even in translation. Nevertheless, the stylistic features that are probably most noticeable to the English reader are the related elements of *repetition* and *dramatic movement*. The poet calls us to view Israel and the actions of Yahweh on a cosmic-historical stage vast enough to include all the nations of the world as seen from the vantage point of Yahweh's divine council. The separate poems are like spotlights cast upon successive portions of this vast stage. The movement and direction of the spotlight is announced by the repetitions of key words and themes.

For example, the poet opens (40:1–2) with a scene in the heavenly council, where Yahweh is pictured as enthroned among the heavenly beings. To these messengers comes the command:

> Comfort, comfort my people says your God,
> Speak tenderly to Jerusalem
> And cry to her that her warfare is ended,
>   that her iniquity is pardoned.

The spotlight then focuses on the wilderness that surrounds the desolated countryside of Judah; the shift is marked by the threefold repetition of the key theme, "wilderness," or "desert" (40:3). The announcement made by the voice of one of the members of Yahweh's council depicts the dramatic return of Yahweh to his people across the wilderness, preceded by his "glory" as in the Exodus narratives (40:3–5).

The scene shifts again as another voice takes up the message (40:6). The prophet himself answers this voice and a kind of dialogue ensues, tied together by the key word, *grass*. In the following section (40:9–11) the location of the scene is spelled out: Jerusalem is in the spotlight, and Yahweh's command is that Jerusalem announce the return of Yahweh and of his exiled people to their homeland. The major connective word in this announcement is a favorite of Second Isaiah's: *behold!* The effect is the unveiling or revelation of something new and startling and dramatic:

> Behold your God!
> Behold, Lord Yahweh comes with might,
>   and his arm rules for him.
> Behold, his reward is with him,
>   and his recompense before him.
> Like a shepherd he leads his flock,
>   in his arm he gathers the lambs,
>   in his bosom he carries them,
>   the nursing ewes he gently guides. (40:9c–11)

Just as an individual strophe or stanza is frequently held together by the repeated key ideas or words, so a whole series of strophes or scenes can be held together by an overall theme. In 40:1–11, this overall theme is provided by the repeated commands to "speak," "cry," "lift up your voice," so that the whole series of poems revolves around the theme of Yahweh's "word," which "stands for ever" (40:8).

What can be said concerning the historical background of Second Isaiah's message? As we have seen, the narrower historical horizons of the pre-Exilic prophets are here tremendously expanded. We are drawn into a stage of dramatic activity that is cosmic in scope. Only one historical figure is mentioned by name, the Persian conqueror Cyrus. The other main characters in the drama are Yahweh, Israel, and the pagan nations among whom the Jews are dispersed.

The events and circumstances that lie behind the production of this great prophetic word are relatively clear. The Jewish community in Babylon had, by the middle of the sixth century B.C., become the real religious and intellectual center of Judaism. Among the exiles the old sacred writings of the prophets, historians, and lawgivers had been collected and edited. The Pentateuch, or five books of the Torah, had begun to take shape as a distinctive body of literature, and to this was attached the Deuteronomic history of Joshua through Second Kings. Oracles of the great prophets were gathered together into separate scrolls by their followers.

At the same time, new modes of worship were evolving among the exiles. Substitutes for the old Temple liturgy were found in prayer, sermon, and scripture reading. Prophetic leaders like Ezekiel held the exiles together and gave them a sense of community and continuity as well as a hope for the future. Community centers for study of the Torah (which eventually evolved into the synagogue) began to emerge. Such rites as circumcision and Sabbath observance were emphasized as the Jewish people struggled to maintain their identity in a foreign and pagan environment.

It must have been difficult, however, to maintain the spirit and morale of the exiles, for the years continued to pass with no visible break in the vast political structure that held them away from their homeland. The people must often have asked, in the spirit of the psalmist, "How can we sing the Lord's song in a foreign land?" (Psalm 137:4). Viewed from our perspective, however, the Babylonian Empire was not long-lived. Its power began to decline after the death of Nebuchadnezzar in 562 B.C., and by 550 B.C. a new force was rapidly rising upon the world scene: the power of Cyrus the Persian.

In a series of lightning strokes that even from our distance in history appear amazing, Cyrus took over the Median Empire, Syria, most of Asia Minor, and even portions of Central Asia. Within little more than a decade he controlled an enormous empire which surrounded the Babylonian homeland, and by 540 B.C. he was poised and ready to conquer Babylon itself.

It was just at this time, about 540 B.C., when a weakened Babylon lay open to the impending attack of Cyrus, that the great prophet whom we know as Second Isaiah spoke. Like the prophets before him, Second Isaiah addressed himself to the current crisis, interpreting events to his contemporaries in the light of Yahweh's sovereignty and covenant relation to his people. But since the fortunes of the conquered Jews were now bound up with the fortunes of the Babylonian nation and the plans of Cyrus, the prophet expanded the world of his discourse to address the nations and the whole historical and cosmic order.

Reduced to a series of propositions, the message of Second Isaiah can easily be outlined, but this would efface both the spirit and the impact of his magnificent poetry. Let us instead comment briefly on the assigned passages, noting the cumulative effect of the whole series of strophes.

Isaiah 40 begins with the familiar words, "Comfort, comfort my people, says your God." The setting is the divine council, where Yahweh is pictured as enthroned among his heavenly host. To his host, Yahweh addresses these words, sending through them a message of strength to his exiled people (in the Hebrew, the word *comfort* is in the plural imperative).

The message is that the years of exile are nearly over, for the people have suffered more than enough for all the sins charged against them by former prophets (40:2). Yahweh himself shall return across the wilderness to his suffering people, his presence symbolized, as in the Exodus accounts, by his "glory" (40:3–5). Even though the people have been as dead as withered grass, they shall be re-created, because Yahweh is faithful to his word (40:6–8). Together with Yahweh's return, the prophet foresees the return of the people of Israel to their homeland, being led and carried by their God as a shepherd takes his sheep to the fold (9–11).

The first theme of the prophet, then, is the promise that the tides of history will turn and draw Israel back to her homeland. There follows a poem on the might and sovereignty of Yahweh as world-creator, standing above all the forms of being which exist, including all the gods of pagan nations (40:12–26). This emphasis on the total sovereignty of Yahweh as creator was peculiarly an achievement of Israel's thinkers and prophets in the Exilic period. The total destruction of Judah and the dispersion of her people throughout the world meant that either the Jews must surrender their faith in Yahweh altogether, or they must expand their conception of his power and being to comprehend all the movements of nature and history. Precisely this expansion is visible in Second Isaiah, for he challenges Israel to grasp the total range of Yahweh's activity as it applies to her own destiny and the destiny of the rest of the world's peoples. This bold faith must replace the self-pity of the exiles (40:27–31).

The prophet then turns to address the pagan nations, challenging them to understand, as Yahweh's prophet does, the frightening events of recent history. The very rise of Cyrus to power was Yahweh's work, and only his people can understand the purpose that lies behind Yahweh's act (41:1–4). The response of the nations is to call upon their gods for help. But this is vain, for these are merely idols which men have set up (41:5–7). Israel alone can understand and respond to events, for Israel is Yahweh's servant (41:8–10). To Israel, redemption and victory are promised, and Yahweh's creative power is again celebrated (41:11–20). The nations are again challenged to respond with some understanding of the baffling movements of time and history, but only silence comes forth (41:21–24). It is Yahweh who led Cyrus to his present pinnacle of power, from which he will grasp even Babylon as his possession (41:25–29).

The nucleus of Second Isaiah's message is already transparent. Yahweh is about to rescue his people from exile and restore them to himself in a mighty act that will be a second exodus. He holds all the nations and even the mighty Cyrus in his hand. The future that had seemed to close up like a dark tunnel is suddenly illuminated for the Jews, and their destiny as Yahweh's people is assured.

One highly significant and somewhat enigmatic theme remains to be further explicated. This is the "Servant of Yahweh," alternately addressed and described in a series of poems throughout Second Isaiah that scholars have labeled "the Servant Songs."

Two questions have been much discussed in connection with these songs: (1) Are they integral parts of Second Isaiah, written by the same author? (2) Who is the Servant intended to represent? The most weighty scholarly opinion now supports the unity of Isaiah 40–55, including the Servant Songs. The theological and stylistic motifs noticed in the Songs are present quite consistently throughout the whole body of Second Isaiah.[10]

But who is the Servant? On this question there is no full agreement as yet. The major alternatives are that: (1) the Servant represents Israel, or some part of Israel (perhaps Isaiah's "faithful remnant"); and (2) the Servant represents an individual figure, such as a prophet, or even the Messiah. Those who argue for the interpretation of the Servant as Israel point to a number of passages in which the identification is certainly Israel (41:8–10; 43:8–13; 43:13–44:4; 44:6–8, 21–23; 44:24–45:13; 48). Supporters of the individual interpretation point to a number of passages in which the Servant is not identified with Israel (42:1–4; 49:1–6; 50:4–9; 52:13–53:12).[11] One of these passages, the famous description of the suffering of the Servant (52:13–53:12), will concern us later.

Another difficult problem concerning the Servant, and one which must be answered in any interpretation, is the temporal question: Is the Servant a figure who is past, present, or future in the prophet's understanding? If he is strictly a past figure, then a messianic interpretation is excluded, but so is an interpretation relating the Servant to Israel in exile. If the Servant is primarily a present figure to the prophet, then he could be either an historical individual or a symbol for sixth-century Israel. If the Servant is a future figure, then he could be a symbol for either the Messiah or an ideal prophet, or for Israel as a whole. There is no strictly linguistic answer to this question of time, for the Hebrew use of tenses is extremely flexible, especially in prophetic literature, where a vision of the future can be described as though it had already become a reality.

Granting that the possibilities of interpretation are many, we would venture to suggest the following interpretation, which we will then apply to the Suffering Servant poem in 52:13–53:12. (1) The Servant is primarily a *role*, not the description of any single individual. This role, in the prophet's understanding, can be assumed alternately by Israel, by a portion of Israel, and even by an individual. The role is both an actuality and an ideal: Israel *is* the Servant and has been the Servant; yet Israel has been blind and deaf (42:18–19), and thus has failed to be the ideal Servant. Within Israel an individual prophet or a portion of the community (the "righteous remnant") can be the Servant and have the task of calling all Israel to be the Servant in an ideal fashion (49:1–5). This ideal Servant group can even be a messenger to the rest of the nations (49:6).

(2) As is already implied above, the prophet's sense of time is quite fluid. The Servant is alternately past, present, and future. Israel has suffered as Yahweh's Servant in the past (52:13–53:12); Israel suffers now as Yahweh's Servant in exile (49:1–4, as well as in 52:13–53:12); and Israel is called to be the Servant to bear Yahweh's message to the nations in the future (42:1–4). As set forth in (1) above, however, it is not just Israel as a totality which functions as the Servant. Individual prophets have suffered greatly in the past (see Jeremiah), and in that respect have acted out the role of Servant; in the future more suffering is in store for such individuals. It is even conceivable that one man could suffer as Yahweh's Servant, as in the interpretations that stress the suffering of Jesus of Nazareth as fulfilling the Servant role.

In the famous passage that describes the Servant's sufferings at length (52:13–53:12), the difficulties of interpretation come to focus. There the Servant seems to be an individual who suffered certain definite pains and who had certain definite features. He was not comely or handsome; he was ignored and despised by his contemporaries; he silently bore oppression and punishment. Yet no one came to his aid. He was buried among the graves of the rich and the wicked, although he himself was innocent. Yet Yahweh restores his life and makes him victorious over his enemies. Indeed, it was Yahweh himself who made the Servant suffer and who now accepts his suffering as making possible the redemption to "many."

> By his knowledge shall the righteous one, my servant,
> Make many to be accounted righteous;
> And he shall bear their iniquities.

It is possible to apply all of this to Israel in exile, especially when we take into account the way in which the community itself could be credited in Hebrew thought with a personality and a definite selfhood.[12] The community of Israel was put to the ultimate test in the Exile: Israel suffered destruction and death, affliction and oppression by the mighty. while the nations ("the many") looked on. Perhaps the prophet thinks particularly of the suffering of the innocent within Israel—the widows and children, the pious poor of the countryside whose fields were devastated by the Babylonian conquerors. Surely the judgment of Yahweh fell heavily upon some whose crime was not evident. Israel seemed indeed, to many in the Exile, to have paid "double for all her sins" (40:2). There was also the innocent sufferer who stood, like Jeremiah, between God and his people, but who also was driven into exile. Perhaps the prophet had such innocent sufferers in mind.

Even more clearly, however, the prophet now calls the whole community of Israel to understand the past suffering as having a function and a meaning: Israel was being refined in the furnace of suffering so that now and in the future, once she returns to her homeland, she can speak as Yahweh's Servant to the nations. The suffering of the Servant can thus be transmuted into redemption and truth, if Israel can now recognize her identity as Yahweh's people.

The Servant theme thus pulls together past, present, and future and interprets the whole drama of history to exiled Israel. More a vocation than a biography, the Servant Songs call upon the vanquished people to cast self-pity aside and to face the terror of history with the courage of faith, for Yahweh's ancient words of promise will stand forever. Second Isaiah's promise of release becomes a challenge to faith and obedience for all Israel and for every individual within her community. Because of Yahweh's sovereign power over all creation, Israel can in fact "prosper" and "be exalted." But it is the exaltation that is won through suffering which Israel must now seek. Only then can she truly learn to be the Servant.

Following the moving description of the sufferings of the Servant, Second Isaiah concludes his work with a series of triumphant passages in which Israel's imminent restoration is celebrated (Isaiah 55). In this chapter, the exiled people are called to respond in joy and faith to the new life that Yahweh opens to them. That life is symbolized by all that sustains man: water, wine, milk, bread—all suggesting the Promised Land flowing with milk and honey (55:1-2).

The promised return will in some sense mean a renewal of the covenant with David (II Samuel 7), in which the continuity of Judah's dynasty and Temple were assured. Now deprived of both king and Temple, the people will find a new mission as Yahweh's representative toward the nations (55:3-5).

The prophet does not imagine that a trusting response to this message of hope and forgiveness will be easy. But Yahweh's graciousness exceeds Israel's hopes and overcomes her despair and sense of abandonment(55:6-9). As he so often does, the prophet supports this confidence in Yahweh's eternal word with a celebration of Yahweh's lordship over nature: just as the rain inevitably falls from the sky and the seeds ceaselessly grow from the earth, so Yahweh's word acts in history as a real power:

> so shall my word be that goes forth from my mouth;
> it shall not return to me empty,
> but it shall accomplish that which I purpose,
> and prosper in the thing for which I sent it. (55:11)

This announcement of the power of Yahweh's word unified Second Isaiah, for it was this theme of Yahweh's proclaimed word that dominated the opening scenes (40:1-11).

The conclusion is a hymnic celebration of the return of Israel from Exile, which closes this great prophet-poet's work like a shout of joy in which all nature shares (55:12-13).

Second Isaiah's work has drawn together all of the past themes of Israel's faith—the covenant with Moses, the promises to David, the law's demands, and the people's faithlessness—into an enormous dramatic panorama that celebrates Yahweh's immediate rule over the actualities of history in the sixth century B.C., promising a return to the homeland following Cyrus's conquest of Babylon. At the same time the prophet has opened up new themes that were to be remembered and pondered over in the centuries that follow, for in the enigmatic figure of the Servant, the prophet has asked one of the most inescapable questions that arise out of man's experience of life: what is the meaning of human suffering? Jeremiah had asked that question as well, and in the anguish of his own life, he found no answer. Second Isaiah suggests that there is an answer, and that this answer is to be found when man courageously affirms his suffering and offers it as a step toward the fulfillment of the purpose of God.

Some Questions for Discussion: Professor Peter R. Ackroyd, writing in *The Interpreter's One-Volume Commentary on the Bible,* notes that Isaiah 40:1–2 "constitutes the equivalent of a prophetic call narrative." Why do you, or don't you, agree with Professor Ackroyd's statement? If you agree, how do you account for a "prophetic call" near the middle of the Book of Isaiah?

What promises are made in 40:1–5? What meaning do you attach to 40:4? Why do you think the language in 40:4 should be taken figuratively, not literally? What is the meaning of the metaphor, "All flesh is grass"?

According to verse 11, what will the Lord do for his people? With whom can God be compared? Why should Israel not say "My way is hid from the Lord/and my right is disregarded by my God"?

What examples of repetition can you find in chapter 41? Are they effective? Why, or why not? What will happen to Israel because it is the Lord's servant? What will happen to Israel's enemies?

Note the many metaphors in chapters 40–44. With what is

Israel compared? Who is the Servant? What reasons can you give for your answer?

Summarize chapters 40:1–44:8. What promises have been made? What will be the fate of the Israelites?

What trials of the Servant are recounted in 52:13–53:12? Now who do you think is the Servant? Why?

What is the purpose of Isaiah 55:1–5? What note of warning is sounded in 55:6–9? What is the purpose of 55:10–13? Why would these verses give great comfort to the people of Israel?

Suggested Activities: Many biblical scholars refer to chapters 40–55 as Second Isaiah, noting the differences between those chapters and 1–39. Examine chapters 1–55. What differences do you note between the so-called "First" and "Second" Isaiahs? Write a short paper in which you explain why chapters 1–39 and 40–55 were not written by the same person.

Second Isaiah gives cause for hope to the exiled Israelites. Consider how the messages in chapters 40–55 might be dramatized. Then write a script for the drama. Who will be included in your cast of characters? What will they do? What will they say?

Besides a drama, explain what other art forms might be used to convey the messages of Second Isaiah.

Many people claim that chapters 40–55 of "Second Isaiah" are near the top—if not at the top—of the list of the most powerful and beautiful writing in the world. Discuss the power and beauty of chapters 40–55, giving reasons why you think they are, or are not, powerful and beautiful.

Ezra and Nehemiah (Ezra 1; 4:1–5, 24; 5–6; Nehemiah 2; 4; 6; 8)

The conquest of Babylon by Cyrus of Persia, so strikingly prophesied by Second Isaiah, was accomplished with little difficulty in 539 B.C. Indeed, Cyrus himself claimed that the Babylonian god Marduk had appointed him to be the city's conqueror and had aided him so that the city simply opened its gates to Cyrus without a battle.[13] When Babylon and its immediate surroundings were added to Cyrus's already enormous domain, the result was the largest empire the world had ever seen. In the Near East, Egypt remained outside Persian control, only to be conquered by Cyrus's successor, Cambyses, in 525 B.C.

The Persian Empire which was thus constructed was administered both efficiently and humanely. Unlike the Babylonians and Assyrians before them, the Persians supported the religious cults of their conquered subjects as a matter of regular policy. The results of this humane and politically astute policy for the Jews were almost immediate. According to Ezra 1, in the first full year of his reign, 538 B.C., Cyrus issued an edict permitting the return of Jews to Jerusalem for the purpose of restoring the ruined Temple of Yahweh. This mission was undertaken under the leadership of a Jewish court official with the Babylonian name Sheshbazzar.[14] While the conditions surrounding this first return from Exile hardly matched Second Isaiah's rhapsodic predictions, the prophet's description of Cyrus as Yahweh's "messiah" and "shepherd" (Isaiah 45:1; 44:28) seems almost justified. Under the aegis of Cyrus and his successors, the Jewish community in Judah was restored and its Temple and capital city rebuilt. The Persian monarchs could not have known it, but one of their most enduring gifts to human history was this restoration of Judaism so routinely provided for in their imperial policy.

We have no reason, therefore, to doubt the basic authority of the Cyrus edict referred to in Ezra 1, even to the restoration of some of the Temple furnishings which is also related (1:5–11). The preservation of such a list of liturgical articles would be the task of priests, and its recording for posterity in the Book of Ezra fits well with the interests of the author of Ezra-Nehemiah, whom we call "the Chronicler."[15]

In spite of Persian encouragement, the first mission to rebuild the Temple was not successful. The work seems to have languished for a number of years, largely because of the hostility of the mixed Jewish and pagan population that now inhabited the province, including Judah (Ezra 4:1–6). The project had to be renewed under a new leader, Zerubbabel, in 520 B.C., during the reign of Darius I (522–486 B.C.). Zerubbabel, whose name is also Babylonian, managed to guide the rebuilding through to its completion five years later, but only in the face of strong local opposition. It is this struggle to complete the Temple that is related in Ezra 5–6.

It is important to try to reconstruct the reasons for local hostility to the rebuilding of the Jerusalem Temple. It should be recognized that the inhabitants of Judah and of the one-time Kingdom of Israel to the north had so lost contact with Hebrew religious traditions that Judaism must have seemed an alien religion to them. Most of the inhabitants of the Northern Kingdom had been deported and replaced by deportees brought in from other countries conquered by the Assyrians. Their religion was a mixture of pagan and Hebrew elements. The spiritual descendants of these northerners were the Samaritans, whose religion was deemed heretical by Jews of the more orthodox traditions. Even Judah had lost contact with the central stream of Jewish faith, for this had been preserved and extended by the religious elite who were in exile in Babylonia.

To these religiously based hostilities we might add the political friction that developed when the Persians installed a new governor over Judah, drawn from among the Jewish community in exile. Such was the background of both Sheshbazzar and Zerubbabel, who were Babylonian Jews under royal appointment to rule Judah in the name of the Persian Empire.

A third reason for hostility toward the returned exiles was an economic one. The small community that was left in Judah after the exiles' departure had confiscated the exiles' land. This confiscation was probably motivated by the need to survive in a famine-stricken country, rather than by simple greed. Nevertheless, the prospect of exiles or their descendants reclaiming their property was not welcome.

It is political hostility, rather than intra-Jewish controversy, that is reflected in Ezra 5–6. When Zerubbabel began to push the Temple rebuilding toward completion in 520 B.C., the project was visited by two imperial officials who questioned the legitimacy of rebuilding the Temple, perhaps fearing an attempt at revolt.[16] One of these officials, Tattenai, was governor of the Persian province of Beyond the River, which included all the territory of Syria-Palestine west of the Euphrates River (Ezra 5:3–4). The Jews working under Zerubbabel explained the history of the Temple project, assuring Tattenai that Cyrus had supported the rebuilding by imperial edict (5:9–16). Tattenai wrote an official inquiry concerning the matter to the imperial capital (5:6–17), and soon received a reply which legitimized the Jewish rebuilding project (6:1–12).

These documents, which the Chronicler includes as copies of official correspondence and edicts, have been regarded by some as not authentic, but the tendency is increasingly to accept most of them as genuine. The language of the whole section of Ezra in which the documents are contained is Aramaic rather than Hebrew (Ezra 4:7–6:18). This adds a note of authenticity, for Aramaic, a Semitic language closely related to Hebrew, had become a common language for international dealings in the Persian Empire.

The completion of the Temple in about 515 B.C. is reported in the concluding verses of Ezra 6. The Jewish community now had a geographical and cultic center around which the community could gather again. The importance of this development can scarcely be overemphasized. Nevertheless, many obstacles still remained; not the least of these must have been the disheartening slowness of the return and the rebuilding as bands of exiles trickled back to Judah. The mood of the returnees is perhaps best reflected in their ready acceptance of a wave of messianic excitement that began around 520 B.C. At this time a number of revolts had broken out across the Persian Empire, and a good many Jews must have thought that the end of Persian domination was in sight. Beliefs that a messiah was about to appear accompanied the speculation about the expected overthrow of Persia, and these beliefs were encouraged by two Jewish prophets, Haggai and Zechariah, who even identified the governor, Zerubbabel, as the Messiah (Zechariah 4; Haggai 2:20–22). While the expectation was not fulfilled, the excitement certainly helped spur the Jewish community to complete the Temple.

The next information we have concerns a period more than fifty years later and centers around the figures of Ezra and Nehemiah. Under these leaders, the defense walls of Jerusalem were restored and a far-reaching religious reform was introduced. The details of these accomplishments are difficult to reconstruct, however, owing to the rather confused way in which the Chronicler has transmitted his records and traditions to us. If one reads Ezra and Nehemiah straight through, the impression is that Ezra preceded Nehemiah in Jerusalem, but that to some extent their missions overlapped. This might be credible, but there are still numerous displacements of material. In the following account, we are accepting the reconstruction of John Bright, although admitting that other solutions are possible.[17]

According to our reconstruction, the career of Nehemiah preceded that of Ezra by a good many years and was concerned primarily with one project—the rebuilding of the defense walls of Jerusalem. Our best source here is the memoirs of Nehemiah, which give a vivid first person account of his activities (Nehemiah 1:1–7:5).

Nehemiah tells us that he was a personal servant to the Persian king, Artaxerxes I, and that he managed to gain the king's hearing for a petition that the Jerusalem walls be rebuilt (Nehemiah 2:1–6). The king acceded to the request and sent Nehemiah to Judah with authority and means to carry it out (2:7–8). Nehemiah arrived in Jerusalem in 445 B.C., equipped for the project, but immediately learned that local hostility to the Jerusalem Jews had by no means died out. Nehemiah relates in vivid detail his secret reconnaisance of the ruined walls by night (2:11–16) and his attempt to persuade the Jerusalem community to support him in rebuilding the defenses (2:17–18). Adversaries appeared immediately, however; Nehemiah was opposed by Sanballat, governor of Samaria, Tobiah, also a Persian official, and Geshem, an Arab king from Transjordan (2:10, 19).

The story of the rebuilding of the city walls in Nehemiah 4, drawn from Nehemiah's personal memoirs, is a classic of story-telling. At length the wall was finished and Nehemiah's courage was rewarded by the knowledge of that accomplishment, although he piously ascribes the success to God (Ezra 6:17).

Some time after Nehemiah's successful mission, another Jewish leader was sent to Jerusalem under imperial orders. Ezra, described as a "priest" and "scribe" (Nehemiah 8:1, 2, 9), was charged with the task of reforming and purifying the corrupt and divided Jewish community in Palestine. This reformation was carried out in accordance with the type of Jewish belief and practice which had evolved in Babylonia, stressing strict observance of the laws of the Pentateuch or Torah and the avoidance of any kind of mixing with Gentiles through marriage.

The date of Ezra's mission in Jerusalem remains uncertain; he arrived in either 428 B.C. or 398 B.C. The former date would make his mission overlap with Nehemiah's term as governor of Judah, and this overlapping is assumed in Ezra-Nehemiah.[18] Far more important than the precise date of Ezra's work is the effect of his mission. With imperial backing, Ezra imposed upon the Palestinian Jewish community the Mosaic law as passed down from early times and elaborated in the Exile. He called the whole Jerusalem community together and read aloud from "the book of the law" (probably some portion of the Pentateuch) and called upon the people to subscribe to this as the basis of their religious and social community. Each day for a week Ezra recited the law from his scrolls brought from Babylonia while the people observed the Feast of Booths or Tabernacles by listening to his reading (Nehemiah 8). It is a mark of the condition of the Jerusalem community that even the language of the law, the Hebrew of the pre-Exilic community, was not understood. Aramaic had so completely replaced Hebrew as an everyday language that interpreters had to stand beside Ezra and give a free Aramaic translation (8:7–8).

If the language of the law was strange, the concepts and commands contained in the Pentateuch must have been stranger still. Ezra's contribution in the development of Jewish religion is very great, therefore, for we must credit him with gaining final approval for those practices which have become the characteristic marks of Judaism ever since. Most important of these was the establishment of written scripture as the basis for all social conduct and religious belief. This was the beginning of the canonization of a certain collection of books known as "the Bible." Next in importance were the various ceremonial practices such as circumcision, Sabbath observance, and detailed dietary laws which served to define and protect the Jewish community from outside influences. The result is a religion that is capable of being practiced anywhere in the world, with neither a national nor a cultic structure being absolutely necessary. The reform of Ezra did more than unify the Palestinian community against its opponents; it also made possible the survival of Judaism as a world religion throughout the future centuries of the Jews' dispersion throughout the world.

Some Questions for Discussion: Ezra 1:1 makes an allusion to Jeremiah 29:10. What does the Jeremiah passage tell us about the duration of the Babylonian Exile? What changes took place in Babylon which led to the release of the exiles? We know from other records that Cyrus claimed to be the one chosen by the Babylonian god Marduk as ruler of the world. In light of this fact, what does Ezra 1:23 indicate about Cyrus's religious beliefs? How do you think the exiles would react to Cyrus's proclamation? Why might many of them choose to remain in Babylon?

Recall that groups of people were taken into exile and some were left in Judah. Recall also what happened in Judah afterwards. (Refer to II Kings if necessary.) Where would you expect the religious traditions of the Israelites to have been preserved more zealously? Why? How do you think the exiles would be greeted on their return by those living in Judah? What problems might the returning exiles encounter? What proposal is made by "the adversaries of Benjamin and Judah"? What reason is given for this proposal? Who might these "adversaries" be? How did the returned exiles respond to their proposal? What were the results of this decision (Ezra 4:4–24)? How does this account help us to understand the hostility between Jews and Samaritans so evident in Jesus' time?

What role did Haggai and Zechariah play in the rebuilding of the Temple? In this second attempt at rebuilding the Temple, what kind of opposition is encountered? How is the completion of the Temple celebrated? What significance would the re-building have for the future of Judaism?

Why was it easy for Nehemiah to gain an audience with the king? Why is Nehemiah sad? How does the king respond to Nehemiah's request? How does the writer first suggest that there is trouble ahead for Nehemiah? How does Nehemiah 2:12 intensify this foreshadowing? What persuasive techniques does Nehemiah use in speaking to the people?

Enumerate the ways by which Nehemiah's opponents seek to prevent the success of Nehemiah's enterprise and the methods by which Nehemiah frustrates each of their attempts. Beginning with Nehemiah's despondency and the king's concern in 2:1–2, can you discover any pattern of organization in the writer's account of Nehemiah's fortunes? How does this arrangement increase the tension or suspense of the story?

What does Nehemiah 8:9 indicate about the respective roles of Ezra and Nehemiah? What does the need for translators (Nehemiah 8:7) indicate about the changes that have occurred? In his portrayal of Nehemiah, what characteristics does the writer depict in the Jewish leader? Cite evidence of each one.

Select two literary devices that Nehemiah employs rather obviously; cite passages in which they are used and comment upon their contribution to the credibility of his account. What attitude toward God sustained Nehemiah and his people as they labored against public opinion in building the Jerusalem wall? How does this attitude and the accomplishment of en-closing the city foreshadow the mission of Ezra in Nehemiah 8? What attempts were made to annihilate Nehemiah? How does the device of relating each attempt separately enhance Nehemiah's final success? What does the mounting tension add to the narrative? Nehemiah 8 relates Ezra's exhortation to the people. Where and how does the style differ from Nehemiah's story of his own experience? Comment upon the appropriateness of each style to its content. In your opinion, which style retains longer the aura of solemnity and portrays its protagonist with heroic stature? Why do you think so?

What parallels do you see between the return of the Jews to Palestine in the fifth and six centuries B.C. and the migration of Jews to Palestine in the twentieth century? What differences do you note?

The Last Judgment (Joel 2:28–3:21)

The Jewish community reacted in various ways to the catastrophic shock of the Babylonian Exile and its aftermath. One response was described above: Judaism once again became a theocracy. The leadership passed from the defunct house of David to the priesthood, and every effort was made to have obedience to the Torah become a reality among the entire community. There was a deep consciousness of sin—of alienation from God—but the Jewish community had not lost hope. Finally acknowledging that the prophets had been right, the Jews came to understand their Exile as a deserved judgment for having disobeyed God's just demands. But they knew those demands were to be found in the Torah, and therein lay their hope. God may have temporarily absented himself from his people, but he did not leave them without hope. The Torah was still theirs; the means of restoring the relationship between God and his people lay in their hands. Thus the sixth and fifth centuries were an extremely creative period in which Judaism became the community of the Torah, so that the Jew—no matter where he lived, no matter what king/government he was forced to swear allegiance to, no matter how far removed he was from the Jerusalem Temple—could maintain his religious identity through adherence to the Torah.

Another response to the Exile within the Jewish community was also initiated by the prophets. Men like Jeremiah, Ezekiel, and "Second Isaiah" saw the Exile as a necessary precondition to the initiation of the new age. The community would have to be purged of its sin before God could work through those who had survived his judgment to establish the new Israel, which would flourish because it would be enabled to adhere perfectly to his will. In this age, the law of God would be written on the flesh of the human heart. God would then be with his people again, restoring them to even greater heights of power and glory so that all the world would know that he is the one and only living God.

This messianic dream, however, was never realized. Many Jews responded to the Exile by disassociating themselves from the Jewish community and merging into the enticing culture of pagan society. And although the agony of the Exile officially came to an end in 538 b.c., when the Persian king Cyrus overthrew the Babylonian Empire, the new age did not dawn upon the pioneering band of Jews who returned and attempted to reestablish themselves in Palestine. They encountered hostile neighbors, cities still in ruins, periodic droughts, and a relatively barren land. Only through the semi-benevolent rule of the Persians were they able to reestablish a small community near Jerusalem. Life was in many ways far more bitter than it had been during the Exile.

The extreme disappointment felt when the messianic age was not realized produced two opposite effects within the Jewish community. The first was, in effect, a denial of the relevance or the immediacy of the messianic age. The Jew should not concern himself with it; he should expend all his energy on keeping the Torah, and indeed if there was such a future age, that was God's concern, not his. The second response to the delay of the messianic age was just the opposite, and concerns us here in this passage from Joel. Instead of denying the immediacy of a new age, some elements within the Jewish community affirmed it with even greater fervor.

Thus we are left with this strange and extremely interesting division within Judaism which was produced by the trauma of the new age's not being realized during the post-Exilic period. The dominant group adjusted to the disappointing circumstances by a new understanding of God that saw him as no longer active in history at the national level. He had acted in history through

Moses, creating his people as a theocratic community by giving them the commandments; now it was up to each Jew to establish and maintain his own relationship with God by turning to the Torah. As Nehemiah built the wall around Jerusalem, Ezra built a "fence" around Judaism so that it could survive the threat of being totally assimilated into a hostile, pagan, mythological environment. The voice of prophecy was silenced (see also Zechariah 13:2–6); new voices could only threaten the community which desperately needed stability and order to survive.

But another element within the Jewish community—an "underground" one, if you will—produced a remarkable body of writings over a period of about six hundred years (400 B.C.–200 A.D.): the so-called "apocalyptic" literature. Besides Joel, we could cite Isaiah 24–27, Zechariah 12–14, Daniel, the Dead Sea Scrolls, and a non-canonical group of writings in the Pseudepigrapha.[19] This group also maintained that the Torah should be strictly kept, but for a different purpose: so that one could be among the righteous "elect" who would be saved when God came with the host of heaven to judge the world. For the first time in Jewish thought, we encounter a highly developed cosmic dualism (doubtlessly derived from the dualistic influence in Persian religion), in which the forces of evil are portrayed in striking—often bizarre—mythological imagery. This constitutes an ingenious explanation for the delay of the messianic age which is derived out of the suffering that the Jews endured at the hands of their Gentile neighbors. Before the new age could begin, it was necessary to do more than purge the Jews of their sins; evil had to be wiped out at a universal level. The enemy nations that persecuted the Jews seemed embodiments of the evil powers that ruled the world. The mythology of fallen angels (Satan, Lucifer, and so forth), who acted as demonic spirits opposed to God's will, was developed during this period and taken with utmost seriousness. But the fallen angels' day of reckoning would soon come; God would destroy them along with the enemy nations they represented. Thus apocalyptic literature consists of two major motifs: warfare and judgment. By these means God would reestablish his rule over those demonic forces—cosmic and historical—who threatened his creation.

Joel is an early representative of apocalyptic literature, probably deriving from the fourth pre-Christian century. He identifies the day of the Lord with the time Yahweh will act to establish the new age. It will begin with the bestowal of Yahweh's spirit upon all flesh (the context, however, equates "all flesh" with all members of the Jewish community) so that they will prophesy. Moses had said, "Would that all Yahweh's people were prophets, that Yahweh would put his spirit upon them" (see Numbers 11:24–30), and Joel sees this hope from the past being fulfilled in the age to come.

In pre-monarchic times, the divine spirit was given to one man (that is, the judge) empowering him to lead Israel in confronting the military crisis at hand. This concept of individual spirit possession was further developed with the advent of the monarchy, when it became a permanent possession of the king at his anointing, empowering him to govern with justice, wisdom, and strength. During the Exile, this concept becomes democratized so that the spirit is possessed by the entire people of God. In Ezekiel 36:26–27, it is God's spirit that will enable his people to return to the Torah and obey it with all their hearts. In this context, the possession of the spirit is no longer associated with a divine empowering to meet a military crisis.

What tradition is Joel developing when he maintains that the spirit will be poured out so that the entire community can *prophesy*? As we pointed out above, prophecy, which heralded the continuing action of God in history, was abolished during the time of Nehemiah and Ezra (450–400 B.C.) because it was felt that new insights would threaten the stability that the Jewish leaders were trying to achieve. The concept of God's continual action in history was replaced with the idea that God had acted once and for all in history through Moses by revealing the Torah to his people. The apocalyptic movement, however, denied that God had ceased to act. There would come a day when he would intervene to establish his kingdom, when evil would be destroyed and all the righteous could live in peace and security. Joel is heralding that day. It will be preceded by the pouring out of the spirit so that the entire community, like the prophets of old, will know that God is about to act momentously in history. Thus the first effect of spirit possession in Joel is a new awareness of God's immediacy and activity among his people. This does not, however, rule out the earlier attributes of spirit possession that we discussed above. It should be remembered that in apocalyptic thought, Yahweh was about to intervene as a warrior who could overcome the forces of evil. The gift of the spirit would enable God's people to join the divine host in this final Armageddon. Furthermore, as in Ezekiel, the possession of the spirit would enable the community to keep the Torah completely so that they would remain pure and thus be acceptable recruits for God's army.

It is instructive to compare the Day-of-the-Lord concept in Joel with that which is presupposed in the first two chapters of the eighth century prophet Amos. Amos envisions the coming day when historical retribution will be meted out against all nations which have transgressed the divine will. He is by no means describing the end of the age; he is simply maintaining that Yahweh's righteous will is going to become effective in history. Joel is developing the same Day-of-the-Lord motif, but the cosmic and mythological characteristics are much more pronounced in this later prophet. The darkened sun, the moon turned to blood, the stars no longer shining—all herald the coming onslaught. God's people should prepare for the day, pounding their plowshares into swords, their pruning hooks into spears (see Isaiah 2:4; Micah 4:3). The vanquished nations of the world will be herded into the valley of Jehoshaphat, where they will be condemned for the iniquities committed against God's people. The new age will then begin, when all peoples will acknowledge Yahweh as their righteous and all-powerful king. The restored community between God and man will also be reflected in the natural order: "the mountains shall drip sweet wine, and the hills shall flow with milk. . . ." The ultimate result of the Day of the Lord will be a return of all creation to its primeval innocence, as in the Garden of Eden.

Some Questions for Discussion: What does Joel prophecy? What might be the "latter days" or "last times"? What impact do such terms have on the overall effect of the narrative? The phrase "the Day of the Lord" is spoken five times in this short book. What might it mean or refer to? What kind of "judgments" does Joel mention? Why do you think these judgments were necessary? What might "afterward" in 2:28 mean? What is the God/man relationship espoused here?

What kind of language does Joel use to indicate the intensity and finality of the judgment to come? How does this language increase the power of Joel's message? Several times Joel uses the metaphor of hills and valleys to contrast the people of God with the enemies of Judah. What is symbolized by the hills? the valleys? How effective do you think these metaphors are? Can you think of other literary works in which these metaphors are used? Why do you think they are such popular metaphors? What are some modern take-offs on this metaphor ("the ladder of success," "the pit of despair," etc.)?

Look carefully at 2:28-29; then think back to the time of the judges and kings. Do these verses indicate a change in the relationship of God to *all* of his people? Explain. Why might such a change have come about? What political attitudes are found in today's society that reflect this philosophy of the apocalypse in political rather than religious terms? Can you think of political groups today that believe in total destruction of existing society and the rebuilding of a new society on the ashes of the old? Is it ever justifiable to seek to change society through destructive means which involve the innocent as well as the guilty? Explain your answer.

CHAPTER 13

The Literature of
the Post-Exilic Period

Short Stories: Ruth, Jonah, Esther, Daniel

In the books of Ruth, Jonah, Esther, and Daniel, one major practical and theological problem is dealt with: How should Jews relate to their Gentile neighbors? The answers that were offered to this question by the post-Exilic community varied as circumstances and events changed, and this variety of responses is clearly visible in the four books we are now considering.

It should be understood that the problem of relations with Gentiles presented itself in an entirely different form after the Exile. The post-Exilic Jews were deprived of their national structure by the policy of first the Babylonian and then the Persian empire. No longer was a man an Israelite because he was a citizen of Israel or Judah, and no longer could he react to foreign hostility or pressure by military attack. After the Exile, the Jews survived only as a religious community, with its headquarters in the rebuilt city of Jerusalem and its members scattered throughout the Near Eastern world. There was no possibility of attacking the Gentiles, and no possibility of escaping them either, for they were everywhere around the Jews.

Not that the situation of Jews in the Persian Empire was one of physical danger—ordinarily it was quite possible for the Jews and other ethnic and religious groups to carry on their internal affairs without much official hostility or repression. But the very lack of overt threats to the Jews' lives and property generated another and more insidious danger—assimilation. It would have been quite easy for the Exilic and post-Exilic Jewish communities to vanish by abandoning their beliefs and practices and intermarrying with Gentiles. We have seen how Ezekiel, Second Isaiah, Ezra and Nehemiah—each in his unique fashion—attempted to stave off the death of Judaism through assimilation, calling the exiles and their descendants to remember the law and covenant of Moses and the continuing activity of Yahweh in history. Ezra and Nehemiah in particular took steps to assure the relative isolation of the Jews from their surroundings by solidifying the community in Judah and emphasizing the observances contained in the Mosaic legal tradition. One of the most important of these steps was the prohibition of marriage with Gentiles.

Yet there was another strain in Jewish response to the Gentile problem, represented especially by Second Isaiah. This prophet had insisted that it was Israel's task to be "a light to the Gentiles" (Isaiah 49:6), to bring Yahweh's law and justice to the Gentile nations. This function of witnessing to Yahweh's existence and teaching his commandments could hardly be carried out by a community that was sealed off from the Gentiles, and it could hardly be carried out if the Gentiles were not deemed worthy of Yahweh's love.

Throughout the centuries following the Exile, then, the Jews were thrown into an increasingly cosmopolitan setting in which they struggled to retain their identity as a religious community. It was not until the second century B.C., as reflected in the Book of Daniel, that we hear of a clear instance of intensive persecution of the Jews. Throughout most of the period, the Jews were primarily concerned with the more subtle threats and baffling theological problems involved in holding the community together while witnessing to the Gentiles about Yahweh's being and goodness.

Another threat may have been a subtle loss of concern for the events of history by the Jews. The years seemed to move by slowly after the Persian Empire was established. No startling events occurred to suggest an imminent change in the Jews' situation in the world. Even with the conquests of Alexander the

Great in the latter part of the fourth century B.C., nothing seemed to change significantly. The Jews simply exchanged one master for another. It must have been difficult for the Jews under these circumstances to perceive any activity of Yahweh in history. One result of this mood seems to have been an increased emphasis on Yahweh's mighty deeds in the past, especially in the time of Moses. The present time seemed by contrast barren of events, a time for reflection and waiting. It is understandable, therefore, that three of the four books which we will now consider (Ruth, Jonah, and Daniel) have as settings periods that were in the remote past for the authors: Ruth is set in the days of the Judges, Jonah in the time of the Assyrian Empire before the Exile, and Daniel in the Exile. Through their imaginative treatments of the past, the authors attempt to speak to present Jewish problems and to convey their messages with a suggestion of authority derived from antiquity.

THE BOOK OF RUTH

No biblical writer has told a story more beautifully than the author of Ruth, which is set "in the days when the judges ruled" and concerns the affectionate relationship between Naomi, a Hebrew woman from Bethlehem, and Ruth, her Moabite daughter-in-law. The author points out his tale very clearly by including a genealogy at the end (4:18–22), which traces the lineage of King David to this Moabite woman whose loyalty and kindness are so strikingly portrayed in the story.

According to the story, Naomi and her husband had been forced to migrate to Moab as the result of a famine. The family lived in Moab for some years, and the sons married Moabite women. First Naomi's husband died and then the two sons died, leaving Naomi alone in foreign territory.

Naomi decided to return to Judah, but advised her daughters-in-law, Ruth and Orpah, to remain in Moab among their own people. Orpah finally accepts Naomi's advice, but in a well-known speech Ruth refuses to desert her mother-in-law:

Entreat me not to leave you or to return from following you; for where you go I will go, and where you lodge I will lodge; your people shall be my people, and your God my God; where you die I will die, and there will I be buried. (1:16–17)

The original readers of Ruth must have been impressed, as later generations have been, by this beautiful protestation of affection and fidelity. It was all the more striking that this speech should be ascribed to a pagan foreigner—but that is precisely the author's purpose.

As the story continues, we see the two women settling in Bethlehem and living in such absolute poverty that they can live only by gleaning the grain that the harvesters leave in the fields (1:19–2:7). Hebrew law commanded that something be left in the fields for the poor folk to gather (Leviticus 19:9–10), and Ruth and Naomi take advantage of this merciful provision.

The narrator describes the engagement of Ruth to be married to Boaz, the owner of the land where the women are gleaning grain. The kindness of Boaz is such that he even allows Ruth to gather grain from among the standing sheaves (2:14–16), and she is moved to try to arrange a marriage with him. Ruth finds Boaz sleeping at the threshing floor, lies down near him, and tells him to spread the skirt of his cloak over her. This gesture represented a man's willingness to marry a woman. Boaz is willing to do this, but first a kinsman of Ruth's dead husband must be given the opportunity to marry her (3:6–13).

The scene that follows has as its background the Hebrew laws with respect to inheritance. The nearest male kin of a deceased man had the right and the duty of marrying the deceased man's widow (see Leviticus 25:25; Deuteronomy 25:5–6). At the same time, the person undertaking such a "levirate marriage" acquired the deceased man's property. In accordance with this practice, Boaz goes to the city gate, where legal business was transacted, to meet Ruth's nearest kinsman. This kinsman replies that he does wish to acquire the real estate which will be Ruth's inheritance, but he does not want to marry Ruth, since this action would diminish his estate for his children.

Boaz, who is also related to Naomi's family, now undertakes to marry Ruth and to acquire her inheritance. The author makes clear, in spite of the detailed legal formalities he recounts, that there is true affection in this union. The idyllic tone continues to the end. Ruth bears a son to Boaz and Naomi helps to care for him.

There is no question that post-Exilic readers must have enjoyed this lovely tale for its intrinsic beauty, but it also is quite obvious that the author is conveying a message. Through his story, the author calls into question the harsh demands of Ezra and Nehemiah that the Jews of their time must divorce their foreign wives (Ezra 10:1–5; Nehemiah 13:23–27). Not only does the author view such marriages as tolerable, he goes much further and suggests that Gentiles are capable of deep love and fidelity. He even depicts David as the descendant of a foreign-born woman, suggesting that God cares less for proper genealogy than some of Israel's leaders did.

Some Questions for Discussion: Where and when did the story of Ruth take place? Why does Naomi urge her daughters-in-law to return to their mothers' houses? What is their initial response to the request? How does she persuade Orpah to leave? Why doesn't Ruth leave Naomi? What is the meaning of "your people shall be my people, and your God my God"?

Why does Naomi tell people to call her Mara? Why does Ruth go to the field of Boaz to glean? What does this action tell you about the financial well-being of Naomi and Ruth? How does Boaz react when he first sees Ruth? What does he already know about her? What special favors is she granted?

From his words alone in 2:4–16, how would you characterize Boaz? What impression of Ruth do you receive from her words alone? How would you characterize Naomi? Why?

What is the significance of Ruth's suggesting to Boaz that he spread his skirt over his maidservant? Why can't he marry Ruth immediately? Why does the next of kin not buy the parcel of land? What does Boaz do after the kinsman refuses to buy the land? What happens to Boaz, Naomi, and Ruth? What is the significance of the genealogy in 4:18?

In *The Interpreter's One-Volume Commentary on the Bible,* Professor Herbert G. May writes:

> The book of Ruth is an exciting short story, possessing almost rustic simplicity and charm. Unlike the story of Joseph, with which it may be compared for literary excellence, it contains no note of dissension or intrigue. Unlike the story of Esther, it has no villain. It maintains the reader's interest through the credibility of events and persons; the characters appear as real folk, and the author has remarkable sensitivity in depicting motivation. He draws no moral, but leaves his teaching obviously implicit.

Do you agree with Professor May's assessment of Ruth?

Suggested Activities: Select a scene from the story of Ruth for dramatization and explain why you selected it. Write directions for portraying the characters for your actors.

Write a modern version of Ruth. What is the purpose of your story? What is the nationality of each of the major characters? If they share the same nationality, what barrier(s) do they have to overcome?

THE BOOK OF JONAH

If the Book of Ruth conveyed its universalistic message through an idyllic romance, the author of Jonah makes a very similar point through a delightful use of irony. Even though the Book of Jonah is to be found among the Minor Prophets in the Old Testament canon, the writing is really a thoroughgoing satire on a prophetic book and on a certain attitude toward Gentiles common in post-Exilic Judaism.

The author begins soberly enough with one of the standard editorial cliches found in prophetic books: "Now the word of the Lord came to Jonah the son of Amittai, saying, 'Arise, go to Nineveh, that great city, and cry against it; for their wickedness has come up before me'" (1:1-2). The prophet Jonah is otherwise no more than a name to us; he is mentioned as a counselor to

Jeroboam II in the eighth century (II Kings 14:25). Thus the name is real enough, but the idea of a Hebrew prophet addressing the capital of the Assyrian Empire arouses a slight suspicion that the Book of Jonah is actually fictional. This suspicion grows as the story unfolds.

Jonah does not behave like a true and faithful prophet. Instead of obeying Yahweh's command to travel to Nineveh, he quickly books passage on a ship traveling in precisely the opposite direction, thinking that in this way he can get away from Yahweh (1:3). The very idea is comical, and it is surely intended to satirize the beliefs of narrow-minded Jewish exclusivists who would limit Yahweh's presence and power to one particular spot on the globe.

Jonah's attempt to flee from his prophetic mission by sailing the Mediterranean leads to the best-known episode in the story in which the prophet is swallowed by a whale or (more precisely) a "great fish" (1:17). Jonah's journey had not gone unnoticed by the Lord; Yahweh "hurled a great wind upon the sea . . . so that the ship threatened to break up" (1:4). This led the pagan sailors to cry to their gods for aid and to lighten the craft by throwing their cargo overboard (1:5). Meanwhile Jonah, alert as always to Yahweh's activity, sleeps in the hold (1:6).

The turning point comes when the pagan sailors cast lots to determine who is responsible for this sudden storm, and Jonah is chosen. Jonah admits his identity and the purpose of his mission, which is to flee from the presence of "Yahweh, the God of heaven, who made the sea and the dry land" (1:9). If Jonah notices that there is an absurdity implicit in his statement, he does not betray it. He even suggests that it would be best to throw him overboard, since the storm has arisen because of him. The pagan sailors shrink from the idea and attempt to row out of the storm and toward the land. Finally, however, they give up the attempt and throw Jonah into the sea, first praying that Yahweh will not hold them guilty for doing the only possible thing to save their lives. The sea's raging ceases and the pagan sailors offer sacrifices to Yahweh (1:14–15). How sensitive and sensible these sailors are in contrast to the foolish prophet of Yahweh!

Now follows the famous "great fish" episode, which unfortunately is all that most people know of the story. Yahweh "appointed a great fish to swallow up Jonah"; (even the fish is more obedient than Jonah!) "and Jonah was in the fish's belly three days and three nights" (1:17). At this point we find a psalm or hymn which Jonah sang as he prayed from within the fish for deliverance. The psalm has nothing to do with the progress of the prose narrative, and it may have been inserted by another author. Eventually, Jonah is rather ignominiously delivered onto dry land by the fish (2:10).

Unable to escape Yahweh, Jonah journeys to Nineveh. The city is described as "an exceedingly great city, three days' journey in breadth" (3:3). Jonah begins to travel across this city, the very heartland of Gentile wickedness, and to threaten imminent destruction in accordance with Yahweh's message (3:4).

To one who has read the prophetic literature of the Old Testament, noting Israel's constant rejection and persecution of the prophets for conveying a similar message from Yahweh, the results of Jonah's preaching are positively amazing. Nineveh repents. "The people believed God; they proclaimed a fast, and put on sackcloth, from the greatest of them to the least of them" (3:5). The king himself calls for abject fasting and repentance, dressing every citizen and even the animals in the symbolic sackcloth (3:6–9). The author here carries his satire to the highest possible pitch, to the delight of his readers.

Yahweh's response to Nineveh's repentance is immediate: he changes his mind and withdraws his plan for the city's destruction. The story could end here, for any sensible prophet would rejoice in the success of his mission and return home. But Jonah, as the author has made clear, is not a sensible prophet. Indeed, Jonah is very disappointed that this great Gentile city will be allowed to stand. Surely here is a biting satire on those Jews who did not want Israel to be "a light to the nations," and who continued to hope, with persistent vindictiveness, that the Gentiles would come to a miserable end whether they believed in Yahweh or not.

In any case, Jonah scolds God for being so merciful (". . . I knew that thou are a gracious God and merciful, slow to anger,

and abounding in steadfast love, and repentest of evil" [4:2])
and asks God to take his life away. Jonah hopes for the worst and
goes outside the city to await Nineveh's downfall (4:5).

Yahweh's mercy extends even to foolish prophets, for the author
tells us that the Lord caused a plant to grow up and shield Jonah
from the fierce rays of the Mesopotamian sun. So Jonah waits in
comfort for the city's destruction. But Yahweh is not yet through
with Jonah. In the night he allows a worm to kill the plant, and by
the next day Jonah feels himself near death from the heat and the
disappointment.

"Do you do well to be angry about the plant?" Yahweh's gentle
question to Jonah prepares us for the beautifully shaped conclusion to the tale. "I do well to be angry," Jonah replies, "angry
enough to die!" Yahweh then contrasts Jonah's pity and concern
over the dead plant with his completely heartless attitude toward
Nineveh, ". . . that great city, in which there are more than a
hundred and twenty thousand persons who do not know their
right hand from their left, and also much cattle." The Lord's reply
to Jonah is this memorable question: "Should not I pity Nineveh?"

The characters and events in the Book of Jonah, as in all satires,
are overdrawn to the point of comedy. The normal state of affairs
in a prophetic book is turned upside down, so that a stupid and
vindictive prophet is found addressing good people who are only
too ready to repent and believe in Yahweh. The fact that these
good people of Nineveh are Gentiles adds to the irony and also
suggests the precise state of mind of some Jews in the post-Exilic
community. To them comes a startling message through this book.
Gentiles, whether they are sailors or city-dwellers, do not lie
beyond the reach of Yahweh's mercy, for Yahweh is more merciful
than those who proclaim themselves his people. The Gentiles *can*
see the light of Yahweh; they *can* repent—even if Yahweh's own
prophet is very slow to learn.

> *Some Questions for Discussion:* What does the Lord command
> Jonah to do? How does Jonah respond? How does Jonah's
> response immediately characterize him for the reader? What
> irony do you see in the actions of the "heathen" sailors as com-

pared to Jonah's actions? What point is the narrator making with these comparisons?

How does the incident of Jonah being swallowed by a great fish affect the narrative? Does the inclusion of such an obviously hyperbolic detail detract from the story? Why might a biblical author have used a fictional story?

How large is Nineveh? How does the size of the city further exaggerate the story? How does Nineveh respond to Jonah? How does the response of the people of Nineveh compare to the response of other peoples in the Old Testament to whom prophecy has been delivered? Is the response of Nineveh characteristic of "human" nature? Why, or why not? Do you see any irony in Nineveh's acts of repentance? What does the irony contribute to the narrative? Explain the symbolism in the incident of Jonah and the plant. What attitude toward "heathen" peoples is conveyed by this incident?

Compare Jonah to other prophets you have studied in terms of his attitude toward 1) his mission, 2) the Lord, 3) himself, 4) the people to whom he is sent to prophesy, 5) his own people. How does Jonah measure up to the other prophets? How is the Lord portrayed in this story? Is God portrayed consistently with the portraits you have seen in other Old Testament literature? Cite examples of consistencies and inconsistencies you find.

How effective is the characterization of Jonah? Is he a stereotyped character? Why do you think the author characterized him in such a way? Might he be intended as a symbol? of what? What purpose do you think the author intended for this story to serve? How do you think the Israelites might have reacted to this story? Is there a "moral" here similar to morals we find in fables? What is it?

Suggested Activities: In *The Interpreter's One-Volume Commentary on the Bible,* Professor Roland E. Murphy writes: "The humorous satire of the book will not disguise the fact that this little work is one of the most important in the OT. There is no greater theological mystery than the mercy of God, and the author was brave enough to caricature a narrow-minded Israelite mentality in order to preserve the sovereign freedom of Yahweh."

Discuss the value of the Book of Jonah. Why do you, or don't you, think it is one of the most important in the Old Testament?

Satirize one of the incidents in any of the books of the Old Testament that you have read thus far. How well do you need to know the book and its characters before you can write a satire?

How effective is your satire? To answer that question, you might ask at least three of your classmates to read what you have written and to give you an honest critique of it.

THE BOOK OF ESTHER

Of all of the books in the Old Testament canon, the Book of Esther is the least religious in its tone and language. God is not mentioned by the storyteller, even where the narrative would seem to demand it (for example, 4:14). No reference is made to famous characters of the Jewish past, such as Moses and David, although there is an oblique reference to the hostility between Saul and Agag the Amalekite (see I Samuel 15). The book has all the qualities of folk legend—artificially constructed names to give the appearance of authenticity, great elaboration of details, an almost comic degree of exaggeration, the struggle between a villain who is all bad and a hero who is all good, and a sense of poetic justice which decrees that the villain die on the very gallows he built for the hero.

The real hero of this elaborate folk tale is the Jewish people as they attempt to survive against overwhelming odds in a Gentile world. Specifically, the Book of Esther purports to set forth the historical events that lie behind the Jewish celebration of the Feast of Purim, which was introduced in the late Old Testament period. The feast, like the book, is of uncertain origin, but its central theme is clear. At Purim, the Jewish community celebrates its survival of persecution through feasting and drinking and rejoicing. Episodes from the Book of Esther are presented in dramatic form to the accompaniment of much merriment and delight. Mordecai, the Jewish hero of the story, is cheered and Haman, the villain, is cursed. The Talmud directs that celebrators of Purim should drink enough wine so that they cannot tell the difference between the shouts of "Cursed be Haman!" and "Blessed be Mordecai!" It is undoubtedly this air of riotous festivity that led to the exclusion of the Deity from the text of Esther, for the Jews wished to avoid any possibility of disrespectful use of the divine name.

The story of Esther, shorn of its lavish and enjoyable details, concerns events in the Persian capital of Susa during the reign of Xerxes I ("Ahasuerus," 1:1). The king has added Esther, a beautiful Jewish girl, to his harem following a nationwide beauty contest. Esther's guardian, the aged Mordecai, is a minor official in the palace. Mordecai, the story suggests, is a descendant of Saul, while his archenemy in the royal court is Haman, a cruel pagan who descends from the hated Amalekites.

The adversaries crash head-on when Mordecai refuses to bow down to Haman. The furious Haman plans a massacre of all the Jews in the empire. A date is set on which the Gentiles will fall upon the Jews and wipe them out. Mordecai begs for Esther to intercede with the king. On his part, Haman prepares the gallows for Mordecai.

Meanwhile the king has discovered that Mordecai once saved his life by reporting an assassination plot. The king prepares to honor Mordecai for his fine deed, and asks Haman's advice: "What shall be done for the man whom the king delights to honor?" Of course Haman has no idea that his enemy Mordecai is slated for honors, and he thinks that he himself will be the honored one. He gives an effusive description of the wealth and prestige that should be given. The plot reaches its desired denouement as Mordecai is honored and Haman's anti-Jewish plot is discovered. Mordecai becomes vizier of the kingdom while Haman perishes on his own gallows.

The sequel is unexpectedly bloody and suggests that the Book of Esther was written after the Maccabean Revolt, which resulted from harsh persecution of the Jews. Not only do Esther and Mordecai prevail upon the king to withdraw the decreed massacre of the Jews, they obtain his permission for the Jews to massacre Gentiles to their hearts' content. Tens of thousands of Gentiles are killed in the capital and in the provinces. The book concludes with a description of the resulting feasting and rejoicing among the members of the Jewish community throughout the empire. The days specified for this festival are the thirteenth and fourteenth of Adar (February-March), which coincide with the date of the Purim festival.

The Book of Esther is shocking in one sense, for it celebrates (as Jonah the prophet wished to do) the downfall of enemies of the Jews. But we should remember that the story of Esther is precisely that—a story. It is a story, moreover, that does no more than picture the Jews as turning the tables upon their persecutors and carrying out in fiction the sort of massacre they have so often suffered in fact in the somber centuries of their history. If the book gives us little history and less religious inspiration, it does offer a penetrating glimpse of the psychology of a powerless and beaten people who bravely demand their right to be themselves.

Some Questions for Discussion: What is the time and geographical setting of this story? What do the details in verses 6–7 add to the story? Why is Queen Vashti dethroned? How is Esther introduced into the story? What "queenly" characteristics does she display before she is made queen? How does the incident in 2:21–23 foreshadow later happenings in the story?

What do chapters 4 and 5 add to Esther's stature? What qualities of character are revealed? What qualities are revealed in Haman as he prepares to attend the Queen's banquet? How has the author contrived for the goodness of Mordecai to be made known to the king? How does Haman interpret the king's question regarding honoring a favorite subject? What perfect irony is involved in his response?

What elaborate scheme does Esther devise to reveal Haman's villainy? How is dramatic tension built into the scene at the banquet table? Compare the characteristics of Mordecai and Haman. What do you discover? Does the "all good" and "all bad" characterization tell you anything about the author's purpose in this story? What poetic justice is achieved in Haman's execution?

Why do you think the Lord's name is conspicuously absent from this narrative? What meaning might this story have for Jewish listeners (look particularly at 3:8)? What Jewish feast was established by Esther? What does it commemorate?

If she had been of the opposite sex, how would Esther's decisions and actions have varied? Would she have accomplished her purpose as well as she did?

Suggested Activity: Select one chapter from the Book of Esther and rewrite it as a script for a play to be presented to your classmates. Consider how you will reveal the thoughts, emotions, and qualities of various characters with techniques of costuming, dialogue, soliloquy, gestures, and stage lighting. How will you build suspense into the incident you choose to dramatize? Present the plays in the sequence of the story.

THE BOOK OF DANIEL

The fortunes of the Jews changed little between the accession of Cyrus in 538 B.C. and the end of the Persian period approximately two hundred years later. Colonies of Jews were dispersed throughout the empire, especially in Babylonia and Egypt, but their ties to the Palestinian homeland remained strong. Persian tolerance of the many national religions within the empire enabled the Jews to worship at their Jerusalem Temple and to elaborate the system of legal prescriptions by which their community was governed.

The Persian period came to an end with the conquests of Alexander the Great in the years between 336 and 323 B.C. At Alexander's death, the enormous empire, which he had so rapidly subjugated, was divided among his generals. Judah became part of the Kingdom of the Ptolemies and was ruled from the Ptolemaic capital in Alexandria until 198 B.C. During the century of Ptolemaic domination, there was little external change in the Jews' situation. Their religious observances and domestic autonomy continued to be respected by the Ptolemies. The main change was internal: Greek became more and more widely spoken and many Jews developed a great admiration for the Hellenistic culture fostered by Alexander and his successors. This culture, representing a mixture of Greek and Oriental social and religious elements, stood in stark contrast to the ancient Hebrew faith. As a result, many Jews avoided Hellenization and despised the Jews who accepted this syncretistic culture. Within the Palestinian Jewish community especially, the split between traditional Jews and their Hellenized countrymen became severe, with considerable hostility between the two groups.

In Alexandria, the Jewish community thrived and increased until there were possibly as many Jews living in Alexandria as there were in the homeland. To these Alexandrian Jews, whose language was Greek, the Hebrew Scriptures became increasingly incomprehensible. During the century of Ptolemaic domination, the Alexandrian Jews produced the first comprehensive translation of the Scriptures into another language. This Greek version of the Old Testament, known as the Septuagint, later became the version of the Old Testament used by the Christian Church, and its importance in disseminating knowledge of these writings throughout the Mediterranean world was inestimable.

In 198 B.C., the province of Judah was wrested away from the Ptolemies and came under the control of the Seleucid Empire, whose capital was in Syria. The situation of the Jews began to worsen, for they were subjected to heavy taxation as the failing Seleucid kingdom attempted to oppose the growing power of Rome. The Seleucid rulers also attempted, with increasing intensity, to unify the tottering empire by imposing Hellenistic culture on all of their subjects. The Jews' situation changed from precariousness to outright danger under the Seleucid ruler Antiochus IV Epiphanes (175–163 B.C.). Antiochus attempted to hold his weakening realm together by fostering Hellenistic culture to an extreme degree. He insisted on the worship of Zeus and imagined that he himself was the local manifestation of Zeus, as indicated by his assumed title "Epiphanes," meaning "manifestation." His Jewish subjects despised Antiochus and came to fear him as well, as indicated by their nickname for him, "Epimanes"—the madman.

It must be remembered that there were severe tensions within the Jewish community itself, for there were some Jews who were perfectly willing to encourage Hellenistic culture and to forget the peculiar observances of the Jews. These Hellenized Jews were ranged against the conservative or orthodox group who would rather die, as they eventually proved, than surrender one iota of the law passed down from the fathers. The situation was ripe for a nasty civil war, and Antiochus shortly precipitated the conflict by plundering the Temple in 169 B.C. At the time, two poorly qualified and thoroughly dishonest Hellenized Jews were vying for the office of high priest by paying large sums to Antiochus, who willingly sold the office to the highest bidder.

When fighting broke out among the Jews over these events, a Seleucid army was dispatched to Jerusalem. The city was taken with terrible butchery, and a garrison of Seleucid soldiers was established in a citadel near the Temple called the Acra. Now Judaism was actually proscribed by Antiochus in 168 B.C., and his soldiers were used to enforce the ban. Copies of the Scriptures were destroyed, the circumcision of infants was outlawed, and finally, as the ultimate insult, swine were sacrificed before an image of Zeus in the Temple itself. It was this sacrilege which was spoken of in the contemporary Book of Daniel as "the abomination of desolation."

Antiochus' cruel and insulting actions precipitated a bloody revolt, led by a family of conservative Jews under one Judas Maccabeus ("the Hammerer"). In a few short years the Seleucids were driven out of Jerusalem, except for the garrison in the Acra. In December 164 B.C., just three years after Antiochus profaned the Temple, the sacred area was cleansed and rededicated by the Jews. This victory is celebrated each year in December as the Feast of Hanukkah ("Dedication").

It is against the background of these events that the Book of Daniel must be read. Its author lived through the frightening persecution under Antiochus, and his heart is clearly on the side of those brave Jews who faced death rather than accede to the king's demands. In order to strengthen the morale of those who resisted the persecution, the author of Daniel collected a series of folk tales about Daniel, a legendary hero who had stood up against the Babylonians in the time of the Exile. These stories comprise the first half of the Book of Daniel. Despite the Exilic setting, the stories are clearly addressed to the dangers and temptations faced by the Jews during the persecution under Antiochus IV.

The six stories about Daniel and his friends are found in Daniel 1:1–6:28. Most of the tales are in Aramaic, rather than Hebrew, for this was the common language of Palestine from the Persian period on. The theme of all of the stories is the courage and faithfulness of the Jews as they remain obedient to the law in a pagan environment.

In the first tale, Daniel and his friends are brought into the king's palace to be trained as courtiers or pages. They are offered the rich food prepared for the king, but refuse to eat it because it is not "kosher." A contest is held to determine whether one can remain healthy on the diet of vegetables and water which the young Jews eat, and it is found that they are healthier and fatter than those who eat the king's food (1:1–16).

Daniel and his friends, who are endowed with great wisdom, now become interpreters of dreams to King Nebuchadnezzar. In the second tale, Daniel's ability to interpret dreams is put to the ultimate test: he is told to interpret a dream without knowing what the dream was. Whereas Nebuchadnezzar's Babylonian wise men cannot do this, Daniel is able to recount to the king his own dream, and then to offer an interpretation. It is to be noted that Daniel himself ascribes his wisdom to the Lord, for the author's lesson is that God will support his faithful people through the worst ordeals and the most impossible situations.

The interpretation of the king's dream (2:36–45) is a cryptic and somewhat confused survey of history from the time of the Babylonian Empire until the Seleucid period. Doubtless the author kept the message deliberately cryptic in order to avoid persecution over the story. In the interpretation, Nebuchadnezzar represents the Babylonian Empire (2:36–38), which is succeeded by an "inferior kingdom," probably intended to be the Median Empire, and then by the Persians ("bronze," 2:39). Then comes the Alexandrian conquest, represented by "iron," which "breaks to pieces and shatters" (2:40). The Ptolemies and Seleucids are the successors to Alexander, and they are represented by iron and clay. Now comes Daniel's concealed prophecy of the downfall of the Seleucid Empire:

> . . . the God of heaven will set up a kingdom which shall never be destroyed, nor shall its sovereignty be left to another people. It shall break in pieces all these kingdoms and bring them to an end, and it shall stand for ever. . . . (2:44)

This was the message of hope that the author of Daniel offered the persecuted Jews: hold out and be faithful to the end, for God himself will overthrow your persecutors and establish his own kingdom.

The third tale concerns Daniel's three friends, Shadrach, Meshach, and Abednego, who are commanded to worship a great golden idol which Nebuchadnezzar erects. If they do not they will be thrown into a fiery furnace. These young men defy the king's order to worship the idol (certainly a symbol for Antiochus' idol in the Jerusalem Temple), but are preserved in the terrible furnace by an angelic being ("like a son of the gods," 3:25). Nebuchadnezzar himself praises the Lord when he sees this:

> Blessed be the God of Shadrach, Meshach, and Abednego, who has sent his angel and delivered his servants, who trusted in him,

and set at nought the king's command, and yielded up their bodies rather than serve and worship any god except their own God. (3:28)

The lesson thus conveyed to the persecuted Jews is transparent.

The fourth tale again concerns the interpretations of a dream which Nebuchadnezzar relates to Daniel. He dreams of a great tree which is chopped down to a stump at the command of an angelic being. The stump remains, bound with iron, among the beasts of the fields. Daniel tells the king that this means the onset of royal madness: the king will become mad and live among beasts in the field for a time. Such madness has not been ascribed to Nebuchadnezzar in historical records, but his successor, Nabonidus, was thought to be mad by his contemporaries. A Dead Sea Scroll text indicates that this story was first told of Nabonidus. In any case, the point is clear that the greatest king can be "cut down" if God so decrees, and this surely was meant to apply to Antiochus and his cohorts.

The fifth tale has the well-known theme of a mysterious hand that appears out of nowhere and writes upon the wall. The setting is a royal banquet at which Belshazzar, son of Nabonidus, and his lords drink wine from bowls and goblets plundered from the Jerusalem Temple (a clear reference to Antiochus' plundering just before the Maccabean Revolt broke out). None of the king's wise men can interpret the enigmatic writing on the wall, and so Daniel is brought before the assembly. Belshazzar is told that his kingdom shall not stand, because he has dishonored the God who rules over the affairs of all men. Specifically the Aramaic words upon the wall are *Mene, Mene, Tekel,* and *Parsin.* These can be interpreted to stand for weights or money: "a mina, a mina, a shekel, and a parsin" (two half-shekels). They also may be read as verbs: "to number," "to number," "to weigh," and "to divide." The weights probably stand for the successors of Nebuchadnezzar, who are of less and less value until the kingdom is finally "numbered, weighed, and divided" to the Medes and Persians. Again, the handwriting on the wall is really intended for Antiochus, whose days as ruler of the Jews are numbered.

In the last of the six tales, which is set in the reign of Darius the Persian (mistakenly referred to in 5:31 as "Darius the Mede"), the greatest possible threat is faced and overcome by Daniel. Daniel has been appointed to rule one of the satrapies, or provinces, of the Empire, but is viewed with jealousy by the other satraps. They find that Daniel, obedient as always to the law, regularly prays thrice daily to the God of Israel, kneeling and facing toward Jerusalem. As a result, he is thrown into a den of lions, for the king has decreed that no petitions shall be made except to him.

As before, Daniel is delivered because of his faithful obedience and trust in God. An angelic being shuts the lions' mouths and the pagan king himself must acknowledge the lordship of Daniel's God,

> for he is the living God, enduring for ever;
> his kingdom shall never be destroyed,
>   and his dominion shall be to the end.
> He delivers and rescues, he works signs and wonders
>   in heaven and on earth,
> he who has saved Daniel from the power of the lions. (6:26–27)

The second part of the Book of Daniel is closely related in theme to the dream-interpretation motif in the prose tales. The author here presents a series of four visions through which God showed to Daniel the meaning of the present persecution and opened to him the mysteries of the future.

The literary genre represented by the visions of Daniel is known as *apocalyptic;* its importance in Jewish and Christian religious literature makes an outline of its typical characteristics desirable. Among the most common features of apocalyptic literature are the following:

Historical setting—Apocalyptic literature arises out of the despair of the Jewish community in the Persian and Greek periods, and it holds out the hope of a glorious future in which the suffering community will be restored and rewarded.

Appeal to history—Apocalyptic writers saw in the salvation history of the past a pattern of God's action, and projected this pattern into the future.

Jewish nationalism—The literature often expresses outright hatred of Gentiles at whose hands the Jews have suffered. In the case of Christian apocalyptic, such as the Book of Revelation in the New Testament, the hatred is directed against the persecuting Roman Empire.

Anonymity and pseudonymity—The decline of prophecy in the post-Exilic period made it necessary to add anonymous apocalyptic passages to prophetic books already in existence (for example, the Isaiah Apocalypse, Isaiah 24–27); or to write under the name of an ancient hero, such as Daniel, who is supposedly predicting the future.

Mythological symbolism—The message of the apocalyptic writers is often clothed in rather obscure symbolism drawn from the stock of mythological figures common to the ancient Near Eastern world.

Most of the above characteristics can be readily applied to the visions contained in Daniel 7–12. In the first vision, Daniel sees a series of beasts, four in number, arising out of a great ocean. Their identity is suggested by the dream interpretation in 2:36–45. The lion is Babylonia, the bear is the Median Empire, the leopard stands for the Persians, and the dragon-like beast represents the Greeks and the ten succeeding rulers. The last of ten horns on this beast, the horn with "eyes like the eyes of a man and a mouth speaking great things," stands for Antiochus IV. This horn "made war with the saints and prevailed over them," but its domination was cut short by God ("the Ancient of Days"), who sits in judgment (7:21–22). After the tenth horn is overcome by divine judgment, the kingdom is given to "the saints of the Most High . . . for ever, for ever and ever." The promise of victory over the Seleucid oppressor is obvious, and the author even suggests a restoration of the Jewish nation to a position of power in the world. At the same time there is an implication that this kingdom which God will establish is a kingdom that will transcend all earthly realities and be truly the Kingdom of God.

One very important symbol of the first vision deserves further discussion. This is the figure of "one like a son of man" who comes before the "Ancient of Days" to receive honor and kingship (7:13–14). The most natural interpretation is that this figure stands for Judah, the "people of the saints of the Most High" (7:27). The phrase "son of man" in Aramaic simply means "man" or "human being," and this human figure stands in meaningful contrast to the beasts who precede him. In this context, then, the son of man figure seems to represent the Jewish people, whose victory over the Seleucids is predicted. Yet there is a further history to the use of this figure in Jewish and Christian literature, particularly in the non-canonical Book of Enoch and in the Synoptic Gospels of the New Testament. In Enoch, "the Son of Man" is individualized and appears to stand for a messiah or messiah-like figure. The early Christians identified Jesus with the Son of Man, deriving this identification from a number of sayings of Jesus. Accordingly many Christians have read the Son of Man passage in Daniel as a reference to the Messiah. While this is not impossible, it seems preferable to interpret the figure as a reference to Judah or the Jewish people, at least in the context of Daniel's immediate message.

The second vision of Daniel also uses a series of beasts to symbolize the rulers of the Near East in the centuries preceding the time of the author. A two-horned ram (the Medo-Persian Empire) is overthrown by a he-goat from the west (Alexander the Great). Then a number of horns stand for the Seleucids, one in particular representing Antiochus. When Antiochus sets up the "transgression that makes desolate" in the Temple, he is given only three and one-half years (1150 days) to reign. After that "the sanctuary will be restored to its rightful state" (8:14). The reference is to the setting up of the statue of Zeus in the Temple and to the period that intervened (actually just three years) before the Jews recaptured and cleansed their holy place.

The third vision is an interpretation of a passage in Jeremiah

(Jeremiah 25:11, 12; 29:10) which predicted that the Jews must suffer seventy years of exile after the destruction of Judah. The sort of numerical manipulation found here is characteristic of apocalyptic literature; it reflects the attempts of seers to calculate the time of the end of the present evil period and to convey their predictions in a cryptic fashion.

The passage opens with a long prayer by Daniel in which he expresses the sense of guilt and contrition that is deeply embedded in the Judaism of the post-Exilic period. He confesses that Israel had not kept Yahweh's law but had spurned the covenant and persecuted Yahweh's messengers, the prophets. As a result, great calamity has fallen upon the community in accordance with the will of God. The sanctuary has been made desolate and the heathen nations are ready to drive Israel into oblivion. The prayer concludes with a plea for deliverance in spite of the people's sins.

The answer to the prayer is the announcement, through the angel Gabriel, of the exact length of Israel's term of suffering (9:24–27). In this section Jeremiah's figure of seventy years for the Exile is reinterpreted. The seventy years become "seventy weeks of years" (9:24), with a "week" standing for seven years. The seventy years is thus extended to cover the entire period from the beginning of the Exile until the author's time. Two "anointed ones" are mentioned as coming between Jeremiah's time and the time of Antiochus IV; the references are probably to Zerubbabel and to a high priest of the second century (9:25–27). After the second anointed one comes the desolation of the sanctuary and the cessation of (Jewish) sacrifices. Finally, Daniel is assured the desolator will meet his "decreed end" (9:27).

The fourth and final vision (10:1–12:13) is the most complex of all of the materials in Daniel. The main pattern and underlying themes, however, are identical with the earlier visions. Daniel has a dream or vision in which he encounters angelic beings, Gabriel and Michael. Through them the panorama of post-Exilic history is opened to Daniel, and the rise and fall of major political powers of the Near East in that period is depicted. As the account of history nears the period of the Maccabean Revolt, historical events and personages are treated in increasing detail. We can only guess at the meaning of some of the cryptic references, though the general meaning is clear.

In this section the conflicts of history are presented as earthly reflections of the conflict between angelic beings. Each nation is represented before Yahweh by a patron angel, Judah's angel being Michael. Such speculation on the identity and function of members of Yahweh's council or "host" is frequent in apocalyptic literature. It may result from the influence of Persian religion, which had a complicated angelology.

Daniel hears of conflicts between patron angels in the first part of his vision, but he is given no clear word as to the meaning of these conflicts (10:10–11:1). An interpretation is offered which lists, in cryptic form, various Near Eeastern rulers from the early Persian period on (11:2–19). It is sufficient for our purposes to point out the general sequence: first come the great Persian monarchs (11:2), then Alexander the Great (11:3). Following Alexander's reign, his kingdom is "broken up and divided" (11:4). Next the century of conflict between the Seleucids and the Ptolemies is depicted in considerable detail and precision (11:5–13).

At this point the author introduces a long passage (11:21–45) dealing in similar cryptic fashion with the reign of Antiochus IV Epiphanes, described as "a contemptible person" (11:21). Antiochus' dealings with the rivals for the high priesthood are depicted (11:22–28), and his attack upon the Jews is presented with unusual clarity:

> Forces from him shall appear and profane the temple and fortress, and shall take away the continual burnt offering. And they shall set up the abomination that makes desolate. (11:31)

The author alludes to the Maccabean Revolt as he speaks of "the people who know their God," who "stand firm and take action" (11:32). Through them comes "a little help" (11:34). Yet it is clear that the author of Daniel does not believe that the revolt can fundamentally alter the course of events. Instead, he takes the deterministic view that "what is determined shall be done"

(11:36) and that the abominable actions of Antiochus will continue until the time set for the end:

> . . . he shall pitch his palatial tents between the sea and the glorious holy mountain; yet he shall come to his end, with none to help him. (11:45)

Chapter 12 depicts the end of the present age of persecution and the beginning of the new age of Jewish power. As is frequently the case in apocalyptic literature, these events transcend the ordinary movements of history and suggest the breaking in of an other-worldly kingdom. After a period of climactic suffering that reflects angelic struggles, the dead who fell as martyrs to the Jewish cause will be raised (12:1–3). Those who have been wise and courageous in adhering to the Law of Moses will "shine . . . like the stars for ever and ever" (12:3). The book concludes with two calculations of the exact time of the end (12:7–12) and a blessing upon Daniel himself:

> But go your way till the end; and you shall rest, and shall stand in your allotted place at the end of the days. (12:13)

In concluding our discussion of the Book of Daniel, we should note how radically this understanding of history differs from the prophetic view that prevailed before the Exile. In apocalyptic literature, the movements of history are not at all affected by individual or national decisions; the course of events and the time allotted to their completion is laid out on an enormous timetable in the divine realm. This makes possible the detailed predictions that are characteristic of this genre of literature. The writer is pictured as a seer to whom the heavenly plans are disclosed ("apocalypse" is the Greek word for "unveiling" or "revealing"). Earthly events are not only planned in advance by the Deity, they are pushed forward toward their consummation by the angelic beings who stand as the patrons of individual nations and kings.

This understanding of history contrasts strongly with the prophetic view in which predictions take the shape of threats and promises that are always conditional. Israel was told by the prophets, in effect, that if she continued to rebel against Yahweh she would surely be punished. But the implication is always present that repentance can lead to a change in her prospects for the future. In this view of history, the future is in the hands of man in accordance with his responsibility or irresponsibility in interaction with God and the rest of mankind.

One can explain the apocalyptic view, which has deep connections with the outlook of wisdom literature, as resulting from the historical situation of the Jews after the Exile. Their situation was one of powerlessness; more and more they were forced to stand and wait for the waves of history to roll over their heads and to accept what came in the best possible spirit under the circumstances. Hopes for the future were increasingly elevated to a mythical level, for the real future that awaited the Jews seemed otherwise to be as barren of meaning as the present.

Perhaps the apocalyptic hope for a mythical future was practically the only hope open to post-Exilic Jews. That they maintained this hope in God's eventual faithfulness to his covenant promises is a mark of the courage which the Jews maintained in the midst of the suffering and emptiness that lay upon them as one foreign power after another deprived them of their freedom.

Some Questions for Discussion: What is the purpose of Daniel 1:1–6? How and why were Daniel and his three friends favored by Nebuchadnezzar? Why does Daniel not want the king's rich food? Why do you think the story of Daniel's obeying the dietary laws of the Jews would have been important to people in Exile?

To "stand before the king" meant that a person was available to give the king advice on demand. Why were Daniel and his three friends brought before the king? What impression of the king do you get from 2:2–12? What impression of Daniel do you get from 2:20–24? How does Nebuchadnezzar's command about the interpretation of his dream differ from that of the pharaoh in the Joseph story? How does Daniel interpret the dream? What does the king do?

How does Nebuchadnezzar's action in 3:1 contradict his speech in 2:47? What does he see in the fiery furnace? What does he seem to believe after he commands Shadrach, Meshach, and Abednego to leave the furnace? What is the purpose of the "fiery furnace" episode?

What form of communication does King Nebuchadnezzar use in chapter 4 to address "all peoples, nations, and languages, that dwell in all the earth"? Why might his greeting be considered boastful? How does the Nebuchadnezzar of 4:1–5 differ from the king you met in previous chapters?

What does the tree in Nebuchadnezzar's dream symbolize? According to Daniel, why should the "stump of its roots" be saved? How does Daniel interpret the dream? What is the purpose of Daniel's statement in 4:19? What happened to the king twelve months after Daniel interpreted the dream? What profound effect did Nebuchadnezzar's experience have on him?

What sacrileges did Belshazzar commit? How did Belshazzar behave as he saw the hand write on the wall? Why do you think Daniel repeats part of chapter 4 in 5:18–21? How does Daniel interpret the handwriting on the wall? What is Belshazzar's fate?

Why do the presidents and satraps plot against Daniel? How did King Darius react when he was first told that Daniel had disobeyed his interdict? How does Darius behave when he finds Daniel safe in the lions' den? What do you think is the purpose of the story of Daniel and the lions' den?

In *The Interpreter's One-Volume Commentary on the Bible,* Professor George A. F. Knight writes that Daniel 7:1–28 is "one of the most far-reaching passages in the Bible in its influence. Most of the apocalyptic works produced during the next three centuries use some of its language and imagery." Why do you think this passage is so influential? What is special about it? Summarize the visions of Daniel. Why are they significant?

What is the purpose of 11:2–29? What is predicted in 11:40–45? How do you interpret 12:1–4? What is the fate of Daniel?

Suggested Activities: Select any passage from one of the six stories in Daniel and rewrite it from a different point of view. For example, you might tell the story of the fiery furnace from Shadrach's point of view. As you change the point of view, what details can you leave in? Why can you keep them? What must you leave out? Why?

Discuss the differences in language and literary technique between chapters 1–6 and 7–9.

Of the four short stories—Ruth, Esther, Jonah, and Daniel— which do you think comes closest to qualifying as a modern short story? Discuss your choice, giving reasons why you think it might be published today as a short story.

Wisdom Literature

PROVERBS (PROVERBS 8:1–9:6; 15; 23; 27; 31:10–31)

The Book of Proverbs is a compilation of small collections of Israelite wisdom literature. The collections give some indication of the complex, diverse development of the wisdom movement in Israel, since they are quite different from one another in tone and outlook. Just as in other parts of the Old Testament (for example, Judges 9:7–15), we find in Proverbs examples of an earthy folk wisdom that thrived in Israel throughout its long history. In Proverbs 25–27, for example, we find a non-theological, commonsense approach to life that must have flourished and been developed wherever men met, be it in the marketplace, at the city gate, in the home, or even in battle as in I Kings 20:11. Fundamental to this outlook on life is a pragmatic sense of order and of basic values that has been tried and tested and found valid in the experience of an entire people.

As a result of his study of the proverbs, R. B. Y. Scott has outlined seven literary forms through which the proverbs are expressed.[1] The following is based on Professor Scott's analysis:

1. identity, equivalence, or invariable association;
(Where A is, you will find B also.)

Examples: A friend in need is a friend indeed.

Easy come, easy go.

A penny saved is a penny earned.

Where there are no oxen, there is no grain.

(Proverbs 14:4)

2. non-identity, contrast, paradox;
(A is not really B, or A strangely leads to B.)

Examples: All that glistens is not gold.

Plenty of smoke, but no fire.

Good fences make good neighbors.

. . . a soft tongue will break a bone. (Proverbs 25:15)

3. similarity, analogy;
(A is like B.)

Examples: Like mother, like daughter.

A chip off the old block.

Like cold water to a thirsty soul, so is good news from a far country. (Proverbs 25:25)

4. circumstances contrary to right order, thus leading to futility and absurdity;

Examples: Don't count your chickens before they're hatched.

What's the use of running when you are on the wrong road?

. . . in vain is a net spread in the sight of any bird.

(Proverbs 1:17)

Why should a fool have a price in his hand to buy wisdom, when he has no mind? (Proverbs 17:16)

5. classification and characterization of people, actions, or situations;

Examples: Children and fools speak the truth.

A rolling stone gathers no moss.

. . . a wife's quarreling is a continual dripping of rain (Proverbs 19:13. For other examples, see Proverbs 30:18–31.)

6. indication of relative value, proportion, or degree;
(A is worth B; better A than B; if A, how much more B?)

Examples: A bird in the hand is worth two in the bush.
Better late than never.
Out of the frying pan into the fire.
. . . to obey is better than sacrifice. (I Samuel 15:22)
A good name is to be chosen rather than great riches. (Proverbs 22:1)

7. consequences of human character and behavior;

Examples: Give him an inch and he'll take a mile.
Nothing ventured, nothing gained.
The fathers have eaten sour grapes, and the children's teeth are set on edge. (Ezekiel 18:2)
He who digs a pit (for another) will fall into it (himself), and a stone will come back upon him who starts it rolling. (Proverbs 26:27)

Chapter 27, with its many penetrating insights into the human condition, is typical of the folk wisdom that developed in Israel. It covers a wide range of subjects, from the plague of the contentious wife to the lostness of the man who leaves home (because of her?). Although several of the proverbs have been coupled because of similar literary form (for example, verses 3–4), there does not seem to be any particular grouping according to subject matter. The overall emphasis seems to be on helping the individual to thrive and endure through the ups and downs life brings. The dominant tone is caution and prudence: recognize who your true friends are; don't long for more than life can give; and duck when you see a blow coming your way. A shrewd hardheartedness is invoked, behind which is the feeling that if you don't get them, they'll get you. If a man has foolishly (and compassionately) pledged bond for a stranger, don't let him escape the obligation of making good on the pledge. In essence, the way of life enjoined in this section of Proverbs seems to be: "You've got to look out for Number One, because no one else will."

Such advice, born from a shrewd appraisal of the potential for good and evil which all men are inherently capable of, cuts directly across some of the basic tenets of Mosaic covenant theology. The wisdom literature is more individualistic in its orientation, whereas the covenant ordinances presuppose the primary value of the community over the individual. The covenant ideology called the Israelite toward a selfless compassion for his fellowman so that the bonds of the community could be preserved and strengthened. The wisdom literature acknowledges man's need for community, but only as a means of enhancing his own position within it.

If the discrepancy between Israelite theology and the wisdom movement is as glaring as we have made it out to be, two fundamental questions should be raised: (1) From what sources did the Israelite wisdom movement develop? (2) How was the wisdom viewpoint adapted in Israel so that it became acceptable to those leaders who formulated the Old Testament canon?

A rich variety of texts—mainly from Egypt and Mesopotamia—provides ample evidence that the wisdom movement was an extremely important element within Near Eastern culture long before the origin of Israel.[2] In Egypt especially, this movement seems to have been associated with the royal courts, where the young nobles were trained to be the next generation of rulers and government officials. Basically a life of prudence and moderation is enjoined: don't get caught in an affair, because it could ruin your career; don't overdrink, because your tongue might slip; show proper respect to your superior so that he will speak well of you when the time comes. One finds a patrician's disdain for the uneducated poor (fool) blended with a paternalistic sense of obligation not to take advantage of their plight.

This kind of wisdom, which was preserved and developed in the royal courts by scribes and wise men who acted as tutors to the young nobility and advisers to kings and government officials, most likely came into Israel during the reigns of David and Solomon. It is known that David tried to structure his fledgling court after the Egyptian model, and Solomon's wisdom assumed legendary proportions. So great was his reputed wisdom that later tradition ascribed authorship of the entire Book of Proverbs to him. Proverbs 22:17–24:34 is directly related to an Egyptian wisdom text, "The Instruction of Amen-em-opet."[3] Each text has thirty precepts, nine of which are the same. Thus it seems that the

Israelite writer was familiar with the basic structure and content of the Egyptian piece. In both works the admonitions are given by the father to his son. From "The Instruction of Amen-em-opet," we see that the speaker is supposed to be the king, who is passing on his experience through a series of maxims to his son, the crown prince. Putting the words in the king's mouth is probably a literary device of the Egyptian sages.

Thus far we have considered two types of wisdom literature: (1) royal wisdom—advice to the young nobility on how to live a proper, successful life—which developed in Near Eastern courts, whence it was transplanted into Jerusalem through the Davidic monarchy; and (2) secular wisdom—the hard lessons of life, which the individual must learn if he is to survive and succeed. This latter kind of teaching is quite alien to a seminomadic society in which the individual is not on his own but is afforded the protection and care of his family, clan, and tribe. The outlook is much more compatible with an urban environment, so we would suggest that this secular wisdom was borrowed from the Canaanites and developed after the Israelites had settled in the land.

There were frequent heated encounters between prophets and wise men in the course of Israel's history. The prophets would demand that the will of God must be fulfilled, regardless of the cost, whereas the wise men would formulate their advice on the pragmatic principles of expediency and caution. The split between the two is so basic that one wonders how the wisdom material ever came to be regarded as divinely inspired. The second major section of Proverbs (10:1–22:16) shows us that a major rapprochement between the teaching of wisdom and the teaching of the Torah must have taken place at some point in Israel's history. Some scholars suggest that the most likely time for this to have happened was after the fall of the monarchy in 587 B.C.[4] The scribes and wise men no longer had a royal house to look after, and, being dispersed with the other Jews during the Diaspora, they soon became the respected community leaders wherever they settled. Also it seems that there would have been greater prophetic influence on the thinking of the wise men during this later period.

The tone of chapters 25–29 is secular and shrewd; the tone of 22:17–24:22 is secular, patrician and pedantic; the tone of 10:1–22:16 is religious and pedantic. The dichotomy is no longer between the wise and the foolish but between the righteous and the wicked. The object of scorn is no longer the uneducated poor man who behaves rashly rather than rationally; "the fool" is now the man who deliberately turns away from the teachings of the Torah. He is not only wicked for transgressing the divine commandments, but he is also a fool because such transgressions always result in his ruin. There is an easy assurance on the part of the teacher that righteousness is rewarded and evil will be punished (for example, 11:1–8). The tone is didactic and dogmatic, and, as Job and Ecclesiastes were to point out, the teachings do not always correspond to the realities of life in an unjust world. R. B. Y. Scott suggests that the teacher was able to pontificate without fear of being challenged, because the students were not in a position to object or answer, nor had they yet experienced the realities of life (see, for example, 15:6).[5] Still these maxims are reminiscent of earlier Israelite theology, exhorting the young student to live a just life and thus secure God's protection and care. Unlike his portrayal in the earlier sections of Proverbs, God is seen as ever-present, watching over the thoughts and actions of each man.

What seems to be required from the students is a rote learning of the precepts that led them toward full participation in the covenant community. Most of the proverbs are two-line couplets. It seems likely that the first line was spoken by the teacher, and the students responded by completing the proverb with the second line. There are three basic literary patterns through which these couplets were completed:

(1) contrast: "A soft answer turns away wrath, but a harsh word stirs up anger" (15:1).
(2) repetition: "There is severe discipline for him who forsakes the way; he who hates reproof will die" (15:10).

(3) synthesis: (second line continues and completes the thought begun in the first line)
"The eyes of the Lord are in every place, keeping watch on the evil and the good" (15:3).

The final stage in the compilation of the Books of Proverbs is the introduction in chapters 1–9, which is an extremely interesting and important section. Again the emphasis is on exhorting the student to find wisdom by embracing the Torah. Obedience, rather than intellectual knowledge, is the ultimate sign of wisdom, because (like Socrates) the writer assumes that once the student understands the rightness of the good life, he will then be willing and able to obey. As in 22:17–24:22, the format for instruction is that of a father addressing his son. Although the "father" may still be the wise sage, one can see from the content that a radical change has taken place in the student body. They are no longer the young nobles learning how to govern; instead, they are the boys of the community who are being instructed in the Torah and exhorted to live a righteous life.

An interesting development is reflected in 8:1–9:6, where Wisdom is personified as a female being who appears at the gates of the city to call men to turn to her. The writer had spent much effort in warning his students about the wide variety of wicked enticements through which a woman can bring a man to his ruin. Now he ends his writing by exhorting his students to cleave solely to Dame Wisdom. We see from 8:22ff that there is a mythological development behind this personification of wisdom. She was made before the world was formed, and through her the creation was established (Proverbs 3:19f).

This concept is a result of post-Exilic Jewish theology, which generally emphasized God's transcendence—that is, the distance between the most holy, almighty God and his troubled creation. God was thought to be so holy, so wholly other, that he could only be related to the world through angelic mediaries. Thus we have a widespread development of angelology in this period, as reflected in Daniel and the New Testament. Part of

392 *Teaching the Old Testament*

this development was the splitting off of one of God's characteristics, his wisdom, into an independent being—a female one at that. To stress the right ordering of the world, Wisdom becomes the agent through whom the world was created. She also gives life to all those who embrace her; the invitation is extended openly to all (9:3–6). And the knowledge that brings life to man is found in the Torah. Thus we have a very close identification between Wisdom, who created the world and came down to entice man to find her and live, and the Torah, which was created in the heavens by God and sent down to earth so that man might find life. Since wisdom ultimately is the law of God, the two figures eventually merge. This development is closely related to the concept of the *Word* which is used to introduce the Gospel of John (1:1–18).

In general, women are not sympathetically portrayed in wisdom literature. They are the wily ones, ever-eager to bring man to his ruin. An addition at the end of Proverbs (31:10–31) in which the ideal wife is described makes up for this antifeminine bias. It is an acrostic poem, the first line beginning with "A" (Hebrew *'aleph*), and each successive line working down the Hebrew alphabet.

Some Questions for Discussion: Who is speaking in 8:4–36? What is the basic message of 8:4–36? At what event was Wisdom present? What does Wisdom's house tell you about her social position? What is her invitation and what do you think it means?

What are some of the differences between the wise man and the fool as noted in chapter 15? We learn a great deal about the Lord, since he is mentioned nine times in chapter 15. What view of the Lord do you get from chapter 15? What do you learn about his omniscience, justice, and attitude toward richness and poverty?

What is the message of 23:1–3? of 23:4–5? According to chapter 23, how should you behave toward the stingy? toward a fool? toward a child? Who is speaking in chapter 23? to whom?

What do you think is the most important advice you receive in chapter 27? Why do you think so?

According to chapter 31, what does a good wife do? What kind of woman could fit the description in 31:10–31? How do you think a contemporary woman influenced by the women's liberation movement would respond to this poem?

Suggested Activities: Write a poem or a theme in which you describe a good husband for the twentieth century. Or write a poem or theme in which you describe a good wife for today's world.

Study several of the proverbs that appeal to you, and then write proverbs of your own that you think might be sound advice for people living in the twentieth century.

Read the entire Book of Proverbs, noting the proverbs that you have heard before. Then select a half dozen of them and prepare to explain them to children between the ages of six and nine. How will you state each proverb? How will you explain it to children? How can you be certain that the children understand it?

ECCLESIASTES (ECCLESIASTES 1; 3; 11:1–12:8)

The ancient Near Eastern wisdom movement did much to give a pragmatic orientation to the establishing of social values. Man was the ultimate determiner, and it was his duty to find out what types of behavior worked best and pass his experience on to benefit future generations. When religious sanctions were applied, the wise men would conclude that the gods blessed the courses of action that the wise men had found to be most successful. This is all very good when there is some sense of stability and continuity with the past. However, a considerable portion of the ancient Near Eastern wisdom literature was produced during periods of great turmoil and chaos, when things did not work out the way they were supposed to. One common tactic was to blame disaster on the gods. We have a sizable body of literature of the righteous individual who cannot understand why the gods cause (or allow) him to suffer. An earnest effort is made to explain the existence of evil in a world controlled by just and good gods. The Old Testament example of this genre is the Book of Job. Another response of the more secular wise men was to shrug their shoulders and affirm the meaninglessness of existence. The world is the way it is—without purpose or value—and the individual can only find some degree of happiness after he has accepted the fact that life is ultimately futile. The book of Ecclesiastes reflects this sophisticated cynicism toward life. Excerpts from one Near Eastern parallel will suffice to illustrate this mood of disillusionment and despair:

"[Servant,] obey me." Yes, my lord, yes. ["Bring me at once the] chariot, hitch it up. I will ride to the palace." [Ride, my lord, ride! All your wishes] will be realized for you. The king will be gracious to you. ["No, servant.] I shall not ride [to] the palace." [Do not ride], my lord, do not ride. [To a place . . .] he will send you. [In a land which] you know [not] he will let you be captured. [Day and] night he will let you see trouble.

"Servant, obey me." Yes, my lord, yes. "A woman will I love." Yes, love, my lord, love. The man who loves a woman will forget pain and trouble. "No, servant, a woman I shall not love." [Do not love,] my lord, do not [love]. Woman is a well, woman is an iron dagger—a sharp one!—which cuts a man's neck.

"Servant, obey me." Yes, my lord, yes. "I will do something helpful for my country." Do (it), my lord, do (it). The man who does something helpful for his country—his helpful deed is placed in the bowl of Marduk. "No, servant, I will not do something helpful for my country." Do it not, my lord, do it not. Climb the mounds of ancient ruins and walk about: look at the skulls of late and early (men); who (among them) is an evildoer, who a public benefactor?[6]

This complete ambivalence of values, set within the context of a grim humor that borders on the absurd, is strikingly similar to contemporary art forms, and we wonder that it was produced so long ago. Note especially the final part of the dialogue: what does it matter whether one is righteous or wicked? Death is the great equalizer, and all men—both righteous and wicked—share the same grave.

This tone of cynical despair dominates the Book of Ecclesiastes. The writer, who calls himself Qoheleth (translated "The preacher," or more precisely, "one who speaks in an assembly"), insists from the outset that everything is *hebhel*. This word is usually translated *vanity;* it denotes a mist, fog, or vapor and connotes that which apparently exists but is ultimately unsubstantial. Man is ambitious; he plans and labors and tries to lead a righteous life so that these ambitions might be realized. But man can in no sense control his own destiny. He is part of a cosmic structure which takes little account of his feeble efforts. Man is caught up and swept along in a course of events which is not determined by his actions. He may enjoy some moments of happiness. There will be other times when he is crushed by turmoil and disaster. But in neither case were these events determined by the kind of life a man might lead. Man is a fleeting breath, a slender blade of grass which soon withers and is forgotten—to be replaced by a new offshoot which takes no note of and is not affected by what has gone before. Only the earth is eternal.

As nature has its regular patterns—the tides, the seasons, the measured sequence of night following day—so there is an eternal cosmic rhythm which overwhelms man's sense of historical particularity. "What has been is what will be, and what has been done is what will be done; and there is nothing new under the sun" (1:9).

The biblical concept of history as an eternally new thing being created by a God who is acting to fulfill his unique purposes by responding to the meaningful decisions and actions of men is replaced by a cyclical view of time that is more at home in Near Eastern mythology or Greek philosophy. Man is not called to create and refashion in response to a righteous God who lays claims upon him; his task is rather to accept and conform to the cosmic ebb and flow that far transcend his particular historical moment. "What is crooked cannot be made straight, and what is lacking cannot be numbered" (1:15). It is no use trying to change the world to conform to some preconceived ideal of what is right. There is a certain givenness about the world and society that can only be accepted, even if one does it with shrugged shoulders. One of these givens is evil—an unfortunate circumstance, but there is nothing that one can do.

Although later tradition has ascribed this work to Solomon (1:1), most scholars agree that it comes from the post-Exilic period. In chapters 1–2, the writer has assumed the role of a king to stress his point that the possession of great riches, luxury, and wisdom are for nought because they do not bring pleasure. During this post-Exilic period, through the special influence of leaders like Ezekiel and Ezra, Judaism had generally accepted the doctrine of individual retribution. The Mosaic teaching that God would work out his judgment on the community over a period of several generations was reinterpreted to stress God's judgment on an individual within his own lifetime. This meant that every person's life was determined by the extent to which he obeyed or disobeyed the Torah. Prosperity would come to the righteous and calamity would inevitably befall the wicked.

Ecclesiastes was written to deny this view of a god who automatically rewards and punishes individuals in response to their every action. As we see from the famous "a time to be born and a time to die" passage in 3:1–9, Qoheleth finds that there is a pattern in life which affirms the existence of a transcendent God. But the pragmatism inherent in the wisdom tradition will not allow the writer to accept the doctrine of individual retribution—a doctrine that he was unable to verify through his own experience and observation. Qoheleth was unable to see that this cosmic pattern was in any way determined by the actions of man. We cannot know our beginning (3:11). We cannot know what happens after death (3:21). We cannot know why the righteous suffer and the wicked prosper (7:15). We know only that all flesh must die (3:20).

In the light of Qoheleth's understanding of the universe as tragic, capricious, and impersonal, one might wonder how he can say "There is nothing better for a man than that he should eat and drink, and find enjoyment in his toil" (2:24; compare 3:12). How can a man find fulfillment in his work if he knows that the fruits of his labor might be swept away at any time by the hand of fate? Qoheleth's point is that the source of our happiness should be the realization that the world is beyond our control. Once we acknowledge the limitations of our knowledge and power, we are set free—free to accept the world as it is. We then would no longer waste away our lives in bitter frustration, trying to shape the world into the perfect place it was never meant to be. Once we give up this misbegotten ambition that has been fostered by high ideals impossible to fulfill, we are free to relish the moments that come our way as free, undeserved gifts from God.

In 11:1–12:8, Qoheleth aims his teaching particularly at the young. Youth is the time of idealism, which leads only to frustration. They should accept life as it is. They should work diligently, but not expect any immediate return. The trouble is that most people are ambitious; they act in the hope that some result will occur. Qoheleth's point is that a result might not be realized for a long time, if ever. If we are always trying to achieve a result, our lives will be wasted away in anxiety. *We must enjoy the work itself*, not the wealth it produces, for it could be lost in war or in court; not the house which is built, for it could go up in smoke; not the knowledge which is gained, for knowledge only increases our sorrow. Life's pleasure is found only in the moment—the moment which must be enjoyed for its own sake.

The general viewpoint represented in Ecclesiastes is quite different from that of any other biblical writer. Certainly there is a note of cynicism and despair, born out of Qoheleth's crushed ideals. But he is by no means a nihilist. He discards the notion of an imminent God who mechanically dishes out retribution; but his embracing the present moment and finding fulfillment in it without worrying about what the morrow will bring is not as far removed from the biblical faith relationship as many would assume.

Some Questions for Discussion: According to Professor Harvey H. Guthrie, Jr., writing in *The Interpreter's One-Volume Com-*

mentary on the Bible, the word that is translated *vanity* "denotes a breath, exhaled air that disappears. Over half its occurrences are in Ecclesiastes. It is the equivalent of the name of the first man in the Bible to die, Abel; and this may be no accident. The author restates his theme in 12:8. It is that, *so far as men can observe,* all that makes up life soon vanishes and loses significance." What do you think of the author's theme? What are your reasons for agreeing or disagreeing with it?

What is the message of chapter 1? How does it agree or disagree with the author's theme as Professor Guthrie sees it?

What is your response to the poem that opens chapter 3? What is the message of that chapter? What can man do to be happy? What is his fate?

How do you interpret "Cast your bread upon the waters, for you will find it after many days" (11:1)?

What do you think is the message of the poem in 11:1–4? What is the author's view of life? of youth?

Suggested Activity: Select any chapter of Ecclesiastes and compare it with any chapter in Proverbs, noting differences or similarities in tone, advice, and philosophy.

JOB (JOB 1–14; 19; 28–31; 38–42)

In our discussion of Ecclesiastes, we remarked that there is a considerable collection of ancient Near Eastern wisdom literature concerning the righteous individual who attempts to understand the cause of his suffering. The story of Job is the outstanding example of this literary genre. Most scholars have concluded that the story originated outside of Israel some time around the middle of the second millennium. We find this kernel story around which the rest of the book has been structured in chapters 1–2; 42:7–17. Job is portrayed as a patriarchal figure—an upright man who has been blessed in all things. He has a large family and abundant material possessions. But the gods decide to test him, suspecting that he is righteous only to assure himself the prosperity he covets. Job is buffeted by one inexplicable tragedy after another. He is tempted to renounce the God in whom he has trusted and for whom he has been righteous. But he hangs on, accepting the trials, refusing to curse God and die (2:9). In 42:7ff, Job's fortunes—his family and possessions—are restored twofold because he has proved his righteousness by meekly bowing down before a divine providence which had treated him rather capriciously.

This is essentially the story in its pre-Israelite form, as it was known and passed on by word of mouth throughout the ancient Near East. Its point seems to be that the righteous man will accept whatever fate has been determined for him by the gods. Suffering is understood as a divine testing that must be endured in the hope that the gods will ultimately be merciful. This story beautifully reflects the ancient Near Eastern (especially the Mesopotamian) mentality, characterized by man's feeling eternally insecure before the capricious omnipotence of the gods. Man could humbly question; he could petition the gods for mercy, but his final recourse had to be a passive acceptance of his destiny.

Such a story, charming as it is with its happy ending, is ultimately incompatible with the Israelite world view because it does not accurately reflect the Israelite concept of God. Whereas divine righteousness was always a secondary characteristic to divine transcendence in ancient Near Eastern thought, Yahweh, the God of Israel, was first and foremost a just and righteous God. The gods of the nations could ulitmately have their way—a way which need never be justified—because they were not necessarily responsive to man's actions. The Israelites conceived of Yahweh as ruling over the affairs of man, but *in response to man's actions*. He is a righteous God who has contractually bound himself to his people, and the Israelites know that their destiny is being shaped, not by a divine power that takes little account of their needs and actions, but by the manner in which they respond to God's demands for justice. Thus, whereas the righteous sufferer could be rationalized in ancient Near Eastern thought, he was a complete enigma in Israel. This is why we find the Job of the middle section of the book (chapters 3:1–42:6) standing for the most part like Prometheus—bloody but unbowed—demanding that the God of Israel show him his sin. There is no provision in Israelite thought for a God who acts arbitrarily.

The problem of unjustified suffering became increasingly acute as North Israel and Judah experienced the shock of being subject to, and eventually absorbed into, the mighty empires of the ancient Near East: the Assyrian, Babylonian, Persian, Greek, Syrian, Roman, and so forth. During the Exilic and Diaspora periods, the Jews could not help asking why this had happened. Of course many answers arose. The dominant response was that God was punishing his people for their past sins, thus moving the Jewish community to return to their God by a strict adherence to the Torah. Second Isaiah felt that the Jews had suffered more than they deserved and that through their suffering they were serving God by bringing reconciliation into the world—a reconciliation that would ultimately overcome the oppressors and thus create at the universal level the ancient ideal of the just society. The apocalyptic writers, such as Daniel and Joel, felt that the untold agony of the Jewish community proved that the world was increasingly coming under the control of demonic forces that would ultimately be overthrown on the day of judgment. Men like the author of Ecclesiastes felt that although God had created the world, he was no longer active in history, leaving man to make his own way.

The Book of Job, we would submit, is one of the most profound struggles with the problem of righteousness in the context of evil and suffering that man has ever produced. Although it stems from the wisdom tradition—a tradition which by and large remained alien to the major categories of Israelite thought—in a very real sense the Book of Job is the culmination of biblical thought. An anonymous Jewish writer of the sixth or fifth century has taken this ancient Near Eastern folk tale of the proverbial man of sorrows and has used it as the framework into which he has placed these stunning dialogues between man and his fellowman, between man and his God. The Book can be divided into these five parts:

1. The Near Eastern folk tale prose Prologue, in which the divine council decides to test the motivation of Job's righteousness (chapters 1–2).

2. The Dialogues, in which Job is visited by three comforters who attempt to account for his suffering in terms of the traditional concept of retribution—Job's predicament proves that he has sinned and therefore his only hope is repentance. Job, however, steadfastly maintains that he is righteous; he demands a confrontation with God. He wants God to justify himself— either to point Job's guilt out to him, or to explain why he allows the innocent to suffer (chapters 3–31).

3. The "Elihu speeches," in which a young man who is not mentioned in the rest of the work comes forward to put Job down for his arrogant demands to confront God with his righteousness (chapters 32–37). Scholars debate the degree of profundity in these chapters, but almost all agree that they are a later addition to the work, perhaps inserted by a scribe who was dissatisfied with the defense of traditional Judaism that had been put forward by the three comforters in the Dialogues.

4. The Yahweh speeches (38:1–42:6), which originally followed the Dialogues. In the Dialogues, Job's last speech had concluded with a beautiful description of his righteousness and of his desire to face God and have his situation explained. Yahweh appears, asks Job a series of overwhelming rhetorical questions, and Job repents in dust and ashes. His repentance is not so much an acknowledgment of sin as it is an affirmation of God's transcendent power and love.

5. The prose folk tale Epilogue, in which Job is restored to a prosperous, abundant life (42:7–17).

The Prologue (Job 1–2)

The Prologue begins with a description of Job's background. He lives in the land of Uz, which is located either in Edom, south of the Dead Sea, or in northern Syria. The description of his wealth indicates that he was a seminomadic tribal chieftain, similar to Abraham. He is a completely blameless man, and the author makes it clear that his abundant property and progeny are a result of his righteousness. He has been richly rewarded for having feared God and turned away from evil. The weekly round of feasts described in verses 4–5 epitomizes in a beautiful thumbnail sketch both the righteousness of Job and the well-being and harmony within his family. Although we cannot tell whether the sons are married, they are young adults, each of whom has his own household—like the sons of a king (see II Samuel 13:7–29). The daughters apparently still live with their father. We cannot tell how often the family would gather to feast together, but it is most likely during the seven-day harvest festivals, at which sacrifices to the deity were accompanied by merrymaking and rejoicing. Each of the seven sons would take his turn at hosting for this family occasion, to which even the sisters were invited. Apparently Job did not attend the festivities. Perhaps it was not customary for a father to be entertained in the house of his son. The main intent of the narrator, however, is to convey the pious concern of Job for his children. He would offer a series of sacrifices to atone for any possible inner thought through which one of his sons may have offended God. Note that Job performs the sacrifices himself. This story must have originated in a time before an organized priesthood existed in Israel.

The scene shifts abruptly to the heavens in verse 6, where the divine council is in the process of assembling before Yahweh, just as the princes of a realm would regularly gather in the court of their king. Ancient Jewish tradition suggests that the context of this divine assembly was the New Year's festival at which the destinies of the righteous and the wicked would be determined by inclusion in or exclusion from the Book of Life.[7] The fate of those who were neither totally righteous nor totally corrupt would be determined on the final day of this ten day festival—the Day of Atonement—and it would depend on the extent to which they had repented and sought mercy.

As the divine assembly convenes, Yahweh is immediately ready to proceed with reckoning Job among the righteous, for "there is none like him on the earth." But there is a Satan (adversary) among the gods who is not ready to concede Job's righteousness so quickly. In Hebrew, the word *Satan* is preceded with the definite article, indicating that this is not to be translated as a personal name; it indicates rather a position or function in the divine court. In a sense, the Satan is the "devil's advocate," whose job was to seek out and prosecute the evil that lurks in the heart of man. This position had its counterpart in a royal court with the officer whose job was to spy and check throughout the realm in order to protect his king against plots, insubordination, and overthrow. In the Persian court, this officer was called "the eyes and ears of the king." Thus the Satan in the Book of Job is not yet the leader of the demonic forces that would overthrow God's rule, as we find in later Jewish and Christian thought. In this early story, he is still an important official in Yahweh's council. And the point which the Satan makes here is crucial for an understanding of the entire work: he questions *why* Job is righteous. Of course Job is good, maintains the Satan, because he knows that his righteousness will bring prosperity and well-being upon himself and his entire family. Under these circumstances one would have to be a fool *not* to be righteous. The real test of a man's righteousness would be to remove the divine rewards and see what happens then. Would a man remain obedient when he realized that it gained him nothing? What is the real motivation for a man's maintaining his righteousness before God? Thus, a central question that runs throughout the book is: "Does Job fear God for nought?" Should it not pay off to be religious?

Yahweh is cut to the quick by the Satan's implication that Job's righteousness is ultimately self-serving. He allows the Satan to deprive Job of all his possessions. In a series of chilling catastrophes, Job loses his flocks, herds, servants, and finally his children. Job accepts this sudden change of fate with a quiet faith that still blesses the name of the Lord. Yahweh has been triumphant in the test, for Job has maintained his integrity. But the Satan knows that there is one final test. A man may shrug his shoulders in passive resignation when he loses all he has, but his spirit will surely despair when his body is racked by horrible pain. Again

Yahweh allows this to happen, only admonishing the Satan to spare Job's life. Again Job maintains his integrity, despite his wife's advice to curse God and die. The prose Prologue ends with a description of the visit of the three comforters, who are appalled at the sight of Job in his misery.

Some Questions for Discussion: Describe the divine council. What is its purpose? Who are its members? How is Job regarded by God? How is Job regarded by the Satan? State your opinion concerning the Satan's reasoning about Job. Why do you agree, or disagree, with the reasoning?

What does Job's statement in 1:21 reveal about the kind of person he is? According to chapter 1, what are Job's virtues? When, a few lines later, God is speaking about his servant Job, he repeats word for word the virtues described at the outset. Why do you think the author employs this repetition?

In the original Hebrew text, the one who spoke against Job in the heavenly council was called *the* Satan. The word means "adversary" or "prosecuting attorney," whose job it was to make sure that both sides of a person's life were considered. What difference does it make in the King James translation that the definite article has been left out? What misfortunes immediately befall Job? What does the Prologue indicate to you about the author's view of God and of God's relationship with man? What impressions are you given of God's relationship to man's sufferings?

The Dialogues (Job 3–14; 19; 28–31)

The Dialogues begin with a monologue from Job (chapter 3), addressed not so much to the comforters as it is against life itself. In words very reminiscent of Jeremiah 20:14ff, Job curses the day in which he was born. He wants the world to return to its primeval state of darkness so that he need not face life's dreadful reality. He asks that Leviathan be stirred up, so that the world will return to the chaotic state it was in prior to the creation. In ancient Near Eastern mythology, Leviathan is one name for the chaos monster who is the force that threatens to overturn the created order. Job is saying that if Leviathan would be stirred up and then succeed, all forms of life—including his own, which he abhors—would be crushed out. In fact, as far as Job is concerned, Leviathan has already been stirred up, because the right order of his life has been destroyed by chaos and evil. He yearns only for the final *coup de grace* to be delivered.

In verses 13–19, we find a powerful description of the appealing quality of death. The horror of non-being is glossed over by Job in his despair. Death will bring him a final, eternal rest in which he will no longer be oppressed by life's horrible injustices. In death he will become one with mankind—both great and small; in death he will overcome the horrible isolation and alienation that he now feels. Alive, Job feels utterly estranged from both God and man. In a mood approaching the suicidal impulse, he sees death as the only means of overcoming this estrangement. At the end of the chapter, he returns to a theme that the Satan had referred to in 1:10. Job in his righteousness had been hedged (that is, protected) against adversity. Now, says Job in 3:23, he feels hedged in; the hedge of pain and adversity has cut him off from God and man.

The author of the Dialogues has cast the comforters in the role of explaining Job's plight in terms that are consonant with the faith of the Israelite-Jewish community. Their speeches represent the various attempts of the traditional Judaism of that day to come to grips with the problem of evil. It should be noted that the comforters are portrayed quite sympathetically. The author does not intend for them to be regarded as straw men who are being knocked down in his polemic against the traditional concept of retribution. Rather, the book gives the impression of being a careful weighing of the pros and cons of a very crucial and difficult issue.

Eliphaz, the first comforter, initiates the dialogues in chapters 4–5. Note the beginning verses: his basic assumption is that Job has done nothing wrong, and he therefore begins by justifying suffering in this context. In a way, Eliphaz's opening remarks echo those of the Satan. You were righteous, he says, and comforted others in their trouble, but now that adversity has struck you, it is not quite so easy to remain righteous (see 1:9–11). Still, Eliphaz maintains, no righteous man has ever perished. He is not saying that the righteous live forever, but that they never meet a tragic or untimely end, because, in allowing this to happen, God would be violating his part of the agreement in his covenant with Israel. Eliphaz defends this blatant contradiction to human experience by affirming the other side of the same coin: the wicked are ultimately consumed by the wrath of God (4:7–8). He develops this thesis further in 5:1–13: the wicked may prosper for a while, but they will eventually be brought low by the hand of God. And if this is so, then God surely also eventually vindicates the righteous.

Eliphaz's second argument seems to take account of the inadequacy of his first attempt. In 4:12ff, he tells of a vision in which he is told of the fall of all men. Even the angels in heaven are fallen (a reference to the Lucifer myth): so how can man ever hope to assert his righteousness before God? No man is perfect. In fact man is a pitiful specimen, dwelling in a house of clay destined to fall into ruin at the slightest tremor. He perishes without anyone's taking note, without the world's being any the wiser. Eliphaz is saying that a man can never claim that he is being treated unjustly by God, because he is part of the sinful, fallen creation that can even claim members of the divine host among its number.

The final argument put forward by Eliphaz represents yet another attempt within the Jewish community to resolve the problem of evil and unjust suffering (5:17ff). It is not as fully developed as it is in the Elihu speeches (chapters 32–37), yet it is a very important argument: suffering is a discipline meted out by God especially on those whom he loves. A man's righteousness is thereby tested; he is purged and purified in the process, and if he hangs on, he will be restored to a state of well-being. It should be remarked that this is essentially the viewpoint of the prose Near Eastern folk tale "framework" in the Prologue and Epilogue.

Instead of working consecutively through the Dialogues, we

are going to jump ahead and discuss the speeches of the other comforters. By doing so, our approach will lose some of the dynamics of the increased intensity and tension of the confrontation between Job and his friends, so that they gradually assume the role of accusers rather than comforters. And it will cause some sense of artificiality as the theological arguments of the comforters are enumerated and structured in a manner that is alien to the development of a real dialogue. The author has consistently kept his ear tuned to the natural: he has kept the dialogue unstructured so that points will be repeated and digressions will be made. We find it too confusing and unprofitable to reproduce by discussing the Dialogues one chapter at a time. We would argue that the real development in the book is not a sustained discussion/argument between Job and his friends in which one comforter picks up where the other leaves off. The statements of the comforters are much more random arguments that do not build to a final conclusion. On the other hand, we would maintain that the real development in the Book of Job takes place within Job himself. It portrays a daring reaching out of the mind and the spirit, as Job struggles to transcend the inadequate solutions of his comforters. Thus, after we finish discussing the positions of the comforters, our approach will allow us to trace the development within Job without interruption.

Bildad's speech in chapter 18 is somewhat more irate and less considerate than that of his predecessor. But Job had just said some shocking things, so one cannot blame Bildad for escalating the conflict. He begins by affirming the central concept of biblical faith: God is above all else a just God. Therefore, he concludes, if Job's children perished, they must have been guilty of some sin of which the community at large was unaware. The implication in this context is that Job must be equally guilty, since he also is now suffering. Thus Job's only recourse is to confess his sin (even though it be unknown) and implore God's mercy. The result will be that Job will be restored to his former state of well-being. But this Job cannot do. If he would repent simply to be relieved of his suffering and have his fortunes restored, then Satan would be vindicated in his taunt (see 1:9–11).[8] He would have proved that Job did serve God because of the good life which such service brought with it.

In order to reinforce his entreaty that Job return to the paths of righteousness through repentance, Bildad appeals to the witness of past generations. History teaches us, he claims, that the way of the righteous will ultimately be vindicated and the way of the wicked will perish. Bildad's approach is a powerful support to Eliphaz's first argument. Eliphaz had made a flat, dogmatic theological assertion: Yahweh is a God who blesses the righteous and punishes the wicked. Bildad gives substance to this assertion by pointing to the process of history: the doctrine of retribution had been tested and found valid in Israel over a period of seven hundred years.

The final argument of the comforters is only hinted at in Zophar's discourse in chapter 11. Again the hostility that is expressed at the beginning of his speech indicates the tension that is gradually building up within the Dialogues because of Job's refusal to admit his guilt. Job had constantly called upon God to explain what he had done and why he must suffer. Zophar blurts out that if this would ever happen, Job would discover that he is receiving less punishment than he really deserves. He would be overwhelmed by the presence of God and discover that the ways of the Almighty are ultimately unknowable. God is beyond man's comprehension; he cannot be forced to govern the world according to man's notions of what is right. This is all right; there is certainly an unknowable quality in God within biblical thought. But this stress on divine transcendence can too often be used as an easy out from the problem of evil and suffering. As in Eliphaz's speeches in 4:20 and 22:2–4, it is too easy to move from a transcendent God to a God who is not ultimately concerned about what man does or what happens to man. This approach allows God to remain pure and holy and aloof, not responsible for the evil that befalls man; but it does so at the expense of a central biblical concept of a God who loves his creation and who acts within history in order that it might be redeemed. One might say that Zophar and Eliphaz, concurring with Ecclesiastes, are the founders of the first "God is dead" theology developed to rationalize injustice in the context of a religion that affirms a just God.

We have already noted that Job's opening monologue reflected a suicidal despair—a feeling that only death could overcome his feeling of total isolation from man and God. Let us now trace the development within Job as he moves beyond the denial of the possibilities in life to repenting in dust and ashes after having been confronted by the living God.[9] In chapters 6–7, Job begins by asking that all of his suffering be weighed on a scale against any sins he may have committed. Surely, he maintains, he is suffering far more than he deserves. Once again he longs for the comfort of death, asking that it come quickly before he turns away from God. He then turns on his "friends," berating them for failing to be compassionate. Friends should be faithful and loyal, but these men are like a treacherous torrent-bed and melting snow; they cannot be trusted. Why should they turn away from him, he wonders, for he has not asked for financial aid. All he wants is the truth (6:25). The comforters are able to rattle off the traditional doctrines, but Job does not feel that they have provided answers to his particular situation. They are sitting as judges over him with their doctrine of retribution; instead, Job needs their compassionate concern. He then moves on to describe man's bitter lot on earth: sleepless nights, hopeless days, months of emptiness—all leading nowhere except to a certain death that will blot out all memory of man's existence.

In utter despair, Job begins addressing his complaints directly to God. He feels totally isolated and cut off, facing the threat of death in the context of comforters who don't really care. Job bitterly turns against God, wondering why he is being treated like Leviathan, the sea monster, hemmed in on every side by chaos and terror. In a cutting parody of Psalm 8:3–4 ("When I look at thy heavens, the work of thy fingers, the moon and the stars which thou has established; what is man that thou art mindful of him, and the son of man that thou dost care for him?"), Job asks why man is so important in God's eyes that he must be visited each day with new torment and suffering. He feels like a condemned man, sentenced to live forever and endure the wrath of God. Perhaps the Prometheus myth is in the back of his mind, for Job concludes in 7:21 that only after he is forgiven will he be permitted to die. A man in such agony can be permitted a bit of sardonic humor. Job pictures God finally seeking him out with notification that he had been forgiven, but the news will come too late, for Job will be dead. Suddenly, it is God who is isolated, who searches for the one he loves but is frustrated by the existence of death. Is Job suggesting that the limitations imposed upon the creation cause even God to suffer? Job is jesting here, but the picture of God is gradually changing from a cruel tormentor to one who cares for and grieves over his creation.

In chapters 9–10, Job takes a new tack. He feels that he has a valid case; but he knows that he will never be able to make his point because of the nature of his opponent. He launches into a hymn praising God's power, but there is a strong cynical overtone because it is the very power of God that will crush all of Job's attempts to justify himself. ("Rahab" in 9:13 is another designation for the chaos monster.) Thus God's power in effect causes injustice, because a man would never be given a fair hearing when he tried to present his case against God. Still Job will speak out, regardless of the consequences (9:21ff). He accuses God of governing the world indiscriminately, so that the righteous and the wicked perish together in one undifferentiated mass. God rules the world all right, but not according to any standards of justice which are comprehensible to man. And if God is not responsible for the tragedies and injustices that occur, then who is (9:24)? Is there a demonic force in the world which is beyond God's control? Job has arrived at a difficult dilemma: if God is almighty, then he is not just; if God is just, then he is not almighty.

This is a knotty theological problem that the Book of Job tries to deal with, but here it is not Job's central concern. Rather, he is examining his inability to establish his righteousness before God. Even if he were washed in snow and cleansed with lye, he would still be thrown back in the garbage pit. Gradually Job is beginning to realize that he is going to need help. If only he had access to an "umpire," he dreams, who would be able to provide him with police protection as he made his case. The image is of a powerful figure who would lay ahold of God and restrain him so that Job could make his case without fear of reprisal. Of course this is only a literary device invented by Job so that he can articulate in chapter 10 the defense he would make if he were given the chance. But it does mark a significant turning point in Job's thought: he has admitted that he needs help in justifying himself before God.

Job begins chapters 12–14 with a stinging rebuke of his comforters, who feel that they have a monopoly on wisdom. Their theology is neatly packaged, but it is not true to life. Job is not afraid to tell it like it is: once again he launches into a diatribe on the arbitrary, indiscriminate manner in which God uses his power. Every living thing is in his hands, yet it is plainly evident that their fate is determined by a lofty power that takes little account of their actions. Who do these comforters think they are fooling, wonders Job. Why do they lie in order to defend God? Is God deceived? Does such a glossing over of the facts really serve his best interests? Job would prefer to probe after the truth, regardless of the consequences. He knows that it may cost him his life, but on the other hand it could be his salvation, for no one would dare to confront God unless he were sure he was righteous (13:15–16). He then proceeds to demand, once again, that God make known his guilt to him. But what is the use? Man is so puny and pitiful. Why do you pick on him, Lord? Why do you bother with him at all? Obviously man will come out the loser in any confrontation with you. His only hope is that you will look away and let him enjoy his fleeting days without the continual reminders that he is powerless and pathetic in your hands (14:1–6).

Man's ultimate fate is that he is cut down and blotted out without any trace remaining. Job meditates on this phenomenon, noting that other parts of God's creation can sprout back after they have been cut down. Why cannot man be like a tree from which a shoot will spring up from the remaining stump? But alas, man resembles another aspect of the created order: the dried-up river bed, whose banks will never again be replenished by life-giving rain. But who is to say that the rains will not come? This leads Job to speculate on the possibility of life beyond the grave. This concept had not yet developed within Judaism. After his life on earth, man was thought to inhabit Sheol—the eternal resting place of the dead. But in his agony, Job is forced to probe beyond this. If death were not the end, then tragic suffering would not be so futile and meaningless. If God is the creator, he would surely yearn to be reconciled and reunited with the work of his hands. At death God would call, and Job would be ready to answer. Note the change in Job's mood—in isolation and alienation he had begun with the wish to escape from God's horrible presence, but now he entertains thoughts of being reunited with his creator at death. Job, however, eventually discards this hope as futile (14: 18ff). Had he clung to the concept of life after death, Satan would have won the wager with God because Job would then be suffering and serving for the rewards that would eventually be his in the life to come. In denying the concept of life after death within this context, Job is being faithful to God.[10]

The first round of the Dialogues ends with chapter 14. Job has responded to each of his comforters, and yet no final resolution of his predicament has taken place. The Dialogues continue on through Job's concluding monologue in chapters 28–31. But for the most part they become quite repetitive and dull. The arguments on both sides have already been well laid out. This does not mean that the author is loose, rambling, and verbose. The prolonged Dialogues are a literary device used by the author to point out two things:

(1) the inability and unwillingness of the comforters to reach any fresh, new insight that would help Job in his dilemma. With increasing hostility, they rattle off their doctrines, further isolating Job from any sense of human (or divine) compassion and understanding;

(2) the necessity for Job not only to lash out violently against both God and man for isolating him from community with them, but also to seek after new dimensions of insight because of the inadequacy of the doctrines of the past.

The best example of Job's aggressive probing, which forms the first climax of the book prior to the Yahweh speeches in chapters 38ff, is 19:25f, in the famous "I know that my Redeemer lives. . . ." Job had begun chapter 19 by continuing the description of the pitiful figure he had become within his own community. He openly accuses God of having overthrown him, of having hedged him about so that no one can or will answer his calls for help. He has completely lost his standing within the community so that everyone—family, friends, servants, even orphans of the street— turns away from him in disgust. In desperation he reaches out to his friends, imploring that they be merciful. Note that he refuses to turn to God for mercy. God is at this moment the enemy who has caused all his suffering. But he finds that the comforters are as relentless and vindictive as God himself (19:22); his only hope is the judgment of future generations. Would that his case were hewn upon a rock that would stand forever. He would finally be vindicated, not by God nor the comforters but by generations yet unborn who would acknowledge his righteousness.

This acknowledgment is the best Job can hope for, but it is not enough. We are not at all prepared for what follows. Job is at the deepest level of despair, and at this moment comes his song of triumph: "I know that my Redeemer lives. . . ." There is no scholarly consensus concerning the identity of this redeemer. Some would argue that within a monotheistic culture the redeemer could only be God himself. Job has intensely felt the absence of God throughout the book; but here, it is claimed, he affirms that at his death a reconciliation with the living God will take place. Others interpret the redeemer as a pre-figuration of the role of Christ in Christian theology. We agree with the latter group to the extent that the figure seems to be an entity independent from God; but we would deny that this passage is to be interpreted as a "prediction" of the coming of Jesus Christ. A later religious community can look at this passage and see an element of its faith being fulfilled through it, but we feel that it is unwarranted to move from this to state that the writer of Job had Jesus Christ specifically in mind.

Our interpretation of 19:25–27 depends on 9:33 and 16:18–21. All of these passages, it seems, presuppose a figure who will help Job become reconciled with God. In 9:33, Job refers to an "umpire" who will protect him from divine wrath as he defends his righteousness before God. But he knows that such a hope will never be realized. In 16:18–21, Job moves further, hoping for a "witness" in the heavens who "will maintain the right of a man with God." It would seem that in both of these cases an entity separate from God is presupposed. Notice that in this second passage Job has given up all hope of pleading his own case. Now he will leave it in the hands of a witness in the heavens to move God's heart in his behalf. Note further that in both of these passages Job understands the task in terms of convincing God of his righteousness.

The Hebrew term for "redeemer" in 19:25 is *gō'ēl*. In general, the word refers to a kinsman who would act after one's death in order to maintain the honor and well-being of the family. He would see that a murder is avenged, buy land that the family was in danger of losing, and marry a childless widow within the family to assure that his posterity would continue to exist. By analogy, God is called the *gō'ēl* of Israel throughout the Bible, in reference to his redeeming his children out of Egyptian bondage. But it cannot be a human relative of Job, for the result is that Job will be brought into the presence of God (19:26). Furthermore, Job has given up on man—his friends, his family, even later generations.

The theme of God as the *gō'ēl* is not developed in Job, even in the Yahweh speeches in the end where one would most expect it. Furthermore, the umpire-witness figures discussed above seem to be separate from God. We would suggest that this concept is derived from the imagery of the divine council. The heavenly host was a highly structured institution. We see from Job 1 that it had a devil's advocate, or prosecutor, whose task was to take note of the sins of man and report them before the divine court. From Deuteronomy 32:8–9 and Psalm 82, we learn that there were also patron deities whom God had appointed to rule over each of the nations in his behalf. Could it be that the *gō'ēl* in Job is an extension of this latter concept? Along with a deity over each nation, could it be that each individual was thought to have a lesser deity who acted as his "patron saint," who would act as a counterpart to intercede for man, thus balancing off the testimony of the Satan?

Note, however, that the *gō'ēl* does not defend Job's righteousness before God. He will apparently play a different role from the usual *gō'ēl*. Job seems to be maintaining that, at his death, the *gō'ēl* will bring him into the presence of God. He will finally be delivered from the terrible absence of God which he has been experiencing in his suffering. Job does not know whether he will be justified; he no longer cares. The presence of God will be adequate. Job has finally surrendered his most treasured possession: his fierce autonomy, which is dramatized in his desire to be acknowledged as righteous.[11]

There are two climaxes in the Book of Job: the "Redeemer" passage in 19:25–27, which we have discussed, and the Yahweh speeches in chapters 38:1–42:6. Why do the Dialogues drag on after chapter 19 for twelve more dreary chapters, in which the comforters and Job repeat over and over again the same points that had been made previously? It would seem that the author is trying to be true to life. It would be somewhat artificial for the author to have ended the Dialogues with chapter 19. Moments of faith and insight are often followed by long periods of doubt and despair. Job has affirmed his ultimate trust in God, but this does not make the agony of his present situation any more bearable.

The Dialogues began with a monologue in which Job had yearned for the nothingness of death (chapter 3). It is fitting that the Dialogues conclude with another monologue that stresses Job's tragedy from a new perspective by describing the noble, righteous, prosperous life he once had lived (chapters 29–31). The monologue is prefaced by a beautiful poem on the source of wisdom (chapter 28). It describes all the treasures of the earth that man is able to ferret out through his ingenuity and technology. But wisdom—the ultimate treasure—is beyond man's grasp. He may search throughout the earth, but he will not be able to lay his hand on it. The "deep" and the "sea"—both personifications of forces within nature that were thought to be potentially hostile to God's rule—must admit that wisdom cannot be found with them. Nor can man buy it, even with the treasures that he has wrested from the earth. Wisdom is priceless, not to be compared with the richest of earth's treasures. Wisdom is not for man to possess. Only God knows its source. Final wisdom lies only with God. This poem beautifully anitcipates the message of the Yahweh speeches. (Most scholars agree that 28:28 is a secondary addition, because it is completely antithetical to what the poem, and the whole Book of Job, is trying to say.)

Just as we were given a portrait of the ideal wife in Proverbs 31:10ff, so Job 29–31 depicts the Israelite ideal of the concrete specifics of righteousness. It was a master stroke that the author reserved this for Job's finale, because for the first time we see that he is indeed a good and righteous man—not a nagging, self-righteous individual complaining about his miserable fate. He was respected in his community, and without fail he used his wealth and prestige to aid the impoverished and oppressed. He was eyes to the blind, feet to the lame, father to the poor, encourager to the faint-hearted, and comforter to the afflicted. But now the very rabble whom Job had helped turn upon him, despise him, flee from him, compounding his sense of forsakenness. He is a patrician at heart. He is horrified by the reversal of roles that has taken place in the community: people who were nobodies, who had become somebodies through his benevolence, now scorn him as an untouchable (chapter 30).

Job is still sure that he is suffering unjustly. In chapter 31, he enumerates the various means through which he could have violated his covenant relationship with God. These include not only the negative prohibitions of the commandments, such as swearing deceitfully or committing adultery, but also positive actions (verses 13–23) and even attitudes (verses 24–34) that show his strong sense of concern for the well-being of the total community.

The author has given an exceedingly sensitive portrayal of Job's righteousness, but in the concluding verses of the speech (31:35–37), he wants to be sure that we hear something else. Job asks once more that God appear to hear his case and explain things, saying "I would give him an account of all my steps; like a prince I would approach him." This is Job's tragic flaw. He feels that the quality of his life has made him almost equal to God. He feels that his morality has put God under an obligation, if not to restore him to his former state of prosperity, at least to admit that Job is righteous and to explain why he has suffered. If faith is the acceptance of God on his own terms, then the author seems to be saying that Job's morality has destroyed his faith.[12]

Some Questions for Discussion: What was the intended purpose of the appearance of the three "comforters"? What emotions did Job expect from his friends? Do the men live up to their designation as "comforters"? Why, or why not? How does Job's reaction to his misfortunes change? In chapter 3, Job compares darkness and light several times. What does each symbolize for Job?

In the Prologue, Job says, "The Lord giveth and the Lord taketh away" when he is afflicted with the four misfortunes. In 3:23, Job refers to God again. How has his opinion of God changed? Verse 3:25 appears to contradict the description of Job's faith that is told in the Prologue. What is the "thing which I greatly feared"? Has Job lost faith?

Trace Eliphaz's basic presentation through his speeches. For what reason does Eliphaz say he is sure Job will be saved from his troubles? What does Eliphaz mean by "happy is the man whom God correcteth" (4:17)? What does Eliphaz feel Job's attitude toward his troubles should be? On what grounds does Job disagree with Eliphaz's remark about the wicked being punished?

What are the metaphors in chapter 7 with which Job equates his life? What is ironic about Job's reference to God in verse 20 as "thou preserver of men"?

Trace the basic idea of Bildad's presentation. The word *wind* is used several times in chapters 6 and 7, as well as in Bildad's first speech in Chapter 8. What are the things compared to "wind" and what is the significance of this particular image?

Why does Bildad claim Job is suffering? What does 8:20 imply about Bildad's opinion of Job? Why does Job say he cannot be just with God? Compare 9:17 with 1:21. What is the difference in Job's responses? To what would you attribute the change?

How does 9:22 disprove both Eliphaz's and Bildad's arguments? In 10:3, do you feel Job is being blasphemous? Defend your answer, keeping in mind what you have seen of Job already. To what is God compared in chapter 10? Why?

Trace the basic idea of Zophar's presentation. Of what does Zophar accuse Job? What would Job have to do according to Zophar in order to be spared? Why can't Job accept Zophar's contentions? What does 12:17–25 indicate about Job's opinion of God? In 12:3 and 13:2 Job repeats "I am not inferior to you." To whom is he speaking, and why does he repeat the line?

In 13:5, Job defines wisdom as being the silence of his friends if they would refrain from making their foolish statements. How does this definition of wisdom differ from the definition expressed in the Prologue (1:1 and 8)? In 13:1–16, Job expresses his attitude toward the words of the comforters. What is his attitude and what conclusion does he reach? In 7:5 and 13:28, Job uses several images to describe the afflictions of his body by God. What do these metaphors indicate about Job's mental state? Do you feel Job is talking rationally? Defend your opinion with examples from the text. What does Job mean in 14:7–9 when he compares man to a tree?

Many scholars feel that 13:15, "though he slay me, yet will I trust him," has been mistranslated and should read "He will slay me; I have no hope." In the context of chapter 13, which translation seems most appropriate to you? Why? What does 14:19–20 show us about Job's appraisal of life? How does this differ from what we are told in 1:5 and 20? How does the author imply that Job now doubts even the meaning of existence? According to Job, suffering is not necessarily a sign of punishment for evil. How else may it be viewed?

When Job argues his case like a lawyer, citing his thoughts, actions, and feelings as witnesses, what does it reveal about his concept of God? In other words, what qualities does Job expect God to exhibit in his dealings with men? Why does Job wish that his words were written in a book (19:23)? In chapter 19, Job enumerates the various punishments that God has inflicted on him; most of them seem to be related to Job's alienation from others. Is it really so bad to be ostracized by people who at one time were friendly? Would it be easier to be isolated (physically) completely from society, on an island, for example? Is a psychological isolation harder to adjust to than a physical isolation? Why, or why not?

Do you think that Job would have reacted differently if his three friends hadn't been there to needle him? Why do his friends torment him so? How does the God of Job compare to the God of Abraham? of Moses? of Joshua? Is this a God who doesn't care, or does he care in an aloof, detached way, or does he care too much? Explain your answer. Find some examples of parallelism in chapter 19. Do any of these parallel constructions seem merely repetitious? Which ones? Are any of them effective in the development of the rhythm of a passage? Which ones?

Does the use of military imagery improve your conception of the basic conflict of this drama in chapter 19:11–12? How do you think Job recites 19:23–29? With hope? resignation? determination? another way? Why? Should "I am an alien in their sight" (19:15) be read with acceptance? anger? dejection? another way? Why? In 19:7–12, how and why does Job compare himself to a king?

What courses of action besides the one he has chosen are open to Job? If he once was as great as he claims, would this rejection and isolation do more damage to him than it would have done to someone who had not had such a position of high esteem? Is Job's reaction to his ostracism typical only of people who have held a high position, or would any person, even one of low esteem, react in the same way to this torment? Why do you think so?

How do you think Job says 30:29–31? Softly, because he has been so thoroughly defeated? Loudly, as though cursing God? Loudly, because he is furious with God? Why do you think the

author has let Job carefully enumerate all of his possible transgressions in chapter 31? Whose god does Job's God most closely
resemble in chapter 31? Abraham's? Moses'? David's? Why?
Job's recollections throughout chapter 29 are a comfort to him
in the midst of great suffering. Why are his images of "dew,"
"rain," and "oil" particularly comforting? Can you suggest
other comforting images in this chapter?

Yahweh Speeches (Job 38:1–42:6)

There are two Yahweh speeches, each of which concludes with
a response from Job. Throughout the Dialogues, Job had demanded that God come forward to explain things and to pronounce him righteous. Now God appears, but does not act quite
as Job had expected. God does not seem to be unduly concerned
with Job's miserable situation. Instead of trying to answer Job's
many questions, Yahweh has a few questions of his own. They are
rhetorical questions—none of which he can answer, and the result
is that Job is overwhelmed by God's transcendent power. Job, the
puny mortal, was not God's partner in the creation of the world;
nor is he able to control the forces of nature which God uses
every day in ruling over his creation. Furthermore, Job has no
real knowledge of the animal world; he is not responsible for the
mysterious wonders of their existence, nor is he able to control
and protect them. When asked for a response to these thundering
questions, Job can only cover his mouth with his hand (40:3–5).
He must admit that he cannot challenge God—that the ways of
the Almighty are ultimately unknowable; he is cowed, but beneath his silence lurk resentful questions that have not been
answered. Ecclesiastes' final answer was an uncaring, transcendent God, who was ultimately unknowable to man and beneath
whose power man could be crushed into subservient silence; but
such an answer does not suffice for Job. Therefore Yahweh tries a
new approach in his second speech (40:6–41:34).

As we noted at the beginning of our discussion of this book,
the ideal ancient Near Eastern response to suffering and tragedy
was a meek, faithful acceptance of one's fate in the hope that the

gods would be merciful. But in Israel, Yahweh was conceived as a righteous God who had bound himself in covenant to his people, so that their destiny would be determined by the extent to which they fulfilled his will. Job is the classic example of the righteous person who has suffered unjustly. This is an anomaly from the Israelite viewpoint, and the Job of the Dialogues, holding God to the righteousness presupposed in the covenant agreement, boldly rises up to demand that Yahweh explain what has happened and proclaim him righteous. But it is pointed out in the second speech that Job has been maintaining his own righteousness at Yahweh's expense: "Will you even put me in the wrong? Will you condemn me that you may be justified?" (40:8). Thus it is Job's justified sense of his own righteousness—he is a truly good man—which has alienated him from God. God's response cannot simply be to overwhelm Job with brute power, as he had done in the first speech.

In the second speech, Yahweh invites Job to consider the world from his viewpoint. Job must see that God, if he is truly to be God, cannot be hemmed in and forced to govern the world according to man's limited idea of what is right and wrong. Yahweh then goes on to discuss Behemoth and Leviathan, the personified forces of death and chaos. Behemoth is actually the hippopotamus, but he has come to symbolize the potential force which can bring death and sterility to the land. Leviathan is the crocodile, and as we have pointed out before, he symbolizes the potential for death and destructive chaos within the sea. Note that there is no dualism in these passages. These forces of evil are called "works of God" (40:19), and we sense that they are conceived as Yahweh's playthings, whose presence he tolerates and almost enjoys.[13] The point of this final speech is that Job cannot hope to understand the complexities of the universe, over which Yahweh rules, where evil is a definite reality and yet ultimately subject to God's power.

To this, Job repents in dust and ashes. Prior to his suffering, he had known of God by hearsay through the testimony of prior generations; but now he has met the living God. Why does Job repent? Has he been squelched by God's omnipotent power? It would seem that the answer lies in the difference between the two Yahweh speeches. In the first, Yahweh appeared as a transcendent power who crushed Job into mute silence—a silence which still questions, which does not include an acceptance of life or God on the terms of an all-powerful being who overwhelms all who would question his integrity. The second speech is different. Here it is made clear to Job that the world is governed at a complex level which will always surpass human understanding and that God will not lessen his majesty and mystery by reducing his rule to terms which will be completely comprehensible to man. But Job has learned something else: despite the mystery and tragic agony of the universe, God still cares very much for man, whom he has created.

Job has moved from demanding a righteous God to experiencing a loving God, and this is enough for him. He is left humbled in dust and ashes, realizing that it was his feelings of self-sufficiency and righteousness that had caused his alienation from God—an alienation that is now overcome.

Some Questions for Discussion: In chapters 38 and 39, God speaks to Job. What is the nature of God's monologue? In what form does he initiate his monologue? What is the answer to God's reasoning? How do the ideas presented by each comforter compare to God's speech? How does Job respond to God's speech? Why does God answer Job's questions with questions?

God's appearance out of the whirlwind reiterates a characteristic of God which has already been established. What is this feature of God, and how is it extended by way of the whirlwind? Job reaches a resolution to the conflict of suffering versus righteousness? What is his resolution to all questions concerning God's way? God implies that Job feels that the world was made for man. By what means does God reveal to Job that the world was not made just for man? Cite specific passages.

What purpose is achieved by God as he gives a detailed description of the Leviathan? What is a Leviathan? In essence, God has answered Job. Does he answer the question of the suffering of the righteous, which was the basic conflict? If so, how is the question answered? If not, what is his answer? Is this story simply about a man, one man, and his suffering and his steadfast nature to remain righteous, or does it have a universal theme?

The Epilogue (Job 42:7–17)

Suddenly the prose narrative from the Prologue interrupts to conclude the story. There are several incongruities that are difficult to explain other than on the assumption that the Prologue-Epilogue once formed an independent story that has been used by the writer of the Dialogues-Yahweh speeches as a framework for his thought. First, Yahweh's anger is directed against the three comforters who, in the Dialogues, had defended him against Job's rebellious challenges. What wrong had they done? Perhaps in the original prose story they had joined Job's wife in urging him to forsake God and die (2:9–13). Whatever the original reason for God's wrath against the three men, the writer of the Dialogues-Yahweh speeches has put his sources together in such a way as to make it appear as if God prefers the blunt integrity of Job to the shallow defenses put forth by traditional religion.

A second incongruity is that Job has all his possessions restored twofold, but the point of the Dialogues-Yahweh speeches is that there is no necessary relationship between righteousness and a prosperous life. We cannot explain this except that perhaps the prose story of Job was so well known that the writer of the Dialogues-Yahweh speeches was unable to make substantial changes. But after Job has discovered who God is and has accepted him on his own terms rather than for the rewards which righteousness would bring, the bestowing of riches is surely anticlimactic and almost ironic.

The comforters are commanded to make atonement for their sins through burnt offerings, imploring Job to intercede on their behalf. It is interesting to note that Job's material prosperity is not restored until after he has reestablished a right relationship with his comforters through his intercessory prayer. The children are not restored twofold. Note that particular attention is given to the daughters and to Job's unusual action in allowing them to share a portion of the inheritance along with their seven brothers. Job's death at a ripe old age places him among the other patriarchal heroes of Israel: Abraham, Isaac, Jacob, and Joseph.

Why was Job written? The original purpose of the Prologue-Epilogue seems to have been to extol the virtue of patience and long-suffering in the face of tragic suffering and to give assurance of the ultimate justice and mercy of God. But this explanation does not hold for the main body of the book, since the Job of the Dialogues is by no means passive and patient. Other scholars interpret the book as a polemic against the classical doctrine that suffering is a result of sin. Still others see it as an attempt to justify the ways of God by placing suffering and righteousness within a broader setting. Certainly these are parts of the author's intention, but it seems to us that B. W. Anderson comes very close to the heart of the matter when he writes:

> To some readers it is disconcerting that the Book of Job does not end with an attempt to resolve the problem of suffering, or to cast light on the goodness and omnipotence of God. Assuming that the book is concerned primarily with these questions, some interpreters believe that Yahweh's speech was beside the point and that Job finally had to admit that the problem of God's justice was too great for his understanding. *But the key to the Book of Job is Job's repentance,* and the preceding discourses which come to a climax with the voice from the whirlwind. From the very first, the fundamental issue is Job's relationship to God. The climax of the poem occurs at the very end, when a false relationship based on self-sufficiency is converted into a relationship of personal trust and surrender.[14]

Some Questions for Discussion: Explain your understanding of these concepts after reading the story of Job: faith, righteousness, esteem, self-esteem, innocent suffering. How does Job come to terms with each of these concepts? What are some of the questions raised concerning each of them? How does Job resolve the questions raised? What implications does the Book of Job have for us?

Suggested Activities: You are a reporter for a newspaper, and your editor has heard about the behavior of an unusual man named Job. You are assigned to interview him. What questions will you ask? What do you think his answers will be? Make certain that his answers are consistent with the speech of Job as presented in the Old Testament.

Job has been dramatized many times. If you were to stage it, what would your set design(s) look like? Either draw or make a model of your stage set(s).

What will the leading characters in your stage production of Job wear? Draw pictures of the costumes and defend your design.

Could you realistically put Job and the comforters in modern dress? Why?

Read Archibald MacLeish's *JB*, and then write a paper in which you show how MacLeish changed the Book of Job in his play.

Select any chapter from Job in which two or more characters speak and present it as a radio play. Then listen to the same chapter as dramatized by classmates. How do their characterizations differ from your cast's portrayals? Why do you think the characterizations differ?

Love Songs (Song of Solomon 1–2)

There is no scholarly agreement whatsoever concerning the interpretation of the Song of Solomon. It was one of the last books to be accepted into the biblical canon in the first century A.D., because even then the rabbis were not certain whether it could be designated as sacred scripture. There were at least three factors that made the writing acceptable so that it was finally made part of the Bible: (1) the tradition that the work had been composed by Solomon; (2) the vehement support given by the famous and influential first-century Rabbi Aqiba; and (3) the allegorical approach to scripture that made it possible to interpret the song as expressing the love relationship between God and Israel.

The allegorical interpretation of literature became popular among the Jews through the influence of Greek culture. It was a handy device for reading spiritual meanings into some of the rather earthy material in the Old Testament. One rabbi interpreted "I am very dark, but comely. O daughters of Jerusalem" (1:5) as meaning that Israel was black with sin through making the Golden Calf, and yet comely because she had received the Ten Commandments.[15] Similarly, an early Christian interpreter thought the verse described the nature of a man before and after his conversion.[16] In general, however, the rabbis felt that the entire work was a retelling, through the imagery of human love, of God's actions in behalf of his people. Thus, the maiden's longing for her lover's appearance refers to Israel's yearning for God to deliver her during the period of the Egyptian bondage. The lover coming to summon his bride to come away is seen as a reference to the Exodus (2:8ff)—he wants to see the bride out in "the clefts of rock" (2:14), where Israel appeared before God at Mount Sinai, and so forth. This was the standard method of interpreting the Song of Solomon in both Judaism and Christianity throughout the Middle Ages, although the Christians generally treated the Song as an allegory expressing Christ's love for his church. The weakness of this approach lies in its extreme subjectivity, whereby one can force the desired interpretation out of any passage because its literal meaning was regarded as irrelevant.

As biblical criticism developed in the nineteenth century, the allegorical interpretation was gradually discarded. Several scholars saw no unity in the book other than the common theme of love. They concluded that the Song of Solomon was not telling a story—allegorical or otherwise—and proposed that the book is actually a random collection of secular love songs. But if we look closely at the work, we find a general overall structure that suggests that there is something more than a grab-bag collection. We find a dialogue between the lovers, interspersed with remarks from a "chorus." This has led a significant number of scholars to propose that the Song of Solomon is a drama, loosely based on the Greek model. The text does not include exact specifications of who the principal characters are and of where each speech begins and ends, but there are enough indications in the songs to tell who they are and to provide the rough outline of the story.

According to one interpretation, there are two main characters, King Solomon and a Shulamite maiden whom he had met in his travels through North Israel and brought back to Jerusalem to be his bride.[17] Act I (1:2–2:7) begins with the Shulamite yearning for Solomon's caresses and excusing herself to the court ladies because she is sunburned and fresh from the country. The ladies reply in 1:8; Solomon enters, and a dialogue between the two lovers ensues.

In Act II (2:8–3:5), there are two monologues on the Shulamite maiden's past. First she describes how she had met Solomon as he was traveling through her mountainous homeland, and then she describes a dream in which she searches for her lover through the streets of the city and finally finds him.

Act III (3:6–5:1) describes the wedding itself, introduced by various citizens of Jerusalem as they behold the wedding procession approaching. At the banquet, Solomon praises the maiden, inviting her to leave her home in the north and be his bride. She acquiesces and the marriage is consummated in 5:1.

In Act IV (5:2–6:9), the Shulamite narrates a dream in which she had searched in vain for her departed lover. The court ladies sympathize (6:1), and she is finally reassured (6:2–3)—thus preparing the way for Solomon to return (6:4–9).

Act V (6:10–8:4) describes an encounter between the Shulamite and the court ladies in an orchard in which they encourage her to dance. She complies with their wish, and they admire her beauty as she performs (7:1–5). Solomon is overwhelmed at the sight and vows his love anew (7:6–9), to which the Shulamite invites him to her home on the mountain. The final act describes the royal pair's return to the Shulamite village and their reception by her family.

An alternate interpretation of the Song as a drama posits three main characters: Solomon, the Shulamite maiden, and her shepherd lover. Solomon had discovered her while on one of his journeys through the north and had brought her back to his palace in Jerusalem where he hoped to win her love. But the maiden cannot forget her true love—a young shepherd who waits for her back home. In Act I (1:2–2:7), she is already in Jerusalem, yearning for the shepherd to deliver her from the power of the king. She demeans her beauty before the Jerusalem court ladies and wonders where her lover is pasturing his flock (1:2–7). In 1:9ff, Solomon comes to win her love, but the resulting dialogue is ironic, because the Shulamite can think only of her shepherd and responds to the king's compliments with wistful asides about her lover's beauty. She concludes by appealing to the court ladies not to encourage her to deny her true feelings.

In Act II (2:8–3:5), the maiden describes a time when the shepherd had visited her in her home and they had walked in the nearby fields. Even her dreams show who her true love is. She tells the court ladies how she had gone looking for him through the streets of the city and how she had rejoiced when she found him—so they are wasting their time in encouraging her to love Solomon.

In Act III (3:6–5:8), Solomon has planned a large-scale procession in the hopes that the Shulamite will be won over when she beholds the splendor of the royal court. Solomon approaches and praises her, seeking to win her love (4:1–7). But the maiden's thoughts are elsewhere; in her imagination she hears her lover inviting her to come away with him (verses 8–15). She accedes to his request (verse 16), and the two become one—but only in her imagination. She then recounts another dream in which she had sought her lover but he had disappeared. This depicts her fear that she will succumb to Solomon's advances and thereby lose her true love.

In Act IV, the court ladies question the Shulamite's holding on to this impossible love, and she tells them why the shepherd is so special to her. Solomon then enters to appeal once more for her love, recalling their first meeting: he had surprised her in a nut orchard, been overwhelmed by her beauty, and asked her to dance. In a final effort to win the Shulamite, he gives a glowing description of her beauty. But the maiden remains steadfast, bravely telling the king that she belongs only to her shepherd (7:10–8:4). Act V describes the joyful reunion of the Shulamite and her lover. She recalls how her family had once worried about her but need do so no longer.

Other scholars have wondered how the Song of Solomon ever came to be accepted into the Bible if it originated as a collection of love songs or even as a secular drama of love. Recently discovered texts show us that a dramatized fertility ritual was commonly practiced throughout the ancient Near East. The hero of this cult was Tammuz, whom we know from the condemnations of Ezekiel 8:14 and Isaiah 17:10f to have been a popular figure among many Israelites. According to this myth, Tammuz died and went to the underworld every year as the vegetation began to die. He would be sought out by a female goddess—his lover— and released from the bonds of death. The lovers' reunion culminated in sexual intercourse, thus assuring fertility for another season.[18] Although this ritual was never officially recognized within Yahwism, these scholars propose that it was well known and practiced in Israel. And indeed there are striking parallels between the love lyrics of the Tammuz liturgies and those in the Song of Solomon. The chief motif in both is the goddess's separation from her lover and her yearning for his return. The proponents of this theory have established a religious origin for the Song of Solomon; but since this type of religion was alien to Yahwism, it is difficult to conceive of its being accepted into the Bible, if its pagan background were known.

Let us consider one final interpretation. About one hundred years ago it was noted that wedding ceremonies among Syrian peasants were seven-day festivals in which the bride and groom were treated as king and queen. During the celebration, songs would be sung describing the physical beauty of the bridal pair. Assuming that these practices might well reflect the customs of ancient times, some scholars have proposed that the Song of Solomon is a collection of songs that were traditionally sung at a wedding celebration. This could well explain why the dialogue between the lovers is occasionally interspersed with songs from the other wedding participants (for example, 1:4b).

Chapter 1 opens with a description of the maiden yearning for the embrace of her lover. She wants to be reunited with him, and her anticipation is so strong that she can say that the king, her lover, has already brought her into his chamber. Her friends (the wedding party?) encourage her in her love. She disparages her beauty in comparison to that of her friends, explaining that she is sunburned because her brothers had forced her to work hard in the family vineyard. But now she would prefer to leave the vineyard to follow after her shepherd-lover.

In 1:9ff, a dialogue between the lovers ensues in which each describes the beauty and charm of the other. The maiden is compared to a mare in Pharaoh's stable—something rare, precious, proud, and breathtaking in her splendor. The maiden replies that yes, she will be decked out for a king if her beloved will be her king. His very presence excites her so much that she experiences not the sound of violins but the smell of rare and precious perfumes. In verses 16–17, the lovers continue to trade compliments that express the depth of their feeling. Returning to the theme in 1:5ff, the young woman modestly demurs that she is nothing special: just one of the wild flowers that grow in abundance in that region. Her lover replies—yes, like a wild flower, but the rest are brambles in comparison. Not to be outdone, the maiden compares him to an apple tree whose fruit she desires and enjoys. Again she anticipates the consummation of their relationship in marriage. But, she concludes, the appropriate moment will come; it must not be forced.

The final song of this chapter is the most beautiful and famous one in the book. The maiden has longed for her lover to come and take her away. Now the springtime has come; the moment of fulfillment has arrived. She hears the sound of her lover's approach—bold, swift, eager, exuberant—like a young stag bounding over the hills, bringing with him the life which is inherent in the coming of spring. He appeals for her to come away with him, and she follows. Verse 15 is puzzling. Perhaps the maiden is recalling the refrain of a ditty that they sang as they laughed and joked together. Love is not all wistful yearning and tender passion. There is also the element of carefree play, bordering on the absurd, but beautiful because it happens in the context of love. The song ends with the maiden's simple statement of the totality of their commitment to one another.

It seems most likely to us that the Song of Solomon is a collection of love songs, and if so, this is indeed a remarkable phenomenon. Whereas other ancient Near Eastern love poetry is full of allusions to the gods, there are no references to God whatsoever in the Song of Solomon. Furthermore, ancient Near Eastern religious literature swarms with erotic elements, but there are none in Israelite literature because Yahweh was not conceived of as a sexual being. Secular love poetry seems not to have played an important role in the ancient Near East. The value of human love could only be affirmed by setting it within a divine context, and this indicates the diminution of the worth placed on human worldly life and feelings.[19] The Song of Solomon is blatantly secular because there was no dichotomy between religion and the earthly life, between spirit and flesh, in ancient Israel. The Old Testament—and the Song of Solomon in particular—is an affirmation of the potential beauty of love and sex because they are aspects of the world which God created and over which he rules. As Rabbi Akiba so aptly puts it, the Song of Solomon is of the rarest beauty because it celebrates the holiness of human life.

Some Questions for Discussion: Who is speaking in 1:2–4 and to whom does she speak? What is the message of 1:5–6? For whom is it intended? What meaning do you give to "my own vineyard I have not kept"?

Is verse 8 a direct response to the question in verse 7? Who is speaking in verse 7? in verse 8? What is the basic structure of the poetic verses in chapter 1?

Who is speaking in 2:1? in 2:2? Which of the lovers is being compared in 2:3? By whom is this comparison made?

Professor Robert C. Dentan, in *The Interpreter's One-Volume Commentary on the Bible,* notes that the appreciation of nature expressed in the Song of Solomon is unparalleled in the Old Testament, and he suggests that the expression of joy over nature reaches its climax in 2:8–17. Reread those verses and explain why you agree, or disagree, with Professor Dentan's statement.

Reread the entire Song of Solomon. Why do you think it was included in the Old Testament? How do you interpret it? What do you think is its purpose?

The Psalms

To the reader of the Old Testament who has noted the poetry of the prophets and the poetic compositions inserted again and again into prose narratives, it should come as no surprise that the Hebrews expressed their worship of God primarily in poetry and music. The Book of Psalms sets forth a selection of such liturgical poetry, representing probably only a small portion of the hymns, laments, thanksgivings, and confessions that were sung in the Jerusalem Temple.

Although most scholars would now accept this description of the Psalter as the Temple hymnbook, this insight into the best approach to the psalms has only been won after years of study. Earlier scholars poured over the titles or introductory verses of the psalms with a view to determining date and authorship of each piece. Any allusions to known events in Israel's history were used to connect the separate poems with actual historical personages. Thus debates raged over whether David actually wrote the seventy-three psalms which bear the Hebrew heading *l^edavid* ("for David," or "concerning David"). Such introductions as that affixed to Psalm 51 were often accepted as pointing to the author and time of composition: "A psalm of David, when Nathan the prophet came to him, after he had gone in to Bathsheba."

In a second stage of critical study, Old Testament scholars were inclined to reject all such attempts to assign specific dates and authors to the psalms. In this reaction, the superscriptions were ignored and the whole Book of Psalms was regarded as a very late production, with many of the individual poems dating from the Maccabean period or even later.

Modern study began with an important work by Hermann Gunkel, the German Old Testament scholar. Gunkel's study of the psalms proposed (1) that all of the psalms had been used in a liturgical fashion, in the context of Temple worship, and that they were poems intended for communal use and did not reflect the lives of particular historical individuals or authors; (2) that the psalms could best be studied as variations of a few genres or typical forms of literature. These typical forms (hymn, lament, song of thanksgiving, and so on) are adhered to quite rigidly; through its form, the function of a psalm in the liturgy could be understood.

The approach outlined by Gunkel, known as the form-critical method, is now dominant among Old Testament scholars. No longer do we attempt to determine individual authors or specific historical situations that lie behind each psalm, except where such data are clearly offered within the psalms themselves. At the same time, a more conservative tendency has set in with respect to the dating of the psalms. It is now known that the whole Book of Psalms must have been completed before the end of the third century B.C., and that many of the individual psalms are much older than this.

The assignment of the psalms to certain ritual or liturgical settings in the Temple has shifted attention away from the individual authors—who are generally anonymous in any case—and has focused our attention on the worshiping congregation of Israel. The "I" of the psalms is not David or Elijah or Zerubbabel; it is everyman. This means in turn that each generation and each individual can see himself in the situations so strikingly expressed by the poets; this doubtlessly accounts for the continual appeal of the Book of Psalms to every kind of reader and worshiper in every generation.

The Book of Psalms comprises a number of smaller collections of poems from various times and localities during Israel's history. As it stands now, the whole book is divided into five "books" or sections (perhaps an analogy with the Pentateuch), each section being marked off by a doxology: Psalms 1–41; 42–72; 73–89; 90–106; 107–150. The numbering of the psalms varies between Protestant and Jewish Bibles, on the one hand, and the Roman Catholic Bible on the other. The reason for this is that the Roman Catholic Bible uses the numbering and divisions of the Septuagint translation, while Protestant and Jewish versions depend on the Hebrew text. The differences are noted below:

PROTESTANT AND JEWISH	ROMAN CATHOLIC
1–9	1–9:21
10–113	9:22–112
114–115	113
116:1–9	114
116:10–19	115
117–146	116–145
147:1–11	146
147:12–20	147
148–150	148–150

The Roman Catholic Bible, like the Septuagint, also contains one extra psalm, Psalm 151, which stands "outside the number" according to the note affixed by the Septuagint translators. In the following discussion, we will use the numbering derived from the Hebrew text as used in Protestant and Jewish Bibles; the table above may be used to determine the equivalent psalm in the Roman Catholic Bible.

PSALMS 42–43: A LAMENT

Over one-third of the psalms fall into the classification of laments. Some of these clearly refer to situations of national adversity and pray for deliverance from military enemies, while others appear to be more individual in content, reflecting the distress of sickness, poverty, and loss of honor. A few of the best known psalms of this type are Psalm 22, quoted and alluded to in the New Testament Crucifixion narratives; Psalm 51, used in liturgical contexts in the Christian Churches; and Psalm 130, *De Profundis,* used in Christian burial services.

The song of lament typically includes four main sections:

1. address or invocation to God;
2. description of suffering;
3. supplication for deliverance;
4. a vow or promise by the worshiper.

Psalms 42 and 43 clearly belong together as one song of lament. The song has three stanzas, each concluding with a refrain (42:5, 11; 43:5): "Hope in God; for I shall again praise him, my help and my God." The psalmist's lament is that he cannot undertake a pilgrimage to the Temple because of a serious illness. He prays for restoral and promises to worship God in his Temple when he is healed. The particular sections are:

Invocation (42:1–4)—Here the psalmist describes his longing for God's presence in the Temple, remembering former days in which he "went with the throng . . . with glad shouts and songs of thanksgiving" (42:4). The stanza concludes with a refrain expressing hope in God's power to restore the sufferer (42:5).

Description of suffering (42:5b–10)—The psalmist here laments his bodily weakness as he waits for healing so far from the sanctuary ("Hermon" is in northern Israel). His personal enemies taunt him with his weakness and scornfully ask, "Where is your God?" Even in the midst of such suffering the psalmist does not cease to trust and hope in God's deliverance (42:8, 11).

Supplication for deliverance (43:1–3)—Now the psalmist, having described his suffering and the grounds of his hope and trust in Yahweh, makes direct appeal for healing and restoration. He prays for God to vindicate him before his mocking enemies and allow him to make his pilgrimage to the Temple ("thy holy hill," "thy dwelling," 43:3).

Vow of thanksgiving—The lament typically concludes with a promise that the psalmist will return his heartfelt thanks to God for his deliverance from death and weakness. Frequently the liturgical setting of such thanksgiving is specifically mentioned, as in the present psalm (43:4):

> Then I will go to the altar of God,
>   to God my exceeding joy;
>   and I will praise thee with the lyre,
>   O God, my God.

PSALM 90: A LAMENT

We include this psalm to demonstrate the great flexibility of expression available to the psalmists within the relatively rigid forms they adhered to. Psalm 90 is a community lament that presents the supplicaton of a broken people before Yahweh. But the terms of description and the poet's grasp of the human situation are such that the psalm transcends the life of any individual or nation. What is here expressed is the situation of all humanity in the face of the shortness and uncertainty of human life.

Address or invocation (90:1–6)—The address to God includes reference to endless generations of men, who pass away so swiftly in contrast to God's eternity:

> Before the mountains were brought forth,
>   or ever thou hadst formed the earth and the world,
>   from everlasting to everlasting thou art God. (90:2)
> Thou dost sweep men away; they are like a dream,
>   like grass which is renewed in the morning:
>   in the morning it flourishes and is renewed;
>   in the evening it fades and withers. (90:5–6)

Description of suffering (90:7–12)—It is against this background of the passing of all things human that Israel understands her current suffering:

> For all our days pass away under thy wrath,
>   our years come to an end like a sigh.

Even if a man is extremely healthy he does not live more than eighty years—how then can Israel expect to escape her allotted suffering?

Supplication (90:13–17)—Nevertheless the congregation shakes off the mood of sadness and courageously asks God to establish his people's strength again:

> Satisfy us in the morning with thy steadfast love,
> that we may rejoice and be glad all our days.

The psalm does not end, as so many of the laments do, with a vow. The conclusion is simply a prayer that the eternal God will establish and favor his people after their years of adversity (90:17).

PSALM 23: A SONG OF TRUST

The themes and structure of the songs of trust have a great deal in common with the concluding sections of the laments, in which the worshiper states his faith in God's goodness and mercy toward supplicants. Psalm 23 is one of the most beautiful declarations of trust in all religious literature, making use of the symbols of God as good shepherd and as the gracious host.

The mention of the Temple (the house of the Lord, verse 6) in the concluding verse and the suggestion of a journey in the opening section (verse 4) indicate that Psalm 23 might also be compared to the Pilgrim Songs, in which the psalmist speaks of his journey to the sanctuary (see Psalm 27:1–6; 122). On his journey, the psalmist will need food and water and safe resting places, and he trusts that Yahweh will provide these as a shepherd cares for his sheep. "Soul" in verse 3 refers to physical vitality and should be translated "life": the Lord leads his flock and sustains its life through food and water.

The journey theme is also suggested by the following words, traditionally translated:

> He leads me in paths of righteousness
> for his name's sake.

"Paths of righteousness" actually means "right paths," and this shows Yahweh as a guide to the pilgrim on his journey. Similarly, "valley of the shadow of death" is not a metaphorical expression for human mortality, but should be rendered simply "valley of dark shadows." The reference, if we continue the pilgrim theme, is to dark valleys where robbers lurk and there is no escape for the traveler. Even there, the psalmist believes, Yahweh will defend him as a shepherd drives off a bear or a lion with his staff and club.

Finally the pilgrim reaches his destination, the Temple of Jerusalem, where Yahweh welcomes him with oil and wine like a gracious host. The psalmist vows to stay for the rest of his life in the Temple (see Psalm 27:4), where Yahweh's presence is continually manifested to the worshiping community through the sacred liturgy.

PSALM 72: A ROYAL PSALM

The royal psalms do not follow a particular form and in this sense are not to be regarded as a fixed genre. They are classed together on the basis of function and content, for they were used in the Temple liturgy in royal ceremonials and are alike in focusing on the role which the king played in Israelite religion and society.

Much controversy still continues over the exact nature of the royal ceremonials. Some scholars attempt to reconstruct an annual enthronement festival in which the king's accession to the throne was reenacted, symbolizing the accession of Yahweh to his heavenly throne as Creation's king. Such psalms as 93, 95–99 would be appropriate for such a liturgical celebration of Yahweh's kingship, and certainly this theme was celebrated in post-Exilic Temple rituals. Whether the king participated in such rituals before the Exile is still uncertain, however.

There remains a number of "royal psalms" that do clearly belong to the pre-Exilic Temple liturgy and that set forth the understanding of kingship which prevailed in Jerusalem. Such psalms include Psalm 2, which is part of the liturgy for the enthronement of a king in Jerusalem, and Psalm 72, which is a prayer for the monarch and his kingdom.

It must be emphasized that all people of the ancient Near East understood kingship as a sacred office. In Egypt, the Pharaoh was identified directly with the deity; in Mesopotamia, the king was the deity's adopted son. In Israel, no such direct relation to Yahweh could be ascribed to any man, yet the king was a sacred person through the holy ritual of anointing. The elevated and often exaggerated court language that was used in other Near Eastern countries also colored Hebrew speech concerning the king, as in Psalm 2:7, where Yahweh "begets" the king and makes him "his son" on the day of his accession to the throne. Such exaggerated language made the royal psalms open to messianic interpretations, for the power and wisdom often ascribed to the king in these poems could not be applied to any human being in the normal course of affairs. There is a sense in which these psalms are justifiably applied to the Messiah or ideal king, for the Hebrews themselves recurrently looked for an ideal king who would be another David, and retained this hope in various forms even after the Exile. If the kings whose rule they actually experienced were far from ideal, they hoped all the more strongly that the next generation would see a king who would live up to his role as the governor of God's people.

Psalm 72 is a prayer for the king that displays both the idealization and sacralization of the monarch and the hope that this particular king will indeed bring justice and peace from Yahweh to his people. The psalm opens with a prayer for Yahweh's gift of justice to the king, for the king stood at the head of the judicial process and was the highest authority to whom a case could be appealed. The poor (verse 2) were especially dependent upon the king's sense of fairness. The psalmist then hopes for national prosperity, so long as that prosperity is accompanied by justice and is not won at the expense of the poor (verse 4).

The next stanza is a prayer for the life of the monarch "while the sun endures, and as long as the moon, throughout all generations" (verse 5). This is the type of exaggeration that is natural to courtly language, but it also suggests the extent to which the life and well-being of the king were bound up with the life of his kingdom, for the king was the channel through which Yahweh's blessing flowed to the people. Thus the petitions for natural abundance and peace are appropriately tied to the prayers for the king's life.

Next the poet prays for the strength of the king in the international realm. An enormous dominion is imagined,

> . . . from sea to sea,
> and from the River to the ends of the earth!
> May his foes bow down before him,
> and his enemies lick the dust!
> May the kings of Tarshish and of the isles
> render him tribute,
> May the kings of Sheba and Seba bring gifts!
> May all kings fall down before him,
> all nations serve him!

It is made clear in the next verses that the Hebrews understood such great power as a privilege won only through justice and concern for the poor and weak. The king is again depicted as the last resort and ultimate protector of the downtrodden. This recognition must have been gained through sad experience, to judge from prophetic condemnations of the role of king and aristocracy in oppressing the helpless.

The concluding stanza pulls together the previous themes of the prayer in a triumphant and joyous mood (verses 15–17). The king's life, fame, power, and blessing are again linked to the prosperity and welfare of the kingdom and of the whole natural order. (Verses 18–19 are not part of this psalm, but constitute one of the doxologies which conclude each "book" of the Psalter.)

PSALM 96: A HYMN

The major parts most commonly found in the Old Testament hymn are: (1) a call to praise or worship Yahweh; (2) a statement of the grounds for praise, often introduced with the conjunction "for"; (3) a concluding confession or praise, often leading back to the themes of the beginning section.[20]

The heart of the hymn is the second section. The Old Testament understanding of God and his relation to man is frequently stated in these passages with great beauty and passion. Psalm 96 is an excellent example of such praise-centered theology.

(1) Call to praise (verses 1–3)—As is frequently true of Old Testament hymns, the setting for praise is musical. The psalmist calls upon the congregation and the whole earth to praise Yahweh in song. Israel is to confess Yahweh's victorious acts ("salvation") and "marvelous works" among all nations. The theme is reminiscent of the royal psalm previously discussed. Indeed, the present psalm could be called a celebration of Yahweh's kingship. It might be intended for a New Year's observance—hence the "new song."[21]

(2) The grounds for praise (verses 4–6)—Now the psalmist expresses the reason for Yahweh's lordship and supremacy "above all gods." It is he that created the heavens, while the idols of the Gentile nations are powerless. This theme, and in fact the whole tone of the psalm, is reminiscent of Second Isaiah. In verse 6, the psalmist specifically focuses our attention on the sanctuary, the Jerusalem Temple, where Yahweh is worshiped with "power and splendor."

(3) Statement of praise (verses 7–13)—Now the congregation sings out its praise, calling upon the "families of the peoples" to worship Yahweh. Verses 7–9 contain an interesting example of climactic parallelism in which the opening phrase, "Ascribe to Yahweh," is repeated and built upon by each succeeding line until the stanza is closed by verse 8, which sums up the preceding thoughts. It is interesting to compare Psalm 72:8–11, in which the Davidic king's ideal sovereignty over foreign nations is expressed. In Psalm 96, Yahweh himself has assumed the role and titles of kingship, as was natural in the post-Exilic period.

In the final section (verses 10–13), the previous themes of the psalm are drawn together into a concluding shout of praise. Yahweh reigns as king over creation and history. In him, the sky, the earth, and the sea rejoice. The very trees of the field sing as Yahweh comes to his Temple. Just as he brings order and light into creation, he also brings order into the chaos of history through his judgment:

> Then shall all the trees of the wood sing for joy
> before the Lord, for he comes,
> for he comes to judge the earth.
> He will judge the world with righteousness,
> and the peoples with his truth.

Some Questions for Discussion: Throughout this volume, we have provided questions that we hope will help you examine more carefully what you have read and provide greater insight into the books of the Old Testament. Rather than providing questions for you for the psalms, we suggest that you frame questions which you believe will help your classmates gain better insight into the psalms discussed in this section.

Books on the Bible of Interest to Teachers of English
AN ANNOTATED BIBLIOGRAPHY

compiled by James S. Ackerman

IA.　Recent Translations of the Bible

The Holy Scriptures According to the Masoretic Text. Philadelphia: Jewish Publication Society, 1917.
> Still the standard translation of the Hebrew Scriptures for the American Jewish community until the completion of the new Jewish translation (see *"The Torah . . ."* under IB below).

The Jerusalem Bible. Garden City, N.Y.: Doubleday, 1966.
> A translation of an important new French version by the Dominican Biblical School in Jerusalem, with excellent, somewhat conservative and Christian oriented introductions to each book and with critical notes to the text. Paperback.

The New American Bible. New York: P. J. Kenedy & Sons, 1970.
> This is an excellent, innovative translation, completed in 1970 by members of the Catholic Biblical Association of America, with critical notes to the text representing liberal Roman Catholic scholarship. Paperback.

The New English Bible with the Apocrypha. New York: Oxford University Press and Cambridge University Press, 1970.
> Hailed by many as the greatest new translation; translated by English biblical scholars and poets. Paperback.

Oxford Annotated Bible with the Apocrypha: Revised Standard Version. Edited by H. G. May and B. M. Metzger. New York: Oxford University Press, 1962.
> American translation completed in the 1950s—attempting to preserve the style and cadence of the King James Version while updating the vocabulary—with critical notes to the text representing liberal Protestant scholarship. A paperback edition of the Revised Standard Version, without critical notes, is available from Meridian.

IB.   Translation of Parts of the Bible

The Anchor Bible. Edited by W. F. Albright and D. N. Freedman.
Garden City, N.Y.: Doubleday, 1964—
An interfaith translation by leading American and some European
scholars, which will comprise some forty volumes when completed.
Each volume contains full introduction and critical notes.

Four Prophets (Amos, Hosea, Isaiah, Micah). Paraphrased by J. B.
Phillips. New York: Macmillan, 1963.
Not as successful as Phillips' superb *The New Testament in Modern
English,* but still worth noting when teaching the prophets.

The Torah: The Five Books of Moses. Philadelphia: Jewish Publication
Society, 1962.
The first volume (to be published in three parts) of the New Jewish
Bible—another of the excellent new translations based on the most
recent scholarship.

II.   Abridged Bible Versions

Abbott, Walter M., Gilbert, A., Hunt, R. L., Swaim, J. C., eds. *The
Bible Reader.* New York: Bruce, 1969.
Includes a broad selection of biblical literature, using many different
translations (though mainly the Revised Standard Version), but the
choice often seems to be based on religious significance rather than
literary value. The critical notes to the text, however, make this book
a must for the public school teacher of literature because they represent interpretations held by both conservatives and liberals within
the Protestant, Roman Catholic, and Jewish communities. Paperback.

Bates, Ernest S., ed. *The Bible Designed To Be Read As Literature.* 2
vols. London: The Folio Society, 1957.
A rich, fairly complete selection of biblical passages from the King
James Version (except for Proverbs, Job, Ecclesiastes, and Song of
Songs, which follow the Revised Version). No critical notes; one
page introductions to each book; contains a beautiful selection of
thirty-two old master drawings from Dürer, Goya, Rembrandt,
Rubens, etc. Also available in an abridged, one-volume paperback
with selections by C. C. Richardson.

Capps, Alton C., ed. *The Bible As Literature.* New York: McGraw-
Hill, 1971.
An anthology of biblical texts taken from the Revised Standard
Version, arranged by categories (epic literature, lyric poetry, rhetoric, wisdom literature, prophetic literature), then broken down into
sub-categories according to literary genre. Each genre is preceded
by a one- to two-page (rather inadequate) introduction. Paperback.

Chamberlain, Roy B. and Feldman, H., eds. *The Dartmouth Bible.* 2nd (Sentry) ed. Boston: Houghton Mifflin, 1961.

An extensive selection of texts from the King James Version, with excellent introductions to each book and critical notes placed at the end of each book. Paperback.

Frank, Joseph H., ed. *Literature from the Bible.* Boston: Little, Brown, 1963.

Selections from the King James Version, chosen for their own literary value and their influence on other literature, with suggestions for readings related to the Bible by theme or allusion. Good introduction to each book of the Bible. Paperback.

Harrison, George B., ed. *The Bible for Students of Literature and Art.* Garden City, N.Y.: Doubleday, 1964.

Selections from the King James Version including most passages encountered as images, allusions, or themes in literature and art, with excellent introductory essay and with helpful notes and index at end. Large print, good format for schools. Paperback.

III. Bible Commentaries

Black, Matthew, and Rowley, H. H., eds. *Peake's Commentary on the Bible.* New York: Nelson, 1962.

An excellent example of liberal Protestant scholarship, with 285 pages of helpful introductory articles on archeology, history, form criticism, Near Eastern culture, languages, the Bible as literature, etc., and 780 pages of finely done verse-by-verse commentary on the biblical text. Recommended for school library.

Brown, Raymond E., S. S., Fitzmyer, J. A., S. J., and Murphy, R. E., O. Carm., eds. *The Jerome Biblical Commentary.* Englewood Cliffs, N.J.: Prentice Hall, 1968.

A monumental work, representing liberal Roman Catholic scholarship, with 1000 pages of excellent verse-by-verse commentary and almost 500 pages of introductory articles. The slight overemphasis on New Testament thought and the strong theological concern do not undermine the value of this book for the teacher of literature. Recommended for school library.

Cohen, A., ed. *Soncino Books of the Bible.* 14 vols. London: Soncino, 1945–52.

Recommended until a one-volume Jewish commentary on the Hebrew Scriptures appears. Each page gives Hebrew text, English translation, and brief critical notes which incorporate many of the insights and interpretations of Jewish scholars from the Talmudic and Medieval periods. Recommended for school library.

Guthrie, Donald, Motyer, J. A., Stibbs, A. M., and Wiseman, D. J. *The*

New Bible Commentary Revised. Grand Rapids, Mich.: Wm. B. Eerdmans, 1970.

The best example of contemporary conservative and evangelical-Protestant scholarship. Contains 1200 pages of critical notes on the biblical text; use in conjunction with other commentaries. Recommended for school library.

Laymon, Charles M., ed. *The Interpreter's One-Volume Commentary on the Bible.* Nashville: Abingdon, 1971.

Contains 970 pages of excellent verse-by-verse commentary of scholars of Protestant, Roman Catholic, and Jewish backgrounds, though dominated by liberal Protestant scholarship. Text includes many useful pictures and close-up maps. Also 300 pages of introductory articles which are especially useful to a teacher of literature (including 80 pages of articles on "The Making of the Literature"), with 16 excellent maps and a 90-page index. Recommended for school library.

Tucker, Gene M., et al. *Interpreter's Handbook of Old Testament Form Criticism.* 3 vols. New York and Nashville: Abingdon, forthcoming.

Includes brief introductions to the seven major blocks of scripture with each passage being analyzed according to its structure, genre, setting and intention. Recommended for school library.

Wright, George Ernest and Fuller, R. H. *The Book of the Acts of God.* New York: Doubleday, 1957.

Though not a verse-by-verse commentary, this is a very readable attempt to analyze specific biblical literature (both Old and New Testament) within the context of Israel's history. Written for the Christian layman and with Christian viewpoint. Critical scholarship useful to teachers. Paperback.

IV. Bible Dictionaries

Buttrick, George A., et al., eds. *The Interpreter's Dictionary of the Bible.* 4 vols. New York: Abingdon, 1962.

By far the best available dictionary, with almost 4000 pages covering people, places, concepts, objects of the Bible, with bibliographies at the end of each article. Written by an international team of over 250 experts on the Bible and ancient Near Eastern culture. Includes many pictures and maps. Recommended for the school library.

Cornfeld, Gaalyahu, ed. *Pictorial Biblical Encyclopedia.* Tel Aviv: Hamikra Baolam Publishing House, 1964.

Excellent articles, stressing biblical institutions (political, economic, military, religious) and history, as uncovered by recent archeology. Lavishly illustrated (black and white) to give the student a real feeling for the culture out of which biblical literature was produced. Recommended for the school library.

Hastings, James. *Dictionary of the Bible.* (Rev. ed. by Frederick C. Grant and H. H. Rowley.) New York: Chas. Scribner's & Sons, 1963. Contains 1059 pages of very well done articles, though in fine print with no illustrations except maps. Contains much usable background information for teachers, but it is often highly compressed and hard to read quickly, thus not highly attractive for general student use.

McKenzie, John L., S. J. *Dictionary of the Bible.* London: Geoffrey Chapman, 1965. Nicely edited, highly readable—the work of one of America's foremost biblical scholars. The best dictionary for the student to begin with. Available in paperback from Bruce-Macmillan. Recommended for the school library.

Tenney, Merrill C., ed. *The Zondervan Pictorial Bible Dictionary.* Grand Rapids: Zondervan, 1967. Contains 916 pages with 5,000 entries compiled from 65 scholars, giving an excellent presentation of the conservative viewpoint. Nicely illustrated: 7 maps with overlays. Recommended for school libraries to be used with other Bible dictionaries.

Young Reader's Dictionary of the Bible. Nashville: Abingdon, 1969. For use with the Revised Standard Version. Stresses names, places, and some of the basic biblical concepts. Format, sketch illustrations, and level of information aimed at the junior high school student.

V. Bible Atlases

Aharoni, Yohanan and Avi-Yonah, M. *The Macmillan Bible Atlas.* New York: Macmillan, 1968. Contains 264 maps covering every conceivable topic from "The Economy of Palestine," "The Rivers of the Garden of Eden," and "Jesus' Visits to Jerusalem" to detailed close-ups of important battles —all with excellent format and simple descriptive text. Just too much for the beginning student, but the teacher's dream for the bright student who would probe further.

Grollenberg, Lucas H., O.P. *Atlas of the Bible.* (Translated and edited by Joyce M. H. Reid and Harold H. Rowley.) New York: Thomas Nelson & Sons, 1956. Contains 406 stunning black-white pictures of the land (including aerial photographs) and the artifacts recently unearthed, set within a 100-page description of the history of Israel and the early Christian community, making this a very impressive reference for classroom use. The 35 maps included in the book are academically solid, but difficult to read because so much information is crammed into them.

May, Herbert G. *Oxford Bible Atlas*. Oxford: Oxford University Press, 1964.

Contains 26 superb full-page maps with accompanying page of text describing the historical background depicted on the maps—all of this sandwiched between two amply illustrated articles, "Israel and the Nations" and "Archaeology and the Bible." Many of the maps are reprinted in the back of the *Oxford Annotated Bible*. Available in paperback.

Negenman, Jan H. *New Atlas of the Bible*. (Translated by Hubert Hoskins and Richard Beckley and edited by Harold H. Rowley.) Garden City, N.Y.: Doubleday, 1969.

The text giving historical background is somewhat flat, but the book's format is lavish and very attractive for the student. Many fine color pictures of the land, with maps whose color differentiation consistently follows present-day land use and ground cover. The first chapters alone, with beautiful pictures of ancient manuscripts (Hebrew Bible, Greek New Testament, Rabbinic Bible, Dead Sea Scrolls, etc.) and examples of ancient writing techniques make the book worthwhile for the teacher of literature.

Wright, George Ernest and Filson, F. V. *The Westminster Historical Atlas to the Bible*. Rev. ed. Philadelphia: Westminster, 1956.

Excellent text on historical background with easy to read maps emphasizing tribal and national boundaries, though not as many photographs (88) as in the other atlases. The eighteen color maps are available in a separate folder for students and in large-scale for classroom use.

VI.   Bible Concordances

Ellison, John W. *Nelson's Complete Concordance of the Revised Standard Version Bible*. New York: Thomas Nelson & Sons, 1957.

Compiled by computer. Hebrew and Greek equivalents not given, so there is no way of determining if two similar words in English may go back to the same Hebrew or Greek word, or, on the other hand, if the same English word may be used to translate several different Hebrew or Greek words.

Young, Robert. *Analytical Concordance to the Bible*. (Rev. ed. by William B. Stevenson.) 22nd ed. Grand Rapids, Mich.: William B. Eerdmans, 1955.

Based on the King James Version. Each English word is subdivided according to the various Hebrew and Greek words which it renders. The Hebrew and Greek words are transliterated into English script, and an index of these transliterated words at the back enables the reader to determine other English words used to translate the original Hebrew or Greek word. Recommended for the school library.

VII. Introductions to the History, Religion, and Literature of Ancient Israel (Christian Old Testament, Jewish Bible)

Anderson, Bernhard W. *Understanding the Old Testament.* 2nd ed. Englewood Cliffs, N.J.: Prentice Hall, 1966.
The best written introduction to the Old Testament, with emphasis on the religious dimension of the literature.

Archer, Gleason L. *A Survey of Old Testament Introduction.* Chicago: Moody Press, 1964.
A conservative interpretation of Old Testament literature and religion, with the first 150 pages discussing problems of inspiration and historical authenticity, and the last 300 pages discussing the literature itself.

Beebe, H. Keith. *The Old Testament.* Belmont, Calif.: Dickenson, 1970.
Attractive layout, with stress on literary forms and techniques (though sometimes at expense of historical continuity), makes this a good introduction for the teacher of literature.

Buck, Harry M. *People of the Lord: The History, Scriptures, and Faith of Ancient Israel.* New York: Macmillan, 1966.
A fine treatment of Israel's literature, based on close analysis of selected passages. For a beginner, it's sometimes hard to see the forest for the trees, but highly recommended for the enthusiast who would dig deeper.

Driver, Samuel R. *An Introduction to the Literature of the Old Testament.* New York: Charles Scribner's & Sons, 1909.
Though many intrepretations have changed since this book was written seventy years ago, it is a classic—still useful for the teacher who prefers paperbacks to expensive hardcover textbooks. Paperback.

Gottwald, Norman K. *A Light to the Nations.* New York: Harper & Row, 1959.
A wide-ranging yet thorough introduction, written with great literary sensitivity.

Napier, B. Davie. *Song of the Vineyard.* New York: Harper & Row, 1962.
The book is subtitled "a theological introduction to the Old Testament," which is essentially correct, but the writer has tremendous insight and captures the spirit of the literature through his fine analysis. A good book for a teacher of literature to begin with.

Sandmel, Samuel. *The Hebrew Scriptures.* New York: Alfred A. Knopf, 1963.

Written by an eminent liberal Jewish scholar. Format is difficult to follow, since the books are discussed in the sequence of their final editing rather than the historical era they describe. Thus Genesis through II Kings is discussed after the prophets and wisdom writers, virtually at the end of the book.

West, James King. *Introduction to the Old Testament.* New York: Macmillan, 1971.

An excellent analysis of biblical literature, beginning with Genesis, working sequentially through the Old Testament, and concluding with the apocryphal (deutero-canonical) material. This book and a companion *Introduction to the New Testament* by Donald J. Selby are available in one volume: D. J. Selby and J. K. West, *Introduction to the Bible.*

Young, Edward J. *Introduction to the Old Testament.* Rev. ed. Grand Rapids, Mich.: William B. Eerdmans, 1960.

Not available to the writer of this bibliography, but reputedly the best conservative introduction to the Old Testament.

VIII. Background to the Culture of Ancient Israel (Old Testament)

A. *Ancient Near Eastern Civilizations*

Eliade, Mircea. *Cosmos and History.* New York: Harper & Row, 1959.

An important book, clearly describing the mythic thought of ancient man and its relationship to the temporal and spatial archetypes which are often important in biblical thought, beautifully contrasting ancient man's return to primordial time and sacred space through myth and ritual with the development of historical thought in Israel. Paperback.

Eliade, Mircea. *The Sacred and the Profane.* New York: Harcourt, Brace & World, 1959.

Only secondarily related to the Bible, but useful for the teacher of literature for its discussion of archetypal-mythic patterns. Paperback.

Frankfort, Henri. *Before Philosophy.* Baltimore: Penguin, 1959.

This book should be part of everyone's library. It cannot be highly enough recommended for the teacher who would understand the cultural background (Egyptian and Mesopotamian) out of which Israelite thought developed. Contains an excellent chapter on myth. Paperback.

Frazer, James G. *The New Golden Bough.* (Notes and foreword by Theodore H. Gaster.) Garden City, N.Y.: Doubleday, 1961.

An abridgement of Frazer's classic twelve-volume work describing similar patterns of belief and ritual practices in ancient societies throughout the world. Paperback.

Hooke, Samuel H. *Middle Eastern Mythology.* Baltimore: Penguin, 1963.
After an introductory chapter on types of myth, the book describes the major bodies of ancient Near Eastern mythology (Mesopotamian, Egyptian, Canaanite, Hittite), with almost half the book devoted to biblical literature. Paperback.

Kramer, Samuel N. *History Begins at Sumer.* Garden City, N.Y.: Doubleday, 1959.
A delightful, popularly written account of 37 "firsts" in man's recorded history, for the student who wants to learn more about the earliest Mesopotamian civilization. (Sample firsts: The First Schools, First Case of "Apple-Polishing," First Case of Juvenile Delinquency, First Animal Fables, etc.) Paperback.

Kramer, Samuel N. *Mythologies of the Ancient World.* Garden City, N.Y.: Doubleday, 1961.
A fine anthology describing the mythologies of ancient Egypt, Mesopotamia, Canaan, Greece, India, China, Japan, Mexico, etc. Paperback.

Moscati, Sabatino. *The Face of the Ancient Orient.* Garden City, N.Y.: Doubleday, 1962.
Brief descriptions of the history, religion, and especially the literature of the Sumerians, Babylonians, Assyrians, Egyptians, Hittites, Canaanites, Hurrians, Israelites, Arameans, and Persians. Paperback.

Pritchard, James B. *The Ancient Near East.* Princeton: Princeton University, 1958.
An excellent collection of texts and pictures of artifacts related to the culture of ancient Israel. Paperback.

Sandars, Nancy K. *The Gilgamesh Epic.* Baltimore: Penguin, 1960.
Though the poetry is changed into prose, this is the most readable translation of the ancient Mesopotamian classic. Paperback.

B. *Archeology and Ancient Israel*

Albright, William F. *Archaeology and the Religion of Israel.* Baltimore: Johns Hopkins Press, 1956.
Crammed full of interesting information, but written for the advanced student of the Bible—by the dean of American biblical scholars.

Frank, Harry T. *Bible Archaeology and Faith.* Nashville and New York: Abingdon, 1971.
Clearly and interestingly written (at college freshman level), with fine introductory chapters on problems faced by archeologists in the Near East and the methodology which they have developed. Results

set within historical framework, showing how our knowledge of each age is enhanced. Good format and maps. Recommended for school library.

Wright, George Ernest. *Biblical Archaeology*. Philadelphia: Westminster, 1960.

The best popular description of how archeology has enhanced our understanding of biblical history and culture, written by one of America's foremost scholars. Paperback. Recommended for school library.

Wright, George Ernest, Campbell, E. F., Jr., and Freedman, D. N. *The Biblical Archaeologist Reader*. 3 vols. Garden City, N.Y.: Doubleday, 1967–70.

An excellent anthology of popularly written articles, by eminent scholars, showing how archeological discoveries have vastly expanded our knowledge of the culture in which Israel lived. Articles on such topics as Solomon's temple, slavery in the ancient Near East, etc. Crammed. full of interesting information for the bright pupil who wants to probe further. Paperback.

C. *The History of Ancient Israel*

Albright, William F. *From the Stone Age to Christianity*. Baltimore: Johns Hopkins Press, 1957.

Chapters 3–6 comprise a monumental synthesis of ancient near Eastern history and thought, centering on ancient Israel, by a writer who has a scope of expertise broader than that of any other scholar. Paperback.

Anderson G. W. *The History and Religion of Israel*. New York: Oxford, 1966.

One of the very best brief (210 pages) descriptions.

Baron, Salo W. *A Social and Religious History of the Jews*. Vols. 1–2. 2nd edition. New York: Columbia University Press, 1952.

The stress in these volumes (which begin a series running already through 13 volumes, up to the Reformation) is on the development of Judaism after the Exile, and continues through the Talmudic period in the early Christian era.

Bright, John. *A History of Israel*. Philadelphia: Westminster, 1959.

The best history available, rich in detail and yet highly readable. A revised edition will soon be ready.

Cornfeld, Gaalyahu. *From Adam to Daniel: An Illustrated Guide to the Old Testament and Its Background*. New York: Macmillan, 1962.

Lavishly illustrated, with an excellent, comprehensive text describing the history and culture of Israel within the context of ancient Near Eastern civilizations. A companion volume, *From Daniel to Paul*, is available for New Testament studies. Recommended for school library.

Orlinsky, Harry M. *Ancient Israel.* 2nd ed. Ithaca, N.Y.: Cornell University Press, 1960.

A fine, brief treatment of the history of ancient Israel. Paperback.

Vawter, Bruce, C. M., ed. *Background to the Bible Series.* 12 vols. Englewood Cliffs, N.J.: Prentice Hall, 1966–.

This excellent series, eight volumes of which are related to the Old Testament (*The Bible and Archaeology, The World of the Patriarchs, The World of Moses, The World of the Judges, The World of David and Solomon, The World of the Prophets, The World of the Restoration, The World of Palestinian Judaism*) sets the given biblical period within its broader cultural and historical context, noting the problems which remain yet to be resolved and discussing the main interpretations of the evidence. Written for the well-read layman.

D. *The Life and Institutions of Ancient Israel*

Heaton, E. W. *Everyday Life in Old Testament Times.* New York: Scribner's, 1956.

Popularly written descriptions of nomadic, town, home, country, industrial, military, civil, professional, and religious life in ancient Israel.

Pedersen, Johannes. *Israel: Its Life and Institutions.* 2 vols. London: Oxford University Press, 1926.

A classic description of the ancient Hebrew mind and of Israelite religious, social, and political institutions, by a noted Danish scholar.

Vaux, Roland de, O.P. *Ancient Israel.* (Translated by J. McHugh.) New York: McGraw-Hill, 1961.

An encyclopedic treatment of ancient Israel's religious, social, and political institutions, crammed full of facts and references, including an extensive bibliography. More thorough and systematic than Pedersen, but not as interesting.

E. *The Thought of Ancient Israel*

1. General

Chase, Mary Ellen. *Life and Language in the Old Testament.* New York: W. W. Norton, 1955.

The book, which is a perceptive and well written sequel to *The Bible and the Common Reader,* is an excellent introduction for the teacher without extensive background in biblical literature. The three parts of the volume consider "The Ancient Hebrew Mind," "Imagination in the Old Testament," and "Language in the Old Testament."

Childs, Brevard S. *Myth and Reality in the Old Testament.* Naperville, Illinois: Alec R. Allenson, 1960.

A beautiful discussion of myth, showing how it relates to the notions of time and space. Takes six Old Testament passages to show how

Israel uses myth, "breaking" it in order to express her monotheistic faith.

Gaster, Theodor H. *Myth, Legend, and Custom in the Old Testament.* New York: Harper & Row, 1969.

A valuable reference work, methodically working through the Bible, chapter by chapter, showing how parallel folklore from other widely diverse cultures can throw light on the literature of ancient Israel. Written as an expansion of Sir James G. Frazer's *Folklore in the Old Testament.*

Ginzberg, Louis. *The Legends of the Jews.* 7 vols. (Translated by H. Szold.) Philadelphia: Jewish Publication Society, 1946–61.

There is a one-volume abridgement of this classic, describing the tremendously rich lore which developed within Judaism through oral interpretations, written down in the early centuries of the Christian era.

Kaufmann, Yehezkel. *The Religion of Israel.* (Translated by Moshe Greenberg.) Chicago: University of Chicago Press, 1959.

An abridgement of a monumental eight-volume work produced by an eminent conservative Israeli scholar, rich with insights and presenting a wide range of alternative conclusions to those of main-line liberal scholarship. For the advanced student of the Bible.

Muilenburg, James. *The Way of Israel.* New York: Harper & Row, 1961.

This superb, beautifully written little book explores the uniqueness of Israelite thought with great literary sensitivity. Recommended for the school library. Paperback.

McKenzie, John L., S.J. *The Two-Edged Sword: An Interpretation of the Old Testament.* Milwaukee: Bruce, 1956.

A profound, yet clearly written treatment of the rich variety of thought within the Old Testament. One concludes this book with a real feel for the literature of ancient Israel.

Robinson, H. Wheeler. *Corporate Personality in Ancient Israel.* Philadelphia: Fortress, 1964.

A very important 35-page study of the relationship between the individual and the community in ancient Israelite thought. Paperback. (Facet Book Series)

von Rad, Gerhard. *Old Testament Theology.* 2 vols. (Translated by D. M. G. Stalker.) New York: Harper, 1962–65.

A superb treatment of the varying streams of ancient Israelite thought, for advanced students of the Bible. A section of volume 2, *The Message of the Prophets,* is available in paperback.

Wright, George Ernest. *The Old Testament Against Its Environment.* Naperville, Illinois: Alec R. Allenson, 1950.

Though somewhat outdated, this is still an excellent treatment, popularly written, of the contrast between the culture of Israel and that of her Near Eastern neighbors. Paperback.

E. 2 *Early Israelite Literature*

Buber, Martin. *Moses*. New York: Harper & Brothers, 1958.
The first chapter on Saga and History is extremely important for the teacher of literature, sketching out an alternative to the source theory which seems particularly applicable to the Exodus traditions. Stresses oral tradition. Paperback.

Gunkel, Hermann. *The Legends of Genesis*. New York: Schocken, 1964.
A brilliant analysis of the process of oral tradition and how it has shaped the form of the stories in Genesis. Paperback.

Gaster, Theodor H. *Passover: Its History and Traditions*. Boston: Beacon, 1962.
A very useful little book, popularly written. Particularly useful when the class is studying the Exodus traditions and wants to know more about the Passover celebration. Paperback.

Westermann, Claus. *The Genesis Accounts of Creation*. Philadelphia: Fortress, 1964.
An excellent, close literary analysis of Genesis 1–3 in 40 pages. Paperback. (Facet Book Series)

E. 3. *Prophecy in Ancient Israel*

Buber, Martin. *The Prophetic Faith*. New York: Harper & Row, 1960.
A sensitive, compelling, brief treatment of the prophets, preceded by five chapters of religious and historical background prior to the prophetic age. For the intermediate student of the Bible. Paperback.

Heschel, Abraham J. *The Prophets*. Philadelphia: Jewish Publication Society, 1962.
The first third of this important book describes the background and thought of the seven most important prophets, the second third treats the major theological concepts, and the final third analyzes the psychological nature of prophetic experience. Clearly written, but for advanced students of the Bible.

Napier, B. Davie. *Prophets in Perspective*. Nashville: Abingdon, 1962.
An excellent, brief, simple treatment of the role of the prophet in Israelite society. Rather than describe the prophets one at a time, the final chapter concludes with the major themes of prophetic thought.

Robinson, Theodore H. *Prophecy and the Prophets in Ancient Israel*. London: Gerald Duckworth & Co., 1953.
A brief, clearly written description of the life and thought of each prophet, preceded by a section on the nature and origin of Israelite prophecy.

Scott, R. B. Y. *The Relevance of the Prophets*. Rev. ed. New York: Macmillan, 1968.

A classic. Like Napier, Scott is interested in the sociological, political, theological, and literary dimensions of prophecy rather than in a biography of each prophet. Paperback.

Vawter, Bruce, C.M. *The Conscience of Israel*. New York: Sheed & Ward, 1961.

A fine treatment of the classical prophets of the eighth and seventh centuries, but does not include those before (e.g., Elijah) and those after (e.g., Ezekial and Second Isaiah).

E. 4. *Wisdom in Ancient Israel*

Murphy, Roland J., O. Carm. *Seven Books of Wisdom*. Milwaukee: Bruce, 1960.

An excellent, brief, clear treatment of Israel's wisdom literature, unfortunately out of print.

E. 5. *Poetry and the Psalms of Ancient Israel*

Gunkel, Hermann. *The Psalms*. (Translated by Thomas M. Horner.) Philadelphia: Fortress, 1967.

A brief (41 pages) form-critical analysis of the literary genres in the Psalter, done by one of the greatest twentieth century biblical scholars. Paperback (Facet Book Series).

Guthrie, Harvey M., Jr. *Israel's Sacred Songs: A Study of Dominant Themes*. New York: Seabury Press, 1966.

Not a commentary which discusses each psalm in detail, but this superb book is of tremendous value in understanding the mentalities which produced the various types of psalms.

Mowinckel, Sigmund. *The Psalms in Israel's Worship*. 2 vols. (Translated by D. R. Ap-Thomas.) Nashville: Abingdon, 1967.

One of the most influential works of twentieth century biblical scholarship, written for the advanced student of the Bible. Dividing the psalms into separate categories according to structure, Mowinckel imaginatively portrays the liturgical setting which produced this literature. The psalms reveal the heart of Israel. Some of M's conclusions are not universally accepted, but this work uniquely opens up the Israelite mentality.

Terrien, Samuel. *The Psalms and Their Meaning for Today*. Indianapolis: Bobbs-Merrill, 1952.

A fine introduction to the Psalter, written with great sensitivity and clarity.

E. 6. *The Future Hope: Messianism and Apocalyptic (Including the Dead Sea Scrolls)*

Bright, John. *The Kingdom of God*. Nashville: Abingdon, 1953.

An excellent popular summary of biblical thought, written from a Christian perspective. Paperback.

Charles, Robert H. *Eschatology.* New York: Schocken, 1963.

This reprint of the 1899 classic is sub-titled "The Doctrine of a Future Life in Israel, Judaism and Christianity." Clearly written, and particularly valuable because of its discussion of some of the noncanonical Jewish literature which developed within the same milieu as the Dead Sea Scrolls. Paperback.

Cross, Frank M., Jr. *The Ancient Library of Qumran.* Rev. ed. Garden City, New York: Doubleday, 1961.

The best treatment of the Dead Sea Scrolls and the community which produced them. Written for advanced students of the Bible. Paperback.

Frost, Stanley B. *Old Testament Apocalyptic.* London: Epworth Press, 1952.

Particularly valuable for its stress on apocalyptic as a recrudescence of Near Eastern and early Israelite mythic thought, but only for advanced students of the Bible.

Gaster, Theodore H. *The Dead Sea Scriptures.* Garden City, New York: Doubleday, 1956.

A collection (with translation and excellent brief introduction) of the Dead Sea Scrolls, closely related to the thought in Daniel and in some parts of the New Testament.

Klausner, Joseph. *The Messianic Idea in Israel.* (Translated by W. F. Stinespring.) London: George Allen & Unwin, 1956.

A detailed discussion of the messianic hope, as it is found both in the Old Testament and in non-canonical and Mishnaic Jewish Literature —done by an eminent Jewish scholar. For advanced students of the Bible.

Mowinckel, Sigmund. *He That Cometh.* (Translated by G. W. Anderson.) New York: Abingdon, 1954.

A classic by the noted Norwegian scholar—traces the idea of the Messiah out of the Near Eastern ideal of kingship as it was incorporated into Israel by the Davidic kings and transformed by the prophets. Also discusses the "Suffering Servant" passages in Second Isaiah and the developing "Son of Man" concept. For advanced students of the Bible.

E. 7. *The Apocryphal (Deutero-Canonical) Literature*

Goodspeed, Edward J. *The Story of the Apocrypha.* Chicago: University of Chicago, 1939.

A very brief, clear, concise introduction to each apocryphal book.

Metzger, Bruce M. *An Introduction to the Apocrypha.* New York: Oxford University Press, 1957

A slightly more advanced treatment of the apocryphal literature, but still well within the grasp of the beginning student of the Bible. Contains valuable final chapter on the influence of the Apocrypha on western literature, art, and music.

IX. History of Translations of the Bible

Bruce, F. F. *The English Bible: A History of Translations from the Earliest English Versions to the New English Bible*. New York: Oxford University Press, 1970.

An slightly more advanced treatment

Historical background and style analysis of all the great English translations from Wycliffe to the present day. The book has been revised to include the most recent translations, though the New American Bible could not be treated in detail because the text was not yet available to the author.

Kenyon, Sir Frederic. *Our Bible and the Ancient Manuscripts*. Rev. by A. W. Adams. London: Eyre & Spottiswoode, 1958.

A revised edition of the 1895 classic; nine chapters describe the ancient versions of the text (Hebrew, Greek, Latin, Syriac, etc.) and their history. The last three chapters describe the various English translations. Includes 48 photographs of ancient texts. For the advanced student of the Bible.

Lewis, C. S. *The Literary Impact of the Authorized Version*. Philadelphia: Fortress, 1967.

A very fine essay (34 pages), challenging the notion that the King James Version has heavily influenced the language, imagery, style, and rhythm of later English writers. Paperback (Facet Book Series).

MacGregor, Geddes. *A Literary History of the Bible from the Middle Ages to the Present Day*. Nashville: Abingdon, 1968.

An excellent treatment of the English translations, done with greater attention to literary qualities than Bruce's book.

Rauber, Donald F. "Regii Sanguisis Clamor ad Coelum: The Condition of Modern Biblical Translations," *Catholic Biblical Quarterly*, Vol. 32 (1970), 25–40.

A sensitive essay of the perils of translation, affirming the importance of the King James Version for more closely approximating the rhythm and style of the Hebrew text than many modern translations.

X. Influence of the Bible on Western Literature

Fulghum, Walter B. *A Dictionary of Biblical Allusions in English Literature*. New York: Holt, Rinehart and Winston, 1965.

A useful book—lacking, however, in references to twentieth century literature. Paperback.

Gaer, Joseph and Siegel, B. *The Puritan Heritage: America's Roots in the Bible*. New York: New American Library of World Literature, Inc., 1964.

A popularly written description of the influence of biblical concepts on American culture (settlement, government, law, education, medicine), particularly valuable for its fine concluding 75-page chapter on American literature. Very useful for the teacher of literature. Paperback only.

Nelson, Lawrence E., *Our Roving Bible: Tracking Its Influence through English and American Life*. New York: Abingdon-Cokesbury, 1945.

A sprightly, entertaining, though somewhat superficial cataloguing of the influence of the Bible on Western culture—from the Christianizing of Beowulf to H. L. Mencken to advertisements in *Collier's Magazine*. Could still be useful for the teacher of literature.

XI. "Literary" Analysis: esthetic, thematic, and source

Bertman, Stephen. "Symmetrical Design in the Book of Ruth," *Journal of Biblical Literature*, Vol. 84 (1965), 165–68.

A fine, brief analysis of the literary structure of Ruth.

Bickermann, Elias. *Four Strange Books of the Bible*. New York: Schocken, 1967.

An excellent analysis of Jonah, Daniel, Ecclesiastes, and Esther.

Bullinger, Ethelbert W. *Figures of Speech Used in the Bible*. Grand Rapids, Mich.: Baker Book House, 1968.

Reprint of an 1898 exhaustive encyclopedic (1022 pages) treatment of more than two hundred kinds of literary devices (e.g., ellipsis, acrostic), with illustrations from all parts of the Bible. The heavy bias toward conservative interpretation at times interferes with purely objective literary analysis.

Campbell, Joseph. *The Hero with a Thousand Faces*. New York: Pantheon Books, 1949.

An important book for the teacher who would understand the thought forms of ancient literature; divided into two major headings: The Adventures of the Hero, The Cosmogonic Cycle.

Chase, Mary Ellen. *The Bible and the Common Reader*. New York: Macmillan, 1944.

This book is not too good on the historical and cultural background of the Bible, but it is sometimes suggestive in its literary analysis. Includes Old and New Testaments.

Chase, Mary Ellen. *The Prophets for the Common Reader*. New York: W. W. Norton, 1963.

A popularly written work (companion volume to *The Psalms for the*

Common Reader), with sections on the nature of prophecy, biographies of the prophets, the literature of prophecy, and selections from the writings of the prophets.

Cope, Gilbert, *Symbolism in the Bible and the Church*. New York: Philosophical Library, 1959.

An interesting discussion of biblical imagery and symbolism, including the archetypes of creation, male and female, and suffering, stressing psychological interpretation.

Crook, Margaret B., ed. *The Bible and Its Literary Associations*. New York: Abingdon, 1937.

An anthology of essays, valuable to the teacher, providing overall literary analysis of biblical (Old and New Testaments) and apocryphal literature, descriptions of how the Bible was written down and its influence on medieval literature, concluding with essays on the King James Version and its influence on Milton, Baxter, Bunyan, Fox, DeQuincey, and Hardy.

Crook, Margaret B. *The Cruel God*. Boston: Beacon, 1959.

An excellent book on Job—proof that literary experts can reach profound understandings of biblical literature.

Crook, Margaret B. "The Book of Ruth," *Journal of Bible and Religion*, Vol. 16 (1948), 155–60.

Not available to the author, but certainly worth looking at.

Frye, Northrop. *Anatomy of Criticism*. Princeton: Princeton University Press, 1957.

Although no biblical passages are dealt with in detail, this classic of literary criticism (especially the third essay on archetypal criticism) is particularly helpful for analyzing and understanding the themes of biblical literature.

Frye, Northrop. *The Educated Imagination*. Bloomington: Indiana University Press, 1964.

Six brilliant lectures on myth, metaphor, and the art of creating and responding to literature. Appropriate for all teachers of literature, but especially for those who would teach the Bible. One scholar has written that the Bible will not be understood properly if it is approached as literature. After reading Frye, I would say that the Bible can only be properly understood if it is approached as literature—as the creative response of the poet, whose job, says Frye, "is not to tell you what happened, but what happens: not what did take place, but the kind of thing that always takes place" (p. 63). Paperback.

Frye, Northrop. *Typology of the Bible*. New York: Harcourt Brace Jovanovich, forthcoming, 1975.

Frye, Northrop, Lee, H. A., Lee, A. A., and Jewkes, W. T. *The Garden and the Wilderness; The Temple and the Ruin; The Marriage of*

Earth and Heaven. New York: Harcourt Brace Jovanovich, 1973–74. Two books covering the archetypes of the Old Testament, and one on the New Testament. Paperbacks, illustrated for high school students, containing Bible selections, modern retellings, with modern and ancient analogs.

Good, Edwin M. *Irony in the Old Testament.* Philadelphia: Westminster, 1965.
An excellent treatment of ironic style in the Old Tesatment, analyzing the Genesis stories, Jonah, Saul, Isaiah, Ecclesiastes, and Job.

Graves, Robert and Patai, R. *Hebrew Myths: The Book of Genesis.* Garden City, N.Y.: Doubleday, 1964.
A useful book for the teacher of literature, describing the Near Eastern lore and especially the rabbinic traditions which parallel the Genesis stories; intended as a companion to Graves' *The Greek Myths.*

Henn, T. R. *The Bible as Literature.* New York: Oxford University Press, 1970.
An expansion of "The Bible as Literature" article in *Peake's Commentary.* An uneven melange, often suggestive, with good chapters on translation and on Job. Some teachers have found the book quite helpful; others not.

Hone, Ralph E., ed. *The Voice Out of the Whirlwind: The Book of Job.* San Francisco: Chandler, 1960.
An excellent anthology, including introductions by Davidson and Jastrow, sermons by Kierkegaard and Newman, essays by Blake, Goethe, Carlyle, and Ciardi, and modern adaptations by Wilder, MacLeish, and Frost. Paperback.

Kermode, Frank. *The Sense of an Ending: Studies in the Theory of Fiction.* New York: Oxford University Press, 1967.
An excellent study of apocalyptic thought and form as it occurs in the Bible and in contemporary literature.

Lowth, Robert. *Lectures on the Sacred Poetry of the Hebrews.* 2 vols. (Translated by G. Gregory.) Hildesheim, Germany: Georg Olms Verlag, 1969.
A welcome reprint of the Anglican bishop's epic-making lectures on Hebrew poetry (given in 1787) dealing with metaphor, allegory, comparison, and personification as techniques, the sublime and sententious as characteristics, the ode, idyll, elegy, proverb, and drama as forms and including a well-known analysis of Hebrew meter. Rich with insights, full of comparisons with other classical literature.

Moulton, Richard G. *The Literary Study of the Bible.* New York: AMS Press, 1970.
A partial reworking of a book first written in 1899, useful for the

teacher in its analysis of literary types found in the Bible. See also his more dated *The Bible as Literature*. New York: T. Y. Crowell, 1896.

MacDonald, Duncan B. *The Hebrew Literary Genius*. Princeton: Princeton University Press, 1933.

An appreciation of the literary types and content of the Old Testament, written by a man who applies understanding of life in the contemporary Middle East to the parallels in thought, custom, and literary style which he finds in biblical literature.

Montgomery, Robert M. *An Introduction to Source Analysis of the Pentateuch*. Nashville: Abingdon, 1971.

A programmed learning student textbook where, in fifty frames, the student can learn the four-source theory through sample textual evidence on which it is based. The preface makes clear that, after understanding the theory, the student is then free to accept or reject its validity. Paperback.

Raglan, Lord Fitz Roy. *The Hero: A Study in Tradition, Myth and Drama*. New York: Vintage, 1956.

Tries to establish the thesis that folk tales are one form of traditional narrative, and are ultimately derived from myth rather than history. Although extreme, his discussion is helpful for noting the mythic qualities attached to biblical heroes.

Rauber, Donald F. "Literary Values in the Bible: The Book of Ruth," *Journal of Biblical Literature*, Vol. 89 (1970), 27–37.

A superb treatment of the literary movement and structure in the Book of Ruth; full of insights.

Robinson, Theodore H. *The Poetry of the Old Testament*. London: Gerald Duckworth, 1947.

Though recent discoveries have added to our understanding of poetic forms in ancient Israel, this book will be extremely useful for the teacher of literature. The forms of Hebrew poetry are described and then analyzed as they occur in Job, Psalms, Proverbs, Song of Songs, Lamentations.

Rylaarsdam, J. Coert. *Guides to Biblical Scholarship: Old Testament Series*. Philadelphia: Fortress, 1971.

So far there are five 80-page paperbacks in this excellent series, two related to the Old Testament: Norman Habel, *Literary Criticism of the Old Testament* and Gene M. Tucker, *Form Criticism of the Old Testament*. Both books are popularly written descriptions of the literary approach taken by contemporary biblical scholars; must reading for the teacher of literature.

Samuel, Maurice. *Certain People of the Book*. New York: Alfred Knopf, 1955.

Striking, sensitive portrayals of figures from the Bible (even obscure ones like Balaam and Ahasuerus); very appealing to secondary school students.

Sander, Paul S. *Twentieth Century Interpretations of the Book of Job.* Englewood Cliffs, N.J.: Prentice Hall, 1968.

Essays by Toynbee, Gilbert Murray, and others, full of literary insights and interesting comparisons. Paperback.

Sypherd, Wilbur O. *The Literature of the English Bible.* New York: Oxford University Press, 1938.

A brief description of each book of the Bible (Old and New Testaments) with scant literary analysis. Contains useful brief sections on the English translations of the Bible and on Hebrew poetry.

Trawick, Buckner B. *The Bible as Literature: The Old Testament and Apocrypha.* 2nd ed. New York: Barnes & Noble, 1970.

A handy reference book, valuable for its summary descriptions of the canonical and non-canonical literature of ancient Israel. To some extent summarizing the results of recent critical scholarship. Some, though not much, literary analysis is given. Paperback.

Via, Dan O., Jr., ed. *Guides to Biblical Scholarship: New Testament Series.* Philadelphia: Fortress Press, 1969–70.

Excellent, popularly written, brief (80 pages each) accounts of the literary methodology taken by contemporary biblical scholars. Includes Edgar V. McKnight, *What is Form Criticism?* Norman Perrin, *What is Redaction Criticism?* and William A. Beardslee, *Literary Criticism of the New Testament.* Paperbacks.

XII. The Bible as Literature in the Classroom

Ackerman, James S. and Jenks, A. W. with Jenkinson, Edward and Blough, Jan. *Teaching the Old Testament in English Class: A Guide for Junior and Senior High School Teachers.* Bloomington, Indiana: Indiana University Press, 1972.

Introduction, critical notes, and discussion–study questions, to one hundred and thirty Old Testament passages, including chapters on the early historical background and the writing of the Bible.

"Hebrew Literature." University of Nebraska English Curriculum Study Center. Lincoln, Nebraska.

Five units, part of the "God and Man" series, developed for the seventh grade curriculum. Students read eight Old Testament narratives (Abraham and Isaac, Jacob and Joseph, Moses, Joshua and Jericho, Samson, Ruth, David and Goliath, David and Jonathan) and consider characters, setting, plot, and literary devices. A student packet and a teacher packet contain questions and background material. Quite well done.

Whitney, John R., and Howe, Susan W. *Religious Literature of the West*. Minneapolis: Augsburg, 1971.
Background information on a wide range of selected Old Testament, New Testament, apocryphal, rabbinic, and Muslim writings. Each passage includes "search cues" and "reflection questions." This excellent book is the result of four years of experimental development of teaching materials at Pennsylvania State University.

Other recommended books not available to the author: *

Church, Brooke P. *The Golden Years: The Old Testament Narrative as Literature*. New York: Rinehart, 1947.
Culler, Arthur J. *Creative Religious Literature: A New Literary Study of the Bible*.
Dinsmore, Charles A. *The English Bible as Literature*. Houghton-Mifflin, 1931.
Jones, Howard Mumford. "The Bible from a Literary Point of View," in *Five Essays on the Bible*. New York: American Council of Learned Societies, 1960.
Reid, Mary Esson. *The Bible Read as Literature*. Cleveland: Howard Allen, 1959.
Wild, Laura H. *A Literary Guide to the Bible*. New York: Doran, 1922.
Wood, I. F., and Grant, E. *The Bible as Literature*. New York: Abingdon, 1919.

* Taken from a list kindly sent to me by Roland Bartel, Professor of English, University of Oregon.

NOTES

BACKGROUND ON THE OLD TESTAMENT

Early Israelite History

1. The stele of an Egyptian pharaoh who reports having destroyed Israel during an excursion into Palestine around 1230 B.C. (James B. Pritchard, *The Ancient Near East: An Anthology of Texts and Pictures* [Princeton University Press, 1958], p. 231.)

2. See S. N. Kramer, *History Begins at Sumer* (Garden City, N.Y.: Doubleday-Anchor, 1959).

3. The idea that each city-state served only one god is an oversimplification. Although the city-state was thought to belong to one major god, under him there was a vast hierarchy of minor deities who were charged with the direct oversight of various aspects of temple service.

4. It is clear that Abraham began his journey to Canaan from the region around Haran in Upper Mesopotamia. We also know that Haran remained the home territory for many of Abraham's relatives (e.g., Laban) who did not migrate into Canaan. This has caused many scholars to doubt the tradition that Abraham originally came from Ur. It is possible, we would think, that Abraham's family may have left Ur at an earlier time and settled in Haran—from whence Abraham wandered into Canaan. The debate, however, is not germane to our discussion, since both areas would have been under the influence of Sumero-Akkadian culture.

5. Although *Amorite* is a broad term which covers many related groups of Semitic peoples, we have retained it in order to identify Abraham within a larger migratory movement of which his journey was but a minute part. Before going to Canaan, Abraham's family seems to have been related to Aramean clans which wandered around the region of Haran (see Deuteronomy 26:5).

6. One should not picture Abraham as a nomadic bedouin who rode camels far into the desert. It has been recently found that the camel was not domesticated until the end of the twelfth century. Thus the description in Genesis of the patriarchs riding on camels represents the assumption of a later age that camels had always been available for long journeys. (See W. F. Albright, *The Archaeology of Palestine* [Baltimore: Penguin paperback, 1956], pp. 206–208.)

7. See W. F. Albright, "Abram the Hebrew: A New Archaeological Interpretation," *Bulletin of the American Schools of Oriental Research,* No. 163 (October, 1961), pp. 36–54. For a portrayal of ass nomads entering Egypt from the Negeb region, see Plate 2 of James B. Pritchard, *The Ancient Near East: An Anthology of Texts and Pictures.* Princeton: Princeton University Press, 1958. Paperback.

8. For a concise description, see John Bright, *A History of Israel* (Philadelphia: Westminster Press, 1959), pp. 86–93.

9. See G. E. Wright, *Biblical Archaeology* (2nd ed.; Philadelphia: Westminster Press, 1962), pp. 66ff. The census lists contained in Numbers 1 and 26 indicate that about 600,000 fighting men participated in the Exodus from Egypt. If one were to include their families, the total population would be over 2 million persons. How could such a group have been served by two midwives (Ex. 1:15)? Wright notes that in the greatest battle of his career, the Egyptian Pharaoh Ramses II fielded an army of about 20,000. W. F. Albright has pointed out that the total population of Western Palestine in 1400 B.C. was about 500,000, and suggests that these lists in Numbers actually represent the census of the United Kingdom which was taken during the reign of David (II Sam. 24). ("The Administrative Divisions of Israel and Judah," *Journal of the Palestine Oriental Society,* vol. 5 20–25.)

10. See Deuteronomy 9:4ff.

11. Our knowledge of Canaanite culture has been greatly expanded by the discoveries at Ugarit (modern Ras Shamra) on the north Syrian coast of the Mediterranean. For a brief description, see Sabatino Moscati, *The Face of the Ancient Orient,* ch. 6.

12. See Albrecht Alt, "The Settlement of the Israelites in Palestine," in *Essays on Old Testament History and Religion* (translated by R. A. Wilson). Garden City, N.Y.: Doubleday-Anchor, 1968.

13. See G. Ernest Wright, *Biblical Archaeology,* ch. 3. Different arguments for this theory are presented by Yehezkel Kaufmann, *The Religion of Israel,* ch. 7.

14. See G. E. Mendenhall, "The Hebrew Conquest of Palestine," in

The Biblical Archaeologist Reader Vol. 3 (ed. by Edward F. Campbell, Jr. and David Noel Freedman), Garden City, N.Y.: Doubleday-Anchor, 1970, pp. 100–120.

15. See Mendenhall, "The Hebrew Conquest of Palestine."

16. A similar governmental structure, in which the number twelve (or six) is of central importance, can be found in the almost contemporary Greek Delphic League and Italian Etruscan League.

17. They eventually gave their name (Palestine) to the entire southern half of Canaan, the northern half being traditionally called Syria.

Israel's Literature From Oral Tradition to Printed Bibles

1. See Hermann Gunkel, *The Legends of Genesis* (translated by W. H. Carruth), New York: Schocken Books, 1964, pp. 3–12.

2. Compare Deuteronomy 6:21–23 and Josh. 24:2–13.

3. *J* is the first letter of *Yahweh* in German spelling.

4. Some scholars maintain that P was written during the century after the Jews returned from exile.

5. We are excluding from our discussion the tale of Ruth, which does not form a part of the Deuteronomic historical narrative.

6. We are not suggesting that the books in the Writings first became authoritative about A.D. 90. The recently discovered Dead Sea Scrolls would indicate that most of the books in this collection were already regarded as sacred in the second century B.C. and even earlier (see G. E. Wright, *Biblical Archaeology* [Philadelphia: Westminster Press, 1962], pp. 216–20). Certain books, however, were still disputed, and the synod's purpose was mainly to arrive at a final decision concerning them.

7. The Bible in its entirety was published by Miles Coverdale shortly after Tyndale's death.

ANALYSIS OF THE LITERATURE OF THE OLD TESTAMENT

The Origins of Man

1. Note that the first story ends and the second story begins in Genesis 2:4. The division is represented here by the letters *a* and *b*.

Letters in parentheses at the end of textual references indicate the source of the text. P is the Priestly writer; J is the Yahwist; and E the Elohist.

2. A fragment of the poetic version is preserved in Job 38:4–27.

3. For the important role of the divine council in the Old Testament, see Psalm 29; 82; Job 1; Daniel 7:9ff; I Kings 22:19ff; and Isaiah 6:8.

4. See E. A. Speiser, *Genesis,* Anchor Bible Series (Garden City, N.Y.: Doubleday, 1964), p. 19ff.

5. Here again God is speaking to the members of his host.

6. See notes on Gen. 1:1–2:4a.

7. See above. Or it may go back much earlier to periods when it was being constructed (about the twenty-fourth—twenty-third centuries or eighteenth century B.C.).

Patriarchal Legends

1. See Gunkel, *The Legends of Genesis,* pp. 25–34.

2. Abraham is called Abram in the early stories, and Sarah is called Sarai.

3. The Babylonians were later called Chaldeans.

4. This is probably an allusion to the Tower of Babel story (Gen. 11:4). What men had there attempted in vain to achieve for themselves is here being freely given by God's gracious power.

5. Verses 15–19 were added to the story by a later hand.

6. See Speiser, *Genesis.*

7. See Early Israelite History, note 7.

8. Although Bethuel, Rebekah's father, is mentioned in verse 50, this is probably a textual error. It would be quite unusual for the son to be named before the father. Verse 28 tells of Rebekah's returning to her mother's household. In verse 53 there is no mention of gifts for Rebekah's father. He had probably died before this story took place.

9. Though the major narrative is from J, there are occasional editorial glosses by P, who also added the final section (Gen. 27:46–28:9).

10. See also Speiser. The imagery in this dream is not of a ladder, but rather of the stairway of a Mesopotamian ziggurat tower (see discussion of Gen. 11). The high temple at the top of the tower was thought to be the place of occasional divine revelations. God is pictured standing above the peak of this tower (the "gate of heaven") with his angels ascending and descending as they proceed to carry out his orders for governing the universe.

The Story of Joseph

1. See Gerhard von Rad, *Genesis: A Commentary,* translated by John H. Marks (Philadelphia: Westminster Press, 1961), p. 342.

2. See Gerhard von Rad, "The Joseph Narrative and Ancient Wisdom," *The Problem of the Hexateuch and Other Essays* (New York: McGraw Hill, 1966), pp. 292–300.

3. This is not only true of the Hyksos period, when the land was ruled by Semitic people. The presence of Semitic people in high positions of power is also attested during the New Kingdom.

4. In general, rather than conflating J and E, the editor has taken sections from each source and arranged them consecutively. See von Rad, p. 343; Speiser, pp. 292ff.

5. See Speiser, *Genesis,* pp. 289ff.

6. See Speiser, *Genesis,* pp. 292ff.

7. See Roland De Vaux, *Ancient Israel, Its Life and Institutions,* translated by John McHugh (New York: McGraw Hill, 1961), pp. 59ff.

8. On *Sheol,* see the explanatory notes on Gen. 49:28–50:26.

9. See von Rad, *Genesis: A Commentary,* p. 359.

10. A very close parallel to this story exists in Egyptian literature. In "The Story of Two Brothers" (J. B. Pritchard, *The Ancient Near East: An Anthology of Texts and Pictures* [Princeton Univ. Press, 1958], pp. 12–16), the younger brother is forced to flee for his life, after rebuffing the advances of his brother's wife, who then accuses him of the attempted seduction. Eventually, however, his innocence is proved.

11. It should be noted that the term *Hebrew* is almost always used in the Old Testament by foreigners or by Israelites who are describing themselves to foreigners. It has been recently found that *Hebrew* was not an ethnic term in the ancient Near East during the second millennium B.C.; rather it was used by the settled urban peoples to designate rootless, seminomadic peoples, who appeared on the fringes of the communities, moving from place to place. Thus the term *Hebrew* designates a very large social group, of which the descendants of Abraham were but a very small part (See John Bright, *A History of Israel* [Philadelphia: Westminster Press, 1959], pp. 84ff).

12. See Speiser, *Genesis,* p. 308.

13. Pritchard, *The Ancient Near East,* pp. 24ff.

14. Speiser, *Genesis,* p. 316.

15. Geographically Egypt is most vulnerable to attack from the north (Canaan). From at least the early part of the second millennium

B.C., Egyptian foreign policy required precautions against invasion from the north.

16. Chapters 40–42 are almost entirely E. Verses 27ff, the one insert from J in chapter 42, stand out as a noticeable intrusion into the story because it duplicates the brothers' discovery of the returned money to their grainsacks (v. 35).

17. See Speiser, *Genesis*, pp. 328ff, who points out that 43:14, 23b are intrusive editiorial additions into the story.

18. von Rad, *Genesis: A Commentary*, p. 382.

19. The text of verse 32 is somewhat ambiguous. Joseph would be seated by himself not because he was a Hebrew—he is now an Egyptian—but because of the dignity of his office. The verse seems to be explaining the separation between Joseph's brothers and his Egyptian servants. See Speiser, *Genesis*, p. 328.

20. The mention of the money being put in the brothers' sacks is most likely a later insertion—a carryover from Gen. 42:25—since no mention is made in verses 11ff of the discovery of any money. See Speiser, *Genesis*, p. 333.

21. von Rad, *Genesis: A Commentary*, p. 388; Speiser, *Genesis*, p. 335.

22. Speiser, *Genesis*, p. 334.

23. The use of this list to describe the descendants of Jacob who entered Egypt at this time can be shown to be secondary through the inconsistencies within the text. E. A. Speiser writes: "According to the data in Genesis xxxviii, Perez was born to Judah after the latter's three older sons had reached adulthood. Here Perez is recorded as having two sons of his own, who in terms of the total elapsed time could have been Judah's great-grandchildren. Yet at the time of Jacob's migration to Egypt, Judah's brother Joseph had been there only 22 years (combining [Genesis] xxxvii 2 xli 46f, and xlv 6: 13 years in Egypt plus 7 years of plenty and 2 years of famine). The chronological discrepancy disappears, however, once it is established that the present list had originally nothing to do with the record of the migration to Egypt." (Speiser, *Genesis*, pp. 344ff.)

24. Speiser, *Genesis*, p. 345.

25. See Pritchard, *The Ancient Near East*, pp. 183ff.

26. See II Sam. 16:16; also von Rad, *Genesis: A Commentary*, p. 402.

27. von Rad, *Genesis: A Commentary*, p. 405.

28. See De Vaux, *Ancient Israel*, pp. 56ff.

29. von Rad, *Genesis: A Commentary*, p. 425.

30. The "Stopover" in Abel-mizraim is apparently the place of Jacob's burial in the J narrative. In verse 5 Jacob speaks of a tomb which he had made for himself, as opposed to the tomb purchased by Abraham. This rough spot in the narrative had to be edited by P (verses 12–13) in order to bring the burial place into conformity with his tradition. See von Rad, *Genesis: A Commentary*, p. 426.

31. See Pritchard, *The Ancient Near East*, pp. 234–236.

32. This is the meaning of the phrase "to be born on the knees." See Speiser, *Genesis*, p. 230.

Moses and the Exodus

1. Pritchard, *The Ancient Near East*, pp. 85f.

2. Scholars are uncertain of the location of Moses' sojourn. The "land of Midian" (Ex. 2:15) is to the east of Sinai. Probably a better location for the episodes which follow is the southern region of the Sinai Peninsula, which is the traditional site of Mount Sinai (see G. E. Wright. *Biblical Archaeology* [2nd ed.; Philadelphia; Westminster Press, 1962], pp. 60–64).

3. F. M. Cross, Jr., "Yahweh and the God of the Patriarchs," *Harvard Theological Review*, Vol. 55 (1962), pp. 225–260. Such a title would need an object following the verb. From the common title Yahweh Sabaoth (Lord of hosts), Cross suggests that the original title may have been "God who creates the divine host."

4. See B. S. Childs, *Myth and Reality in the Old Testament, Studies in Biblical Theology*, No. 27 (London: SCM Press, 1960; Chicago: Allenson, 1960), pp. 58–63.

5. Although most of the narrative comes from J, the regulations governing the celebration of the Passover are mostly from P.

6. All of the plagues can be given a natural explanation. Only the first plague, in which the waters of Egypt are turned to blood, occasions some difficulty. The original plague seems to have been a sickness which killed so many fish in the Nile that the water became impotable. Though the Nile becomes reddish during a certain period each year, any Israelite who had lived in Egypt would know that the water is not thereby spoiled. But it is easy to see how this might later enter the tradition.

7. Not even high Egyptian officials were permitted to appear before the king. It would not be likely, then, for the leader of a band of recalcitrant slaves to make such repeated appearances.

8. See Martin Noth, *Exodus: A Commentary* (Philadelphia: Westminster Press, 1962), pp. 87–92.

9. In Ex. 13:17, the highway is called "the way of the land of the Philistines." This statement would be geographically correct after the Philistine invasion in the late thirteenth century, but in its present context it is an anachronism—the result of several generations of oral narration in which the traditions continued to develop as they were passed from one generation to the next.

10. See Ex. 3:1ff. The Elohist consistently called Mount Sinai "Horeb."

11. Num. 14:14; Deut. 31:15.

12. See Noth, *Exodus: A Commentary*, p. 109. There are problems involved in this interpretation, however, since there were no known active volcanoes on the Sinai Peninsula at that time; the nearest active volcanoes were in the land of Midian (along the eastern shores of the Red Sea and Gulf of Aqabah). On the other hand, it should be pointed out that the precise location of Mount Sinai is not agreed upon among scholars.

13. Num. 10:33ff.

14. Ex. 15:1–18 is one of the earliest Israelite songs—even earlier than the accompanying prose narrative in chapter 14. Its beauty is self-evident. Structurally it follows the canons of recently discovered Canaanite poetry from the latter part of the second millennium. In another prose-poetry account of a single event (Jud. 4–5), the poetic version is also anterior to the prose narrative.

15. See L. E. Toombs, "Clean and Unclean," *The Interpreter's Dictionary of the Bible* (New York: Abingdon, 1962), Vol I, pp. 641–648.

16. Ex. 19:13 seems to have originally implied that a trespasser would be killed by Yahweh's wrathful holiness. But a later addition to the verse indicates that he was to be stoned to death by the Israelite community.

17. It is difficult to determine whether the theophanic imagery surrounding Mount Sinai is that of a volcano or of a violent thunderstorm.

18. Although the Hittite suzerainty treaties suggest convincingly that covenant renewal took place within the context of remembering the Exodus deliverance in the Passover festival, some Old Testament scholars maintain that covenant renewal was originally a separate festival which took place at a different time of the year.

19. An alternate form of the Decalogue can be found in Deut. 5:7–21.

20. Evidence that these laws did not all originate prior to Israel's settling in Canaan can be found in Ex. 22:5, where it is assumed that Israelites are owners of vineyards. There are other laws in this code which presuppose an agricultural, rather than a seminomadic, background.

21. Pritchard, *The Ancient Near East,* pp. 138–167.

22. See discussion of the Elohist on page 30.

23. The sudden appearance of Joshua in the story is a carryover from Ex. 24:13.

24. The story of the Levites' being called upon to slay those who had sinned (Ex. 32:25–29) is obviously a later addition. In verses 30ff the punishment had not yet been effected. The Levite story was probably added to legitimatize their claims to hold sacred office (see Num. 25:6–13, which similarly attempts to explain how the family of Phinehas was elevated to the priesthood).

The Fall of Jericho

1. See G. E. Wright, *Biblical Archaeology* pp. 78–80; and K. M. Kenyon, *Digging up Jericho* (London: Benn, 1957), pp. 256–265.

2. Miss Kenyon (*Digging up Jericho,* pp. 259–262) notes the possibility of erosion and remarks that the process of erosion is arrested only after a new town is built upon the destroyed remains.

The Judges

1. W. F. Albright, "The Song of Deborah in the Light of Archaeology," *Bulletin of the American Schools of Oriental Research,* No. 62 (1936), pp. 26–31.

2. Verses 7, 12, and 15 indicate that the composer was not Deborah.

3. A further problem in this context is the relationship between Jael, the slayer of Sisera, and Heber the Kenite. In 5:24b, a secondary line which violates the metric structure of the poem, Jael is called Heber's wife. Otherwise there is no mention of Heber in the poem. In 4:11, 17b, Heber is described as living near Hazor and Kedesh, and at peace with Jabin of Hazor. A brief look at a map of ancient Palestine shows that Sisera would never have fled through the heart of Israelite territory to Kedesh when he could have stopped off at Hazor along

the way for safety, and when Kedesh was three times the distance of Harosheth-hagoiim, his own fortified city. We can only conjecture that Heber the Kenite (or his wife) showed his allegiance to the Israelite cause by betraying Jabin's forces, and that Jael, who lived somewhere along Sisera's path of escape through the Esdraelon valley (and one hundred years later than Heber the Kenite), has become Heber's wife in the process of conflating the two traditions.

4. See F. M. Cross, *Studies in Ancient Yahwistic Poetry* (Johns Hopkins Ph.D. Dissertation, Baltimore: 1950), pp. 5–42. Our rendering of the song of Deborah is based largely on Cross' translation. For other studies of Hebrew poetry related to the song of Deborah, see J. M. Myers, "Introduction and Exegesis of the Book of Judges," *Interpreter's Bible,* Vol. 2 (New York: Abingdon-Cokesbury, 1953), pp. 717–729; and C. F. Burney, *The Book of Judges* (New York: Ktav Publishing House, 1970), pp. 94–176.

5. As scholars have noted, it is quite strange that there is no mention in this song of Judah, one of the most powerful tribes, whose presence or absence would surely have been felt. Does this mean that Judah did not become a part of the Israelite tribal league until after 1125 B.C.?

6. G. F. Moore, *A Critical and Exegetical Commentary on Judges* (*International Critical Commentary* series) (New York: Charles Scribner's Sons, 1901), p. 161. See also Jud. 8:4–17.

7. The writer had thought that this was an original insight until he recently discovered that Julius Wellhausen had made the same suggestion a century earlier.

8. J. L. McKenzie, *The World of the Judges* (Englewood Cliffs, N.J.: Prentice Hall, 1966), p. 129.

9. The Midianites were earlier a seminomadic people whose permanent home lay south of Edom and east of the Gulf of Aqaba. From there some clans seem to have wandered north along the edge of the Arabian desert, while others would journey west into the Sinai peninsula. Israelite tradition acknowledges some kin relationship with the Midianites (Gen. 25:2). The ties were particularly close and permanent with the Kenites, a Midianite clan into which Moses married and which joined with Israel in entering Canaan (Jud. 1:16). In fact it was Heber the Kenite (or his wife) who played an instrumental role in helping Israel defeat Jabin of Hazor (see The Judges, note 3). On the other hand the Israelites did not have the same close ties with the Midianite clan which wandered along the Arabian desert east of the Transjordan (Num. 25; 31).

10. W. F. Albright, "Islam and the Religions of the Ancient Orient," *Journal of the American Oriental Society,* Vol. 60. (1940), p. 283.

11. R. Kittel, *Great Men and Movements in Israel,* translated by C. A. Knoch and C. D. Wright. (New York: The Macmillan Company, 1929), p. 61.

12. It is strange, however, that no mention is made of Issachar. Could the note in Gen. 49:14–15 give us some indication of the tribe's fate during this period?

13. Note how similar the description of the tent's collapse (". . . a cake of barley bread tumbled . . and came to the tent, and struck it so that it fell, and turned it upside down, so that the tent lay flat") in 7:13 is to the death of Sisera in 5:27. J. M. Myers (in *Interpreter's Bible,* pp. 729, 735) suggests that the earlier form of Gideon's exploits may well have been a narrative poem.

14. R. Kittel, (*Great Men and Movements in Israel,* pp. 67f) points out that the custom of using the names of great warriors in battle cries has been retained by Arabs until recent times. Their spirit was thought to convey power to the troops through the mentioning of the name.

15. It has been noted that having a torch, a pot, a horn, and a weapon would be too much for each man to handle. One solution is that two sources have been conflated—one in which the soldiers had horns, the other in which they carried torches and pots. It would seem equally possible that some soldiers had horns while others were carrying the torches and pots.,

16. Since Jephthah was a Gileadite (literally in Hebrew "a son of Gilead"), the author calls his father "Gilead." Apparently the father's name was no longer remembered. On the other hand one could argue that since Jephthah was the son of a whore, his father never was known. In this case his expulsion by his "brothers," the sons of his "father's" real wife, would be a reference to his being excluded from the community as illegitimate by the tribal elders.

17. H. W. Hertzberg, *Die Bücher Josua, Richter, Ruth* (Part 9 of *Das Alte Testament Deutsch* series) 2nd edition (Göttingen: Vandenhoeck & Ruprecht, 1959), p. 216.

18. We know from Num. 21:27–30 that the disputed land north of the Arnon had once belonged to the Moabites before it was taken by Sihon the Amorite. We also know from Num. 22–24 that Balak had cast longing eyes in that direction before deciding that discretion was the better course. Furthermore, we know from the ninth century Mesha

stele that the Moabites eventually were able to drive Israel from this area. We can only surmise from Jud. 10 that the Ammonites, who are closely related to the Moabites (see. Gen. 19:30–38) and who seem to have been more powerful than the Moabites during Jephthah's time, were asserting the claims of both groups to the land over against Israel.

19. Some scholars, pointing to the last verse of this chapter, regard this story as a cultic legend which has been incorporated into Israelite tradition in order to explain the four-day mourning festival. That is, the festival came first and then the story was developed in order to explain the festival. Given Israel's abhorrence of human sacrifice, one finds it difficult to see how the story would have become a part of the tradition had the event not really happened.

20. There is no mention in Jud. 11:29 of Jephthah's sending to Ephraim for help. It is most likely that the "I" in Jud. 12:2ff does not refer to Jephthah, but to the people of Gilead (see Jud. 11:12, 27) who could well have called upon Ephraim before finally turning to Jephthah for help.

21. The taunt "you are fugitives of Ephraim, you Gileadites, in the midst of Ephraim and Manasseh" (12:4b) is apparently an obscure reference to Gilead's area being settled by an offshoot of the tribe of Ephraim.

22. See Genesis 18:1–15, I Samuel 1:1–20.

23. Some children were apparently dedicated by their parents as Nazirites for their entire lifetime. The laws in Num. 6:1ff, however, provide for adults fulfilling the vows of a Nazirite for a specified period of time.

24. Most scholars would omit "his father" in verse 10 as a later addition.

25. McKenzie, *The World of the Judges*, p. 153.

26. Our approach to the story of Samson's riddle has been greatly influenced by C. F. Kraft, "Samson," *The Interpreter's Dictionary of the Bible*, Vol. 4 (New York: Abingdon Press, 1962), p. 199.

27. There is some confusion concerning when the Philistines began to panic. The Hebrew text of verse 15 begins "on the seventh day"; the Greek and Syriac texts read "On the fourth day." It is probable that "seventh" is secondary due to the influence of verse 17, where Samson finally reveals the secret to his bride on the seventh day. But if the Philistines did not approach her until the fourth day, why had she been beseeching Samson in tears all seven days? It would seem

most likely that the bride had been trying all week long to get Samson to share his secret with her, and that her earlier motive was simply female curiosity. These attempts then became more desperate after the groomsmen had threatened to kill her.

28. For a brief summary, see Kraft, in *The Interpreter's Dictionary of the Bible,* p. 200; for more detail, see C. F. Burney, *The Book of Judges,* pp. 391–408.

29. McKenzie, *The World of the Judges,* p. 158.

The Early Monarchy

1. We are following the unpublished views of Professor Frank M. Cross, Jr. of Harvard University.

2. *Understanding the Old Testament* (Englewood Cliffs, N.J.: Prentice Hall, 1966), pp. 122–126.

3. On polygamous marriages, see O. J. Baab, "Marriage," *The Interpreter's Dictionary of the Bible,* Vol. 3, pp. 280f.

4. Hans Wilhelm Hertzberg, *I and II Samuel: A Commentary* (Philadelphia: Westminster Press, 1964), p. 28.

5. We are following in part the proposal of Hertzberg, *I and II Samuel,* pp. 25f.

6. Whereas the Hebrew text reads "Elkanah went," the Greek text reads "they went." Furthermore, "Elkanah" in the Hebrew text could be designating his entire household.

7. On the hardening of the heart as a problem of divine determinism vs. man's free will, see p. 104.

8. See Jud. 10:1–5; 12:8–15.

9. Some scholars believe that this is the beginning of the "Saul source," whereas others maintain that the editor is using a separate source which traced the history of the Ark (I Sam. 4–6; II Sam. 6).

10. The problem here is how literally to take I Sam. 4:6–7, where the fearful Philistines maintain that the Ark had never been used in battle against them before.

11. See *The Story of Joseph*, note 11.

12. See I Kings 13:3, 5; II Kings 20:8–9; Isa. 7:11, 14.

13. Another explanation for the origin of the saying "Is Saul also among the prophets?" can be found in I Sam. 19:18–24.

14. Hertzberg, *Samuel,* p. 93 note b, recalling that Gideon routed the Midianites with three hundred men, makes the very plausible suggestion that the number one thousand was later added to the text.

15. We see from II Sam. 12:24ff that it was common practice for kings to have two names: perhaps one given at birth and the other given at his accession to the throne. Other kings of Judah having dual names: Uzziah-Azariah, Jehoahaz-Shallum, Eliakim-Jehoiakim, Jehoiachin-Coniah, Mattaniah-Zedekiah.

16. See Wright, *Biblical Archaeology*, pp. 124ff.

17. Gerhard von Rad, *Old Testament Theology*, translated by D. M. G. Stalker (New York: Harper & Row, 1962), Vol. I, 48–56.

18. See I. Mendelsohn, "Familiar Spirit," *The Interpreter's Dictionary of The Bible*, II pp. 237–238, and the bibliography cited there.

19. There being no official Israelite doctrine with respect to the afterlife or the abode of the dead, the Hebrew depended upon widespread ancient beliefs and folklore in picturing the state of the departed. The dead were believed to reside in a region under the earth called Sheol. This was not a place of punishment, nor was it thought of as a meaningful existence. It is from this shadowy dreaming state that Samuel has been summoned. See T. H. Gaster, "Abode of the Dead," *The Interpreter's Dictionary of the Bible*, I, pp. 787–788, and the bibliography cited there.

20. See Albrecht Alt's classic studies, "The Formation of the Israelite State in Palestine," and "The Monarchy in the Kingdoms of Israel and Judah," in *Essays on Old Testament History and Religion*, translated by R. A. Wilson (Doubleday-Anchor: Garden City, New York, 1968), pp. 223–335.

21. See W. F. Stinespring's notes, *ad loc.*, in *The Oxford Annotated Bible* (New York: Oxford University Press, 1962). My dependence upon these excellent notes is frequent, though I have not wished to burden the reader with too many references to them.

22. The role of the prophet at Mari, on the Upper Euphrates, is particularly interesting in comparison with biblical prophecy. See A. Lods, "Une tablette inédite de Mari, intéressante pour l'histoire ancienne du prophétisme sémitique," *Studies in Old Testament Prophecy*, ed. H. H. Rowley (Edinburgh: T. & T. Clark, 1946), p. 103–110; Martin Noth, "History and the Word of God in the Old Testament," *The Laws in the Pentateuch and Other Studies*, translated, D. R. Ap-Thomas (London: Oliver & Boyd, 1966), pp. 179–193.

23. The law which forbade the marriage of half-siblings (Lev. 18:9) is considered by most scholars to be later than the period of this narrative. In early narratives such marriages are reported as though they were not remarkable (e.g.. Gen. 20:12).

24. The list of David's sons is given in II Sam. 3:2–5. His second son, Chileab, appears to have died young, since he is never mentioned in later narratives.

The Divided Monarchy and the Rise of Prophecy

1. See Martin Buber, *The Prophetic Faith* (New York: Harper & Row, 1960), pp. 67–70.

2. Mircea Eliade, *Cosmos and History: The Myth of the Eternal Return,* translated by Willard R. Trask (New York: Harper & Row, 1959), ch. IV.

3. See Roland De Vaux, *Ancient Israel, Its Life and Institutions,* pp. 333–336.

4. See Benjamin Mazar, "The Aramean Empire and Its Relations with Israel," *Biblical Archaeologist,* XXV (1962), pp. 98–120.

5. In one Canaanite depiction of Baal which has been excavated, he is pictured as a young man holding a spear and a club, the handle of the spear being formed of forked lightning. See G. Ernest Wright, *Biblical Archaeology,* p. 109. Wright's whole discussion of Canaanite religion in Chapter VII of the same volume is valuable for the student of the Old Testament.

6. NB also the covenant narrative of 18:30–32 (see Ex. 24); the miraculous feeding of Elijah in the wilderness as he returns to Horeb (Sinai), 19:4–8; and Elijah's mysterious death or disappearance, like that of Moses east of the Jordan (II Kings 2:1–18).

7. See S. V. McCasland's article, "Miracle," *The Interpreter's Dictionary of the Bible,* III, pp. 392–402.

8. See John Gray's translation, "a sound of thin silence," in his *I and II Kings: A Commentary* (Philadelphia: Westminster Press, 1963), p. 362.

9. Note the analogies to the sending of a true prophet in the story of Isaiah's call, Isa. 6.

10. See the discussion of John Gray, *I and II Kings,* pp. 416–417. Gray himself thinks the stories are basically independent.

11. John Gray compares the title given by Muhammed to a great general: "The sword of Allah." (*I and II Kings,* p. 426.)

12. As suggested by H. B. MacLean, "Jehu," *The Interpreter's Dictionary of the Bible,* Vol. II, p. 818.

13. See G. Ernest Wright, *Biblical Archaeology,* p. 159. The text of the inscription is translated in Pritchard, *The Ancient Near East,* pp. 188–192.

The Prophetic Movement

1. We are following the reading of the Septuagint "sons of God," which has been confirmed by one of the recently discovered Dead Sea Scroll texts.

2. For an excellent discussion of how the divine council concept is related to monotheism in Israelite thought, see G. E. Wright, *The Old Testament Against Its Environment* (Chicago: Alec R. Allenson, 1950), pp. 30–41.

3. See H. Wheeler Robinson, "The Council of Yahweh," in *Journal of Theological Studies,* Vol. 45, 1944, pp. 151–157.

4. For a fuller treatment of prophetic ecstasy, see J. Lindblom, *Prophecy in Ancient Israel,* Philadelphia: Fortress Press, 1965.

5. This interpretation is from the unpublished lectures of Professor Samuel Terrien, Union Theological Seminary, New York.

6. There are two other visions in 8:1–3 and 9:1–4.

7. Amos 1:4, 7, 10, etc. Note the articles on the subject by D. R. Hillers and P. D. Miller in *The Catholic Biblical Quarterly,* 26 (1964), pp. 221–225 and 227, (1965), pp. 256–261.

8. The Hebrew word $t^e h\hat{o}m$ ("deep") is etymologically related to Tiamat, the personification of chaos in the Babylonian creation story.

9. See pp. 20–23; 119–120.

10. See our discussion of Hebrew poetry above in pp. 124–129.

11. R. S. Cripps, *A Critical and Exegetical Commentary on the Book of Amos* (London, 1960), p. 124.

12. Cripps, . . . *Amos,* p. 136. Sophocles' *Antigone* indicates that this was a belief widely held in the Mediterranean world.

13. See pp. 113–114.

14. In North Israel the original inhabitants of the land are traditionally referred to as "Amorites" rather than "Canaanites."

15. "Jezreel" is the place where Jehu conducted his purge against the house of Omri in 842 B.C. Although the purge was undertaken due to the instigation of the prophets, its excesses were so great and its results so devastating that the bloody event was still remembered one hundred years later. Hosea is saying that the house of Jehu will be punished. Jeroboam II was the last great ruler from this line: his son Zechariah was assassinated after ruling six months, thus fulfilling the prophecy. The second child is a sign that God's judgment, which had been withheld for so long, will soon fall and there will be no deliverance. The third child, whose name bears the most ominous sign of all,

is a message to Israel that the covenant relationship had been terminated, since she had not been faithful to its conditions. One might wonder at a prophet giving his children such strange names, but we know that Isaiah did the same thing (Isa. 7:3; 8:1). This falls in the same category as a symbolic action—undertaken in order to reinforce the power of the word so that what is spoken will surely come to pass.

16. For a more thorough description of the various interpretations, see H. H. Rowley, "The Marriage of Hosea," *Bulletin of the John Rylands Library,* Vol. 39 (1956/57), pp. 200–233.

17. See Pritchard, *The Ancient Near East,* pp. 278–280.

18. We are following the Septuagint translation, which includes the transitional word "saying" between 5:15 and 6:1.

19. For example, James M. Ward, *Hosea: A Theological Commentary* (New York: Harper & Row, 1966), pp. 114–126, maintains that Hosea is not rejecting the people's repentance in 6:1ff. In fact the prophet is saying that the knowledge of God which they are seeking in verse 3 is precisely what God requires of them. What Hosea is doing in verses 4–6 is lamenting the inconstancy of their desire to know God. Israel's loyalty flickers on and off as the need arises, and therefore is no loyalty at all.

20. Ward, *Hosea,* p. 195.

21. Most biblical scholars generally divide the Book of Isaiah between two, and sometimes three, prophets: "Isaiah of Jerusalem" (chs. 1–39), who lived in the eighth century, and "Second Isaiah" (chs. 40–66), who prophesied when the Jews were exiled in Babylon. Some scholars go further by assigning chapters 56–66 to a "Third Isaiah," who seems to have prophesied in Palestine shortly after the Jews returned home from Babylon.

22. Thorleif Boman, *Hebrew Thought Compared with Greek,* translated by J. L. Moreau (London: SCM Press, 1960), pp. 129–154.

23. For a fuller discussion of the Jerusalem Temple, see chapter 8 of G. E. Wright, *Biblical Archaeology.* Note also II Sam. 6:2.

24. John L. McKenzie, *Dictionary of the Bible* (London: Geoffrey Chapman, 1965), p. 789.

25. Rudolf Otto, *The Idea of the Holy,* translated by J. W. Harvey (New York: Oxford University Press, 1950), pp. 8–40.

26. The sexual connotation in the term *beloved* as a designation for Yahweh is quite shocking. In this context the best translation seems to be *friend.*

27. See Isa. 36–37. For a good discussion of the problems in these chapters see J. Bright, *A History of Israel,* pp. 282–287.

28. On the Davidic covenant, Bright, *A History of Israel,* pp. 23–25.

29. B. S. Childs, *Myth and Reality in the Old Testament. Studies in Biblical Theology* No. 27. London: SCM Press, Ltd., 1962, pp. 69–72.

30 See Ps. 2; 20; 21; 72; 89:19–37; 110; 132.

31. On the anointing of kings, see pp. 165–166.

32. For a superb treatment of this topic, see James Muilenburg, *The Way of Israel,* New York: Harper & Brothers, 1961.

33. See Sennacherib's own account in Pritchard, *The Ancient Near East,* pp. 188–192.

34. See Bright, *A History of Israel,* pp. 268–287.

35. Bright, *A History of Israel,* pp. 288–291.

36. See G. Ernest Wright's "Introduction to the Book of Deuteronomy," *The Interpreter's Bible,* Vol. II, pp. 311–330.

37. See Gerhard von Rad's sensitive discussion of Jeremiah in his *Old Testament Theology,* Vol. II, pp. 191–219.

The Fall of Judah: Exile and Restoration

1. We are not necessarily arguing that Jesus used this title in order to proclaim himself as the messianic deliverer. It could well be that, if he used this title, he deliberately chose it because of its ambiguity ("apocalyptic warrior" or "an ordinary man") in order to preserve his "messianic secret."

2. W. F. Albright, *Archaeology and the Religion of Israel* (Baltimore: Johns Hopkins Press, 1956), p. 165f.

3. Albright, *Archeology . . . ,* p. 166f.

4. See H. Wheeler Robinson, *Corporate Personality in Ancient Israel,* Philadelphia: Fortress Press, 1964.

5. See Robinson, *Corporate Personality,* p. 24.

6. For a discussion of the meaning of "clean" and "unclean," see Robinson, *Corporate Personality,* pp. 95–96.

7. See A. R. Johnson, *The Vitality of the Individual in the Thought of Ancient Israel* (Cardiff: University of Wales Press, 1964), pp. 23–27.

8. See James Muilenburg's "Introduction to Isaiah 40–66," *The Interpreter's Bible,* Vol. V, pp. 381–419, especially pp. 384–392.

9. See Muilenburg, in *The Interpreter's Bible,* pp. 388–392.

10. Muilenburg, in *The Interpreter's Bible,* pp. 406–407.

11. Muilenburg, in *The Interpreter's Bible,* pp. 408–414.

12. See H Wheeler Robinson, *Corporate Personality in Ancient Israel, Werden und Wesen des Alten Testaments,* ed. J. Hempel (Beiheft 66, *Zeitschrift für die alttestamentliche Wissenschaft,* 1936), pp. 49ff.

13. See the Cyrus Cylinder inscription, Pritchard, *The Ancient Near East,* pp. 206–208.

14. See Arthur Jeffrey's notes, *Oxford Annotated Bible,* p. 573, in which the stages of the return from exile are clearly set forth.

15. Scholars identify the author of Ezra-Nehemiah with the author of the Books of Chronicles. See Raymond Bowman's "Introduction to Ezra and Nehemiah," *The Interpreter's Bible,* Vol. III, pp. 551–569.

16. Bowman, in *The Interpreter's Bible,* p. 607.

17. John Bright, *A History of Israel,* pp. 356–386.

18. Bright, *A History of Israel,* pp. 363–365.

19. R. H. Charles, ed. *The Apocrypha and the Pseudepigrapha of the Old Testament,* 2 vols. (Oxford: Clarendon Press, 1913); T. H. Gaster, *The Dead Sea Scriptures,* Garden City, N.Y.: Doubleday Anchor, 1956.

The Literature of the Post-Exilic Period

1. R. B. Y. Scott, *Proverbs–Ecclesiastes,* Anchor Bible, Vol. 18 (Garden City, N.Y.: Doubleday, 1965), pp. 5–8.

2. Pritchard, *The Ancient Near East,* pp. 234–258.

3. Pritchard, *The Ancient Near East,* pp. 237–243.

4. See "Wisdom" by S. H. Blank, in Vol. 4 of *The Interpreter's Dictionary of the Bible,* ed. by G. A. Buttrick, et al. (New York: Abingdon Press, 1962), pp. 852–861.

5. Scott, *Proverbs–Ecclesiastes,* p. 24.

6. "A Pessimistic Dialogue between Master & Servant," in J. B. Pritchard's *Ancient Near Eastern Texts Relating to the Old Testament* (Princeton: Princeton Univ. Press, 1950), p. 437f.

7. M. H. Pope, *Job,* Anchor Bible, Vol. 15 (Garden City, N.Y.: Doubleday, 1965), p. 9

8. See S. Terrien, *Job: Poet of Existence* (Indianapolis: Bobbs-Merrill, 1957), pp. 108–117.

9. One footnote does not suffice to underscore the influence of Professor Samuel Terrien—both in his lectures and his writings—on the interpretation of Job. His insights have so permeated our thinking

that almost every sentence in the treatment of Job should be footnoted and eventually attributed to him. This is particularly true of the interpretation of the development within Job. See his works: *Job: Poet of Existence,* Indianapolis: Bobbs-Merrill, 1957; "Job: Introduction and Exegesis," in *The Interpreter's Bible,* Vol. 3. New York: Abingdon Press, 1964, pp. 875–1198; and his notes in the *Oxford Annotated Bible.*

10. Terrien, *Job: Poet of Existence,* p. 130.

11. Our interpretation of this chapter is heavily dependent upon S. Terrien, *Job: Poet of Existence,* pp. 142–155.

12. Terrien, *Job: Poet of Existence,* pp. 183–188.

13. Terrien, *Job: Poet of Existence,* p. 237f.

14. Bernhard W. Anderson, *Understanding the Old Testament* (Englewood Cliffs, N.J.: Prentice Hall, 1966), p. 518.

15. H. H. Rowley, "The Interpretation of the Song of Songs," in *The Servant of the Lord and Other Essays* (London: Lutterworth Press, 1952), p. 192.

16. Rowley, ". . . Song of Songs," p. 196.

17 For the clearest presentation of these dramatic theories, see S. R. Driver, *An Introduction to the Literature of the Old Testament,* 10th edition (New York: Charles Scribner's Sons, 1900), pp. 437ff.

18. Driver, *An Introduction to the Literature of the Old Testament,* pp. 10e–12e.

19. I received this insight from one of my students, Miss Sharon Shurts.

20. See Artur Weiser, *The Psalms: A Commentary,* translated by Herbert Hartwell (London: SCM Press, 1962), p. 53.

21. Weiser, *The Psalms,* p. 629.

INDEX